P9-CLD-910

MODERN CHINA'S SEARCH
FOR A POLITICAL FORM

The Royal Institute of International Affairs is an unofficial body which promotes the scientific study of international questions and does not express opinions of its own. The opinions expressed in this publication are the responsibility of the author.

Modern China's Search for a Political Form

Edited by

JACK GRAY

Senior Lecturer in Far Eastern History, University of Glasgow

Issued under the auspices of the
Royal Institute of International Affairs

OXFORD UNIVERSITY PRESS

LONDON NEW YORK TORONTO

1969

Oxford University Press, Ely House, London W.1

GLASGOW NEW YORK TORONTO MELBOURNE WELLINGTON
CAPE TOWN SALISBURY IBADAN NAIROBI LUSAKA ADDIS ABABA
BOMBAY CALCUTTA MADRAS KARACHI LAHORE DACCA
KUALA LUMPUR SINGAPORE HONG KONG TOKYO

© Royal Institute of International Affairs, 1969

Printed in Great Britain by
The Camelot Press Ltd., London and Southampton

DS
761
.M6

CONTENTS

115228   EMORY AND HENRY LIBRARY

ABBREVIATIONS

Note: The following abbreviations are used throughout this book. In addition abbreviations for particular sources relating to individual chapters are explained there at the first instance.

CB	US Consulate-General, Hong Kong, *Current Background.*
CCP	Chinese Communist Party.
CKMT	Chung-kuo Kuomintang (Chinese Nationalist Party).
CQ	*China Quarterly.*
CWR	*China Weekly Review.*
CPR	Chinese People's Republic.
CYB	*China Yearbook.*
FLP	Foreign Languages Press.
JPRS	*US Joint Publications Research Service.*
KMT	Kuomintang.
PD	*People's Daily (Jen-min Jih-Pao).*
NCNA	New China News Agency.
NCH	*North China Herald.*
PLA	People's Liberation Army.
SBTS	*Scholarly Book Translation Series.*
SCMM & *SCMP*	US Consulate-General, Hong Kong, *Survey of China Mainland Magazines* & *Survey of the China Mainland Press.*
TFTC	*Tung-fang tsa-chih* (Eastern Miscellany).

CHINESE ADMINISTRATIVE TERMS

Hsiang	Rural district, each consisting of a number of villages.
Hsien	County.

FOREWORD

THE chapters composing this volume originated as contributions to the Working Group on China and the World of the Royal Institute of International Affairs. The Group, composed of academics, public servants, journalists, and others professionally interested in the study of modern China, and representing various disciplines, meets to discuss papers contributed by members. Each annual programme has a general theme, chosen to make use of the actual research being pursued by a majority of its members at any one time. The theme which forms the title of the present work was that of the programme for 1965–6.

The character of the book is related to the nature of the Group and its work. The Group brings into a closer relationship research in progress upon a number of mutually-supporting subjects, enabling each specialist to put his own work in the perspective of that of his colleagues, and so providing for each separate line of research the broad background which, in a comparatively undeveloped subject, does not yet exist in published work.

In editing the papers for publication, we have tried to supply for the reader who is not a specialist on China a volume which will, like the work of the Group, have both breadth and depth. The individual contributions represent specialist research, much of it of a pioneering kind; but the authors have tried to make this research available to the non-specialist by relating their work to the general theme, and by putting the results of research in the context of more general discussion, which will make the force of this research obvious and its details comprehensible. We hope also that, as the sharing of ideas within the Group has helped us as members by broadening the range of our knowledge and by enriching our sense of relevance, it may do the same for specialist colleagues who read the volume.

The essays as a whole are historical rather than analytical. This is justified by the fact that history has conditioned the course of the communist revolution in China with peculiar strength. A unique national tradition underlies the revolution and influences it; the most radical changes in China cannot wholly destroy—and may even in some respects revitalize—the greatest moral, political, and scientific tradition outside Christendom. The experience of the present Chinese leaders during the agonies of the decay of this tradition is so far from our own experience of politics that we must bring to its study a strenuous effort of historical imagination.

Jerome Ch'én begins with the story of China's struggle to reach national unification and integration. He has singled out for special scrutiny four interrelated problems which have become increasingly urgent over the last century: problems for which, as he shows, interdependent solutions had to be found before China could take her place among modern nations. The other essays deal with some of the different attempts that have been made in China so far to find such solutions.

Mark Elvin's paper describes the first and in some respects most significant attempt at the employment of representative institutions in China, made possible by the widening and the modernization of the traditional social responsibilities of the Chinese gentry, under the immediate influence of foreign attitudes and institutions exemplified in the foreign areas of Shanghai. This attempt was ended by civil war, but it at least reminds us of the possibility in China of successful representative government, and suggests that in more peaceful conditions the evolution of such representative government might have taken place and that Chinese society was not wholly inimical to such a development.

Martin Bernal examines the first socialist thought in modern China, vague, utopian, based more on traditional than modern values, but showing in its anarchist as well as its moralistic tendencies certain characteristics which have proved lasting and which still affect the thinking of the Chinese communists, and form a vital part of the content of the present Great Proletarian Cultural Revolution.

Jean Chesneaux's study of the Federalist movement in the years around 1920 introduces one of the fundamental and abiding problems of Chinese politics—that vast size and variety, imperfect integration and disruptive local loyalties make fully centralized government impossible even now; and at the same time shows the strength of the tradition of national unity which prevented the radicals from accepting a federal solution. The problem is not wholly solved. The course of the present crisis has strongly suggested that the ancient geopolitical rifts could still open, in a familiar pattern, under a sufficient strain.

Patrick Cavendish, in dealing with the formative years of the Nationalist regime, describes the fundamental dilemma of etatism *versus* social mobilization. The gulf between the Chinese élite, alienated by their education, by the acceptance of foreign culture, and by life in modern Westernized cities, and the illiterate conservative mass of the population goes far to explain the futility of Nationalist government. The Nationalists destroyed the effectiveness of their own reforming administration by destroying the mass organization through which alone they could have made their legislation effective. Again, the problem is still a live one; the present crisis was actually precipitated by the determination of Mao Tse-tung to free his mass organizations from domination by the bureaucratic party hierarchy, met by the stubborn rearguard actions fought by the *apparat* to maintain a minimum of hierarchical control.

If the Nationalists found that central legislation was not enough, it was partly because, as *Sybille van der Sprenkel* shows, law as a means of social control in China was traditionally not only underdeveloped but positively discouraged. She shows also that the tradition is still strong. Paradoxically, it both feeds the anarchist elements of Chinese communism and strengthens its totalitarian proclivities. It has very recently revealed its strength in the cult of the 'good official' by liberal playwrights in China in the early 1960s, and in the anomic activities of the Red Guards in 1966.

The most dramatic of China's twentieth-century problems was the failure of government to control the military. *John Gittings* analyses the way in which the Communist Party, as perhaps one of its greatest achievements, created an army loyal to civilian policy-makers. It is an achievement now for the first time seriously threatened as a consequence of the Cultural Revolution.

James Macdonald's chapter deals directly with Chinese communist political methods, and is a study of Communist attempts to bridge the gulf between the élite and the mass. He analyses the efforts made to create a new élite loyal to the general aims of the Chinese Communist Party, but responsive to the wishes, the interests, and the fears of the unsophisticated rural population. His analysis shows the determination of the party (or of its left wing) to shorten the period of tutelage by a process of mutual education between leaders and led. This, too, is a topical theme: the Cultural Revolution is, in the last analysis, an attempt to eliminate those factors which threaten to bring the process of mutual education to an end, factors which Mao Tse-tung identifies as the 'three great differences'—between town and country, industry and agriculture, and mental and manual labour.

George Moseley's chapter supplies another dimension of the problem of the form of state: the question of the relations between the Chinese nation and the peoples of non-Chinese race who form the rest of the 'Chinese world'. His chapter forms a bridge between the papers in this volume on the internal political organization of China, and the theme of the Group's current programme on the international framework of the Chinese revolution, a programme which we hope may provide a new volume, complementary to the present one.

In a symposium of this kind, it was not to be expected that there would be complete unanimity among the different specialists, and no attempt has been made to impose it. Nor, as the reader will appreciate, have the different authors all been writing at the same moment, which, because of the revelations about past happenings which have been made during the recent unfolding of events, makes it more likely that there should appear to be some disparity of view. In the circumstances, each essay must represent a contribution at the time of writing.

The Editor warmly expresses his gratitude to his colleagues in the Group, and in particular to Sybille van der Sprenkel for the unstinting and careful collaboration which she has provided in the preparation of this volume.

The debt which the Group owes to the RIIA will be obvious to readers of this volume; but in addition, all members of the Group owe and wish especially to acknowledge their dept to Miss Hermia Oliver of Chatham House for the assistance and advice she has so freely given in the editing of these papers. Our gratitude is also due to Geoffrey Shillinglaw, both for compiling the index and for help in many other ways, and to John Gittings for his part in the creation and running of our programme in its earlier stages.

April 1968   J. G.

I

Historical Background

JEROME CH'ÊN

THE PROBLEM

WHEN in 1915 the question of the form of the state (*kuo-t'i*) was raised by Yüan Shih-k'ai's supporters, Liang Ch'i-ch'ao, the fervent advocate of a constitutional monarchy before 1911, voiced his opposition to it in a memorable article, 'How strange the so-called question of the form of state!'[1] *Kuo-t'i*, according to him, is never perfect, since it is always based on an imperfect *fait accompli* and nothing else. 'Is not any attempt to judge the merits and demerits of a polity on political principles and to choose one in preference to another', he asks, 'the greatest folly on earth?' Folly alone is no disaster; 'the endless disaster our country can suffer would be to show one's predilection for one particular polity and proceed to create a *fait accompli* in order to fulfil it.'[2] In Liang's view, as a student of politics or a politician, his duty is to accept rather than to discuss the adequacy of a polity.

Perhaps influenced by his study of Liang, Professor Levenson, too, deems it odd that this question should have been raised in 1915. *Kuo-t'i*, he argues, is an expression of Japanese origin, *kokutai*. But the Japanese term 'was a living word; *kuo-t'i* was a contrivance. To speak a living language, one must say that the Hung-hsien reign [Yüan Shih-k'ai's abortive monarchy] was supposed to be a revival of Chinese *kokutai*. But how could a Chinese *revive* in China a new and foreign importation?'[3]

Liang's objection to the discussion had its political reasons, as Levenson's had its semantic ones. Mao Tse-tung in 1940, however, entertained a diametrically opposite view. He plunged right into

---

[1] 'I-tsai so-wei kuo-t'i wen-t'i che', full text in Pai Chiao, *Yüan Shih-k'ai yü Chung-hua min-kuo* (Yuan Shih-k'ai and the Republic of China) (Taipei, 1960), pp. 315–39; see also J. Levenson, *Liang Ch'i-ch'ao and the Mind of Modern China* (London, 1954), pp. 179–81.

[2] Pai Chiao, p. 217.

[3] Levenson, *Confucian China and Its Modern Fate* (London, 1964), ii. 137.

the problem by describing *kuo-t'i* as the relative positions of the classes in a nation and *cheng-t'i* (political form) as the pattern of power structure. He thought that China should adopt a dictatorial coalition of all the revolutionary classes (as *kuo-t'i*) and the system of democratic centralism (as *cheng-t'i*) to form a New Democratic Republic.[4]

The propensities of these authors apart, *kuo-t'i* and *cheng-t'i* have been since 1895 the liveliest issues in Chinese political thought. Broadly speaking, the argument began with the advocacy of a constitutional monarchy in 1898 which at length gained grudging acceptance by the Manchu dynasty after 1905. The revolution of 1911 and the Republic of 1912 did not put an end to it, as the Hung-hsien empire of 1915–16, the restoration fiasco of 1917, and the Manchukuo farce of 1932 showed.[5] Even within the framework of republicanism there were disputes and disagreements; hence the hurriedly created Republic of 1912 and the *San-min-chu-i* (the Three Principles of the People) Republic of 1929, followed by the New Democratic Republic of 1949. All these, however, were centralist. After the first world war there was also the federalist movement[6] which, though yielding nothing of lasting significance, had its influence on the political scene of the time. One common feature of all these movements was that, before their acceptance, they were regarded by the government in power as subversive, and consequently suppressed. All, except for constitutional monarchism, had to resort to arms in order to obtain a hearing. Once accepted and adopted, they themselves became repressive for the sake of their own preservation.

The problems facing us in this historical introduction are therefore: (1) Why were these changes in the form of state necessary? (2) What did the reformers and revolutionaries expect to achieve through them? (3) How did a new polity fail to fulfil its promise and to preserve itself? To answer these questions we must analyse the destructive and constructive forces at work throughout the period of 1895–1949 and take stock of what has been destroyed and what has been created during this time.

---

[4] Mao, *Hsüan-chi* (Selected works) (Peking, 1961), ii. 660–70.
[5] *From Emperor to Citizen: Autobiography of Aisin-Gioro Pu Yi* (Peking), i. (1964), chs. 3–5; ii. (1965), ch. 6.
[6] See ch. 4 below.

1895

Why 1895? Let us quote Liang Ch'i-ch'ao again: 'Our country's awakening from a dream of 4,000 years took place after the defeat of 1895, the cession of Taiwan, and the indemnity of 200 million [taels]'.[7] What Liang calls awakening may be taken to mean the collapse of the restoration movement inaugurated at the end of the T'aip'ing rebellion and the beginning of China's modern nationalism. The restoration movement gave the Chinese a false sense of security and its collapse in a manner as traumatic as the shattering defeat of 1895 by Japan evoked a deep anxiety over the survival of the country. A consequence of this was the birth of China's nationalism.

The restoration had not, in the three decades between the Anglo-French Expedition and the Sino-Japanese war, endeavoured to change the imperial polity of the Ch'ing empire. Its sole aim was to make use of Western technology in order to strengthen the Confucian empire. It did not succeed in modernizing either Chinese agriculture, so as to make it the chief supplier of free labour and free capital, or China's education and civil service, so as to provide technologically suitable personnel for the use of modern enterprises. As a result, China's capital formation in this period had to rely on the tax revenue from commodities, the maritime customs and *likin* (inland tariff barriers), and the management of modern enterprises had to be entrusted either to Confucian scholars or to people who had had associations with foreigners or foreign businesses in China. Admittedly, young students were sent abroad to study, but none of them had as yet attained sufficient eminence to make an impact either on Chinese politics or on the economy.[8] The reliance for revenue on maritime customs and *likin*, limited as they were, not only retarded the rate of capital growth but also affected China's foreign policy. Li Hung-chang could, for instance, in a memorial presented to the throne on 21 June 1883, argue against a war with France on the ground that once started, the war would pare to the quick China's customs and *likin* revenue.[9] The Confucian 'universal man',

[7] *Wu-hsü cheng-pien-chi* (The coup d'État of 1898) (Peking, 1954), p. 1.
[8] The first group of students sent in 1871: see a memorial by Tseng Kuo-fan & Li Hung-chang on 26 June 1871 in T'ung-chih, ed., *Ch'ou-pan i-wu shih-mo* (The management of barbarian affairs) (Taipei, 1963), ch. 82, pp. 46b–52a. See also below, p. 19.
[9] Chung-kuo Shih-hsüeh-hui, *Chung-Fa Chan-cheng* (The Sino-French war) (Peking, 1962), v. 159.

essentially an amateur, was ill suited for specialized jobs in modern enterprises; his ignorance of such matters tended to give ample opportunities for irregularities, even if he himself was incorruptible. In the end, most of the new enterprises, e.g. the Mawei Shipyard, the Kiangnan Arsenal, the Hanyang Foundry,[10] and the Merchant Steam Navigation Company, were either embarrassed by lack of funds or ruined by corruption, or both. The defence services suffered the same fate, a fact brought into sharp relief in 1894–5.

CONFUCIANISM

The restoration policy, apart from offering China nearly a generation of external peace and internal order, considerably modified Confucianism both as a world view and the basis of government. The *t'i-yung* (essence-utility) dichotomy was in itself an admission of the existence of another culture and of the partial inadequacy of the Confucian education. But as *t'i*, in the words of Levenson, 'Confucianism was the essence of civilization, an absolute[11] which, by the eternal law of its being, was still capable of encompassing the spiritual, aesthetic, and political life of man.' The defeat of 1895 changed this. In his fourth 'letter' to the emperor, dated 30 June 1895, the radical reformer K'ang Yu-wei put forward a novel view of the world order:

> The pressure upon us from the nations of the Great West represents a changed situation which China has not known in thousands of years. Previously, barbarian invasions from all directions meant no more

---

[10] The foundry was a typical case of technological ignorance. The furnaces were ordered by Chang Chih-tung when he was viceroy at Canton, but he was transferred to Wuch'ang before their arrival. As his successor at Canton, Li Han-chang, refused to continue the foundry project, Chang had to take the furnaces to Hupei, where the high phosphorous content of the iron ore of Tayeh rendered the furnaces useless. Fresh orders for Siemens Martin had to be sent.

The distance between the Tayeh mines and the river is 45 *li* and that between Tayeh and Hanyang about 250 *li* up the river. Four or five days were required to transport a ton of iron ore to the foundry at a cost of 2 taels. Coal had to come from P'inhsiang to Kiangsi at the cost of 5 taels per ton (7 taels for a ton of coke). To produce a ton of pig iron, estimated price 22 taels, the foundry needed 1·7 tons of iron ore and 1 ton of coke and these alone cost 10 taels or more to transport, nearly 50 per cent of the price. See Chang Chih-tung, *Chang Wen-hsiang-kung ch'üan-chi* (Complete works of Chang Chih-tung) (Taipei, 1963), chs 29, 34, 39 & 390 and Kuang-hsü, *Ch'ing shih lu* (The veritable records of the Ch'ing dynasty) (Tokyo, 1937), ch. 21, p. 7a.

[11] *Confucian China*, ii. 14.

than the menace of a strongly armed force; state craft and literature did not come into play. Now the nations of the Great West vie with us in the art of government and surpass us in knowledge.[12]

This recognition of the coexistence of culturally equal, if not superior, nations of the West was brought home to the Chinese by Article 51 of the Sino-British Tientsin treaty of 1858 which forbade the use of the word *i* (barbarian) as a description of the Europeans and by the bitter experience of China's repeated defeats. For achieving her proclaimed goal—the wealth and power of the nation[13]—China had to emulate not only Western technology but also Western political principles and general knowledge. The first step in this direction was to interpose a constitution between Heaven and Its Son, thus placing the monarch under both the Mandates of Heaven and the people. As a constitution is concrete, more definite, less elusive, *vox populi* threatened to displace *vox Dei*.[14] True, the identification of Heaven with the people dates back to the times of the *Book of History, Book of Odes*, and Mencius and the nationalists at the turn of the century made no claim of originality in this. K'ang Yu-wei's request for a constitution was couched precisely in Confucian terms, borrowing authority from the *Spring and Autumn Annals*.[15] None the less, the interposition made two significant changes in Confucian political thinking. First, the monarch became the supreme representative of the interests of the people who, in turn, represented all there was to represent of the nation. In K'ang's own words, Emperor Kuang-hsü decided to adopt reform measures for the sake of *China* (Chung-kuo, not the Great Ch'ing),[16] and in Liang Ch'i-chao's words, his sole aim of reform was 'to preserve the country and to protect the people', 'the waxing or waning of the monarchical power being of no consequence'.[17] In other words, Kuang-hsü in 1898 was the rallying point of patriotism, not just loyalty, while the reformers themselves, in their effort to save China, were patriots, not just loyal vassals. This was no insignificant change. Both the monarch's

---

[12] Chung-kuo Shih-hsüeh-hui, *Wu-hsü pien-fa* (The 1898 reform) (Peking, 1953), ii. 175.

[13] On the whole subject of the realization of the link between a country's wealth and its power and the preoccupation of China's modernizers with the duty of government to promote these, see Benjamin Schwartz, *In Search of Wealth and Power; Yen Fu and the West* (Camb., Mass., 1964).

[14] Levenson, *Confucian China*, ii. 12. [15] Ibid. pp. 236–7.

[16] Ibid. i. 413. [17] *Wu-hsü cheng-pien-chi*, pp. 148 & 157.

B

role and the reformers' commitments were new. And it was precisely because of their commitment to save China rather than the dynasty that they were charged with treason in the edict of 29 September 1898:

> Again we have heard that the rebel party illegally set up a Pao Kuo Hui [the Society for National Preservation], advocating the preservation of China instead of the Great Ch'ing. Their rebelliousness and treachery has certainly aroused our intense anger.[18]

Secondly, the bureaucracy was considered by the reformers as inadequate for the task of achieving the 'wealth and power of the nation'. The proposed changes in the examination system and the civil service were directed not so much against corruption and irregularities as against the training of universal men for specialized jobs. Specialization and usefulness with particular reference to the wealth and power of the nation were the two cardinal goals of China's new education. Although it was still superficially within the Confucian tradition that good administration depended on good men, the reformers scarcely understood, as their opponents did, that, like the changed concept of the monarch, this, if put into practice, would in time have undermined the entire structure of the traditional bureaucracy.

What the reformers proposed to do in the guise of Confucianism was to dismantle the two institutional pillars of the Confucian state—the monarch and his civil service.

The failure of the Boxer rebellion in 1900 and the defeat of despotic Russia by constitutional Japan compelled the Confucian monarchy to yield to these demands. The main contents of the government-sponsored reform after the Boxer catastrophe were the adoption of a constitution and the reorganization of the administrative and educational systems. Thereafter Confucianism ceased to be institutionally meaningful in Chinese politics. When this happened, the death-bed of Chinese culturalism became the birthplace of her nationalism. Seeing nationalism as an irrepressible force, the alien Manchu dynasty in the first decade of this century made a desperate attempt to identify its own interests with those of the nation in the vain hope of taking the wind out of the sails of revolution. This eleventh-hour effort came too late.

Since institutional Confucianism was jettisoned by even the

---

[18] *Wü-hsü pien-fa*, ii. 103.

most conservative of China's political forces in the 1900s, Confucianism remained only as a 'faith' and a body of ethical precepts. In the eyes of its defenders, it was a badge of identity all Chinese should wear;[19] in those of the iconoclasts, it was a brake on progress that should be removed.[20] To say that Confucianism is a faith which can be developed into an organized religion comparable to Christianity is to force the master's doctrines into an un-Confucian framework, an arbitrary effort with no hope of success. Worse still, its advocates in 1916–17 were either semi-literate soldiers or were soon to be discredited in the farce of the 1917 imperial restoration. But the ensuing attack on Confucianism launched by Ch'en Tu-hsiu, Wu Yü, Li Ta-chao, and Lu Hsün, though vehement, did not suggest a way by which Confucian ethics could be replaced by other standards. Indeed, the iconoclasts themselves had no clear view on what new moral standards China should have adopted. As a result of this weakness, some people stuck to traditional moral principles while others simply had no idea what code of conduct to follow. The general outlook was a moral confusion in which warlords, compradors, and opportunistic politicians throve. Furthermore, there was no established legal system which might have helped to improve the situation.[21] Excesses of various descriptions therefore went on unabated. Against this background Chinese leaders attempted moral rearmament in forms such as the New Life Movement, which made no bones of reviving Confucianism *in toto*, and rectification campaigns which accepted some of the Confucian values.[22]

The moral chaos had one dire consequence for Chinese politics in so far as everyone could trim Confucian standards to suit his own purposes. The Hung-hsien reign was supported and opposed entirely on Confucian moral grounds; so was the 1917 imperial restoration. Tuan Ch'i-jui in Peking, Sun Yat-sen in Canton, Wu P'ei-fu in Loyang, and even Chang Tsung-ch'ang, the bandit warlord, in Shantung, all justified their views and actions by quoting from Confucian classics. Later, the right wing of the

[19] Ibid. pp. 231 ff.; Fengkang Chi-men Ti-tzu [not usually romanized 'Chi men-ti-tzu'], *Sanshui Liang Yen-sun hsien-sheng nien-p'u* (A chronological biography of Liang Shih-i of Sanshui) (Canton, 1939), ii. 538; Levenson, *Confucian China*, ii. 15.

[20] See writings of this period by Ch'en Tu-hsiu, Li Ta-chao, Wu Yü, and Lu Hsün.

[21] See below, ch, 7.

[22] *Cheng-feng wen-hsien* (Documents of the rectification campaign) (Hong Kong, 1949), pp. 80 & 87–88.

Kuomintang interpreted the Three Principles of Dr Sun Yat-sen in the light of Confucianism, identifying the principles of nationalism, democracy, and livelihood, which were obviously inspired by practical needs and Western ideas, with the teachings of the great master and his disciples. A typical example of this is Chang Ch'i-yün's book, *Min-tsu Ssu-hsiang* (Nationalistic thought), published in Taipei in 1951. According to him, Dr Sun was a great thinker because he was a latter-day Confucius; his principles were profound because they represented a revival of Confucianism. The republican polity Dr Sun designed was in Chang's view a Confucian state. Coming after the abolition of the monarchy and the traditional bureaucracy and education, these views and their practice, if they meant anything at all, were anachronistic.

NATIONALISM

The retreat of Confucianism and its eventual abandonment were only one side of the coin; the other was the growth of China's nationalism as a force disruptive and destructive of the *ancien régime* and constructive of a new state. Although the stimulus to this growth came from China's inability to deal successfully with the foreigner by force of logic or arms, it drew nourishment in its infancy from self-examination—what was wrong with China and what was wrong with the Chinese?

The trend of introspection was set in motion with the famous Rehabilitation Programme (*shan-hou chang-ch'eng*) of January 1861[23] and went on throughout the period of restoration, but its characteristic then was not so much what was wrong as what was lacking. The confidence, or complacency in the tradition, hence in the dynasty which represented it, remained largely unshaken; the question of replacing either the fundamentals of the tradition or the dynasty did not yet arise. The shock of defeat in 1895 made the Chinese élite realize that unless the country itself could be preserved, the fate of its tradition was doomed. As Professor Schwartz puts it, 'if in the last analysis, one must choose between the preservation of the state and preservation of Confucian values, which shall give way?'[24] What was at stake, then, was not just

---

[23] *Ch'ou-pan i-wu shih-mo* (The management of barbarian affairs), *Hsien-feng*, ch. 71, 17b–26a. Excerpts in S. Y. Teng & J. K. Fairbank, *China's Response to the West* (New York, 1963), pp. 47–49.

[24] Schwartz, p. 19.

Confucian values, but also the Confucian institutions which made up the state. Once the question was posed thus, culturalism was on its way out while nationalism was on its way in.

Before the dust of 1895 had had time to settle, the Boxer blunder was committed. Since the captain himself was scuttling the ship, the crew had to save it by jettisoning him. What then was the ship? On introducing the concept of China to replace the Great Ch'ing, it was realized, much to the dismay of politically-conscious Chinese, that China was not a nation, nor were her people citizens of a nation-state.[25] To redress the situation, the alien rule of the Manchus had to be removed so that full control over their own fate could be restored to the Han Chinese.[26] This explains why the Chinese nationalism of the constitutional-monarchy vintage was superseded by anti-Manchuism. When the Manchus were overthrown, the Han Chinese, it was argued, would be able to modify the tradition, adopt new plans, achieve 'the wealth and power of the nation', and eventually stand *vis-à-vis* the foreigner as his equal. To prove the capabilities of the Han Chinese in fulfilling all this, the nationalists of the 1900s revived the myth of 'the descendants of the Yellow Emperor',[27] representing a racialist view which had played only an insignificant part in orthodox tradition.

If this line of argument was valid, the only answer to China's manifold problems was a revolution to clear away the obstacle on the path towards the promised land, the Ch'ing dynasty, and to let the 'better race' take over the helm of power. The more cautious and conservative, however, rejected the premises that the Chinese were slaves of the Manchus and that the overthrow of the dynasty was a precondition of national salvation. They thought rather that the root of China's weaknesses lay in the physical, moral, and intellectual inadequacies of the Chinese,[28] which could be remedied only by education and by a reform of the educational system.

---

[25] Chang Nan & Wang Jen-chih, eds., *Hsin-hai ke-ming ch'ien shih-nien chien shih-lun hsüan-chi* (Selection of topical articles from the decade before the 1911 revolution) (Peking, 1962–3), i. 63, 87, 91, 262, 428–9, 436; Shih Chün, ed., *Chung-kuo chin-tai ssu-hsiang-shih ts'an-k'ao tzu-liao chien-pien* (Selected reference material on the intellectual history of modern China) (Peking, 1957), p. 632.

[26] See below, p. 307.

[27] Chang & Wang, i. 60, 94–98, 273, 295 & ii. 484, 528, 653, 668–70, 721.

[28] Ibid. i. 8–16, 428–9, & 436, and Yen Fu's views in Chung-kuo Shih-hsüeh-hui, *Wu-hsü pien-fa*, iii. 41 ff.

Drastic alterations of any kind in the existing political order were unnecessary, premature, harmful.

The issue was joined. Education and discipline were admittedly necessary, but the question was whether they should be preceded by a revolution to remove the main obstacle to making both China and her citizens strong.[29] The revolutionaries insisted that they should be, but the inefficacy of the republican system after 1912 proved them to be wrong and threw the issue wide open again. The monarchists argued in favour of a restoration on the ground that the Chinese were not politically mature enough to be citizens of a republic and proceeded to put their convictions into practice; the republicans stuck to their guns, later introducing remedial measures such as the Nationalists' tutelary period[30] and the people's democratic dictatorship of Mao Tse-tung.[31] Below this level, there were also pure educationists like Yen Fu, Liang Shu-ming, and Dr James Yen who believed that the obliteration of ignorance was the only cure for China's ills. All these conflicting views were put forward for achieving only one end—'the wealth and power of the nation'.

After 1919 a mighty new factor pushed its way into Chinese nationalistic thinking, the idea of anti-imperialism. Before that date, all nationalists blamed China's poverty and frailty on her own faults; since then, they have also blamed the imperialists. The injection of this factor changed the meaning of Chinese nationalism. After 1919 it was no longer enough for a nationalist to seek 'the wealth and power of the nation'; he had to be anti-imperialistic at the same time. Therefore those who had striven to strengthen the Confucian empire without being hostile to the imperialists, e.g. Tseng Kuo-fan, Li Hung-chang, and Chang Chih-tung, were labelled 'traitors'; those who had done nothing to improve the conditions in the country or to resist the imperialists, e.g. Yüan Shih-k'ai, Tuan Ch'i-jui, and Wu P'ei-fu, were 'claws and fangs' of their foreign masters; and after 1945 even those who tried to strengthen the republic without adhering to the anti-imperialistic cause, e.g. Chiang Kai-shek, were called 'thieves selling their country'. But anti-imperialism had its more construc-

---

[29] See below, p. 139.   [30] See below, p. 154.

[31] The definition of the people, Lenin's identification of the party with the class, and the implied infallibility of the party were all designed to restrict the people's political power and guarantee a 'wiser' use of power.

tive role to play. It gave China a clear concept of her sovereign rights, and a cohesive power to rally her people around the government. The unity of the nation became almost entirely dependent on it; so did the prestige of the government and its leaders in consequence.[32]

A paradoxical situation existed. China's poverty and frailty, in the majority opinion, was caused partly by imperialist encroachment, yet the efficacy of her anti-imperialism depended among other things on her 'wealth and power': therefore the salvation of China lay not in a head-on clash with the imperialists but precisely in achieving 'the wealth and power of the nation'. Hence the memorialists of 1861 advised the throne to 'resort to peace and friendship when temporarily obliged to do so; use war and defence as your actual policy', and 'to suppress the T'aip'ings and Nien bandits first, get the Russians under control next, and attend to the British last'.[33] Replace the 'T'aip'ings and Nien bandits' with the 'communists', the 'Russians' with the 'Red imperialists', and the 'British' with the 'White imperialists' and the policy of 1861 would become Chiang Kai-shek's *an-nei jang-wai* (stabilizing the internal situation before dealing with external problems) of the 1930s. In fact, from 1895 to 1949 the prime and consistent concern of the Nationalists in power, whether anti-imperialists or not, was nation-making, especially the state institutions—the drafting of a

---

[32] The vicissitudes of the KMT and Chiang illustrate this. The party's anti-imperialism reached its height in the Manifesto of the 2nd National Congress (*Hsüan-yen hui-k'an*, Collected declarations (Shanghai, 1928), p. 176) and this was sustained throughout the first phase of the Northern Expedition (July 1926–April 1927). The Nanking Incident of March 1927, when KMT troops killed and looted foreign residents there, provoking violent reactions from the powers concerned, dampened this enthusiasm and the Tsinan Incident of May 1928, when Japanese garrison troops challenged Chiang's army, causing Chiang to back down, showed a further decline in the enthusiasm. Thereafter the Declarations of the National Government on 7 July 1928 and of the 3rd National Congress of the KMT in March 1929 spoke of unification, reconstruction, and strengthening before the hope for a diplomatic victory could be fulfilled (Chang Ch'i-yün, *Chung-hua min-kuo shih-kang*, An outline history of the republic of China (Taipei, 1954), vi. 261). After 18 Sept 1931, when the Japanese occupied Manchuria, and the formulation of Chiang's 'revolutionary philosophy' which advocated a policy of 'patience and determination' the party had almost abandoned its short-lived anti-imperialism (*CYB, 1937*, pp. 283, 289, & 321); not until after the Sian coup and Chiang's statement made at Kuling on 19 July 1937, which announced China's decision to resist Japan, did the party and its leaders resume their anti-imperialist stance. The prestige of both the party and Chiang stood high during the Japanese war.

[33] Teng & Fairbank, p. 48.

constitution, the rebuilding of a civil service, the reorganization of the nation's defences, and the reconstruction of its economy, under the overriding goal of 'wealth and power'.

CONSTITUTION

To the statesmen of 1912 a constitution represented two important prerequisites for the smooth administration of the country—consolidation of the gains of the revolution by restraining the powers of the conservative and the military, and the replacement of the Confucian orthodoxy which had hitherto been the fundamental principle of the state with a new concept, legitimacy. Plainly, these two were closely connected and were the *raison d'être* of the 1912 provisional constitution. Equally plainly, the bludgeon of Yüan Shih-k'ai exposed the complete inadequacy of this. Yet it was precisely this tattered piece of paper that the politicians and warlords of the 1920s tried to make effective after the death of Yüan Shih-k'ai.

In such constitutional issues as the presidential succession of 1916, the parliamentary elections of 1917, and the presidential election of 1923, two new and rather ambiguous concepts, *fa-t'ung* and *hu-fa* (respectively the constitutional tradition and protection of the constitution), call for a brief examination. In concrete terms, *fa-t'ung* means a respect for the constitutional tradition dating from the 1912 provisional constitution which was particularly revered (but usually ignored in practice) by the Peking government from 1916[34] till the proclamation of the 1923 constitution,[35] and by Sun Yat-sen and his followers from 1917 to the Reorganization of the Kuomintang in 1924.[36] In abstract terms, however, its meaning is obscure. It is an over-simplification to say that 'The Provisional Constitution, representing the spirit of the times, was a symbol of change and a promise of modernization. It was due to this quality that it was . . . always held in some measure of affection by those who were genuinely republican.'[37] The genuine republicans, it must be remembered, flourished in both the Peking and Canton governments; Li Yüan-hung, Tuan Ch'i-jui, and Ts'ao K'un were no less convinced of the permanence of the republican form of state than Sun Yat-sen, Lu Jung-t'ing,

[34] *Cheng-fu kung-pao* (Government Gazette, hereafter *CFKP*), 29 June 1916.
[35] Ibid. 18 Oct 1923.   [36] See below, pp. 140 ff.
[37] Ch'ien Tuan-Sheng, *The Government and Politics of China* (Harvard, 1950), p. 70.

and T'ang Chi-yao, though for different reasons. It is through their different and often irreconcilable interpretations that the significance of *fa-t'ung* may be grasped.

Let us look at a few examples. On the question of the presidential succession of 1916, Tuan Ch'i-jui preferred the application of the 1914 Constitutional Compact to the revival of the 1912 provisional constitution in the hope that by this one stroke he could reduce Li Yüan-hung, the presidential successor, to a mere Acting President while keeping his power as the Premier free of interference from parliament.[38] His later attempts to revise the parliamentary Election Law, to influence the election of the Anfu parliament, to constrain Li Yüan-hung's power, and to unify the country by force[39] helped to show that considerations of power were behind all his constitutional wrangles. Ironically, it was he who as the provisional executive in 1924 formally abrogated the 1912 constitution.[40]

Another example was the question of whether to incorporate the organization of provincial government in the draft constitution of 1917. A practical consideration here was whether the stipulations of the constitution would be observed by the disobedient military leaders of the provinces who had previously evinced their opposition to the incorporation.[41] In the parliament which undertook to draft the constitution, those who represented provincial interests, the Progressive Party, were therefore at loggerheads with those who did not, the Kuomintang splinter groups, and this resulted in an ugly brawl between them which abruptly terminated the work of drafting.[42]

The 1923 constitution may have been technically better than that of 1912, but in the process of its drafting, the distinction between *fa-t'ung* and *hu-fa* became clear. Wu P'ei-fu, the pillar of the military strength of the Chihli clique, was in favour of preserving the *fa-t'ung*, hence mildly opposed to the making of a new constitution, in order to court the adherence of the south and to

---

[38] Ch'ien Tuan-sheng & others, *Min-kuo cheng-chih shih* (History of political institutions under the Republic of China) (Shanghai, 1946), i. 190–1; Shen Yun-lung, *Li Yüan-hung p'ing-chuan* (A critical biography of Li Yüan-hung) (Taipei, 1963), p. 78; Yang Yu-chiung, *Chin-tai Chung-kuo li-fa shih* (A history of legislation in modern China) (Shanghai, 1936), pp. 281–3.

[39] Yang Yu-chiung, pp. 280–3; and Hsü Tao-ling, *Hsü Shu-cheng hsien-sheng wen-chi nien-p'u ho-k'an* (Essays and chronology of Hsü Shu-cheng) (Taipei, 1962), pp. 133–7.

[40] *TFTC*, 10 Jan 1925.   [41] *CFKP*, 6 Jan 1917.   [42] Ibid.

effect a peaceful unification of the country,[43] while Ts'ao K'un, the leader of the clique, was anxious to have a new constitution which would facilitate his election to the presidency.[44] To make sure of his success, Ts'ao gave his constitution a federalist bias in both political and economic terms and each of those who voted for him a cheque for $5,000.[45] Ts'ao's personal interests in constitution-making were plain enough; Wu's, however, were more subtle. Even if he did not aspire to become President himself, his personal power and prestige as the master of central China were undoubtedly what he wanted to preserve. He knew perfectly well that his enemy in the north, Chang Tso-lin, though defeated by him in 1922, was grudgingly waiting to seize any opportunity to stage a come-back, and he was afraid that such an opportunity would be in the offing if the new constitution and presidential election were to provoke the 'protectors' of the 1912 constitution in the south to take military action. Under such circumstances, his own troops would be sandwiched between two enemies, fighting on two fronts. Hence he preferred the vague 'constitutional tradition' to a definitive constitution. Again, personal interests overrode everything else.[46]

[43] Wu P'ei-fu, *Wu P'ei-fu hsien-sheng chi* (An anthology of Wu P'ei-fu) (Taipei, 1960), p. 384 and Li Chien-nung, *Tsui-chin san-shih-nien Chung-kuo cheng-chih shih* (A political history of China in the past thirty years) (Shanghai, 1930), p. 506.

[44] Art. 73, 1923 constitution (Chien Tuan-sheng, app. C), which in the final analysis required a mere simple majority of those present in the parliament at the presidential election to have a candidate legally elected.

[45] Ch'ien Tuan-sheng, p. 78.

[46] This speculation is based on Wu's personal views on the constitutional problem. In 1914 he was sent by Yüan Shih-k'ai to discuss the articles concerning defence with Yüan's Japanese adviser on the constitution and he thought: 'Since the draft constitution was a translation of an existing foreign constitution which did not suit the Chinese national characteristics and since arguing over each point with him would have meant running the risk of being disobedient to my superiors, I adopted the best policy of keeping my mouth shut' (Wu P'ei-fu, p. 287). The mildness of his opposition to the 1923 constitution can be interpreted in his concept of loyalty. After the defeat of 1924, Wu met Yoshida, the Japanese consul of Tientsin, who suggested that he should co-operate with Tuan Ch'i-jui, the erstwhile leader of the Anhwei clique of warlords, so as to stabilize the situation in the north. This Wu rejected by saying: 'Since each nation has its own history and national characteristics, its concept of nationhood is often peculiarly its own. China is an old country with a history of 4,000 years and a permanent, unalterable, unwritten "constitution", i.e. the eight virtues of filial piety, brotherhood, loyalty, faithfulness, propriety, righteousness, incorruptibility, and sense of shame. When these eight virtues prevail, the "constitution" of the country is established and the country itself prospers; when one of them is destroyed, there would be no standard [of judgement] left by which the nation can be united. . . . If I were to accept, my honourable consul, your suggestion to co-operate with Tuan and betray

In all these examples the underlying motive for opposing constitutional revision was personal power and self-interest with which restrictive stipulations might interfere, especially if they were made unambiguous. The suitability of the provisional constitution of 1912, in the eyes of the warlords, lay in its vagueness (e.g. the relationship between the President and the Cabinet, and the parliament and the election of the President) and omissions (e.g. the organization of provincial government)[47] which made it the least troublesome for the militarists to observe and utilize. To make it even more vague, they invented the term *fa-t'ung*, to reintroduce the old concept of orthodoxy into the new one of legitimacy. Although both were restrictive, they did not restrict (and by implication therefore justified what was not restricted) specifically the same things. A constitution must, for instance, restrict the political ends, as well as the means for their fulfilment, of the activities of the citizens; the orthodoxy, i.e. the Confucian tradition, seldom restricts the means. What could not be justified constitutionally might be justified in Confucian terms. In other words, what might not be legitimate could still conform to the orthodox way of doing things. It was because of this additional flexibility (this double standard, to put it bluntly) implied in the term *fa-t'ung* that we find many political activities of the warlord period (1916–28) being justified in either constitutional or Confucian terms or both, and indeed several attempts had been made to include the establishment of Confucianism as a state religion in the constitution.[48] But the vagueness, the flexibility, was used to serve self-interest or personal power.

Under the banner of *hu-fa*, Sun Yat-sen, supported by some of the southern warlords, set up a rival government in Canton which lasted continuously from 1917 to 1923. Sun's own motives, e.g. the preservation of the Republic, may have been altruistic; those of his supporters were definitely not. The warlords who participated

Ts'ao, what could be preserved out of the correct relationship [between Ts'ao and me]? More than that, my integrity as a vassal (*ch'en*) [to Ts'ao] would be ruined and myself would be unsuited for the weighty burden of state affairs. People often say that the lord-vassal relationship died on the day the Republic was founded. In my view, this is quite wrong' (ibid. pp. 407–8). Wu made no distinction between a constitution and the orthodoxy.

[47] Full text of the constitution in Chang & Wang, *Hsin-hai ke-ming* . . . , viii. 30–36.

[48] The 1923 constitution, being highly eclectic in nature, had a half-hearted reference to this in Art. 12.

in the Canton government were interested only in their own preservation or territorial expansion in the context of Tuan Ch'i-jui's, and later Wu P'ei-fu's, policy of unification by force. Again, just because it omitted to mention the organization of the provincial government, the 'territorial barons' in the south found it convenient to uphold the 1912 constitution and could do so without contradicting their other policy—a federation of autonomous provinces. Sun's interests tallied with theirs in so far as he wanted to preserve the 1912 constitution, but ran counter to them because of Sun's insistence on unification under a strong central government. For Sun the protection of the constitution was a nationalistic policy; for his supporters it was regionalistic.

The conclusion the revolutionaries of the 1920s drew from the havoc played by the unscrupulous distortion or open defiance of the constitutions was that the Chinese people were not yet ready for constitutional rule. A few took exception to this view, but to no avail. Therefore the elusive idea of a 'tutelary phase' as being necessary after the military phase of a national revolution became a fact when the Kuomintang unified the country in 1929. From that date to the collapse of the National government in 1949, except for a brief interval in 1948 and 1949, China was ruled by the Compact of the Tutelary Phase of 1931, which gave her a government of five powers (*yüan*).[49] The imbalance of power among them is well known, and with the consequence that the Legislative *Yüan* was almost powerless over the Executive *Yüan*. Even in the executive branch of the government, power dwelt wherever Chiang Kai-shek happened to be. When he was the President he was concurrently the commander-in-chief of all the armed forces (before December 1931 and after September 1943); when he was not, the President (who was Lin Sen) was deprived of the command. Corresponding to the fluctuations in the power of the President, the chairman of the Executive *Yüan* grew in importance under Lin Sen and shrank to a subsidiary position under Chiang Kai-shek.[50] In such circumstances, one is left to wonder whether the National government was, as the Compact of 1931 says, controlled by the Kuomintang or by Chiang, by the strength

[49] See below, p. 154 and Ch'ien Tuan-sheng & others, ix. 206–7. Full text of the constitution drafted in 1936 and adopted in 1948 in *Li-fa yüan kung-pao* (The Gazette of the Legislative Yüan), no. 62.
[50] Ch'ien Tuan-sheng & others, i. 223.

of its organization or by the armed forces under his command. The frequent civil wars, anti-communist campaigns, and eventually the Japanese war created conditions favourable to further military ascendancy and enhancement of Chiang's personal power. In addition to being the chairman of the Military Commission, he was made the chairman of the Supreme Defence Council when in 1937 it superseded the Political Council and he succeeded Lin Sen as the President of the government. To justify all this, Chiang revived Confucianism and used it to explain his policies. In the absence of a constitution, the orthodoxy tended to invade all the territories of legitimacy.

The history of Chinese constitution-making seems to indicate two internal obstructive forces—the Confucian orthodoxy, and the might of arms in support of factional interests, the former justifying the use of the latter and being made more persuasive by the latter. Together they reduced all the constitutional endeavours to futility. This diarchy did not come to an end until the power of the Communist Party organization, with the help of nationalistic and socialistic mass propaganda, succeeded in controlling and using the gun for its destruction. Only then, in 1954, did a more effective constitution become a possibility, as will appear in Chapter 7.

CIVIL SERVICE

Towards the end of the last century, the expansion of the modern functions of the Ch'ing government revealed the inability of the traditional education and examination systems to provide suitable people for selection for official posts. Modern enterprises, too, were in need of people with modern, specialized training. Apart from its inherent limitations, the traditional examination system, as is well known, was fraught with irregularities. The institutional limitations and the malpractices of the existing system prompted the reformers of 1898 to cry out for an overhaul of China's education, from the cultivation of people's talents by setting up modern schools to the reform of the examinations, in order to bring about changes in the civil service.[51] The plans of 1898 were implemented, *mutatis mutandis*, after the Boxer uprising.

When the system of modern schools was generally introduced in 1902, the government was aware of the economic difficulties entailed—the regular hours of attendance and in some cases

[51] Chung-kuo Shih-hsüeh-hui, *Wu-hsü pien-fa*, iii. 21.

regular residence at the school would deprive the student of an opportunity of gainful employment. Moreover, the expense of uniform, textbooks, and residence represented an outlay not many could afford. Therefore the original idea was initially to provide free education at state schools and colleges; not until 1907 was the question of a fee contemplated. The middle school, it was suggested, might charge 1 *yuan* per month and the college 2 *yuan* as tuition. But during the first year of the 1902 plan complaints came from all provinces, beseeching the government to revise its decision on free education on the ground of financial stringency. The new plan of 1903 continued to provide free primary education but left the amount to be charged for tuition at the middle school and college to the discretion of the local government. The universities, too, were to collect a tuition fee from their students.[52]

After the revolution of 1911, the financial hardships endured by the government colleges and schools remained unrelieved. Hence the Ministry of Education announced that from 1916 state primary schools were to collect a monthly tuition fee of 0·2 *yuan* and state colleges 0·5 *yuan*.[53] The private school had always been fee-paying. What had initially been envisaged as free education now became costly in the eyes of many, thus linking wealth and education more closely than ever.[54] Modern education in China, therefore, tended to decrease upwards social mobility.

Another, even more expensive, kind of education was study abroad,[55] which became so fashionable in the 1900s as to warrant the publication of a periodical (the *Yu-hsüeh i-p'ien*)[56] for those who were already abroad and those who intended to go. Several of its contributors urged Chinese students to study, preferably, in the United States or Europe, or, as a second choice, in Japan.[57] Ostensibly, this was for the good of the nation; but the successes of those who had contacts with foreigners[58] and those who had had

---

[52] On all this see Shu Hsin-ch'eng, *Chiao-yü-shih tzu-liao* (Material on the history of education) (Peking, 1962), i & ii.

[53] *Chiao-yü-pu kung-pao* (Gazette of the Min. of Education), 2nd yr, no. 12 & 3rd yr, no. 11.

[54] This tendency had already existed in the second half of the 19th century, as pointed out by Prof. Ping-ti Ho in his 'Family vs Merit in the Ming and Ch'ing Dynasties', in J. Menzel, ed., *The Chinese Civil Service* (Boston, 1963), p. 31.

[55] A Chinese student in Japan in 1903 needed 300 taels per year (Chang & Wang, *Hsin-hai ke-ming* . . . , i. 391).

[56] 'Translations and essays while studying abroad'.   [57] Chang & Wang, i. 394.

[58] Sheng Hsüan-huai, T'ang Ching-hsing, Cheng Kuan-ying, and Hsü Jun.

foreign education[59] undoubtedly gave food for thought. Three categories of Chinese students—members of the imperial clan, government students, and the self-financed private students who formed the great majority—therefore went to study in those countries. In 1905–9 the number of Chinese students in Japan leapt from 3,000 to 13,000,[60] and by 1919 there were more than 1,700 Chinese students in the United States.[61]

This resulted not only in the replacement of traditional degree holders in the high places of the government by school-trained personnel, but also in the predominance of foreign-trained students. The imperfect statistics below (gathered from the Who's Who section of the *China Yearbook* of 1919 and 1924) will help to show this.

	1919	*1924*
American-trained	32	81
European-trained	13	48
Japanese-trained	100	43
Chinese school trained	43	51
Traditional degree holders	37	24
Total	225	287

Note: Military leaders are excluded from this table and it must be noted that the information of personal educational background in the 1919 *Yearbook* is far from complete

It is not surprising that since the traditional examination system had been abolished in 1905, more and more intellectuals with a different kind of training came up to replace traditional degree holders. What is unexpected, however, is the speed with which they were replaced, at first by the Japanese-trained and then by the American- and the European-trained scholars. The passport to eminence seems to have been a degree or a certificate of a college abroad rather than a mere Chinese diploma. The Japanese-trained, particularly those in the 1900s, were responsible for the upsurge of Chinese nationalism, whereas the American- and European-trained, particularly those in the decade 1910–20, were responsible for the cultural revolution in the 1920s. This was because of the cultural similarity of Japan and China and of the

[59] Yung Wing, T'ang Shao-i, Liang Tun-yen, and Chan T'ien-yu.
[60] Levenson, *Liang Ch'i-ch'ao*, p. 81.   [61] *The Times*, 9 July 1919.

cultural difference of America and Europe. In other words, while those who had been students in Japan in the period 1900–10 were politically alienated, those who returned after study in Europe or America in the next decade were culturally alienated. Both types of alienation produced a class of pioneers the basis of whose claims to distinction and leadership differed from those of the traditional élite. The superficiality of their training was largely ignored. As Kuo Mo-jo complained early in the decade 1910–20:

Haven't we got in places like Shanghai and Peking a large number of people who have been to the United States for two or three years, decorated with 'doctors' and 'MAs', and come back full of pride and conceit to take up posts like government commissioners, university professors, and chief editors of publishing houses?[62]

Later Lu Hsün described them—sarcastically, as in his short story *Li-shui* (Water Conservancy)—as 'high-class Chinese' (*kao-teng hua-jen*).[63]

Wealth was, then, a necessary condition for achieving eminence through alienation. For the talented but poor, the outlets for their ambition seem to have been (1) to form some sort of association with foreign business firms so as to become rich (e.g. Yü Hsia-ch'ing);[64] (2) to attend a free state school in the hope of winning a scholarship to study abroad (e.g. Lu Hsün);[65] and (3) to join the army (e.g. the warlords of the decades 1910–20 and 1920–30). Ch'en Hsiao-fen's reminiscence is most revealing: 'After the abolition of the traditional examination system scholars had to look for other ways for a living. Some went to study abroad and others became boarders at schools in the cities. But the majority of them, the poor, joined the army.'[66] Consequently three new classes of people emerged in modern China—the business associates of foreign firms who supposedly understood foreign trade and industry, the culturally-alienated intellectuals who were pioneers of political and social reforms, and the new soldiers. The first two categories, it must be borne in mind, had one common characteristic—their admiration of some aspects of the foreign way of life with which they were familiar.

[62] *Mo-jo wen-chi* (Collected essays by Kuo Mo-jo) (Peking, 1958), vi. 177.
[63] *Ch'üan-chi* (Complete works) (Peking, 1961), ii. 329–45.   [64] *CYB 1924*, p. 1220.
[65] Preface to 'Na-han' (To Arms), *Ch'üan-chi*, i. 3–4.
[66] People's Political Consultative Council, Hupei Branch, *Hsin-hai shou-i hui-i-lu* (Memoirs of the 1911 uprising) (Wuhan, 1957), p. 68.

The selection of Chinese associates of foreign firms for government posts began soon after the Opium war. As the government extended its modern functions in the field of economy and diplomacy, the selection, too, was extended. Under Li Hung-chang and Chang Chih-tung many such men rose to high positions in the civil service (Sheng Hsüan-huai and Ts'ai Hsi-yung, for example). This trend continued after the 1911 revolution and gained momentum after 1928. But for a ministerial post, one had to have foreign education, not just association with foreign firms. The appointment of foreign-trained students to the rank of minister began with T'ang Shao-i and Liang Tun-yen. In the decades 1910–20 and 1920–30 a few foreign-trained scholars rose to a similar eminence, as seven of them were ministers or vice-ministers in 1919 and four in 1924. The smallness of these numbers was due to the complexities of warlord politics which tended to exclude and discourage modernized men from joining the government. In 1934 the total number of ministers and vice-ministers increased to 30, of whom 18 were foreign-educated, and in 1943 the number went up to 37, of whom 21 were foreign-trained.[67]

The growing number of foreign-educated staff in the Nationalist central government of Nanking after 1929 was not matched by a similar development in the local governments.[68] Here we must admit a lack of statistics to substantiate this point, but it is probably not far wrong. The continued complexities of provincial politics in the 1930s tend to strengthen this impression. The diarchy of the culturally-alienated leaders in the centre and parochial leaders in the provinces and districts was partly responsible for the lack of understanding and other difficulties between them. The provinces and districts remained the spheres of influence of warlords, local gentry, their relatives and friends, and Chinese-trained scholars and people of 'equivalent academic experience'.[69] This state of affairs had been created in 1912, and neither the efforts of Yüan Shih-k'ai and Chiang Kai-shek to make uniform the organization of local governments nor the civil service examinations from 1916 on did anything to improve it.

The traditional method of selecting civil servants was undermined;

[67] *CYB 1935* and *China Handbook* (New York, 1943).
[68] *CYB 1943*, pp. 868–72.
[69] Ch'ien Tuan-sheng & others, i. 99–100 & 256–7, and Chou Ku-ch'eng, *Chung-kuo she-hui chih chieh-kou* (The structure of Chinese society) (Shanghai, 1935), p. 347.

the new scheme was not an effective substitute. This was the basic cause of the disintegration of the civil service in the Republican period. Add to this the serious shortage of qualified people for various government posts, the financial chaos, and the military interference in civilian administration, none of which was conducive to an unobtrusive growth and consolidation of the civil service. The only hope in this period lay in the utilization of the members of the Kuomintang itself to staff the civil service after 1929, but even they were ill trained for the task of building up a modern and robust bureaucracy.[70] Without reliable civil servants, no government could function efficiently or achieve lasting stability. For an efficient and stable government, as for a definitive constitution, China had to wait until the victory of the communists.

One other group of intellectuals remains to be considered—the frustrated ones. Documentation here is hard to find, except for the biographies of communist leaders (whose early background is often unsatisfactorily recorded) and novels and short stories such as Yeh Shao-chün's *Ni Huai-chih* (1928). These people were ambitious and talented, but poor, unable to achieve distinction in any recognized field of activities for a variety of reasons; they found most of the doors of society closed to them; even the work-study scheme in France[71] at the end of the first world war did not offer them a real chance of rising to eminence. They were radicals, sensitive to and indignant over social injustice and anxious to redress it through a drastic change in the social and political order. Most of them came from relatively comfortable homes of steadily declining fortune,[72] as Lu Hsün so vividly depicted: 'Had anyone sunk from relative comfort to poverty? In the process of such a transformation, I think, one sees clearly the true faces of men.'[73] In the decade 1900–10 the ladder of success, as Lu Hsün could visualize it, was a free state school, study abroad, and then service to the nation, but by the decade 1910–20, especially after the May Fourth Movement,[74] Mao and his generation of frustrated young men and women realized that a social revolution was necessary,

---

[70] Huang Shao-hsiung, *Wu-shih hui-i* (Memoirs at fifty) (Shanghai, 1945), i. 182.

[71] Sponsored by a group of leading scholars for those who wished to study in France (see Ch'ên, *Mao and the Chinese Revolution* (London, 1965), p. 52).

[72] Compare, say, the family fortunes of H. H. K'ung and Lu Hsün. See Yü Liang, *K'ung Hsiang-hsi* (Dr H. H. K'ung, a famous financier) (Hong Kong, 1955).

[73] *Ch'üan-chi*, i. 3.   [74] See below, p. 333.

among other things, for putting the right people in the right places in order to enrich and strengthen the nation. In two or three decades these frustrated young men and women of China identified their personal interests with those of the country, determined, through different means, to fulfil themselves as well as the needs of their country. It was they who in the 1920s and 1930s went to the grass-roots of society, to work among the peasants and workers, disciplining themselves and arousing the revolutionary fervour of the lower classes at the same time. With the support of the peasants and workers they formed the real opposition to the authorities in the 1930s, changed the social and political structure of large parts of China in the 1940s, and made the nation in the 1950s.

DEFENCE

It was for the defence of the metropolitan area after the destruction of Li Hung-chang's armed forces in 1895 that the Manchu government decided to train a new army at Hsiaochan, and to reorganize four others, under the command of Jung-lu. Five years later, after the Boxer uprising, the new army was the only one which had survived. It owed its survival to its good fortune in being stationed in Shantung instead of in Chihli, so that it was not engaged against foreign troops, and to its leader's refusal to transfer it to Chihli, in spite of repeated imperial urgings.[75] From 1901 onwards this was the only effective force for the defence of Peking and the dynasty; it was therefore expanded and many of its officers were to become prominent leaders on the eve of the 1911 revolution.[76] Without a single exception, the Hsiaochan group of officers fought for the Manchu throne in 1911; with very few exceptions, they became great warlords afterwards. Their transformation from imperial officers to warlords was brought about by the removal of imperial rule and hence of the Confucian legal and political restraint; this was made even more obvious after the war against the Kuomintang in 1913 and against Yüan Shih-k'ai in 1916.

Their concentration in the north was in contrast to that of the Japanese-trained officers in the south at the time of the 1911 revolution. These two groups of soldiers were different in so far as the southern ones had been affected by anti-Manchu nationalism

[75] J. Ch'ên, *Yuan Shih-k'ai* (London, 1961), pp. 48–51 & 70–71.
[76] For the membership of the group, see below, p. 40.

and after the revolution they had to fight against the revolutionary secret societies in order to gain control over their respective provinces. The fact that, having just overthrown the Manchus in a concerted effort with the revolutionaries, they could at once turn against their comrades in arms can be explained only by the shallowness of their 'nationalistic', or more precisely racialistic, understanding. Once the Manchus had been removed, the southern warlords found themselves to have more in common with the soldiers in the north than with the revolutionaries in the south.

What were the qualities they shared? What kind of men were the warlords?

Of the 1,300 officers of the rank of brigadier and above who flourished in the period 1911–28, sketches of whose biographies are available, 117 were trained in Japan, 29 at the Tientsin Military School, 61 at the Paoting Military Academy, and 20 were traditional degree holders. Altogether those so educated made a total of about 227. In addition, there were also trainees and graduates of provincial military schools. But the grand total of educated officers was in the region of 370–400. In other words, the proportion of the educated is unlikely to have exceeded 30 per cent, and the rest were mostly illiterate or semi-literate people of extremely modest origins. This general lack of education forced them to rely on their secretaries who, to judge from the warlords' public statements which they wrote, were mostly traditional scholars either indifferent or antagonistic to modern ideas and modern thought.[77]

The warlords were superstitious men, hostile to science and new ideas and stout in their defence of the Confucian tradition. Generally speaking, they were completely ignorant or ill informed about modern political thought, possessing no political or ethical criteria other than the rudiments of the Confucian canons by which to judge the wisdom or folly of a policy or an action. Confucianism to them was the only yardstick of legitimacy, and legitimacy meant respectability. Those who followed it were doing things in a legitimate or respectable way, and those who did not were illegal and contemptible. Here lay the distinction between a warlord and a bandit leader, and also the reason for the bandit leader's anxiety to become a warlord.

[77] Sources of information about the facts and figures in this section are so widely scattered as to make references impossible or too clumsy. For details, see my review article, 'Defining Chinese Warlords and their Factions', *SOAS Bulletin*, Oct 1967.

Unfortunately, their understanding of Confucianism, as of nationalism for that matter, was shallow. This was responsible for the inconsistency between their words and deeds. They were always anxious to apply Confucian yardsticks to others, not to themselves, for their own compliance with Confucianism was taken for granted. As a consequence, all their public statements appear to have been didactic, with emphasis on instruction rather than explanation. Their leniency to themselves and censure of others made them appear self-righteous and suspicious of their colleagues. Self-righteousness and suspicion are frequent sources of temper. When a powerful military leader was ever ready to lose his temper, and to inspire awe by losing it, the country might be expected to suffer from constant civil wars.

These warlords were bad Confucians and bad nationalists. Fittingly, they were the people in control of China during the interregnum between the collapse of the Confucian empire and the rise of the nation-state. They were products of a China without a stable polity and also helped to prolong such a state of affairs.

The lack of a stable polity throughout this period does not mean that the warlords made no effort to give one to China. In fact, since the collapse of the Hung-hsien dynasty, they had been concerned primarily with the question of unification, to achieve which three proposals were put forward at different times. Tuan Ch'i-jui and his Anhwei clique advocated unification by force, Feng Kuo-chang and his Chihli clique advocated unification by peaceful means, and the southern warlords advocated a federation of autonomous provinces, all with one overriding consideration in their mind—namely self-preservation. To understand this, we must have a clear idea of the deployment of the troops of these three groups, and their territorial interests. The Anhwei clique before 1920 dominated Shensi, Inner and Outer Mongolia, Peking, the Tientsin–Pukow railway zone, Anhwei, and Chekiang; the Chihli clique controlled south Chihli, Honan, Hupei (hence the Peking–Hankow railway zone), north Hunan, and the lower reaches of the Yangtze; the southern warlords fortified themselves in south Hunan, Kwangsi, Kwangtung, Kweichow, and Yunnan. The places where the influences of the north and south met were the arc stretching from south Shensi, through Szechwan, west Hupei, north Hunan, to Kiangsi and Fukien, to form what may be called the 'civil war belt', to the south-west of which were poised the southern troops and, to the north-east the forces of the Chihli clique. The armies of the Anhwei clique, not to speak of the Manchurian clique, were farther to the north-east behind those of the Chihli clique. It is small wonder that the Anhwei clique should have advocated unification by force in order to let the Chihli clique fight the south, thus killing two birds with one stone; by the same token, the Chihli clique insisted upon unification by peaceful means. The southern warlords, being too weak to aspire to unification, countered these grandiloquent proposals by their federalism. However convincing they might sound, these proposals completely failed to achieve anything but more factional feuds.[78]

The best hope of ending this state of affairs was the reorganization of the Kuomintang and the training of a new politically-indoctrinated army at Whampoa so that the former should control the latter and the latter could be used to destroy the warlords. The prerequisite of this process was the unity of the Kuomintang, which would guarantee the party's ideological leadership and organizational strength over the military. As long as the party was united, devices such as political indoctrination of the soldiers and the political supervision of the officers could function properly. In addition, the party could also work among the masses in the areas under its domination, thus making the soldiers depend on the politically-conscious masses and respect their interests. Unfortunately, the Kuomintang split after the death of Sun Yat-sen and thereafter rival factions solicited the help of the army, thus opening the flood-gates to military supremacy over the party. The result was that both the Kuomintang and its army were weak.

With a weak party and a weak army, the Northern Expedition was launched in July 1926 and had to be suspended half-way to allow the party strife to be resolved. The interval of eight months between the first and second phases of the Expedition clearly revealed the inadequacy of both the political programme and the organization of the Kuomintang for the tasks it had set itself. By the middle of 1928 the warlords' regime was nominally brought to an end, partly by hard fighting and partly by bribery. In the part of China affected by the expedition, many warlords continued to survive; in the part not so affected, things went on as usual. Out of the 82 armies in China in 1928 only 9 were under the direct control of Chiang Kai-shek and could be regarded as having had

[78] Ch'ên, *Mao and the Chinese Revolution*, chs 2–5.

some political training. The country remained basically divided, civil wars could not be stopped, and imperialist encroachment went on unabated. The vision of wealth and power remained as distant as ever.

ECONOMY

Cultural and political disintegration had their equivalent in the field of the economy—the prosperity of smallholders which the restoration leaders had striven hard but not entirely successfully to achieve was now a thing of the past as agricultural depression began. The war and indemnity of 1895 left the government with enormous foreign debts secured on the revenue of the maritime customs, while *likin* and salt gabelle, due to embezzlement and other irregularities, were yielding less and less. This, in the context of expanding public expenditure because of new defence and reform measures, upset the balance of the budget.[79] For example, in the 1911 budget the total revenue was estimated at 297 million taels whereas total expenditure was 339 million.[80] The main hope for an increase in revenue lay, not in tariff or *likin*—the principal sources of finance of the government's modern projects since the 1860s—but in land tax and salt gabelle, two of the most rigid sources of taxation. On the expenditure side, indemnity and loan service took 16·6 per cent and defence 37·7 per cent. The cumulative effect of this was the ramification of agricultural surtaxes (*fu chia shui*), an increasing burden on the peasants, and the concentration of landownership.[81]

The fall of the Manchu government meant the loss of the unity of financial administration. Since there existed no clear distinction between central and local revenues, the warlords simply retained whatever proportion of tax collections they needed for their own use. In 1913 the government expected more than 32 million *yuan* from the provinces; in fact only 5 million was received.[82] Peking, therefore, had to live on borrowed money while planning for the use of force to unify the country and get itself out of this predicament.

[79] Chao Feng-t'ien, *Wan-ch'ing wu-shih-nien ching-chi ssu-hsiang-shih* (Economic thinking in the last 50 years of the Ch'ing dynasty) (Peking, 1939), pp. 6–18.

[80] Liu Chin-tsao, *Ch'ing-ch'ao hsü wen-hsien t'ung-k'ao* (A documentary history of the Ch'ing dynasty) (1915), ch. 66, pp. 8245b–8246b.

[81] Liu Shih-jen, *Chung-kuo t'ien-fu wen-t'i* (Problems of land taxes in China) (Shanghai 1935), pp. 161–2.

[82] *CFKP*, 1912, *passim*, being telegrams from the military governors of the provinces.

This was partly the cause of the 1913 civil war. After the war the government's revenue from the provinces more than doubled and went up to 20 million *yuan* in 1916.[83] On the death of Yüan Shih-k'ai the situation reverted to 1912 and in later years it became steadily worse.[84] Even the salt gabelle, which had been reorganized in 1914–15 and placed under the inspection of foreign officials, was now tapped by the warlords as the following table shows:

The Interception of the Surplus of the Salt Gabelle
(ooo yuan)

Year	Total surplus	Amount detained
1918	71,671	15,000
1919	75,183	26,000
1920	64,020	24,000
1921	70,474	18,000
1922	78,862	31,000
1923	89,800	30,200
1926	64,287	47,672
1927	—	52,557

Sources: *CYB, 1923*, 755–8 & *1924*, 738–9; *The Times*, 4 Feb 1920, 8 July 1927, & 17 Feb 1928.

The general picture was that after 1922 the government succeeded in getting almost nothing from the provinces. In 1923 Ts'ao K'un, pursuing his policy of winning warlord support by conceding provincial autonomy, formally agreed to the land-tax becoming a purely provincial tax, so that the central government lost what had been in imperial times by far its greatest source of revenue.[85]

The financial dilemma of Peking may be stated thus: its existence depended on its ability to borrow abroad, its ability to borrow depended on its hope of solvency, its hope of solvency depended on its ability to subjugate the warlords by force or by bribery, and its ability to subjugate the warlords depended on its credit in the international money market. The more it borrowed the heavier its interest burden became, and the more it had to spend on defence

[83] Chia Shih-i, *Min-kuo hsü ts'ai-cheng-shih* (A history of the public finance of the Republic of China) (Shanghai, 1917), 70–72 and *TFTC*, 10 Dec 1928, 11.

[84] *TFTC* 10 Dec 1928, p. 11 and *The Times*, 2 Aug 1924.

[85] See below, Chapter 4.

in the hope of getting more money from the provinces. The general
trend was inevitably one of budgetary expansion.

Budgetary Expansion

(m. yuan)

Year	Revenue	Expenditure
1914	382·5	357·0
1925	461·6	634·0
1935	770·0	957·0

Sources: *TFTC*, 10 Oct 1920, 113; Chia Shih-i,
i. 41, and Sun Huai-jen, *Chung-kuo ts'ai-
cheng chih ping-t'ai chi ch'i p'i-p'an* (The
maladies of China's public finance)
(Shanghai, 1937), 11–14.

Budgetary expansion gained speed after 1929 when the maritime customs, now autonomous, salt gabelle, now successfully
reorganized, and consolidated tax (*t'ung-shui*), now replacing the
abolished *likin*, became the mainstays of the government's income,
while defence and loan service remained the principal outlays.
The budget was far from balanced and the deficit was financed by
the issue of domestic loans.[86] However, as the country moved
towards administrative and monetary unity, there was hope of
putting the finance of the central government on a healthier basis
in the early 1930s. The Japanese war of 1937 once again threw it
out of gear. The loss of the coastal provinces cut tariff and salt
gabelle from the reckoning; land tax in kind was restored to its
traditional role as the principal source of income;[87] and as the war
went on, note issuing had to be relied upon to pay for China's
defence. By the time of its collapse, the National government was
totally bankrupt; as the American Ambassador, Dr J. L. Stuart,
declared, only 5 per cent of its expenditure came from normal
revenues 'but more than this amount was expended in its collection'.[88] The *fa-pi* or the gold dollar notes, its legal tender, were
rejected by the people. Neither the *assignats* after the French
revolution nor the mark after the first world war met with a
sadder fate than Chiang Kai-shek's *fa-pi*.

[86] The *Yin-hang chou-k'an* (Bankers' Weekly), xix/44.
[87] *China Handbook, 1944*, p. 187, and Chia Te-huai, *Min-kuo ts'ai-cheng chien-shih* (A
brief history of the public finance of the Republic of China, 2nd ser.) (Shanghai,
1947), i. 86.
[88] *Fifty Years in China* (New York, 1954), p. 226.

Defence Budget in the Japanese and Civil Wars

Year	(per cent) Total expenditure	Chiang's expenses
1944	51	18·94
1945	69	38·33
1946	60	16·81
1947	55	14·88
1948	64	

Sources: Chang Chia-ao (Kia-ngau), *The Inflationary Spiral* (Camb., Mass., 1958), pp. 47, 71–72; Wu Kang, *Chiu-chung-kuo t'ung-huo p'eng-chang shih-liao* (Source materials on monetary inflation in old China) (Shanghai, 1958), p. 153.

Government's Reliance on Note Issuing, 1947

(per cent of revenue)

January	70·9	April	53·4
February	66·2	May	49·8
March	73·7	June	62·8

Source: Gen. A. C. Wedemeyer's report, US Dept of State, *United States Relations with China* (1949), p. 782.

In the provinces the financial situation was even more chaotic, due to the desire of the warlords for self-preservation and territorial expansion. To take the strongholds of their factions, for instance: Honan, of the Chihli clique, increased its military expenditure from 4·5 million *yuan* (60 per cent of the total expenditure) in 1919 to 17 million (85 per cent) in 1925; in Chekiang, of the Anhwei clique, the increase was from 2·5 million (just under 40 per cent) to 10 million (70 per cent); in Kirin, of the Manchurian clique, it was from 3 million (just under 60 per cent) to 9 million (60 per cent); in Szechwan, on the civil war belt and shared by several warlords, the increase was from 6 million (63 per cent) to 26 million (86 per cent).[89] In six years military expenditure had been quadrupled. And how was this met? The revenue of the 21st army in Szechwan, although the extreme case, may help us to understand:

[89] Chia Shih-i, i. 140–2 & ii. 148–50.

	1930	*1931*
	(*yuan*)	
'Cruel taxes' (*k'o-tsa*)	10,976,247	8,539,772
Opium	13,652,686	10,551,853
Salt gabelle	4,778,661	3,894,417
Stamp duties, tobacco & wine taxes		3,453,071
Others		108,805
Total	31,319,172	33,400,226

Source: Feng Ho-fa, *Chung-kuo nung-ts'un ching-chi tzu-liao* (Source materials on Chinese rural economy) (Shanghai, 1933–5), i. 829.

The main items here are the 'cruel taxes', opium, and salt gabelle which, translated into more general terms, meant extortionate taxes on agriculture, tax on or monopoly of opium, and the interception of taxes earmarked for the central government. In addition, there were two other important sources of income which are not included here, namely corvée and the issue of local currency.

According to Professor J. L. Buck and Chia Shih-i,[90] not since 1912 had there been any noticeable increase in the amount of land tax throughout China except Szechwan. The rule and exception in fact represented two different ways of extortion—agricultural surtaxes and land-tax collection in advance. The surtaxes were resorted to by the warlords along the lower reaches of the Yangtze—in Kiangsu 147 kinds, in Chekiang 73 kinds, and in Hupei and Kiangsi 61 kinds. In these provinces the surtaxes exceeded land tax proper by 26 times in Kiangsu, 3·8 times in Chekiang, 86 times in Hupei, and 9·5 times in Kiangsi.[91] This was the state of affairs before 1934, five years after the founding of the Nanking government, Chekiang, the model of agrarian reform, had 457 kinds of extortionate taxes instead of 73! Land-tax collection in advance was not confined to Szechwan alone, but Szechwan was by far the worst case, as the table[92] on p. 32 shows.

[90] Buck, *Land Utilization in China* (Chicago, 1937), pp. 453–4 and Chia Shih-i, i. 146–8.

[91] *Han-hsüeh ts'ung-shu* (Sweat and blood series), vii/1, pp. 54–55; Liu Shih-jen, pp. 172–3; Sun Hsiao-ts'un, 'K'o-chuan tsa-shui pao-kao' (Report on extortionate taxes), *Nung-ts'un Fu-hsing Wei-yuan-hui pao-kao* (Report of Committee on Agrarian Revival), no. 12, p. 6.

[92] Tsou Fang, 'Chung-kuo t'ien-fu fu-chia ti chung-lei' (Kinds of surtax on the land tax of China), *TFTC*, xxi/14 & *Ching-pao* (Peking Gazette), 31 July 1934.

Tax Collection in Advance in Szechwan, *1934*

Collector	*Years in advance*	*Annual no. of collections*
20th Army	50	6
21st Army	22	4
24th Army	25	2
28th Army	74	14
29th Army	66	12
New 6th Division	58	10
23rd Division	60	3
A Kweichow division	33	3

Sources: Szechwan yüeh-pao (Szechwan monthly), nos. 28 & 29; *Shen-pao yüeh-k'an* (Shen-pao monthly), iv/6; Feng Ho-fa, i. 286; and *Han-shüeh ts'ung-shu*, no. 7, *T'ien-fu wen-t'i yen-chiu* (A study on the land tax) (Shanghai, 1936), i. 52–53.

By 1935 there was still no sign of improvement.[93]

Under these crushingly heavy taxes, the normal crops of rice and wheat of necessity gave way to the more lucrative opium, as a *mou* of land in Hsüp'u of Hunan, for instance, could produce only 5 *yuan* worth of wheat but 30 *yuan* worth of opium.[94] Therefore some warlords relaxed the prohibition of poppy cultivation (e.g. those in Hupei, Hunan, Kiangsu, Kiangsi, and Kwangsi) and others encouraged or compelled the peasants to plant opium (e.g. those in Manchuria, Chihli, Shantung, Kansu, Shensi, Jehol, Honan, Szechwan, Yunnan, Kweichow, Fukien, and Anhwei).[95] Some warlords of Szechwan even went so far as to levy a 'laziness tax' (*lan-chuan*) on those who did not plant opium.[96] What had been almost eliminated before 1916[97] now gained a new lease of life as the percentage of cultivated land devoted to opium increased from 3 in 1914–19 to 20 in 1929–33, while that devoted to barley decreased from 23 to 19 and sorghum (*kao-liang*) from 23 to

---

[93] *Hsin-wen-pao* (Shanghai), 12 Apr 1935.   [94] Feng Ho-fa, ii. 112.

[95] Lo Yun-yen, *Chung-kuo ya-p'ien wen-t'i* (The problem of opium in China) (Shanghai, 1929), pp. 90–91.

[96] Feng Ho-fa, i. 828.

[97] Jordan to Grey, 7 Apr 1911 (FO 371, 1072, no. 16037); Sir Alexander Hosie's report, 15 Apr 1911 (FO 371, 1072, no. 18425); Chang Yu-i, *Chung-kuo chin-tai nung-yeh-shih tzu-liao* (Material for the history of agriculture of modern China) (Peking, 1957), ii. 210–11.

16.[98] Throughout China only Chekiang and Shansi were free from poppy cultivation.[99]

From 1912 to 1923, on the average, seven provinces had been in a state of war; from 1924 to 1930 this average increased to 14.[100] When war broke out, people and their carts and boats were impressed for military service. Wu P'ei-fu, for example, demanded 4,000 carts, 4000 men, and 8,000 mules from a small area of six counties in Shantung for his campaign against Chang Tso-lin in 1924;[101] Feng Yü-hsiang, while in the north-west in 1929, requisitioned a large number of carts which he sold as soon as he arrived at his destination;[102] and as late as 1933–4 the people of Hopei had still to supply 15,000 carts, 4,000 mules and horses, and 60,000 men for military corvée duties.[103]

Apart from heavy taxes, opium, corvée, and the interception of the central government's revenue which we have already discussed, in the years immediately after the 1911 revolution and then after the death of Yüan Shih-k'ai the warlords also issued their own paper currency. In the first period, from 1912 to 1914, the monetary situation was chaotic, but the inflation did not run wild, thanks mainly to the reluctance of the population to accept paper notes. The total issue in the provinces did not exceed 17 million *yuan*;[104] it was therefore comparatively easy for Yüan Shih-k'ai to restore a measure of stability in 1915 and 1916. After his death, however, the situation grew steadily worse, and by 1926 the Manchurian notes alone reached an estimated total issue of 400 million.[105] The success in this endeavour depended chiefly on local conditions, on the people's willingness to accept paper money, and on the warlords' credit and financial urgency. Manchuria, Jehol, Chihli, Honan, Hopei, and Shantung were the worst affected, although all warlords had issued paper money and perhaps only Kiangsu and Chekiang were not plagued by it.[106] Where the people's resistance was strong, there the warlord

[98] Chang Yu-i, ii. 214–15 and *CTB 1928*, p. 526.

[99] Chou Hsien-wen, 'Chung-kuo yen-huo chi ch'i chiu-chi-ts'e' (The scourge of opium in China and its remedies), *TFTC*, xxiii/20 (1926), p. 33.

[100] Chang Yu-i, ii. 599, modified according to my own statistics.

[101] Ibid.   [102] Feng Ho-fa, i. 149.   [103] Ibid. ii. 132.

[104] Wei Chien-yu, *Chung-kuo chin-tai huo-pi-shih* (A history of money in modern China) (Shanghai, 1955), p. 199.

[105] *The Times*, 15 Apr 1926.

[106] E. Kann, 'Review of the Bullion and Exchange Markets in 1927', *Chinese Econ. J.*, Mar 1928, 283–305.

resorted to debasement as a means of obtaining money for the maintenance of his troops. Thus in Szechwan between 1922 and 1926 there was the following incongruous picture:

Composition of Currencies in Circulation (percentage)

Year	Copper wen	Silver coins	Silver ingots	Copper cash (10 wen)	Copper cash (20 wen)	Copper cash (50 wen)	Copper cash (100 wen)	Copper cash (200 wen)	Copper cash (500 wen)	Notes
1922	40	30	5	10	3	2	6	4	0	0
1923	35	35	3	6	2	3	10	6	0	0
1924	20	33	1	3	2	2	17	20	0	2
1925	5	30	0	1	0	1	20	35	0	8
1926	0	34	0	0	0	1	7	42	1	15

Sources: Huang Chu-i, 'Chuan-pei nung-min hsien-k'uang chih-i-pan' (Survey of conditions of peasants in north Szechwan), *TFTC*, xxiv/16, pp. 35–36. See also Feng Ho-fa, i. 838.

Agricultural depression was a natural consequence of these exactions. Total output shrank; so did the total area under cultivation.[107] The wealthy and strong in the countryside refused to pay the irrational levies,[108] shifted the burden to the peasants,[109] or transferred their assets to the cities.[110] As a result, the peasants had to sustain higher rates of rent[111] and standards of interest.[112] Their

[107] The trend of the declining output was not arrested until 1932 (Chang Yu-i, iii. 922). For lack of statistics, we can verify this point only by cotton production. According to H. D. Fong, *Chung-kuo ching-chi yen-chiu* (A study of the Chinese economy) (Shanghai, 1938), i. ii, cotton output in Hopei fell from 1,650,000 picul in 1918–22 to 600,000 picul in 1923–8. This can be supplemented by the decline in the national total output from 10 m. picul in 1919 to 6·7 m. picul in 1928 (*Chung-kuo ching-chi nien-chien* (Chinese Economic Yearbook) (Shanghai, 1934), i. 192–3). The decrease in the total area under cultivation, according to official statistics, was: 1914, 1,578 m. mou; 1919, 1,314 m. mou, 1931, 1,248 m. mou (Fong, i. 160 and Wang Hsiao-wen & others, *Chung-kuo t'u-ti wen-t'i* (Land problems in China) (Shanghai, 1937), pp. 89–90).

[108] *Han-hsüeh ts'ung-shu*, no. 7, i. 115, 118, & ii. 188–9.

[109] Chang Yu-i, ii. 601–4.

[110] Ibid. iii. 675–7 and Ch'ien Chia-chü, *Chung-kuo nung-ts'un ching-chi lun-wen chi* (Essays on Chinese agricultural economy) (Shanghai, 1936), pp. 101–2.

[111] Chang Yu-i, ii. 328–33; Fong, i. 291; R. H. Tawney, *Land and Labour in China* (London, 1932), p. 66. The average rate of rent was 50 per cent of the yield.

[112] Chang Yu-i, ii. 556–8; Ch'ien Chia-chü, pp. 165–6 & 172–3; Tawney, p. 62; Buck, *Chinese Farm Economy* (Shanghai, 1930), p. 159. In 1921–5 the usual rate was 20–30 per cent and in 1932–4 20–40 per cent. About 56 per cent of the rural households needed short-term loans for their finance.

living conditions deteriorated and some of them went to the cities while others joined the army of brigands.[113] On the one hand, concentration of ownership, noticeably in the hands of the war-lords, accelerated; on the other an increasing number of the peasants were forced to leave their farms. The more unemployed, the greater the numbers engaged in soldiering and banditry; therefore the more frequent the civil wars and the more depressed the agriculture of China. As put very simply by Fei Hsiao-t'ung, 'it is the hunger of the people that is the real issue in China'.[114]

Faced with this situation, the Peking government in 1914 attempted to limit the amount of surtax to 30 per cent of the land

[113] C. D. Dittmer ('An estimate of the Chinese standard of living in China', *Q J Econ.*, xxxiii (1918), pp. 107–8) investigated 200 households of the size of 5 persons and an annual income of 100 yuan whose pattern of expenditure was

Per cent

Food	68–83	Fuel & lighting	6–7
Rent	5–15	Other	1·3–6·6
Clothing	3·4–8·5		

This roughly corresponds to Buck's estimates (*Chinese Farm Economy*, pp. 386–7). Prof. J. B. Taylor's figures, quoted in W. H. Mallory, *China: Land of Famine* (London, 1926), pp. 9–10, tend to be too low, in view of the inflationary trend (from 1911 to 1924 the general food prices had increased 150 per cent). See *CYB, 1925*, p. 542. About the migration of peasants, see Chang Yu-i, ii. 636–7 and Fong, pp. 178 & 181; and about their jobs after leaving their farms see Chang Yu-i, ii. 646–9 and Feng Ho-fa, ii. 116.

[114] *Peasant Life in China* (London, 1939), p. 282. This book was based on fieldwork in the Yangtze delta. On the question of concentration of ownership, official statistics tend to exaggerate the proportion of owner-occupiers in the total rural population, while the left-wing sources do precisely the opposite. Tawney (p. 34, quoting the Dept of Agric. and Commerce), for instance, gives the following percentages for 1918: peasant owner-occupiers 50, part-owners 20, and tenants 30 (see also T'ao Hsi-sheng, *Chung-kuo wen-t'i chih hui-ku yü ch'ien-chan* (The background and prospect of China's problems) (Shanghai, 1930), pp. 296–7) whereas the Peasant Dept of the KMT in 1927 gave an entirely different picture:

Per cent

Poor peasants (below 10 *mou*)	75
Middle peasants (10–30 *mou*)	11
Wealthy peasants (over 30 *mou*)	14

Source: Ti-i-tz'u kuo-nei ke-ming chan-cheng shih-ch'i ti nung-min yün-tung (The peasants' movement during the first revolutionary war) (Peking, 1953), pp. 3–5.

Even official statistics betray a sad story. The Legislative Yüan's figures show that from 1930 to 1933 more than 20 m. had become landless.

Percentages of the total rural population

	1930	1933
Owner-occupiers	52	45
Part-owners	22	23
Tenants	26	32

Source: Fong, i. 385.

During the Japanese war there was further concentration of ownership:

tax proper, but this, came to nothing.[115] In 1930 the Nanking government resorted to rent reduction and ownership restriction; after a short and disastrous experiment in Chekiang, this too came to nothing.[116] In 1933 Chiang Kai-shek diagnosed that the malaise of Chinese agriculture was not unequal distribution but poor land utilization.[117] From the long-term point of view this is true, but there was also the problem of short-term relief. By concentrating its attention on the long-term problem the Nanking government was in fact leaving the short-term one to the communists, as 'the real nature of the communist movement was a peasant revolt due to their dissatisfaction with the land system'.[118]

The Nanking government had greater success with public finance. The perennial problem of demarcating central and local revenue and expenditure, dating back at least to 1908, was at last partially solved after the National Finance Conference of 1928.[119] After two attempts in 1932 and 1936, public loans were readjusted in a more orderly manner, but the total indebtedness increased by two and a half times from 1928 to 1934.[120] By 1935, having abolished more than 5,000 items of miscellaneous taxes, the government promised to do away with more still and the monetary unification in that year was a success.[121] These were signs of the modernization of China's public finance system. However, there was still no effective budget, and no diminution in the people's tax burden. Worse still, as the efficiency of the administration did not allow a successful introduction of direct taxes, taxation remained regressive.

In this political, economic, and cultural setting, it is small

n. 114 *cont.*

	Before the war		After the war	
	Landlords (% of total rural popn)	Their land (% of total arable land)	Landlords (% of total rural popn.)	Their land (% of total arable land)
Chengtu	20	50	8	80
Chungking	20	50	2	95

Source: *Hsin Chung-hua* (New China), xii/12.

Sources about landowning warlords are extremely scattered. It suffices to say that all of them owned large areas.

[115] *Han Hsüeh ts'ung-shu*, no. 7, i. 11.   [116] Fong, i. 296–7 & 318–19.
[117] Ibid. 312.   [118] Fei Hsiao-t'ung, p. 285.
[119] Chia Te-huai, i. 18–45 & 46–47.
[120] *Yin-hang chou-k'an*, xix/44 and Sun Huai-jen, pp. 5–6 & 36–39.
[121] Sun Huai-jen, p. 44 and *Shih-shih hsin-pao* (Daily News) (Shanghai), 15 Nov 1935.

wonder that the process of China's industrial growth has been slow and arduous. G. E. Hubbard lists the obstacles to Chinese industrial development as

the absence of central authority able to exert a steady directive influence, the rudimentary means of communication which is all that exists in large parts of the country, . . . an often arbitrary system of local tax barriers, the lack of a single medium of currency throughout the whole country . . . and finally the fact that the industrial centres of China are divided between Chinese and foreign administrative control and the industries themselves separated into two sharply distinguished categories, the Chinese- and the foreign-owned.[122]

All these and many others were retardative and verifiable. But in addition, two other fundamental hindrances—shortage of capital and imperialism—should not escape notice.

In 1936, the peak year of the prewar prosperity, China's national income at factor cost amounted to 26,758 million *yuan*.[123] On the assumption of an average rate of interest of 8 per cent, this gives the total national wealth (including labour) at 335,000 million *yuan*. Total capital in Chinese- and foreign-owned modern enterprises was 5,807·8 million *yuan* in 1936.[124] This makes modern capital investment occupy less than 2 per cent of the national wealth in 1936.

Of the modern capital investment of 5,807·8 million *yuan*, only 3,807·8 million was invested in manufacturing, mining, and transport industries, and only 41 million in capital goods industries, which could not produce enough for maintenance purposes, far less for growth.[125]

Agriculture, the mainstay of Chinese economy, had no share of modern investment at all. Instead, its traditional type of investment was, according to Professor Buck, distributed as in the table on p. 38.

The absence of floating capital for short-term finance, which, if it had existed, would have rescued the peasants from the necessity of resorting to usurious loans, shows the inability of Chinese agriculture to provide capital for industrialization. Previously, in the second half of the nineteenth century, government enterprises

[122] *Eastern Industrialization and its Effect on the West* (London, 1938), p. 193.

[123] UN, *National Income Statistics* (draft), May 1948.

[124] Quoted from Ku Ch'un-fan, *Chung-kuo kung-yeh-hua t'ung-lun* (A general discussion of China's industrialization) (Shanghai, 1947), p. 160.

[125] Ibid. pp. 162–3.

D

Average Investment per hectare, 1921–5[126]

	yuan	per cent
Land	615	74·8
Buildings	128	15·6
Livestock	27	3·3
Farm equipment	23	2·7
Trees	18	2
Seeds & supplies	14	1·6
Total	825	100·0

Source: Buck, *Chinese Farm Economy*, p. 68.

relied upon the maritime customs and *likin* for capital supply, but these were no longer available after 1895. From then on investment in modern industries was left to foreigners, and Chinese businessmen could invest and manage only on a small scale. Consequently, in 1936 73·8 per cent of the investment in modern industries belonged to foreigners and the average value of capital assets of Shanghai factories was between 10,000 and 50,000 *yuan*.[127]

This severe shortage of capital could be resolved either by China's heavy reliance on foreign aid or by a drastic overhaul of her agriculture, or both.

Imperialism was an impediment to China's industrial growth in the sense that the treaties concluded after the wars of the nineteenth century robbed the Chinese government of the power to protect the infant industries. The tariff question was twofold— first, without complete control over it, China could not use it to encourage exports or to discourage imports in order to balance her

[126] Farm investment in Kwangsi in 1933 can be quoted to supplement this:

		Per cent	
Land	50·9	Livestock	5·6
Buildings	32·2	Seeds, fertilizer & fodder	7·9
Tools	2·6	Equipment for handicrafts	0·7

Source: Ch'ien Chia-chü & others, *Kwangsi sheng ching-chi kai-k'uang* (Economic conditions in Kwangsi) (Shanghai, 1935), p. 51.

[127] Ku Ch'un-fan, p. 162.

payments and foster her own industries; second, since it was used as security against foreign loans arising from indemnities and financial chaos, the Chinese government could hardly regard it purely as a protective weapon. Among other things, China had to depend on foreign loans and investment to balance her international payments. The loans were more often than not used for political and military purposes, thus creating more unrest and chaos which caused the government to borrow further—for 'the stabilization of the internal situation' (*an-nei*); the investment reduced the Chinese-owned industries and the rural handicrafts to an ever less competitive position.[128]

Under the impact of growing nationalism, the old culturalistic empire of China disintegrated before nationalism found its suitable political form. Externally, the country had only a nominal independence; internally, the constitution could not be decided, a new robust civil service could not be established, defence could not be properly organized, finance could not be thoroughly reformed, agricultural depression could not be relieved, and modern industries could not be developed. What was old and traditional had been discarded; what was new and modern made a poor showing. The country and its politics were formless. Yet all Chinese nationalists of this period shared one common aim—'the wealth and power of the nation'. They differed from each other on the ways and means of achieving this purpose, thus making nationalism a disruptive and destructive force. None the less, the singleness of their purpose helped to hold the country precariously together and made them eager to introduce into China all that was new and modern—thus making nationalism a constructive force. When this nationalism was given a definitive shape in 1949, the interregnum was over.[129]

[128] Ho Ping-hsien, *Chung-kuo ti kuo-chi mao-i* (China's international trade) (Shanghai, 1939), i. 23–25.
[129] This chapter was written in the spring of 1965, when the significance of the Cultural Revolution was not appreciated by me. Now, in 1968, it may be argued whether Mao's ultimate aim is a 'strong and wealthy' or a morally 'good' China. Readers will do well to bear in mind what Mao said in November 1956 and repeated on 13 November 1966 (the *People's Daily* of that date). He predicted that in 2001 China would become a 'powerful, socialist industrial country'. From all available evidence, I think Mao's strong China and good China are the same thing. In order to be strong, she must also be good. This is why the Cultural Revolution has been hitherto highly moralistic.

THE HSIAOCHAN GROUP

Graduates of the Tientsin Military School (Pei-Yang wu-pei hsüeh-t'ang)

Feng Kuo-chang, Chihli, *aide-de-camp* to Yüan Shih-k'ai, head of Infantry School, later leader of the Chihli clique.

Tuan Ch'i-jui, Anhwei, c.o. of the Artillery Corps, head of Artillery School, later leader of the Anhwei clique.

Wang Shih-chen, Chihli, c.o. of the Engineer Corps, head of Engineering School, later Minister of War.

Ho Feng-lin, Shantung, instructor, later Garrison Commander of Shanghai.

Lei Chen-ch'un, Anhwei, officer, later head of Department of Military Law.

Li Ch'un, Chihli, officer, later Governor Kiangsi and Kiangsu, Chihli clique.

Lu Chien-chang, Anhwei, officer, later Governor of Shensi, Anhwei clique.

T'ein Chung-yü, Chihli, officer, later Governor of Shantung, Anhwei clique.

T'ien Wen-lieh, Honan, officer, later Governor of Honan.

Ts'ao K'un, Chihli, officer, later Governor of Chihli and President, Chihli clique.

Tuan Chih-kuei, Anhwei, officer, later Governor of Fengtien.

Wang Chan-yüan, Shantung, instructor, later Governor of Hupei, Chihli clique.

OTHERS

Chang Hsün, Kiangsi, officer of the Huai Army, later Governor of Anhwei.

Chang Huai-chih, Shantung, officer, later Governor of Shantung.

Ch'e Ch'ing-yun, officer, later Provost Marshal in Peking.

Ch'en Kuang-yüan, Chihli, later Governor of Kiangsi, Chihli clique.

Chiang Kuei-t'i, Anhwei, officer of the Huai Army, later Military Commander of Jehol.

Meng En-yüan, Chihli, officer, later Governor of Kirin.

Ni Ssu-ch'ung, Anhwei, officer of the Huai Army, later Governor of Anhwei, Anhwei clique.

Pao Kuei-ch'ing, Mukden, officer, later Governor of Kirin.

Yin-ch'ang, Manchu, instructor, later *aide-de-camp* to the President, Yüan Shih-k'ai.

2

The Gentry Democracy in Chinese Shanghai, 1905–14

MARK ELVIN

THE first formally democratic political institution in China was the City Council[1] of that part of Shanghai left under Chinese rule at the beginning of this century. I know of no monograph in the English language in which it is mentioned but it is worth study for the contrasts it affords, in an admittedly exceptional part of China, with more commonly-known patterns of Chinese political behaviour.

The genesis of the Council in 1905 must be seen against the background of a steady evolution in local administration in the county of Shanghai since the latter part of the Ming dynasty. At that time the low-level organization needed for taxation and water-conservancy work was done by commoners conscripted on a rota basis, and the 'gentry', who may be approximately defined for this period as 'those who held official titles and academic degrees',[2] were exempted from this often ruinous labour. In the early part of the K'ang-hsi reign in the later seventeenth century the system, which had long been rotten, broke down entirely, presumably partly in conjunction with the increase in the burden of tax and in the size of landed estates that immediately followed the imposition of Manchu rule in the area; and the corvée administrators were gradually replaced by government clerks.[3] Around

[1] The exact title of the City Council varied according to period, viz., 'General Works Board' 1905–9, 'Self-Government Office' 1910–11, 'Municipal Government Hall' 1912–14.

[2] This term is simply used as an equivalent for the Chinese *shen*, and implies no necessary connexion with landholding or rural residence. With the end of the empire in 1912 these titles lost their validity.

[3] On the system that prevailed in the Ming and the early Ch'ing see the *T'ien-hsia chün-kuo li-ping shu* (Documents on the strengths and weaknesses of the commanderies and principates of the empire; 17th cent., Ssu-k'u shan-pen ed., Taiwan reprint), ed. Ku Yen-wu, viii. 74b, 76b, 91b; Yeh Meng-chu, *Yueh-shih pien* (A Survey of the

about the last quarter of the eighteenth century there was a second period of institutional change. Members of the gentry began to take direct personal control of dredging and other projects and were soon in consequence regularly referred to as 'gentry directors'.[4] At the same time customary gentry charitable practices became institutionalized in a rapidly growing number of 'charitable halls' (which later also undertook the first rudimentary beginnings of municipal administration),[5] and the local merchants began to organize themselves systematically into guilds.[6] In the second quarter of the nineteenth century another essentially new type of body appeared in the form of the official 'board' or specialized local agency, usually under a deputy but in which gentry or merchants might also participate.[7] Following the T'aip'ing rebellion in the middle years of the century the gentry extended their power, set up militia, regularly collected supplementary taxes for local projects, and sometimes created semi-permanent boards for hydraulic works.[8] In this last period distinct elements of proto-democratic behaviour appeared. On occasions the gentry would 'publicly select'[9] one of their number to direct a project,[10] and by

Age; late 17th cent.), vi. 12b–13a; *T'ung-chih Shang-hai hsien-chih* (Gazetteer of Shang-hai *hsien* for the T'ung-chih reign, 1871), ed. Yü Yueh (hereafter T'ung-chih Gazet-teer), iv. 18b–22a, 24a, 26b; and Hoshi Ayao, *Mindai sōun no kenkyū* (A study of the grain transport system of the Ming dynasty, 1963), pp. 496–7, 505.

On the collapse of this system see Yeh, vi. 15a–18b; T'ung chih Gazetteer, iv. 26b; Hoshi, p. 509. On corruption and landed estates see especially Yeh, i. 17b–19a.

[4] See T'ung-chih Gazetter, iv. 27ab & 34a ff.; *Shang-hai hsien hsü-chih* (A continuation of the Gazetteer of Shanghai *hsien*, 1918), ed. Yao Wen-nan (hereafter Cont. Gazetteer), v. *passim*.

[5] See T'ung-chih Gazetteer, ii. 21a–27a; Cont. Gazetteer, ii. 31a–40b; *Min-kuo Shang-hai hsien-chih* (Gazetteer of Shanghai *hsien* for the republican period, 1936), ed. Niu Yung-chien (hereafter Republican Gazetteer), x. 1a–4a. On Kiangsu charities generally see Yü Chih, *Te-i lu* (Te-i records) (Shanghai, 1869).

[6] See Negishi Tadashi, *Shanhai no girudo* (The guilds of Shanghai, 1953), pp. 7–14; Cont. Gazetteer, iii. 1a–16a; Republican Gazetteer, vi. 1a–7b.

[7] See Cont. Gazetteer, ii. 22a–31a.

[8] On the militia see Chiang Shen-wu, 'Shanghai *hsien* during the Ch'ing dynasty', in *Shang-hai-shih t'ung-chih-kuan ch'i-k'an* (The periodical of the Shanghai Municipal Gazetteer Office, 1933–5), ed. Liao Ya-tzu (hereafter SHSTCK CK), 2nd yr, ii. 513, 516–18; *Shang-hai tzu-chih chih* (Self-government gazetteer of Shanghai Municipality), ed. Yang I & Ch'ü Ching-p'u (hereafter TCC), Docs A 136ab. On the supplementary taxes see Cont. Gazetteer, v. 1a, 6b, 7ab. On the gentry boards see ibid. 1b–2a, 30b, 31b.

[9] The exact nature of the procedure is not certain, and it seems unlikely in the greater part of the 19th century to have been genuine election rather than some form of public approval of a choice arrived at by other means.

[10] See, e.g. Cont. Gazetteer, v. 7b.

the opening of the twentieth century from the sporadic employment of officially-sponsored gentry discussions there had developed
the almost mandatory use of consultative gentry assemblies both
for determining the quantity of water-conservancy levies and for
advising the *hsien* magistrate on matters of policy.[11] Similarly,
there appeared in the guilds as a method of selecting directors the
use of 'public selection', as opposed to co-option or the tenure of
office in rotation, and by about 1900 this could mean much what
we would understand by 'election'.[12] The guilds also accustomed
their members to regular discussions of policy in special rooms set
aside for that purpose, and in at least one case it can be shown
that it was the opinion of the *hsien* magistrate that a guild policy
was not binding on members unless approved by them at a meeting.[13] When the City Council emerged at the beginning of the
twentieth century it was a fusion of the charity, the guild, the
official board, and the water-conservancy project. The Municipal
Council of the International Settlement and the Mixed Court
there were admired models of administration and law, but democratic inspiration came solely from the home institutions of foreign
countries and not from the Chinese tradition itself.[14]

Underlying the institutional fusion was the social fusion of
merchants and mandarins.[15] Some of the Council's leaders were
predominantly traditional gentry, with their influence rooted in
the educational establishment and in their official connexions. Li
Chung-chüeh, who headed it for many years, was a former *hsien*
magistrate, the author of a work on Singapore, a connoisseur of
antique bronzes and a pioneer of Westernized hospitals and clean
water. Mu Hsiang-yao, who ran the Council's police force, was a
provincial graduate. Yao Wen-nan, the Speaker of the Assembly
in its early years, was chairman of the organization of the local
educational bodies. Others, like Mo Hsi-lun and Lu Wen-lu, had

[11] See T'ung-chih Gazetteer, iv. 40b, 42b, 43a; Cont. Gazetteer, v. 16a, 18b–19a,
20b–21a, 25b–26a; TCC Docs, A 38a, 38ab, 38b, 39b–40b, 40b–41a, 92a, 92ab.
[12] See Cont. Gazetteer, iii. 3b, 6a, 6b, 8a (2 entries), 9a, 9b, 12a, 12b (2 entries), 13a,
13a–14b, 16a; TCC Docs, A 142b; *NCH*, 1905, 16 Dec, 671; 1907, 29 Nov, 516.
[13] On guild discussions see Cont. Gazetteer, iii. 2a, 3b, 9a, 12a. On the need for
members to approve policy see TCC Docs, A 110a–112b.
[14] Chiang Shen-wu, 'The Period of the Separate Municipal Administration of
Shanghai', SHSTCK CK, ii. 4, pp. 1216–22; TCC Docs A 1b, 2a, 2b, 53b, 66ab,
67b–68b; and espec. A 173b. On the Municipal Council see A. M. Kotenev, *Shanghai:
Its Mixed Court and Council* (Shanghai, 1925), pp. 9, 15, 16, 561–5.
[15] See *NCH*, 15 Dec 1905, p. 596; 1910: 21 Jan, p. 129, 8 July, p. 74.

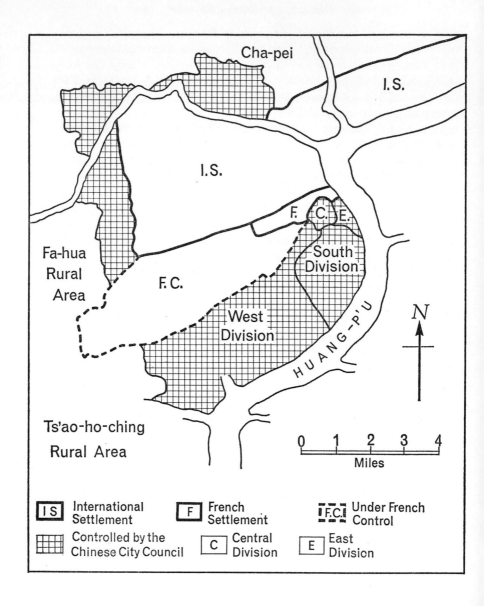

Cha-pei

I.S.

I.S.

F. C. E.

South Division

Fa-hua Rural Area

F. C.

West Division

HUANG-P'U

N

Ts'ao-ho-ching Rural Area

0 1 2 3 4
Miles

I S	International Settlement
(grid)	Controlled by the Chinese City Council
F	French Settlement
C	Central Division
F.C.	Under French Control
E	East Division

made their careers in the administration of charities. The remainder were merchants pre-eminent in the guilds and chambers of commerce. Chu Pao-san was the pioneer of numerous modern industries in the city and a former comprador. Chang Chia-nien and Ku Lu-kuei were leading grain merchants. Shen Man-yün was a banker and later one of the most important revolutionaries. Su Pen-yen was an industrialist and an expert on commercial law. Tseng Chu, the 'merchant *taotai*', was president of the General Chamber of Commerce and leader of the anti-American boycott of 1905. Wang I-t'ing was a comprador, president of the south city chamber of commerce, revolutionary and a distinguished painter besides. Yü Huai-chih had studied at the government's foreign language school in Shanghai and had become a merchant, head of the Piece-goods Guild, an advocate of improved methods of cotton cultivation and a philanthropist.

Many members of the Council were well acquainted with foreign ideas and customs. Chu Yin-chiang was Jardine, Matheson's comprador for dealings in lumber. Yao Po-hsin edited the newspaper *Hsin-wen pao*. Lu Po-hung, manager of the China Electric Light Company and the Chinese Tram Company, and a painter of some quality, was a fluent speaker of French who acted as an official interpreter on occasion. Ts'ao Hsiang, who had won a traditional bachelor's degree, and was a noted book collector, was the Chinese pioneer of Sino-English lexicography.

Although it cannot be proved in every case it seems highly probable that all the members of the City Council possessed official rank, more often than not purchased. Ku Lu-kuei, for example, who represented the rice and bean trade in the south city chamber of commerce, was an expectant sub-prefect, holding the fifth rank, and entitled to wear the peacock feather. Conversely, genuine degree-holders were at home in commerce. Mu Hsiang-yao resigned his Council post in 1908 to manage a timber company.

Finally, many of the Council's leaders were at the head of one or more of the companies of merchant militia that were formed in the years after 1906, and whose members totalled about 3,000 on the eve of the 1911 revolution.[16]

The City Council was distinct from the power structure created

---

[16] For references to these persons see Endnote 1.

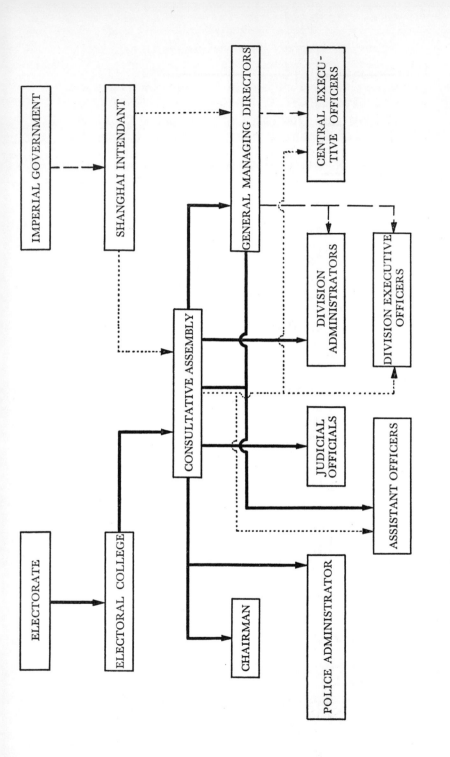

Figure 1. The Selection of the Personnel of the City Council (GEB), c. 1906-8

Key: Elects ——▶ Approves ······▶ Appoints ―――▶

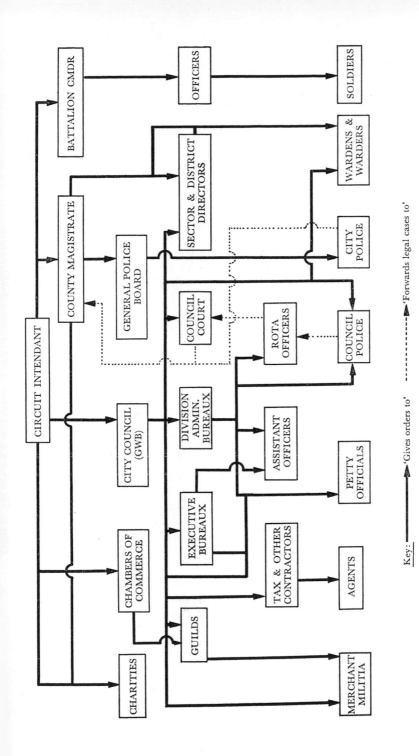

Key: → 'Gives orders to' ------▶ 'Forwards legal cases to'

Figure 2. *The Structure of Local Authority in Chinese Shanghai, c. 1907*

by the Chinese community in the foreign settlements. The leading figures in the latter were Yü Hsia-ch'ing, the best-known comprador in Shanghai, and popularly called the 'Barefoot God of Wealth' in allusion to his enormous riches and equally enormous debts, Wu Shao-ch'ing, the head of the Silk Guild, Chou Chinchen, a banker and the head of the General Chamber of Commerce, and Shen Tun-ho, Director of the Imperial Bank of China and prominent in every kind of charitable cause.[17] A few, like Chu Pao-san and Yü Huai-chih, had a foot in both camps.

The new institution was in many ways strikingly modern. Taking shape gradually, there were separate executive and legislative branches. The directors' committee, composed of 5 'general managing directors' and 2, later 3, 'divisional administrators', was in charge of a substantial bureaucracy, and the assembly, originally of slightly more than 30 and later of 60 members, met first monthly and later four times a year to decide on policy. The executive was not authorized to act or spend money without the assembly's permission, and in important matters the approval of the circuit intendant or the *hsien* magistrate had to be secured.[18]

Besides carrying out special tasks entrusted to it by the imperial officials, such as the suppression of opium dens and the sale of cheap rice in times of shortage, the Council undertook the dredging of waterways, built roads and bridges, removed garbage and night-soil, lit the streets, looked after certain public utilities, charities, and schools, ran its own police force of about 800 men for the area outside the walled city and its own court of justice with elected judges. Its average (arithmetic mean) monthly expenditure rose from about 14,000 *yuan* in 1905 to 28,500 *yuan* early in 1913, most of this being met by taxes on property, boats, and vehicles, by loans, by a public debt and by the renting and sometimes the sale of public land.[19]

---

[17] See Endnote 2.

[18] On the general structure and nature of the Council when it was first created see TCC Regulations, A 1a–2a, arts i & viii; A 6ab, arts ii, viii, xi, xiii, & xv; Docs, A 16oab. For the original draft regulations which were never used see *TFTC*, ii. 10 (21 Nov 1905), *nei-wu*, pp. 194–6.

[19] On the suppression of opium dens see TCC Docs, A 121a–127b; B 74a–76a. On the sale of cheap rice see A 118a–120a; B 68a–73a. On dredging see A 25a–28b, 38a–41b; B 13a–16b. On the construction and repair of roads and bridges see A 21a–14b, 42a–45a, 57a–59b; B 7a–12a; C 10a–11a, 16a–19a. On the cleaning and lighting of the streets see A 60a–63a; B 31a–34a; C 64a–68b. On the waterworks see A 104a–106a. On charities see C 28a–33b. On schools see C 22a–25a. On the police see A 2a,

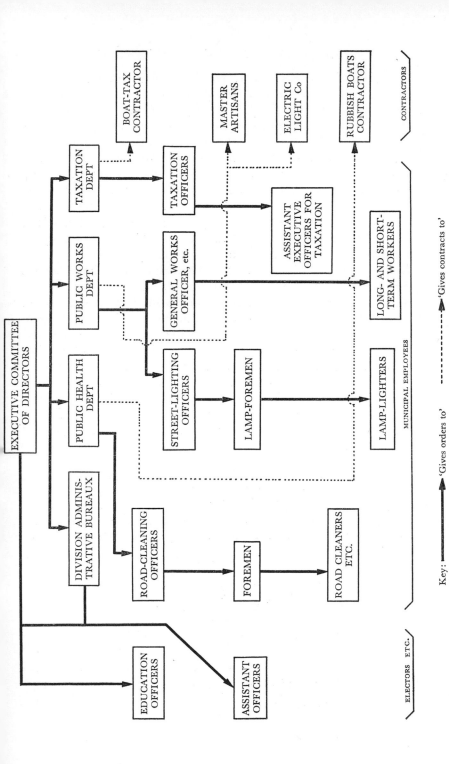

Figure 3. The Lower-level Administrative Structure of the City Council (SGO), c. 1910

Key: ■—— 'Gives orders to'   ■----▶ 'Gives contracts to'

The administrative structure consisted of three parts: one run by those qualified as electors, mostly without pay and somewhat in the spirit of the English JP; one by the Council's professional employees, who ranged from highly salaried members of the gentry having charge of documents, accounts, and planning to semi-literate policemen and humble road-cleaners and lamp-lighters; and one by outside contractors who undertook to per-form certain tasks that demanded specialized local knowledge, such as the levy of tax from boats (which fell into numerous cate-gories and were always on the move), and the removal of the city's night-soil.[20] The high degree of functional differentiation may be traced to the legacy of the nineteenth-century boards.

Subcontracting, which has often been thought to have been a general weakness of Chinese administrative structures,[21] only appeared in the management of the boats which removed garbage. In both the ordinary executive departments and in the Taxation Department there were carefully devised means by which the superior officers kept direct control over their lowest-level sub-ordinates.[22] The Council had a hard time finding honest recruits for its police force, but when it so wished, as in the case of the suppression of opium dens, it was capable of enforcing central government policy with some efficiency upon the population at large. Only organized collective resistance, such as that mounted by the beggar-boats when they were faced with the order to move

3b, 60a, A 53a–54b; B 28a–29a. On the court of justice see A 2a, 2b–3a, & 55a–56b; B 30a; *TFTC*, iii/1 (18 Feb 1906), *nei wu*, pp. 22–24.

On the expenditures see Table 2 (p. 63). The average is calculated from TCC Maps & Tables, Accounts I (Gen. Table).

[20] On those jobs which were reserved for qualified electors (initially gentry and merchant 'directors') see TCC Regulations, A 9a, art. ii; B 7a, art. vi; Docs, A 2b–3a; Regulations, B 7a, art. iii.

On the professional employees see TCC Regulations, A 1b, art. ix; *Ta-Ch'ing Kuang-hsu hsin fa-ling* (The new laws of the Kuang-hsu reign of the great Ch'ing, 1909), ii: Regulations for the Local Self-government of Cities, Towns and Rural Areas, art. lxvi. On the lower level of administration see TCC Regulations, B 8a, arts i & ii; 8b–9a, arts ii & iii; B 10ab, arts i & iv; B 11b–12a, arts v–xxiii. On the self-government bureaucracy after the revolution see ibid. C 1b, arts xiv–xviii.

On the contractors see TCC Docs, A 14a, 22b, 61a–63a, 66a–67b, 143a–b, 162ab; B 97b; C 26a, 26b, 64a–68b; Regulations, B 11a, arts iv & v; B 14b, art. ii; B 15b, art. ii.

[21] As by Muramatsu Yūji in his *Chūgoku keizai no shakai taisei* (The social structure of China's economy, 1948), pp. 363–72.

[22] See TCC Regulations, B 8ab, arts ii, iv, ix, xii, & espec. xv (on wages); 10b, arts v, x, & xi; 11b–12a, arts v–xi, xiv & xv.

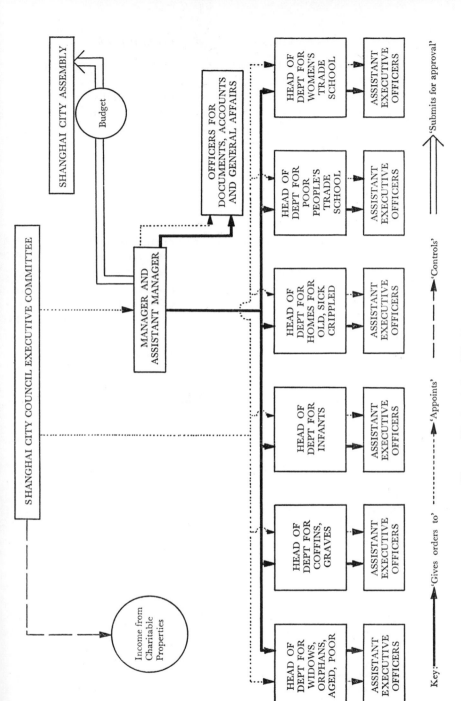

Figure 4. The Association of Charities, c. 1912

SHANGHAI CITY ASSEMBLY

Budget

SHANGHAI CITY COUNCIL EXECUTIVE COMMITTEE

MANAGER AND ASSISTANT MANAGER

OFFICERS FOR DOCUMENTS, ACCOUNTS AND GENERAL AFFAIRS

Income from Charitable Properties

HEAD OF DEPT FOR WIDOWS, ORPHANS, AGED, POOR

ASSISTANT EXECUTIVE OFFICERS

HEAD OF DEPT FOR COFFINS, GRAVES

ASSISTANT EXECUTIVE OFFICERS

HEAD OF DEPT FOR INFANTS

ASSISTANT EXECUTIVE OFFICERS

HEAD OF DEPT FOR HOMES FOR OLD, SICK CRIPPLED

ASSISTANT EXECUTIVE OFFICERS

HEAD OF DEPT FOR POOR PEOPLE'S TRADE SCHOOL

ASSISTANT EXECUTIVE OFFICERS

HEAD OF DEPT FOR WOMEN'S TRADE SCHOOL

ASSISTANT EXECUTIVE OFFICERS

Key:

'Gives orders to'

'Appoints'

'Controls'

'Submits for approval'

their moorings, was apt to prove too much for the police, wardens, petty officials, and militiamen upon whom it could call. The new apparatus meshed with the older system of district (*t'u*) and sector (*tuan*) gentry directors and of district and precinct (*p'u*) wardens, over whom the Council's directors in effect shared authority with the *hsien* magistrate.[23] So essential indeed did it become that some of its opponents accused the Council's leaders of bending the local officials to their wills by threatening to resign if their wishes were not met.[24]

By about 1910 the City Council had elaborated an array of detailed regulative laws that covered most aspects of daily life. These involved, for example, building permits, a highway code and a system of one-way streets, provision for the supervision of the quality of foodstuffs offered for sale to the public and of the safety of boilers in factories, the censorship of plays, films, and songs, and prohibitions on any number of acts thought to be anti-social, such as leaving litter, defecating in the roadway and hanging women's underwear out to dry in the streets.[25] *Pari passu* the old gentry sense of social obligation became transformed into the belief that there was an obligation upon the municipal government to provide for what amounted to a limited welfare state. Speaking of a new institution they had created in 1912 the Council declared:

In the age of the Great Concord there is no doubt that arrangements will have been made to ensure that the old live out their allotted span, that the mature are enabled to grow strong, and that the widowers, the widows, the crippled and the ailing all have someone to take care

[23] On the problem of honest police recruits see TCC Docs, A 2b–3a, 53a–54b, 54ab, 159b, 160b.

On the use of the Merchant Militia against the opium dens see ibid. A 147b. On the use of the regular troops as police see A 20a. For an evaluation of the effectiveness of the campaign against the dens see *NCH*, 1907: 14 June, 648, 21 June, 712, 28 June, 749 & 768, 5 July, 17, 27, & 50; and TCC Docs, A 147b, which admits partial failure. On the beggar-boats see *NCH*, 1908, 17 Oct, 117; TCC Docs, A 20ab.

On the gentry directors (to a first approximation urban *tuan-tung* and rural *t'u-tung*) see TCC Docs, A 98ab & 99a. On the warders (urban *ti-chia*) and wardens (rural *ti-pao*) see A 92a–95a; C 71b–72a & 83a. On the relationship between the wardens and directors see B 43b & 82a, in which it appears that the directors were far from effective in the exercise of control over the wardens for whom they were nominally responsible. Cf. also A 92ab. On the Council's *de facto* authority over the wardens see e.g. A 141a. On its *de facto* authority over the directors see e.g. B 42a.

[24] See TCC Docs, A 159ab.

[25] See ibid. A 138b–150a *passim*; Regulations, A 11a–12a & B 17a–22a; Docs, B 90b.

of them. The establishment of our P'u-yü Hall in a modest way pursues this ideal.[26]

Besides providing cheap rice in times of dearth, the Council paid for the training of medical personnel, supported hospitals, cared for the elderly, infirm, and orphaned through its Association of Charities, in which most of the older charitable halls had been regrouped and reorganized, gave industrial training to the poor, and subsidized municipal primary education (which was often free to deserving pupils).[27]

There was little or no corruption at the higher levels, if we may judge from the published accounts, the total lack of any scandal, and the failure of a hostile government inquiry in 1914 to reveal anything discreditable. An obvious reason is that the Council paid both expenses and handsome salaries, and that its financial operation was modern in the sense that public and private expenditure were kept distinct. The directors and their officers were not obliged, as a *hsien* magistrate was, to pay for essential services out of their own pockets and then recoup themselves by technically illegal means.[28]

The democratic basis grew with time. The elections of 1905 were held in two sessions, one for invited gentry directors and the other for leading businessmen, while further candidate representatives were simply co-opted by the organizers and the final selection from the short-list of seventy-odd persons so compiled made by the local officials. In 1907 those who had been resident in the city for more than five years were entitled to vote if they paid more than 10 *yuan*[29] of local taxes annually. A two-tiered system involving an electoral college was introduced and official

[26] See TCC Docs, C 32a.

[27] On the provision of cheap rice see n. 19 above. On the training of doctors in Western medicine see TCC Docs, C 82b–83a. On support for hospitals see A 69a–71a. On the care of the elderly and other charitable undertakings see C 28a–29a. On industrial training see C 30a–31a. On education see C 87b & 99a.

[28] On the inquiry see TCC Docs, C 107a.

On Council salaries see TCC Regulations, B 6a, art. xii, which states that the General Director was to receive 3,840 *yuan* per annum in salary, directors 1,920 *yuan*, and others a maximum of 960 *yuan*. For an example of the type of expenses paid see TCC Docs, B 57a.

Some corruption among the contractors for boat and for rubbish taxes was admitted. See, e.g. A 162ab & 164a.

[29] 10 *yuan* were worth approx. £1 stg at this time. Rather more than 6 *yuan* would buy 213 $\frac{1}{4}$ lb of rice, 4 *yuan* some 133 $\frac{1}{3}$ lb of local flour, 12 $\frac{1}{2}$ *yuan* some 400 lb of bean oil, and 17 cents 1 $\frac{1}{3}$ lb of pork. See FO 227/1561 Warren to Satow, 24 May 1904.

E

approval (which was in no case ever actually withheld) took the place of official selection. In 1909 the Council followed the newly promulgated imperial *Regulations for the Local Self-government of Cities, Towns, and Rural Areas*, and the electoral college was abandoned. Instead, two rolls of voters were drawn up in such a way that large tax-payers were given greater representation than small ones. The financial qualification was lowered to the payment of any kind of direct tax amounting to 2 *yuan* annually. In 1910, which is the first year for which we have figures, there were 334 A-roll electors and 3,310 B-roll electors, or some 2 per cent of the population affected. The turn-out at the polls was 56 per cent of the A roll and 29 per cent of the B roll. By 1913, the last year for which we have figures, there were 693 persons on the A roll and 8,165 on the B roll in a slightly larger population, and turn-out rose to 58 per cent and 45 per cent for the A and the B roll respectively. In 1912, the only year for which the necessary information exists, the most popular B-roll assemblyman received 55 votes and the least popular A-roll assemblyman was elected with 2.[30] These figures should be put in perspective by remembering that every candidate for the sixty-member strong Assembly was competing against every other candidate, that each elector had only one vote to bestow, and that since (almost) every elector was *ipso facto* a potential candidate, numerous votes must have been scattered across a wide field of unsuccessful aspirants.

The Council Assembly was probably the first Chinese political institution in which open political struggle was regarded as a legitimate and even normal activity. Although there seems to have been a prejudice against parties, and there was no true election campaigning based upon contrasting programmes of action, there was considerable competition at a personal level and, in so far as the making of policy was concerned, no inhibitions about the use of the majority vote. For major disputes within the gentry the Assembly was too small an arena and the traditional method of conflict resolution was still followed. Either the two opposing

---

[30] On the 1905 elections see TCC Docs, A 1ab: Outline of Main Events, A 1a. On the 1907 elections see TCC Regulations, A 3b–4a arts ii, v, & vi; Outline of Main Events, A 8a, 10b; Docs A 6ab & 6b–7a. On the introduction of the imperial regulations see TCC Docs, A 8a & 134b.

On the size of the electorate and the turn-out at the polls see TCC Docs, A 9ab, B 5b–6a, C 3ab & 8ab. On the number of votes needed to elect the municipal congressmen in 1912 see C 6a–7b.

parties would fight a straight 'battle of petitions' until the official authorities delivered a verdict, or a series of public and private meetings would be held until an agreed compromise emerged and the officials could be asked with confidence for their endorsement. Lu Wen-lu, when as an Honorary Director of the Council he attacked the Council's policy in 1908, stated the two possibilities with exemplary clarity in a letter to the intendant. The latter, said Lu, should 'either, after having made a careful examination, reject its proposals or order the scholars and people of the entire county to hold a public discussion in the Hall of Human Relation-ships, and take any action only after public opinion has reached unanimity so as to ensure that whatever is done has a public and not a private character.' On another occasion the governor-general of the lower Yangtze provinces told the Shanghai inten-dant that since the gentry and merchants were 'split into two parties', he should 'collect them for discussions' before making any decision.[31]

Officials were usually extremely reluctant to commit themselves until the local notables had resolved among themselves where a preponderant majority of opinion lay. That this was often called 'unanimity' should not obscure the fact that it rarely was. In the controversy as to whether or not the city walls of Shanghai should be demolished, for example, the following pattern of events un-folded.[32] Firstly, about two-thirds of the City Council and a number of other leading members of the gentry, 31 in all, pro-posed to the intendant that the walls be taken down in order to improve communications. One of the Council minority then headed a petition opposed to this. He was supported by 19 other notables, and a further 54 sent in two other petitions written in a similarly antagonistic vein. One of them demanded a mass meeting

---

[31] On the prejudice against parties see Li, *Ch'ieh-wan lao-jen ch'i-shih-sui tzu-hsü* (Old Still Stubborn's autobiography at the age of 70, 1923), p. 195ab, whom I take as typical. It should be added that a number of leading Council members were in the T'ung-men Hui and/or, after 1912, the KMT. See Kojima Yoshio, 'The great mer-chants and the independence of Shanghai in the 1911 revolution', in *Tōyō shigaku ronshū* (Symposia on Far Eastern history), vi.: *Chūgoku kindaika no shakai kōzō* (The social structure of China during her modernization, 1960), p. 131. On contested elections see TCC Docs, C 9a & B 6a. On majority voting see espec. TCC Regulations, A 5ab, arts xvii, xxviii, xxix (c. 1906).

On Lu Wen-lu see TCC Docs, A 44a: and for the governor-general's remark B 22b.
[32] On which see ibid. A 29a–37a, B 17a, C 12a–15a; and Li, Autobiography, pp. 192b–193b.

of the élite of the entire *hsien*. There ensued an extensive series of consultations, the outcome of which was a massive petition, signed by 92 members of the gentry including 7 demolitionists and 15 of the original opponents of demolition, asking for the opening of four extra city gates as a compromise solution. The intendant then declared that the gentry had 'reached unanimity over their plans' (when they hadn't) and the governor-general felt moved to state that 'Since they have reached unanimity I naturally ought to accord them my approval'. The die-hard demolitionists on the Council thereupon fought a fierce and effective delaying action to stop the compromise plan from being given adequate financial backing, and eventually managed to persuade a new intendant that the whole problem should be discussed again *ab initio* by a meeting of 'the whole body of gentry and merchants'. The con-servationists were sufficiently frightened that the day would go against them, and attached so much weight to the moral force of the decisions of such a meeting that they had it broken up by strong-arm methods before it had properly started. The intendant observed that he had not expected the gentry 'to be so incon-siderate as to quarrel among themselves, lose sight of principles, and get involved in partisan arguments'. The Council, faced with a dangerous loss of face because the governor-general was now insisting that the compromise plan should be carried out since it had been given official approval, had further talks with its advo-cates and it was decided that the Council would itself take over the work of opening the new gates, this being a sort of compromise within the compromise. Before all the new gates had been built, the 1911 revolution supervened and the leading demolitionist, Li Chung-chüeh, lost little time in calling a mass meeting of 3,000 people, most of them his own supporters, and having the proposal to pull the walls down and fill in the city moat carried by acclaim. The approval of the revolutionary military governor was obtained and work begun the following morning. The use of the public meeting, if only to secure a semblance of popular approval, was an underlying theme of the entire controversy.

When political conflicts extended beyond the range of merely gentry interests, either upwards or downwards, more wholly traditional patterns of resolution survived. In the course of the City Council's clash with the local armed forces over who owned the land in between the city walls and the moat, the issues were

argued in petitions, letters, and official orders, in a manner
astonishing to us for the lack of definition of terms and of any systematic examination of the facts, for the absence of any accepted
corpus of law upon which a decision could be based (the local
gazetteer being the nearest thing to it), and for the prevalence of
libellous abuse. When the night-soil brokers who had been put out
of work by the Council's inauguration of a system of contracted
collection instigated riots and burned the new contractor's offices,
the Council simply put them down by force. Here, though, some
new forces were at work. When there were comparable, but not
exactly similar, riots in the West Division, the Council asked the
local Merchant Militia to hold a mass public meeting to find out if
the night-soil carriers had any legitimate grievances; and when a
number of merchants, adversely affected by a Council road plan,
asked for an alteration, the Council was quite prepared to do so once
the merchants had called a meeting of all likely to be concerned
and made sure that there was a genuine general desire for the
change.[33]

   Until 1911 the City Council differed from the provincial assemblies and the National Assembly created in the last years of the
Manchu dynasty in that it operated an administration and it kept
scrupulously out of national politics. With the revolution this
detachment became impossible. The 1910 financial crisis, which
had been triggered by the Stock Exchange machinations of J. A.
Wattie and made possible by the disruption of the normally
reliable Chinese banking system by certain of the foreign banks
lending outside the mechanism of the Chinese Bank Guild, ended
by turning most of the Shanghai merchant community against the
imperial government because of the corrupt and incompetent way
in which the intendant and his superiors handled it.[34] They thus

[33] On the conflict over the moat land see TCC Docs, A 50a–52b, 90ab; B 13a–14a,
20a–27b. On the night-soil workers' riots see C 64a–68b; and for the mass meeting
pp. 67b–68a. On the merchants' request see C 10b & 10b–11a.
[34] On the 1910 financial crisis see FO 228/2506–8. Neither Kikuchi in his 'The
Financial Crisis as a Factor in the Chinese Revolution', in *Chūgoku kindaika no shakai
kōzō*, pp. 73–111, nor M-C. Bergère, *Une crise financière à Shanghai* (1964) has understood
the nature of the crisis but both give useful information. Important references in the
NCH are 1912, 8 June, 672–3 (list of rubber companies); 1909, 13 Nov, 341; 1910:
6 May, 332–3 & 334, 23 Sept, 706 & 734, 14 Oct, 81–82 (on rubber share boom);
and 1912, 19 Oct, 186 (on Wattie). On merchant antagonism to the intendant and
his superiors see FO 228/2506, Muller to Doyen, 12 Oct 1910 & 21 Oct 1910 encl.;
NCH, 1910, 7 Oct, 41–429. On merchants in revolution see *NCH*, 1911: 9 Dec, 650,
30 Dec, 859–60; 1912: 20 Jan, 160; 1913: 13 May, 551.

became easy targets for the extensive campaign of propaganda and subversion mounted by the revolutionaries in the following year. The banker Shen Man-yun in particular contributed heavily to the underground activities of the anti-Manchu T'ung-meng Hui (Revolutionary League), led by Ch'en Ch'i-mei. While the revolutionary societies were the indispensable driving force of the Shanghai revolution, it was the adhesion of the City Council leaders, and their Merchant Militia and police, to their cause that effected the crucial shift in the local balance of power.[35] The year 1912 saw the apogee of the Shanghai self-government. They took over the posts in civilian government vacated by the imperial officials and, after Ch'en Chi'i-mei's resignation at the end of July, in the military government as well.[36]

The revolution was also indirectly the beginning of the end for the Council. The internecine quarrels between the local revolutionaries, the influx of professional criminals into their ranks and the corrupt and tyrannical rule of Ch'en Ch'i-mei as military governor all alienated the sympathies of most of the merchants from the republican cause. One consequence was that they refused to provide money for the 1913 revolutionary uprising against President Yüan Shih-k'ai and this, together with the determined efforts made by the British at Shanghai to see that the local troops were kept loyal to the central government by being paid out of foreign-loan funds, was an important factor making for the up-

[35] On the collaboration of the self-government leaders with the revolutionaries see FO 228/1806 Fraser to Jordan, 6 Nov 1911, 12 Nov 1911 (telegram), 13 Nov 1911 (encl.); *NCH*, 1911: 11 Nov, 337, 338, 349, 367–70, 18 Nov, 413 and encl.; *Municipal Gazette* of 16 Nov 1911; Kojima, pp. 113–14, 123–30; Republican Gazetteer, i. 49a–51b, xiii. 10b–11a; *Chung-kuo Min-kuo k'ai-kuo wu-shih-nien wen-hsien* (Documents issued on the 50th anniversary of the inauguration of the Republic of China), ii.: *Ko-sheng kuang-fu* (The revolution in the provinces, 1963), i. 343–5, 380, 387–9; *Hui-i lu*, iv. 3, 5, 7, 8, 11, 13, 21, 27–29, 38–39, 48; Li, Autobiography, pp. 186b–192b.

On the preliminary underground and front activities see *NCH*, 1910, 8 July, 75; 1911: 29 Apr, 299; 20 May, 499; 1 July, 12, 17; 15 July, 169 (on which cf. Kojima, pp. 126–7); 17 July, 754; *Ko-sheng kuang-fu*, i. 365–6, 370–2. On the subversion of the troops, &c. *Hsin-hai ke-ming hui-i lu* (Recollections of the 1911 revolution, 1961–), iv. 43–45; Chang Kuo-kan, *Hsin-hai ke-ming shih-liao* (Materials on the 1911 Revolution, 1958), pp. 226–7.

[36] Li Ying-shih, a distant relative of Li Chung-chüeh whom the latter had engaged to train the Merchant Militia, controlled the regular troops around the city. See Li, Autobiography, pp. 188b–189a and Republican Gazetteer, xiii. 1ab. Li Chung-chüeh took over most of the former intendant's civil functions (see, besides his Autobiography, *NCH*, 1912, 7 Sept, 700; FO 228/1844 Fraser to Jordan, 6 Apr 1912). Wu Hsing, the Deputy Chairman of the Council's Consultative Assembly in pre-revolutionary times, took over the former county magistrate's functions. (See Kojima, p. 130; Republican

rising's failure.[37] The over-mighty City Council, which had shown its power to influence the course of national events in 1911, was already an object of suspicion to Yüan and the rebellious activities of some of its members, like Wang I-t'ing, in 1913 and the armed neutrality of others, like Li Chung-chüeh at the head of the Merchant Militia and the Amalgamated Fire-Fighting Association, led him to move against it once the uprising had been crushed. His henchman in Shanghai, Admiral Cheng Ju-ch'eng, disbanded the Merchant Militia and early in 1914 the President abolished self-government bodies throughout China. The Council was replaced by a non-elective official board.[38]

The picture presented in the foregoing pages conflicts at almost every point with the generally accepted view of gentry self-government in late imperial China. Teraki Tokuko, for instance, is of the opinion that it was merely 'a legal guarantee of the powers already held by the rural gentry' and 'the legalization of . . . the infliction of extortion'.[39] Seen with respect to the case of Shanghai, the first of these generalizations is clearly an inadequate way of describing the complex gentry-controlled bureaucracy in the city even if its roots were firmly sunk in past institutions, while the second is grotesquely untrue in view of the extensive work done by the City Council in the fields of public construction, education, and charity. The explanation of this apparent anomaly may partly be found in accidental and personal factors, for Li Chung-chüeh, the pioneer of Shanghai gentry democracy, was a man of

Gazetteer, xv. 20a–21a & ii. 1a. Many others took up important posts under these two, e.g. Chu K'ai-chia, Director of the South Ward, who became head of the county's Industrial Department (TCC, Outline of Main Events, C 10a).)

[37] On the criminals see *NCH*, 1911, 1 July, 17; 1912: 30 Mar, 845, 25 Apr, 132; 1913, 29 Mar, 927, 23 Aug, 601, 15 Nov, 516, 13 Dec, 186; 1914, 24 Jan, 246; *Municipal Gazette*, 1912: 15 Feb, 39, 25 Apr, 132; *Ko-sheng kuang-fu*, i. 369; *Hui-i lu*, iv. 2, 12. On merchants' altered attitude see Kojima, pp. 131–2; Republican Gazetteer, i. 51b–52b; *NCH*, 1913: 5 Apr, 91, 19 Apr, 169, 26 Apr, 225–6, 235, 3 May, 358, 10 May, 370, 427, 17 May, 490, 7 June, 748, 19 July, 164; FO 228/2498 S'hai branch HK & S'hai Bank. Corp. to Peking branch, 18 July 1913; Alston to Fulford 20 July 1913; FO 228/4999 Fulford to Alston, 19 & 31 July 1913.

[38] On the course of the 1913 uprising in Shanghai see Li, Autobiography, 219b ff. his biography in Republican Gazetteer, xv. 39b; *NCH*, 1913: 26 July, 296, 2 Aug, 313, 343, 9 Aug, 439, 16 Aug, 529, 11 Oct, 139; FO 228/4999 Fulford to Alston, 12 Sept 1913; FO 228/2502, Fulford to Alston, 12 Sept 1913 encl. from Cheng Ju-ch'eng. On the disbanding of the Merchant Militia see Republican Gazetteer, xiii. 11a. On the dissolution of the City Council see TCC Docs, C 106a–108a; *NCH*, 1914, 28 Mar, 953.

[39] See Teraki Tokuko, 'Local Self-government at the End of the Ch'ing and at the Beginning of the Republic', in *Ochanomizu shigaku* (1962), vi. 18, 19.

enlightened views who had a formidable moral probity, but it would seem above all to reside in a contrast between city and countryside. If we look at many of the rural areas just outside Shanghai, Teraki's assertions seem much more plausible. The City Council was not, on its own admission, altogether popular with the citizenry but there was never any violent popular opposition to its existence as such.[40] This was, however, very much what seems to have happened to self-government bodies in the counties of Huat'ing and Nanhui, in the sub-prefecture of Ch'uansha and indeed in P'utung just across the river. Some of the rioting against local self-government was inspired by Buddhist monks who had lost the use of their temples to schools or police stations, but most of it arose from resistance to the imposition of supplementary taxes. So little loved were the rural self-government bodies that when their leaders sided with the revolutionaries in 1911, as happened in Nanhui and P'utung, the country folk rose up to defend the officials of the Manchu dynasty. In the early years of the Republic we likewise find cases of magistrates being popularly elected in defiance of the local self-government bodies and also of farmers' associations at war with the gentry assemblies.[41] T'ientsin, how-ever, where there was a council in many ways comparable to that at Shanghai, needs to be examined in more detail than I have been able to if it is to be discovered to what extent Shanghai was a unique example of successful gentry democracy.[42]

The general conclusion that emerges from this brief study is that the traditional Chinese social order had, under suitable conditions such as those that existed for a little while at Shanghai, a greater adaptive capacity to the demands of the modern world than it is

[40] On the lack of popularity see TCC Docs, A 6ab.

[41] On the riots against self-government offices see ibid. Docs B 61a; *Hsin-hai ke-ming Chiang-su ti-ch'ü shih-liao* (Historical materials relating to the revolution of 1911 in the Kiangsu area, 1961; Jap. reprint of 1963), pp. 11–12 ff. Teraki, p. 19; *NCH*, 1911, 3 & 10 Mar, 579; *Municipal Gazette*, 1911, 21 Mar, 77; *NCH*, 1911: 9 Sept, 658, 11 Nov, 370, 353, 18 Nov, 436. On the later opposition to self-government bodies see *NCH*, 1913, 5 July, 24.

[42] The Council was not an isolated phenomenon. In 1906 and 1907 there was a spate of self-government associations, public discussion boards, and lawsuit settlement offices, all of which resembled it in one way or another. See *TFTC*, iii/8 (13 Sept 1906) *nei-wu*, pp. 184, 186; iii/11 (9 Jan 1907), *nei-wu*, pp. 277–8; iv/5 (5 July 1907), *nei-wu*, p. 233; iv/10 (30 Nov 1907), *nei-wu* pp. 507–9; & v/5 (23 June 1908), *nei-wu*, pp. 303–4, for examples. On Tientsin see *NCH*, 1906: 23 Nov, 434, 28 Dec, 712; 1907: 2 Aug, 245–6 & 272–4; 25 Oct, 229–31 and *TFTC*, iv/5 (5 July 1907), *nei-wu*, pp. 208–16.

usually credited with possessing. Whether, however, the City Council could have grown into a true local democracy, given the time and unhurried pace afforded by history to the boroughs of England, remains an intriguing but unanswerable question.

TABLE I

The Income of the Shanghai Chinese City Council, 1905–14

(*yuan*)

1.	Locality tax	477,218·827
2.	Vehicle tax	263,122·483
3.	Boat tax	244,855·137
4.	Loans	169,573·022
5.	Public land rents	116,332·788
6.	Public works tax	100,223·792
7.	Public land sales	92,674·019
8.	Supplementary fees	60,915·410
9.	Charity tax	41,462·483
10.	Education fees	34,335·219
11.	Title-deed fees allocated to education	24,767·457
12.	Donations by self-government officials	24,151·423
13.	Cleaning tax	19,800·000
14.	Certificate fees	19,675·099
15.	Commercial boat registration	15,486·595
16.	Electric light fees	8,781·549
17.	Supplementary taxes	8,119·291
18.	Miscellaneous income	6,980·147
19.	Tea-, wine-, & cigarette-shop taxes	4,144·197
20.	Interest from banks	4,129·738
21.	Militia tax	3,190·901
22.	Public funds	3,110·622
23.	Sale of public goods	3,033·534
24.	Advance from the Assoc. of Charities	2,820·976
25.	Businessmen's contributions	2,419·790
26.	Advertisement tax	1,638·059
27.	Education tax	739·246
28.	Small boat registration	701·015
29.	Rebate on purchase of public land	600·000

Total　1,755,002·819

Source: Tzu-chih chih, Accounts. There are errors for the period 1913–14 in the various tables which make it impossible to produce perfectly matching figures from each of them. In this and table 2 the General Table in *Accounts* has been ignored.

TABLE 2

The Expenditure of the Shanghai Chinese Municipal Council, 1905–14

(*yuan*)

1. Public works	517,359·446
2. Police	334,363·029
3. Municipal Council & Assembly	166,668·061
4. Education	162,842·579
5. Loan repayments	137,683·800
6. Charities	125,356·935
7. Street-lighting	122,828·317
8. Public health	117,008·217
9. Court of Justice	61,152·602
10. West Division	49,051·744
11. Interest on loans	47,749·685
12. South Division	47,040·306
13. Purchase of public land	30,768·000
14. Electricity plant	30,322·570
15. Merchant militia	14,524·379
16. Centre Division (walled city)	8,170·034
17. Special expenses	6,546·250
18. Opening South Division	2,976·796
19. Opening West Division	2,852·258
20. Elections	2,251·428
21. Loss through bank failure	1,210·947
22. West Division losses in 1913 rising	695·370
23. Transfer of Council to Public Works, Police, & Taxation Board	589·065

Total   1,990,011·818

Source: as in Table 1. According to which tables one uses in the *Tzu-chih chih*, the overall deficit appears as 232,101·026 or 232,361·627 or 235,008·999 *yuan*.

ENDNOTES

1. On Li see his Autobiography; biography in Republican Gazetteer, xv. 37b–39b; Ch'en Ting-shan, *Ch'un-shen chiu-wen* (Old Hearsay from Shanghai, 1964), A 70; and numerous references in *NCH* where he appears as Li Ping-shu (correctly P'ing-shu) or Li Chung-ku.

On Mu see TCC Docs, A 4a, B 1b; Cont. Gazetteer ii. 38b; Kojima, pp. 121, 123, 130.

On Yao see TCC Docs, A 42a, B 7a, C 28a; Cont. Gazetteer xi. 8a–9a; Republican Gazetteer, xix. 1a; *NCH*, 9 Aug 1913, p. 439.

On Mo see TCC Docs, A 161a; *NCH*, 27 Feb 1910, *Municipal Gazette*, p. 168.

On Lu see TCC Docs, A 96a; Republican Gazetteer, xv. 37ab; Kojima, p. 118.

On Chu see Republican Gazetteer, xvii. 9b–10a; Kojima, p. 119; *NCH*, 1905, 3 Nov p. 245; 1906: 16 Feb pp. 346 & 371, 23 Feb p. 397; 9 Mar p. 534; 1910, 13 Nov p. 415; 1911, 1 Apr p. 43.

On Chang see TCC Docs, A 161a, B 61a; Kojima, pp. 117, 119; *NCH*, 1909, 18 Sept, 667, 1911: 15 July, 169, 8 Sept, 655.

On Ku see TCC Docs, A 4b; Kojima, pp. 117, 119; for his official rank see TCC Docs, A 4b.

On Shen see Kojima, pp. 116, 118, 123, 127–8; *NCH*, 1909, 15 May, 377, 1910, 27 May, 509, 1911: 17 Mar, 637, 15 Apr, 164, 29 Apr, 298, 20 May, 499, 17 June, 754; 1912: 16 Mar, 729, 11 May, 414, 14 Dec, 728; PRO FO 228/1806, Fraser to Jordan, 13 Nov 1911; Li, Autobiography, p. 187a; *Hui-i lu*, iv. 48.

On Su see Republican Gazetteer, xv. 22b–23a, xix. 24a; Kojima, pp. 115, 117–19, 123.

On Tseng see Kojima, pp. 115, 117–19, 123; *NCH*, 1905: 7 July, 52, 18 Aug, 382, 1 Sept, 519, 27 Oct, 229, 15 Dec, 610; 1906, 24 Nov, p. 428; 1908: 23 May, 478; 30 May, 545.

On Wang see TCC Docs, A 7a; Cont. Gazetteer, ii. 52a; Kojima, 117–19, 123, 130; Ch'en Ting-shan, A 70, 131, B 114, 115; TCC, Outline of Main Events, C 6b; *NCH*, 1909, 18 Sept, 667, 1911, 15 July, 169; 1912: 20 Jan, 153, 13 July, 118, 1913, 26 July, 263 & 265; FO 228/1806, Fraser to Jordan, 13 Nov 1911.

On Yü see TCC Docs, B 7a; Republican Gazetteer, xv. 11b–12b, xix. 24a; Kojima, pp. 117, 119, 123, 130; *NCH*, 1906: 16 Feb, 346, 22 Feb, 397; 1912: 11 May, 270, 25 May, 558.

The positions held by the foregoing on the City Council may be found in TCC Maps and Tables.

On the Merchant Militia see FO 228/1603 Chinese encl. No. 65

(1906); *NCH*, 1906: 18 May, 376, 13 July, 83; TCC Docs, C 70ab; *Ko-sheng kuang-fu*, i. 386–8.

2. See e.g. the descriptions of the attempts made to form a 'Chinese Merchants Consultative Committee' in the International Settlement given in *NCH*, 1905, 29 Dec, 707; 1906: 16 Feb, 346, 23 Feb, 396–7 & 427; 2 Mar, 495–6.

On Yü see Negishi Tadashi, *Chūgoku shakai ni okeru shidōsō* (The leading stratum in Chinese society, 1947), pp. 156–64; Ch'en Ting-shan, A 11–12; *NCH*, 1905: 2 June, 467, 28 June, 213; 1906, 23 Nov, 425; 1907: 1 Mar, 473, 4 Oct, 103; 1909: 13 Feb, 382, 27 Mar, 774, 15 May, p. 377; 1910: 2 Sept, 553, 30 Dec, 789; 1911: 1 Apr, 43, 15 Apr, 164, 18 Nov, 413; 1912, 20 Jan, 153; FO 228/1805, 1844 & 2506; Kojima, p. 115; on role in 1911 revolution see Li, Autobiography, 191b–192a.

On Wu see *NCH*, 1905, 15 Dec, 595; 1906, 16 Feb, 346 & 371.

On Chou see ibid. 1906, 13 Feb; 1907: 1 Mar, 473, 15 Nov, 407; 1908, 27 June, 847; 1909: 6 Feb, 317, 15 May, 377; 1910: 22 Apr, 204, 6 May, 336, 23 Dec, 698 & 720; 1911, 1 July, 26; 1912, 16 Nov, 526; 1913: 10 May, 438, 4 Oct, 21; Negishi, Guilds, p. 340.

On Shen see Republican Gazetteer, xvii. 3b; Kojima, p. 115; *NCH*, 1906, 16 Feb, 371; 1907, 1 Mar, 473; 1908, 24 Apr, 215; 1910: 6 May, 336, 13 Nov, 415; 1911: 20 May, 499, 3 June, 596, 17 June, 754; 1912, 11 May, 270.

3

Chinese Socialism before 1913

MARTIN BERNAL

Mao Tse-tung once wrote: 'Before the October revolution not only did we Chinese not know about Lenin and Stalin, we also knew nothing of Marx and Engels.'[1] Other modern scholars have tended to agree that before 1919, when the impact of the Soviet revolution first reached China, the socialist and anarchist movements there were insignificant and futile. There is also no doubt that such movements as there were did not mesh with social or economic realities. The period from 1898 to 1913 was one in which the Chinese peasant population was under increasing economic stress. Landlords and officials became more and more brutal and exacting as the restraints of Confucian morality and the imperial system broke down. In south and central China there was a rapid extension of tenancy and landlessness, and around the treaty ports foreign imports were destroying peasant handicrafts. Even though most Chinese progressives came from landowning and official families, the extent to which they failed to relate these problems to socialism is extraordinary. Almost without exception early champions of socialism insisted that there were no great economic injustices in Chinese society. Their concern with socialism and anarchism was because they saw them as ways to prevent the rise of the injustices and immoralities of impending capitalism.

With the exception of a few individuals mainly concentrated in the minute Westernized bourgeoisie, Chinese of all classes tended to find individualism, liberalism, competition, and 'the law of the jungle' both frightening and immoral. The results they had produced in the West were not altogether attractive and there was no parallel to them in Chinese tradition. Socialism and anarchism on the other hand were less horrific and unfamiliar. Socialism was not only similar to various specific Chinese traditions such as

[1] *Lun jen-min min-chu chuan-cheng* (On the peoples' democratic dictatorship) (Hong Kong, 1949), p. 5. See *Selected Works*, Peking ed., vol. 4.

Ta-t'ung and the *Ching-t'ien* system (pp. 70–72 below); it also resembled orthodox Confucianism with its official concern for popular prosperity and welfare. Anarchism not only resembled the Taoist rural idyll but it also had many similarities to a vast under-current of Chinese culture—the peasant longing for a pure, frugal, and egalitarian millennium which has been expressed in peasant risings and attempts to establish 'communist societies throughout Chinese history'.[2]

During the first two decades of the twentieth century these similarities meant that socialism and anarchism had vast potential support. This was not realized partly because of the difficulties of rousing the peasants to any cause, though the T'aip'ings and Boxers had succeeded in this, but even more significantly because the radicals themselves failed to see the relevance of socialism and anarchism to existing conditions in China. As this was the case, most of them—Sun and his immediate group excepted—saw socialism as something that could wait until the more urgent and constitutional problems were solved.

Nevertheless there were socialist and anarchist stirrings in the period, and they seem worth studying. Firstly, many of the people who thought and wrote about socialism and anarchism before 1913 went on to become important figures in the KMT or CCP in the 1920s and 1930s. This early influence affected their ideas on the subject. Sun Yat-sen, for instance, used the word 'communism' in the sense of Kropotkin's anarcho-communism right up to his death in 1925. It also affected political careers. Wang Ching-wei's extraordinary propensity to refuse office or resign was clearly connected with an anarchist oath he took in 1912.

At another level the writings and activities of the early socialists and anarchists introduced some of the vocabulary of Marxism— 'class', 'bourgeois', 'capitalist', 'communism', &c.—to hundreds of thousands of Chinese. Thus the rapid progress of Marxism-Leninism in the early 1920s was undoubtedly helped by the fact that its terminology was not entirely unfamiliar. Study of the early period also helps one understand the relationship between elements of the Chinese tradition and Western radical thought. These can be seen clearly in the early period when socialists were quite explicit about what they saw as links between the two. Since

[2] Y. Muramatsu, 'Some themes in Chinese Rebel Ideologies', in A. F. Wright, ed., *Confucian Persuasion* (Stanford, 1960), pp. 241–67.

1919, in order to be 'modern' and 'scientific' Chinese radicals have tended not to admit their debt to traditional ideals such as *Ta-t'ung* or the *Ching-t'ien* system. However, political events such as the Great Leap Forward and the Great Proletarian Cultural Revolution suggest that they and the peasant millenarian tradition associated with them persist and are having a great influence on China's search for a social and political form.

In its formative stages Chinese socialism was closely linked to the Japanese socialist movement. Therefore any description of it must include many references to the latter. As there is as yet no satisfactory history of Japanese socialism in a Western language, it is necessary to outline the development of the Japanese movement here.[3]

Japanese socialism originated from two very different sources, the Christian and the liberal. However, in the early years the Christians clearly dominated the movement. The chief reason why so many Christians became socialists or sympathetic to socialism was that their Christianity was often a symptom of a more general revolt against the values and methods of Meiji Japan. Furthermore, by becoming Christians the future socialists had already alienated themselves from their background—they were nearly all Samurai—and from Japanese society. Thus in many ways the adoption of socialism was only one step more on a path of revolt.[4]

All of the Christian socialists seem to have been educated by low-Church American missionaries, many of whom were interested in the 'social problem' which seemed particularly severe in the United States during the last decades of the nineteenth century. It was through their contact with these American Christian reformers either in Japan or the USA, where many of them studied, that the future Japanese Christian socialists first encountered socialist ideas. They were introduced to four or five key books on socialism, by American writers, most of whom, while not socialists themselves, were very sympathetic towards it.[5] The

---

[3] The chapter on Japan in G. D. H. Cole's *History of Socialist Thought*, iii, pt 2 (London, 1960), pp. 930–40, is not very accurate and the articles in English by Katayama Sen are not widely available.

[4] Cyril H. Powles, 'Abe Isoo and the Role of Christians in the Founding of the Japanese Socialist Movement 1895–1905', *Harvard Papers on Japan* (Camb., Mass., 1961), i. 98–99.

[5] The books were: Richard Ely, *Socialism and Social Reform* (London, 1894) and

most influential of these books were popular 'digests' of socialism treating the fundamentals of socialist belief but devoting more space to describing actual socialist politicians and parties. The authors of these books consciously set out to be objective about the controversial topic of socialism, and they succeeded to a very large extent. However, they did have a distinct bias towards socialism. This meant that they emphasized what they considered to be its more favourable aspects—its altruistic and idealist nature, and the writers' opinion that many socialist leaders were less material-ist than they themselves supposed. The writers also played down the violence and class conflict in socialism, saying that these were the preserves of the anarchists. Generally their writings implied that a socialist world was inevitable, but that this would be brought about by parliamentary means, and great portions of the books were devoted to demonstrating the steady increase of the Social Democrat parties in both size and number of votes. These books and the ideas contained in them formed the basis of Japanese socialism, and through the Japanese they exerted a considerable influence on Chinese socialism.

The liberal strand of Japanese socialism was dominated by the brilliant journalist Kōtoku Shūsui (1871–1911). Kōtoku was steeped in the Japanese liberal tradition, he was the foremost pupil and biographer of the Japanese translator of Rousseau, and he himself was very much influenced by the struggle for a constitu-tion and political rights in the 1880s. Thus he always had the deep concern with political liberty that was later to lead him to anarchism. Kōtoku was converted to socialism by the same Ameri-can books but his predilections, unlike those of the Christians, did not tally neatly with the Western authors. Although Kōtoku was equally concerned with the immorality of existing society, he was a materialist who did not shrink from violence and was therefore much more in accord with the Social Democrats themselves than with their religious apologists.

In the late 1890s Christian socialists started labour agitation and trade unions, while Kōtoku and his colleagues began writing articles in support of Western socialism, which gained widespread

French and German Socialism (New York, 1887); W. D. P. Bliss, *A Handbook of Socialism* (New York, 1895); A. Schäffle, *The Quintessence of Socialism* (Eng. trs., London, 1889), the author being a German economist with sympathies towards socialism. The only key book that was not a general survey was Edward Bellamy's novel, *Looking Backward* (Camb., Mass., 1889).

F

publicity.[6] At the same time socialists and socialist sympathizers formed a series of study groups to discuss socialism in general and its possible application to Japan. In 1901 members of these groups decided to link with the new trade unions and form a Social Democrat Party in the approved German manner. Japan in 1901 was far more free than Japan in 1941, but the formation of a Socialist Party was too much for the Meiji government and the party was banned on the day it was founded.[7]

Before it became established in China socialism was often equated with two traditional concepts, *Ta-t'ung*, a legendary golden age of social equality and harmony, and *Ching-t'ien*, a system of land tenure which may have been practised locally at certain periods during the first millennium BC.[8] The classical description of the former concept occurs in a passage in the *Li Chi* (The Book of Rites). The passage gives a picture of an age in which everyone is unselfish, and all men work for the common good rather than for their own interests or that of their families. It is one in which there is care for the old, the young, and the sick, and employment and an equal right to use property for all men and women. Despite its un-Confucian attack on the family, the passage became a generally accepted though little known part of the orthodox Confucian canon.

The concept of *Ta-t'ung* seems to have been part of a complex of cosmological and religious ideas which was incorporated into Confucian philosophy during the third and second centuries BC. As such *Ta-t'ung* was always close to the apocalyptic and millenarian element in Chinese thought which reappeared frequently among the people and less often among the literati throughout Chinese history.[9] This element was the only one in Chinese culture

[6] For a description of the early labour movement see H. Kublin, *Asian Revolutionary; the Life of Sen Katayama* (Princeton, 1964), pp. 105–28, and Kosaka Masaaki, 'Japanese Thought in the Meiji Era', tr. D. Abosch, in the series *Japanese Culture in the Meiji Era* (Tokyo, 1958), ix. 233–4.

[7] Powles, p. 110; Kublin, pp. 146–9.

[8] For the drawing of these parallels see Liang Ch'i-ch'ao, 'Nan-hai K'ang hsien-sheng chuan' (Biography of K'ang Yu-wei), reprinted in *Yin-ping shih wen-chi* (Taipei, 1960), iii, ch. 6, p. 73, and Liang, 'Chung-kuo chih-she-hui chu-i (China's socialism), *Hsin-min k'ung-pao*, 14 Feb 1904, pp. 45–47. See also Chang P'eng-yuan, *Liang Ch'i-chao yü Ch'ing-chi Ke-ming* (Liang Ch'i-ch'ao and the revolutionary movement at the end of Ch'ing) (Taipei, 1964), p. 17.

[9] See J. Needham, 'Time and Social Revolution or Evolution, Ta Thung and Thai Phing', in *Time and Eastern Man* (The Henry Myers Lecture 1964) (London, 1965), pp. 23–31.

which contained the belief that history could be an upward progress culminating in a glorious future. The two orthodox views of history were of a decline from the golden past, or of an alternation between periods of order and chaos. It was true that a few sceptics believed that the past was less civilized than the present but even they did not predict a glorious future. With its associations with the apocalyptic element it was easy to visualize the age of *Ta-t'ung* in the future, rather than in its original position in the past. In the 1850s the T'aip'ing rebels, for instance, clearly linked the age of *Ta-t'ung* with the coming Kingdom of God.[10]

Ta-t'ung became much more widely known among literati in the late 1890s when the reformer K'ang Yu-wei (1858–1927) started using it to describe his own ideals. K'ang's ideal society of the future was one in which the whole world formed a single unit, undivided by race, nation, family or class. The barriers which divide men would gradually and systematically be removed.[11] Within the new world all men and women would be equal, and without private property, brought up in public nurseries and schools and cared for in public hospitals and old-age homes. K'ang seems to have formed the basis for this ideal from his orthodox Confucian background, Buddhism, and the Western concepts of Christianity, science, and progress. He then appears to have looked for traditional Chinese equivalents to his new synthesis. In the late 1880s, in the *Kung-yang* school, a part of the apocalyptic element in Chinese thought, he found a Chinese parallel to Christianity in the school's concept of Confucius as a reformer and a redeemer. He found an equivalent to the Western concept of progress in the school's theory of the 'Three Epochs' in which Confucius by his civilizing influence was supposed to have raised the world from an age of 'chaos', through an age of 'Rising Peace' to an age of 'great peace': *T'ai-p'ing*. Sometime after 1895 K'ang linked the term *T'ai-p'ing* to that of *Ta-t'ung*, and he called the work describing the ideal world of the future, which he had been writing for the previous twenty years, *Ta-t'ung shu*, the 'Book of *Ta-t'ung*'.[12]

[10] 'T'ai-p'ing Chao-shu' (T'aiping Imperial proclamations), in Hsiang Ta & others, eds., *T'ai-p'ing T'ien-kuo* (Shanghai, 1954), i. 92.

[11] K'ang Yu-wei, *The One World Philosophy of K'ang Yu-wei: Ta T'ung Shu*, tr. L. G. Thompson (London, 1958).

[12] Hsiao Kung-ch'uan, 'K'ang Yu-wei and Confucianism', *Monumenta Serica*, xviii (Nagoya, 1959), 113–14, & R. C. Howard, 'K'ang Yu-wei (1858–1927), His

Because of the radical nature of many of his ideas—which included annual marriage and the toleration of homosexuality—K'ang did not dare to have his work published for several years. However, his general ideas were widely publicized by his disciple and colleague Liang Ch'i-ch'ao (1873–1929), and it was Liang who first drew the parallel between *Ta-t'ung* and Western socialism.[13] K'ang's slight knowledge of socialism seems to have come from hostile reports of it in Japanese newspapers, and he does not appear to have seen any clear relationship between it and his own ideas. Liang, who had read Japanese articles sympathetic to socialism, believed that the two were almost identical. He saw the parallel in the very real similarities between the socialist ideal and *Ta-t'ung* and between the two methods of reaching them, both of which involved an inevitable staged historical process. Perhaps because of the bias of his information on socialism, Liang failed to see any discrepancy between K'ang's reaching the glorious future by the peaceful elimination of barriers, and the Marxist achievement of socialism through the intensification of class conflict and violent revolution. In seeing a parallel between socialism and *Ta-t'ung* Liang was only the first in a long line that included Chiang K'ang-hu, the founder of the Chinese Socialist Party, and Sun Yat-sen. Thus the refurbished ideal of *Ta-t'ung* played a great part in the formation of Chinese socialism.[14]

The introduction of Western socialism into China only began after 1902. In that year Liang Ch'i-ch'ao and his reformist supporters founded a publishing house, the Kuang-chih shu-chü (the Extension of Knowledge Book Company), in Shanghai and the magazine *Hsin-min ts'ung-pao* in Yokohama. The market for these books and magazines was largely restricted to the treaty ports and the student communities in Japan and Europe, but some copies were also circulated in the interior.

In 1903 the Kuang-chih shu-chü brought out three books on socialism and in the same year two others were brought out by different publishers in Shanghai. All these books were translations of Japanese surveys of socialism which were themselves modelled

---

Intellectual Background and Early Thought', in A. F. Wright, *Confucian Personalities* (Stanford, 1962), pp. 314–15.

[13] See n. 8 above.

[14] Chiang K'ang-hu, 'She-hui-chu-i yen-chiu hui hsüan-yen' (Proclamation of the Society for Research in Socialism), in *Hung-shui chi* (San Francisco, 1914), p. 25b, and Feng Tzu-yu, *Ko-ming i-shih* (Chungking, 1945), iii. 216.

on the American works mentioned above.[15] The books repeatedly emphasized the European Socialist Parties' moderation and devotion to parliamentary methods. They also stressed the very real connexion between the socialism and the political democracy of the Social Democrats. The books shared the belief expressed in the American works that nearly all the violence in the socialist movement was attributable to the anarchists and nihilists.

It is very difficult to explain why all these books should have come out in the one year 1903. It is possible that the spate was part of the general increase of publications on the West that year that accompanied the patriotic and revolutionary ferment among Chinese students in Shanghai and Tokyo. However, the number of books published on other aspects of European culture did not increase to the same extent.[16] It is even more puzzling that no more books on socialism were published between 1903 and 1911. The only answer to this that I can suggest is that the very limited market for books on socialism had been sated.

However, during the years following 1903 articles on socialism continued to appear and increased in number. Many of these articles appeared in *Hsin-min ts'ung-pao*, some of them describing European socialism and others its relation to China. From these articles one can gain a general understanding of the attitudes towards socialism of Liang and his supporters during the years 1902 and 1905. Liang clearly sympathized with the European socialists; he was distressed by the Western 'social problem' and believed that a socialist solution to it was not only just, but almost unavoidable.[17] Liang was somewhat inconsistent on the question of revolution; at times he maintained that social revolutions were inevitable all over the Western world, at others he thought that they could be avoided in countries like Germany where not only was there a strong Socialist Party but the government itself

---

[15] The books were:
(1) *Chin-shih chih she-hui-chu-i* (Modern socialism), by Fukui Junzo, tr. Chao Pi-chen.
(2) *She-hui Tang* (The Socialist Party), by Nishikawa Kojiro, tr. Chou Pai-kao.
(3) *She-hui-chu-i* (Socialism), by Murai Chishi, tr. Lo Ta-wei. Another translation of the same work was brought out by the Wen-ming ch'u-pan she.
(4) *She-hui-chu-i kai-p'ing* (Gen. critique of socialism), by Shimada Saburo was published by yet another publishing house.

[16] See the chart in Chang Ching-lu, *Chung-kuo chin-tai ch'u-pan shih-liao* (Source materials on modern Chinese publishing) (Shanghai, 1954), ii. 100–1.

[17] Liang, 'Wai-tzu shu-ju wen-t'i' (The problem of the introduction of foreign capital), *Yin-ping-shih wen-chi*, vi. 98.

practised state socialism.[18] Looked at in this way socialism appeared to be not a force for revolution but rather a method for avoiding it through reform. This view was reinforced by the Japanese picture of socialism as a moderate non-violent movement.

To Liang socialism, with its emphasis on social harmony and its devotion to the common good, seemed in many ways more sympathetic and less revolutionary than liberalism and social-Darwinism, with their creeds of individual struggle and competition. As the equivalent to *Ta-t'ung* and the *Ching-t'ien* system, Liang believed that socialism was suitable to the Chinese temperament and applicable to China. Thus socialism appealed to him and his supporters in several different ways.

However, he did not think that the application of socialism in China was urgent. In his eyes China's lack of industry meant that she had no rigid class system and that the social problem had not yet arisen there. Therefore no immediate solution to it was necessary. For Liang the political problem of reforming the government and the economic problem of building up industry were far more pressing, because China would need to solve them before she could effectively resist foreign powers. Liang's programme was for political reform and the creation of industry, to be followed by state socialist measures such as insurance for the workers and railway nationalization. Apart from their intrinsic justice he believed that these measures would be advantageous because they would prevent the 'social problem' from arising and check the danger of a 'social revolution'. Liang's programme did not go beyond state socialism but he was sympathetic to other socialists. Like them he believed that the final stage of world history would be one of 'perfect socialism' or *Ta-t'ung*. He only disagreed with them when they said it could be practised immediately. He thought that it would take centuries for it to be possible in Europe and even longer in China.[19]

While Chinese were absorbing the ideas of the Japanese Christian socialists, changes were taking place within the Japanese socialist movement itself. After the suppression of the ephemeral Social Democrat Party, its members went on with their old activities, agitation, lecturing and above all journalism. Their main aim was to propagate socialism, but they also joined in

[18] Liang, vi. 98.   [19] Ibid.

agitation on immediate political problems, adult suffrage and the Russo-Japanese war. From 1903 to 1905 the Japanese socialists were united in opposing the war. Despite constant harassment from the police, and very little response from the public, they published anti-militarist books and articles, carried on correspondence with leading Russian radicals such as Tolstoy and Trotsky, and gave hundreds of lectures and speeches against the war.[20]

In the midst of this activity many socialists, particularly those in the liberal or 'political' wing of the movement, found time to enlarge their knowledge of Western socialism. Even more translations of Western works appeared and men like Kōtoku began to understand and accept such Marxist concepts as 'economic determinism', and the idea of class conflict being the mainspring of history.[21]

The end of the war in September 1905 removed the challenge which had united the movement. Almost immediately there was a split between its 'political' and Christian wings, each founding its own journal. However, early in 1906 a new and more liberal government came to power and passed a bill allowing limited freedom of association. The 'political' faction of the socialists immediately took advantage of the situation: they came to a compromise with some of the Christians and together they formed a new party which they called the Japanese Socialist Party.

Although the Chinese revolutionary Sun Yat-sen did not expound socialism publicly before 1905, he was conscious of it even earlier than Liang Ch'i-ch'ao and the reformists. Sun first became aware of the Western 'social problem' during his stay in England in 1896–7. Then for the first time he realized that even in a powerful country with political freedom, the people were not prosperous or contented. Over the next few years his impressions of the West led him to the conclusion that the radicals who said that a 'social revolution' was inevitable were correct. But he thought this was only true in the advanced West; in China which had not yet developed, he believed it was still possible to prevent the injustice

[20] H. Kublin, 'The Japanese Socialists and the Russo-Japanese War', *J. Modern History*, Dec 1950, pp. 328–31. Cole, iii, pt 2, p. 935, & Kublin, *Sen Katayama*, p. 230, are mistaken when they state that Lenin may have written to the Japanese socialists. The correspondence between the Japanese and Russian socialists took place when Mensheviks controlled *Iskra*. However, the revolutionary tone of the letters suggests that they may have been written by Trotsky.

[21] Kublin, *Sen Katayama*, p. 154; Kosaka, p. 342.

of the class system and the catastrophe of a violent social revolution. If China could have a bloodless social revolution at the same time as her political revolution, she could avoid the mistakes of the West and become a modern industrial nation without creating a social problem.[22] Thus the main aim of Sun's social policies at this stage was, not the reform of existing Chinese society, but the prevention of a future calamity.

Sun found what he thought was the way to achieve this aim in a group of theories which were widely prevalent at the turn of the century, especially in English-speaking countries. These theories belonged to two related schools of thought known as 'single tax' and 'land nationalism'.[23] From 1897 onward Sun accepted ideas from both these schools. But it is my opinion that before 1902 he was chiefly influenced by the ideas of 'land nationalism'; that all land should be nationalized with full compensation and distributed in small plots to anyone willing to work it. The Land Nationalists believed that this would prevent the excesses of the class system, because the workers could then refuse the conditions offered by the employers and support themselves on the land. It was, I think, these beliefs that made Sun call his policy *P'ing-chün Ti-ch'üan* (Equal Land Rights), a name that he retained after the policy itself had changed considerably.

During the years between 1902 and 1905 Sun became increasingly attracted to the theory of single tax: that all rent on site value should go to the state, and that all other forms of taxation should be abolished. Throughout his life Sun acknowledged his special debt to Henry George, the most famous 'Single Taxer', but evidence from Sun's statements and lectures at the time, shows that even after 1902, he greatly modified Henry George's ideas, or derived his own from other thinkers.[24]

[22] It is unlikely that Sun fully developed this last theory before 1905. The concept of simultaneous 'political' and 'social' (capitalist and socialist) revolutions probably came from the example of the 1905 revolution in Russia which was seen by many in these terms. (See, e.g. Lenin, 'Lecture on the 1905 Revolution', *Selected Works* (London, 1936), iii. 3.) I can find no evidence that Sun expounded this theory before 1905.

[23] See Cole, ii. 370–4 & 383–4. Harold Shiffrin, 'Sun Yat-sen's Early Land Policy', *J. Asian Studies*, Aug 1957, pp. 549–64, 557–61, & Wang Te-chao, 'Tung-meng Hui shih-ch'i Sun Chung-shan hsien-sheng ke-ming ssu-hsiang ti fen-hsi yen-chiu' (An analytical study of Sun Yat-sen's revolutionary thought during the T'ung-meng Hui period), in Wu Hsiang-hsiang, ed., *Chung-kuo hsien-tai ts'ung-k'an* (Taipei, 1960–   ), i. 161–6.

[24] Shiffrin, p. 560; Wang, p. 165.

After its introduction in 1902, Sun's policy of 'Equal Land Rights' became one of the four planks of the platform of his small revolutionary organization, the Hsing-chung Hui.[25] The first use of the term *Min-sheng chu-i* (principle of Popular Livelihood) came in 1905 in the introduction of *Min-pao*, the journal of the newly formed union of revolutionary parties, the T'ung-meng Hui. It was the third of Sun's 'three principles of the people', the first two approximating to nationalism and democracy. There is abundant evidence to show that the T'ung-meng Hui students, who accepted his theories of nationalism and political democracy with enthusiasm, were uninterested in or hostile to the 'principle of Popular Livelihood' and the policy of 'Equal Land Rights'. Again and again Sun talked to different groups about the injustices of the European class system, the coming violent social revolution, and the necessity for China to avert these two calamities. Despite this exhortation, the majority of the students only accepted the 'principle of Popular Livelihood' reluctantly as part of a package deal.

Rather than explain how his policies should be implemented, Sun preferred giving the general principles behind them. However, in a speech in December 1906 he gave some indication of the specific policies he had in mind. These, though similar to those of Henry George, were closer to those of John Stuart Mill. Sun proposed that immediately after the political revolution, all land prices should be fixed, and that landowners should pay to the government any increase in the value of their property brought about by the advance of civilization—the growth of towns and the extension of railways. He thought that with a rapidly developing economy this sum alone would provide sufficient revenue for the state and all other taxes could be abolished.[26]

Sun published no further details of his proposals for another five years, and the picture of his social policies was still further blurred

---

[25] The usual date given for the introduction of the policy is the summer of 1903 at the foundation of the Ke-ming chün-shih hsueh-hsiao. See Feng Tzu-yu, iii. 205–6. I see no reason to doubt Jung Meng-yuan, 'Hsin-hai ke-ming ch'ien Chung-kuo shu-k'an shang tui Ma-ke-ssu chu-i ti chieh-shao' (Introduction of Marxism in Chinese publications before the 1911 revolution), *Hsin chien-she*, no. 3 (1953), p. 10, when he states that it was first used at the foundation of the Viet Nam branch of the Hsing-chung Hui in 1902.

[26] Section on 'Min-sheng chu-i' in Sun's speech reported in *Min-pao* (4 vols, Peking, 1957), x (20 Dec 1906).

by the fact that other party spokesmen wrote articles putting forward slightly different proposals. Most of these articles were written by men with ideas of their own and are dealt with elsewhere. However, one article written by Hu Han-min in May 1906 may represent Sun's own views. Hu was an intimate friend of Sun and at the early stage of their acquaintance Hu's concepts of the 'principle of Popular Livelihood' and of socialism seem to have been entirely derived from Sun.[27] In his article Hu proposed land nationalization, with the government renting it for money to people prepared to cultivate it.[28] This proposal, as the opponents of the T'ung-meng Hui quickly pointed out, appeared to contradict Sun's plan, which was merely to tax the increase of land values.[29] The two proposals were later reconciled and made to fit into a coherent scheme by Chu Chih-hsin, another T'ung-meng Hui supporter.[30] However, it seems likely that Sun had no such master plan and that the two proposals were simply different points on the range of opinions held by him at the time.

Hu Han-min's article also described the position of the 'principle of Popular Livelihood' in relation to socialism. Hu said that their policy was land nationalism, which was in turn part of collectivism (social democracy) as opposed to communism (anarcho-communism).[31]

Sun's sympathy with Western socialism, unlike that of Liang Ch'i-ch'ao, did not extend to state socialism. He firmly believed in the connexion between democracy and socialism. The socialism of the Prussian monarchy was to him only a trick to deceive the workers and to delay, though it could not prevent, the social revolution.[32] Although Sun wanted to minimize its violence in

---

[27] 'Hu Han-min tzu-chuan' (Autobiography of Hu Han-min), *Ke-ming Wen-hsien* (Documents of the revolution) (Taipei, 1954–), iii. 386. Hu clearly stated that before he met Sun he knew nothing about socialism.

[28] Hu, 'Min-pao chih liu ta chu-i' (The Six Great Principles of Min-pao), *Min-pao*, iii, 5 Apr 1906, pp. 12–14.

[29] Liang Ch'i-ch'ao, 'She-hui ke-ming kuo wei chin-jih Chung-kuo suo pi-yao hu?' (Is a social revolution really necessary in China Today?), *Hsin-min ts'ung-pao*, no. 86, reprinted *Hsin-hai ke-ming ch'ien shih-nien chien shih-lun hsüan-chi* (Selection of topical articles from the decade before the 1911 revolution), compiled by Chang Nan & Wang Jen-chih (Peking, 1962–3), ii, sect. i, pp. 346–7.

[30] Chu chih-hsin, 'T'u-ti kuo-yu yü tsai-cheng' (Land Nationalization and Finance), *Min-pao*, 5 July 1907, pp. 67–99, & 25 Sept 1907, pt ii, pp. 34–43.

[31] Hu, 'Min-pao chih liu ta chu-i', p. 11.

[32] Hu attacked the use of 'social policies by constitutional states which have not yet forgotten autocracy' (ibid. p. 11).

China, as a revolutionary himself, he could not share Liang's absolute horror of the social revolution. For Sun, there was no incompatibility between the high moral sense of the Western socialists and their work for a revolution. Sun had no hesitation in identifying the T'ung-meng Hui with the world socialist movement.[33] He looked upon the 'principle of Popular Livelihood' simply as the form of socialism suitable for China. During 1905 and 1906 the unity of the two was so obvious to Sun that he and the other party spokesmen used the two words *Min-sheng chu-i* and *She-hui chu-i* (socialism) interchangeably.[34] Indeed euphony seems to have been the only reason why Sun created the new term. It was simply that it fitted more easily with *Min-tsu chu-i* (Nationalism) and *Min-ch'üan chu-i* (Democracy).

Chinese intellectuals showed more interest in social democracy and Marxism during the eight months from November 1905 to June 1906 than at any time until the 1920s. Over ten articles and translations concerned with Western socialism appeared in five issues of *Min-pao* during these months. There appear to have been several reasons for this rush of interest. It is clear that one factor was the impact of Sun Yat-sen and his 'principle of Popular Livelihood' on the students in Japan. Sun's principle was accepted in all the articles which mentioned the application of socialism to China, although there were some interesting deviations from it.

The other major stimuli on the students were the activities and propaganda of the Japanese socialist movement. The leaders of the T'ung-meng Hui came into contact with two Japanese who called themselves socialists, the Miyazaki brothers. Miyazaki Torazō was an international agitator and an old friend of Sun's, who kept open house for Chinese students in Tokyo.[35] His brother Tamizō, an ardent socialist, was often there and we know that his views were a frequent topic of conversation. However, Tamizō's socialism was not orthodox social democracy. He believed in land nationalization and the free distribution of land to all who wanted it (not Sun's policy of leasing it to the highest bidder). Tamizō had

[33] See his visit to the Headquarters of the Second International referred to in *Le Peuple*, 20 May 1905, p. 1, in an article which was quoted in the Japanese socialist journal *Chokugen*, 6 Aug 1905, p. 3 (reprint, p. 213).

[34] Robert Scalapino & Harold Shiffrin, 'Early Socialist Currents in the Chinese Revolutionary Movement', *J. Asian Studies*, May 1959, p. 334.

[35] See Sung Chiao-jen, *Wo chih Li-shih* (My story), reprinted Taipei, 1962, pp. 89, 95, 129.

his own society for the 'Restoration of Land Rights', the constitution of which he published in *Min-pao*.[36]

The Miyazakis were not part of the main stream of the Japanese socialist movement, with which the Chinese students had no personal contact at this date. The students were, however, interested in the socialists' publications. It was through these that the 'theorists' of the T'ung-meng Hui gained up-to-date information about the Western Socialist Parties, and a much deeper knowledge of revolutionary and particularly Marxist theory.

It was this new knowledge together with the ideas brought in by Sun that made up the basis of the *Min-pao* articles. The most important divergence from, or addition to, Sun's 'principle of Popular Livelihood' as he stated it, the proposal to nationalize all utilities and heavy industries, seems to have been inspired by this new knowledge of Western socialism. The scheme was advocated both by Feng Tzu-yu, the future historian of the T'ung-meng Hui, and by Chu Chih-hsin, the party's most original theoretician.[37] At no point before 1911 did Sun himself propose the nationalization of anything but land; on the contrary, he emphasized that his policy of single tax would liberate private industry from taxation and encourage it to expand through competition. This was the way in which Sun's policy was interpreted at the time and later. It is possible that Sun did not reveal his plans for nationalization in order to avoid antagonizing merchants and would-be industrialists on whom his party depended. However, if that were the case, why should Sun have permitted party spokesmen to propose it? It seems more likely that Sun did believe in public ownership of several utilities and industries and that the following rationale given in 1907 by Hu Han-min was more or less true. Hu said that the party believed that all natural monopolies should belong to the nation, while commerce and industries which were naturally competitive should remain in private hands. This was what Sun had meant by encouraging competition. Hu understood the

[36] Miyazaki Tamizō, 'T'u-ti fu-ch'üan t'ung-chih Hui chu-i shu' (Letter on the principles of the Comrades' Association for the restoration of land rights), letter in *Min-pao*, 22 Jan 1906.

[37] Feng Tzu-yu, 'Min-sheng chu-i yü Chung-kuo cheng-chih chih ch'ien-t'u (Min-sheng chu-i and China's political future), *Min-pao*, 1 May 1906, p. 109, & Chu Chih-hsin, 'Ts'ung she-hui chu-i lun t'ieh-tao kuo-yu chi Chung-kuo t'ieh-tao chih kuan-pan ssu-pan' (Railway nationalization and the official and private management of China's railways from a socialist point of view), ibid. iv. 49.

'natural monopolies' to include gas, electricity, railways, mines, and so on, but he thought land was a far more fundamental natural monopoly than any of these. That was why, according to Hu, the party emphasized its land policy, and had not mentioned its attitude to the other factors of production.[38]

On the other hand, at this stage the brilliant young student Chu Chih-hsin only paid lip-service to Sun's policies and was not much interested in land. He was far more concerned with capital and Marx. In the four articles he wrote in the spring of 1906, he demonstrated a remarkable and detailed knowledge of Western socialism. One of the articles, for instance, consisted of an intelligent assessment of the prospects of the British Labour Party after its success in the election of 1906.[39] Chu disagreed with Sun in his analysis of Europe; he thought that a violent social revolution was not inevitable and that socialism would triumph there by gradual and peaceful means.

Chu's articles also showed that he had a moderately good grasp of Marxist theory. He understood and accepted such Marxist concepts as 'surplus value', 'economic determinism', 'class analysis', and the historical role of class conflict.[40] It is even more interesting to note which points he understood but did not accept, either because Japanese socialists objected to them or through his own independent judgement. Two of these objections are particularly significant because they later became parts of Leninism or Maoism. Chu agreed that the proletariat was to be the main class behind a 'social revolution', but he felt obliged to invent his own term for 'proletarian', because the usual word meant industrial worker, and he believed it was essential to include the peasants in any social-revolutionary force in China.[41] Chu also disagreed with Marx's view that 'all capital is plunder'. While he admitted that the modern Western capitalists accumulated their fortunes by exploiting the workers—according to the law of surplus value—he

[38] Hu Han-min, 'Kao fei-nan min-sheng chu-i che' (To the denouncers of the principle of Popular Livelihood), *Min-pao*, 6 Mar 1907, p. 103.

[39] Chu, 'Ying-kuo hsin-tsung hsuan-chü Lao-tung-tang chih chin-pu' (Progress of the English Labour Party in the new general election), ibid. iii, Shih-p'ing sect., pp. 6–11.

[40] Chu, 'Te-i-chih she-hui chu-i ke-ming-chia hsiao-chuan' (Biographies of German social revolutionaries), pt i, ibid. ii. 6.

[41] Chu, 'Lun she-hui ke-ming tang yü cheng-chih ke-ming ping-hsing' (That the social revolution should be carried out with the political revolution), ibid. 26 June 1906, p. 53.

believed it was possible for small businessmen to do their own work and accumulate capital through their own efforts.[42] Thus Chu implied that the peasants should take part in the social revolution and the petty bourgeoisie need not be its enemy, an interesting anticipation of the present People's Republic with its dictatorship of the people as opposed to the dictatorship of the proletariat. Of course, the parallel is not entirely coincidental; to me it suggests that some of the adaptations of Marxism to un-industrialized countries were both natural and inevitable.

Through their vagueness and inconsistency the articles on the social policies of the T'ung-meng Hui by Sun and Hu Han-min must have caused considerable confusion. The articles by Miya-zaki, Feng, Chu, and others can only have increased the bewilder-ment of anyone trying to discover the precise meaning of the party's social policies. On the other hand, these articles greatly increased the Chinese students' knowledge of Western socialism.

The 'principle of Popular Livelihood' only played a very minor role in the early stages of the crucial literary battle between the reformists and the revolutionaries which lasted from November 1905 to October 1907. At first both sides were principally inter-ested in the revolutionaries' anti-Manchuism and republicanism. Towards the end, however, Liang, baffled in his attacks on the racial and political policies of the T'ung-meng Hui, concentrated on what he believed to be their weakest point—their social policies.

One of the most interesting results of the debate was the modifi-cation and clarification of their ideas, which both sides were forced to make. At the beginning one of Liang's chief weapons was the charge that Sun's policy concentrated on land and did not deal with capital; it showed that Sun could not understand socialism. It was this attack which eventually forced the Revolu-tionaries to clarify their position on the nationalization of 'natural monopolies'.[43] At the same time Liang was sniping at the T'ung-meng Hui for what he considered to be their false advocacy of revolutionary socialism. According to Liang, it was quite obvious to Sun and his followers that the ideas of Marx and Bebel were hopelessly impracticable. Therefore Sun's only motive for sup-

---

[42] Chu, 'Te-i-chih she-hui-chu-i . . .', pt i, p. 13 (n. 40 above).
[43] Hu, 'Kao fei-nan min-sheng . . .', p. 103 (n. 38 above).

porting them must be 'to agitate the dregs of society'.[44] This assault drove Hu Han-min, while defending Marxist socialism, to state that the 'principle of Popular Livelihood' was not socialism but something for which he coined an English word, 'demosology'.[45]

The Revolutionaries counter-attacked by saying that once the T'ung-meng Hui had come out in favour of socialism, Liang had changed his position, while he had previously supported it, he now denigrated it. Although many modern historians believed this change to have been correct, in my opinion it was very much exaggerated.[46] While admiring all socialist morality, since 1903 or 1904 when he realized the distinction between state socialism and social democracy, Liang had proposed the former and believed the latter to be impracticable. After 1905 Liang's fury was not against Marxism, but what he believed to be the hypocritical use of it by the T'ung-meng Hui.[47]

However, in May 1907 there was, I think, a sharp change in Liang's attitude. While searching for ideas with which to fight the Revolutionaries, he read Japanese translations of articles written by the most intemperate American critics of public ownership. In one article Liang appears to have gone a long way towards meeting their views, which attacked the fundamentals of the state socialism and municipalism he had previously advocated.[48] In his next piece, however, he returned to some of his old positions, and remained a state socialist, if a very cautious one.[49]

In the last year of the debate Liang's assault was mainly against the vagueness of the T'ung-meng Hui's social policy. This forced Hu Han-min and Chu Chih-hsin to attempt to fill the gaps left in Sun's very open structure. In an article which has been almost completely neglected by later historians, Chu Chih-hsin did give details of a practical policy. The essence of his scheme was that the fixing of land prices, the nationalization of land, and single tax were three consecutive processes. After land-price fixing the excess

---

[44] Liang, 'Lun k'ai-ming chuan-chih shih-yung yü chin-jih chih Chung-kuo' (Discussion of the suitability of enlightened despotism in China today), *Hsin-min ts'ung-pao*, Apr & May 1906, reprinted in Chang Nan, ii, pt i, p. 172.

[45] Hu, 'Kao fei-nan min-sheng . . .', p. 126 (n. 38 above).

[46] See for instance Jung Meng-yuan, p. 8 (n. 25 above).

[47] Liang, 'Lun k'ai-ming chuan-chih . . .', p. 172 (n. 44 above).

[48] Liang, 'Tsai po mou-pao chih t'u-ti kuo-yu lun' (Another attack on a certain journal's principle of land nationalization), *Hsin-min ts'ung-pao*, May–June 1907, 90–92, sections printed in Chang Nan, ii, pt 2,580–607, & *Yin-ping-shih wen-chi*, vi. 52–53.

[49] Liang (n. 48 above); Chang Nan, p. 600.

price paid in any sale would go to the government. From this, and from foreign loans, the government would establish a fund to buy all land over a period of 40–50 years. Government-owned land would be leased to the highest bidder on condition that he cultivated it himself. The government would also develop industry and housing on its land. Only when this revenue was sufficient could all other forms of taxation be abolished.[50]

It is difficult to say whether Sun had thought out this policy when he first announced the 'principle of Popular Livelihood', or whether he kept it in his mind during the following years. My tentative conclusion is that although Sun had assembled nearly all the elements of the scheme, it was Chu who made a coherent structure of them. I also believe that as Sun continued to talk in the old, vague generalities, it is unlikely that he was influenced by Chu's scheme, even if he read the latter's article.

It is widely recognized that Liang lost the debate with the revolutionaries. Nevertheless, Liang's last articles on the 'principle of Popular Livelihood' were left unanswered. Liang appears to have been defeated on 'racial' and 'political' issues, not on 'social' ones. It would be fair to say that the riot that broke up a meeting of Liang's reformists had more effect than all the writings on social policies put together.[51] However, the articles which made up the debate introduced a mass of Western social and economic concepts to the progressive Chinese reading public.

In late 1906 and early 1907 progressives in both Japan and China were affected by the world-wide movement among radical socialists against social-democracy and towards anarcho-syndicalism that took place after the Russian revolution of 1905.[52]

The change in Japan was initiated and led by Kōtoku Shūsui. In the spring and summer of 1905, inspired by the spectacular deeds of the Social Revolutionaries in Russia whose political theory he imagined to be a form of anarchism, Kōtoku began reading the

[50] Chu, *T'u-ti kuo-yu yü tsai-cheng* (Land nationalization & finance), pt ii, pp. 35–36.

[51] See the description in Li Chien-nung, *The Political History of China*, tr. Ssu-yu Teng & Jeremy Ingalls (Princeton, 1956), p. 217. Li is mistaken on the date of this meeting which actually took place on 17 Oct 1907.

[52] See Lenin, 'Left Wing Communism an Infantile Disorder', *Selected Works*, x. 65. 'The activities of Rosa Luxemburg and the left wing of the German Social Democratic Party after 1905 for anti-militarism and a mass strike'; the overwhelming confirmation of anti-parliamentary syndicalism by the CGT at Amiens in 1905, are all examples of this trend which I believe was triggered, though not caused by, the Russian revolution of 1905.

works of Kropotkin. By August of that year he was calling himself 'a Radical Anarchist'.[53] His new beliefs were confirmed by a stay of eight months in California where he had close contact with anarchists and members of the newly formed International Workers of the World.[54] On his return to Japan in June 1906 he set about converting the Japanese socialists to anarcho-syndicalism. His campaign was extremely successful; many socialists, particularly the younger ones, seem to have been frustrated by the slow moderation of social-democracy and to have accepted it only because Marxism, to which it was firmly attached, was considered the sole 'modern' and 'scientific' form of socialism. Once it appeared that Marxism had been superseded by more 'modern' and 'scientific' theories, many Japanese socialists went over very quickly to the more congenial theories of anarchism and syndicalist 'direct action'. Thus, by early 1907, Kōtoku had gained enough support to split and destroy the Japanese Socialist Party. From then until his arrest in 1910 on the probably false charge of attempting to assassinate the emperor, for which he was eventually executed, the Japanese socialist movement was increasingly dominated by its anarchist wing.[55]

The Chinese students in Japan were also affected. In June 1906 there was a sharp change in the contents of *Min-pao*. As we have seen above, the first five issues of the journal were full of articles on Western socialism. In the sixth issue these stopped, and from then on the magazine included numerous articles on anarchism and terrorism.[56] Historians have generally attributed this shift of interest to the change of editorship which took place at the same time. They also assert that it was because the writers concerned with socialism and Marxism, notably Chu Chih-hsin, left Tokyo to take part in revolutionary activities in China.[57] There were in fact several changes in *Min-pao* when Chang Ping-lin took over the editorship, and the group of Sun's immediate supporters were displaced to some extent. However, in 1907 at least, the division

---

[53] Letter from Kōtoku, 10 Aug 1905, quoted in Hippolyte Havel, ed., 'Kōtoku's Correspondence with Albert Johnson', *Mother Earth*, vi, nos 6, 7, & 9 (Aug, Sept, Nov, 1911), p. 182.

[54] Kōtoku, 'Tobei Nikki' (American diary), reprinted in Shioda Shobei, *Kōtoku shūsui no nikki to shokan* (Tokyo, 1954), pp. 129–46.

[55] Kublin, *Sen Katayama*, pp. 194–208.

[56] Jung Meng-yuan (n. 25 above), p. 11, notes this.

[57] T'ang Leang-li, *The Inner History of the Chinese Revolution* (London, 1930), p. 54.

G

between Chang and Sun was not as sharp as some writers have maintained; articles in favour of Sun and his policies continued to appear throughout the year. The writers interested in socialism did leave Tokyo for China, but not until the spring of 1907. Even after that date, in the thick of revolutionary activities they found time to write on Sun's policies, though not on Marxist socialism. I think that the two major causes for the shift of interest in *Min-pao*, were the beginning of anarchist activity and propaganda in the Japanese socialist movement, and the delayed impact of the Russian revolution.

In the winter of 1906–7 the Miyazaki brothers brought out a magazine called *Kakumei Hyōron*.[58] This magazine, which was specifically aimed at the Chinese students in Tokyo, described revolutionary activity all over the world, but gave particular emphasis to Russian terrorism and anarchist assassination.[59] The Miyazakis also helped T'ung-meng Hui members contact Russian Social Revolutionary refugees in Tokyo. *Kakumei Hyōron* contained descriptions of meetings and discussions between the two groups, and other sources suggest that Russian terrorists in Japan taught Chinese revolutionaries how to make explosives.[60]

Thus the Russian revolution augmented interest in both terrorism and theoretical anarchism, the two being commonly confused. In the summer of 1907 two groups of Chinese established anarchist magazines, one in Paris, *Hsin shih-chi*, the other in Tokyo, *Tien-i pao*.[61] The two differed sharply in their attitudes towards Western culture. The Paris group, led by Wu Chih-hui and Li Shih-tseng (both aligned with the T'ung-meng Hui), wanted the complete destruction of Chinese culture and its replacement by Western science and rationality more or less as outlined by Kropotkin.[62] The group was deeply concerned with issues peripheral to Chinese society such as anti-Christianity.

---

[58] This magazine has been reprinted in the series *Meiji shakaishugi shiryō shū* (Collection of source materials on Meiji socialism).

[59] See Kayano Nagatomo, *Chukaminkoku kakumei Hikyu* (Secrets of the Chinese revolution) (Tokyo, 1941), p. 85.

[60] *Kakumei Hyōron*, 25 Jan 1907, p. 6, reprint p. 198, and Kayano, pp. 49–55.

[61] *Hsin shih-chi*, which ran until 1910, has been reprinted twice, in Shanghai (1947) and Tokyo (1966). Several numbers of *T'ien-i pao* have been republished (Tokyo, 1966). For a general description of Chinese anarchism, see R. A. Scalapino & G. T. Yu, *The Chinese Anarchist Movement* (Berkeley, 1961).

[62] For a description of Wu's philosophy see D. W. Y. Kwok, *Scientism in Chinese Thought 1900–1950* (New Haven, 1965), pp. 33–58.

The Tokyo group was led by a great classical Chinese scholar, Liu Shih-p'ei, and it was almost characteristically concerned with the preservation of Chinese culture—Liu had previously been the editor of a journal entitled *Kuo-ts'ui hsueh-pao* (Journal of National Culture). Nevertheless *T'ien-i pao* contained numerous translations from the Japanese of texts from the broad range of Western socialism. Kropotkin naturally predominated but there were pieces from Marx, Engels, and other Social Democrats. These seem to have been put forward by the Chinese and their Japanese teachers as essential foundation stones for the edifice of modern anarcho-communism.[63]

What the two groups shared was the desire to overthrow the Manchus and a detestation of existing Western society. As individuals the leaders of both groups also shared a propensity to turn away from actual political or social revolution. Either through weakness or under intolerable pressure, Liu Shih-p'ei became an agent of the Manchus, and he ended his political career as an active supporter of Yüan Shih-k'ai's attempt to become emperor.[64] After 1911 and even into the 1920s Wu Chih-hui and Li Shih-tseng remained influential among the radical élite. However, the issues for which they fought—anti-Christianity and a scientific and materialist world-outlook—were of very little relevance to the majority of the Chinese population. In the late 1920s, while still proclaiming their support for an eventual anarchist revolution, both Wu and Li were very active in right-wing Kuomintang politics.

After the revolution of 1911 a new anarchist group called the Hsin-she was founded in Canton. It was led by a charisimatic young man and an ex-assassin called Liu Ssu-fu or Shih Fu.[65] Shih Fu saw himself as a modern international anarcho-communist, and his journal *Min-sheng*[66] was full of the translated works

---

[63] See, for instance, *Tien-i pao*, joint no. 16–19, 15 Jan 1908, which contained sections on: *The Communist Manifesto*; Hyndman, *Theory of Socialist Economics*; chapter from Bliss, *A Handbook of Socialism*; the first chapter of Kropotkin's *The Conquest of Bread*; Decisions of the 4th Anarchist Congress; Malatesta, *A Talk about Anarcho-Communism*; part of Kropotkin's *The Philosophy and Ideal of Anarchism between two Workers*; a history of the evils of elections; a section from Engels, *The Origin of the Family*.

[64] Scalapino & Yu, pp. 32–33.

[65] For Shih Fu and his group see Scalapino & Yu, pp. 39–44, Feng Tzu-yu, ii. 207–12, and Mo Chi-p'eng, *Hui-i Shih Fu* (Taipei, 1962 (?), mimeo.).

[66] This journal was first published under the title *Hui-ming* in Canton in Aug 1913. At the third issue it was forced to move to Macao and changed its name to *Min-sheng*. It

of Kropotkin. However, Shih Fu even more than Liu Shih-p'ei was deeply influenced by Chinese culture and by Buddhism in particular. The name Shih Fu could well be that of a monk or priest, and that of his chief follower, Cheng Yun-o, Pi An, had even stronger Buddhist connotations. A disciple wrote of Shih Fu: 'The headquarters were always thronged with strangers coming with queries for Shih Fu—it was as if he were in the jewelled hall of anarchism, seated on a throne as a great teaching priest.'[67]

The society gained national fame for the twelve prohibitions its members had to abide by: (1) no meat; (2) no wine; (3) no tobacco; (4) no servants; (5) no marriage; (6) no family names; (7) no taking official poses; (8) no riding carriages or rikshas; (9) no standing for parliament; (10) no joining political parties; (11) no participation in military forces; (12) no religion.[68]

Groups all over China were setting up similar conditions and Hsin-she only gained its fame because its conditions were the most stringent.[69] This pattern, though influenced by Western anarchism, particularly in its hostility to taking office, had its roots in the traditional belief that society could be reformed or saved by personal reform and example. It was also influenced by Taoist and Buddhist beliefs that the pure man should withdraw from official positions and responsibilities and help others by teaching and example. Shih Fu's followers were well aware of the similarities between their prohibitions and those of the Buddhist priesthood.[70]

In August 1913 Shih Fu's small group had to flee from Canton to Macao when southern warlords supporting Yüan Shih-k'ai drove out the T'ung-meng Hui administration. Forced out of Macao by the Portuguese the group survived precariously in the foreign concessions of Shanghai. In July 1914 the group attempted to establish an Anarchist-Communist Comrades' association, openly in Shanghai and underground in Canton.[71] They seem to have disappeared after Shih Fu's death in 1915. *Min-sheng* was published sporadically until 1921 and its later publishers built up a

later had to move to Shanghai and some issues were printed in Tokyo. It survived Shih Fu's death in 1915, and sporadic issues were published as late as 1921. For Shih Fu's works see also *Shih Fu Wents'un* (Canton, 1927).

[67] See Mo Chi-p'eng, p. 24.

[68] The group published 10,000 pamphlets setting out these principles, *Min-sheng*, xxx, 15 Mar 1921, p. 4.

[69] See the *Chin-te hui* launched by Wu Chih-hui & others in Feb 1912 (Scalapino & Yu, p. 38); *Min-li pao*, 26 Feb 1912, p. 8.

[70] Mo Chi-p'eng, p. 23.   [71] *Min-sheng*, 18 July 1914, pp. 222–6.

cult around Shih Fu.[72] Even so, there is very little evidence of organizational continuity between the early and later periods.

In 1913 the Hsin-she attempted without success to establish communist communities in the countryside, but its activities and those of the anarchist-communist comrades' association in Canton may well have helped the strength of anarchist trade unionism there in the 1920s.[73]

A far more striking phenomenon during the months of relative political freedom which followed the anti-Manchu revolution of October and November 1911 was the rapid and extensive growth of the Chung Kuo she-hui Tang (Chinese Socialist Party) under its leader Chiang K'ang-hu (1885–1945). Chiang came from an extremely influential official family. He seems to have had a considerable reputation as a classical scholar, but was interested in foreign studies from a very early age.[74] Before 1911 he vacillated between study abroad and official posts in the more modern branches of the Chinese bureaucracy.[75] Although he always held 'advanced' ideas and was a friend of some of the revolutionary leaders, he was not a revolutionary, his general political idea being closer to those of Liang Ch'i-ch'ao and the reformists. His concept of socialism was in fact similar to that held by Liang in 1903. Chiang believed that socialism was essentially idealistic, unselfish, and moderate—its purpose was to avoid conflict rather than to provoke it—and, like Liang at that time, he was unable to see any real difference between state socialism and social-democracy.[76] Chiang's concept of socialism appears to have remained stationary while those of Liang and his revolutionary opponents went forward. However, the very lack of sophistication of Chiang's ideas increased their popular appeal. The political thought of the gentry students and others in the interior was naturally several years behind that of the reformist and revolutionary leaders who had been directly exposed to Japanese influence.

[72] Ibid. 15 Feb 1921, pp. 1–3.

[73] Jean Chesneaux, *Le movement ouvrier chinois de 1914 à 1927* (Paris, 1962), pp. 203–4, 242–3.

[74] *Chiang Ming-ho Chi* (Testament) (Peking, 1927), pp. 18 & 34.

[75] Wu Hsiang-hsiang, 'Chiang K'ang-hu yu Chung-kuo She-hui Tang' (Chiang K'ang-hu and the Chinese Socialist Party), in *Chung-kuo hsien-tai shih ts'ung-k'an*, ii.

[76] For Chiang's ideas see *Hung-shui-chi*, a collection of his speeches and writings. His views as expressed in English in *China and the Social Revolution* (San Francisco, 1914), and his 'Socialism in China' in *The Masses* (New York, 1915), vi/i, issue 41, pp. 18–19, seem to have been modified by his American collaborators.

Chiang began his public advocacy of socialism even before the fall of the dynasty. In June 1911 he went on what he described as a 'lecturing tour' of Chekiang province. His chief topic was 'Women and the Socialist Movement', a theme he took from a Japanese translation of Bebel's *Die Frau und Sozialismus*, a favourite book of his. His lectures were according to Chiang a great success, but, hardly surprisingly, there was official disapproval and Chiang had to flee to the English concession in Shanghai for his safety.[77] Completely undeterred, he continued his activities there. On 10 July he launched a society called the She-hui chu-i yen-chiu Hui (Society for the Study of Socialism).[78] This attracted about fifty members who became the nucleus of the 'Chinese Socialist Party', which was founded two days after Shanghai declared its independence from the Manchu government on 5 November 1911. On that day it was decided to form a national party with headquarters at Shanghai and local branches all over the country. The new party adopted the programme drafted by Chiang:

1. Support a republic.
2. Destroy racial divisions.
3. Reform the law and respect the individual.
4. Destroy the system of inheritance.
5. Organize public organs to spread equal education.
6. Promote directly beneficial enterprises and encourage the workers.
7. Only levy land tax and abolish all other taxation.
8. Limit military expenditure and unite our strength for non-military competition.[79]

At this time Chiang also set forth what he believed the political role of the Chinese Socialist Party to be. It should not in his opinion act as a political party but rather as an educational society, to study and diffuse socialism, and as a pressure group, to persuade the leaders of political parties to implement socialist policies.

[77] Chiang, 'Chung-kao nu-t'ung-pao' (To our Sisters), and 'She-hui-chu-i yü nu-hsüeh chih kuan-hsi' (The relationship between socialism and female education), *Hung-shui-chi*, pp. 6b–17b.

[78] Chiang, 'She-hui-chu-i yen-chiu hui yen-shuo tz'u' (Lecture to the Society for Research into Socialism), *Hung-shui-chi*, pp. 27–29, & *Min-li pao*, 11 July 1911, p. 8.

[79] Chiang, 'Chung-kuo she-hui tang hsüan-kao' (Proclamation of the Chinese Socialist Party), *Hung-shui-chi*, pp. 53–55.

The party spread with astonishing rapidity. Chiang claimed that within the first year it had over 400 branches and 400,000 members.[80] These claims seem extravagant, but from the contemporary press I have so far been able to identify over 200 branches, and if one takes attendance at a party meeting or participation in a party activity as the criterion of membership the figure of 300,000 may not be totally unrealistic.[81] Most of the branches were within a 300-km. radius of Shanghai but they existed as far west as Szechwan and as far south as Kwangtung. There were branches in Peking and Tientsin, but outside these and a few other cities the party does not seem to have been tolerated by the generals of the Peiyang army who controlled most of north China. In south and central China, which were ruled by a medley of ex-Ch'ing-dynasty officials, local generals, and reformist provincial assemblies, the Chinese Socialist Party together with many other radical and reformist groups was occasionally harassed but generally left alone.

The party branches had a wide range of activities; public meetings were held in which lectures were given on such subjects as 'the nature of socialism' or 'the situation of socialism in Europe'. The Socialist Party Daily, Weekly, and Monthly, together with pamphlets issued by the party headquarters, including one with excerpts from *The Communist Manifesto*, were distributed. Some branches even published journals of their own. Branches also established free elementary schools and crèches and tried to organize trade unions. In some places socialist actors and opera singers toured the countryside performing plays with a socialist message. All branches corresponded with the party headquarters, and, in theory at least, sent 5 per cent of their revenue to it.[82]

It is difficult to discover who the members and activists of the party were. Hostile government reports described them as rowdy and low class.[83] Chiang stated that many of the members were illiterate. These, together with the prominent role in the party of

---

[80] Chiang, 'Chung-kuo She-hui Tang ch'ing-yuan kuo-hui shu tsao-an' (Draft of the requests of the Chinese Socialist Party to the National Assembly), *Hung-shui-chi*, p. 105b.

[81] See my *Chinese Socialism to 1913* (Camb. Univ. thesis, unpubl.), pp. 368–76.

[82] Chiang, *China and the Social Revolution*, pp. 26–27, & *Min-li pao* (Nov 1911–Aug 1913).

[83] 'Lin-shih ta tsung-t'ung ming-ling' (The Provisional President's order) [banning the Socialist Party], *Hung-shui-chi*, pp. 117–117b.

actors—one of the most despised professions in Chinese society—
suggest that considerable numbers of artisans and urban unemployed were involved. On the other hand, there is considerable
evidence that most of the party members were not from these
classes. Nearly all the party propaganda seems to have been in
classical Chinese and Chiang himself wrote in a peculiarly esoteric
style. The reports of speeches given at party meetings suggest that
their content was far too complicated and abstract for illiterates.
These pieces of evidence, together with the background of the few
identifiable members—who included Li Ta-chao, a future founder
of the CCP, and the great historian Ku Chieh-k'ang—indicate
that the majority of party members, and certainly the bulk of its
activists, were students or other young men of mainly gentry
origin.[84]

During the period of rapid growth, two groups within the party
began to challenge Chiang's picture of socialism and his concept of
the party's function, and these divisions came to a climax at the
annual conference of the party held in October 1912. The meeting
was attended by the representatives of fifty-eight branches. The
first challenge, which quickly failed, came from the right. It was
the demand by some members that the Chinese Socialist Party
should become a straight political party and put up candidates for
the elections planned for that winter.[85] The group had been
encouraged by a series of lectures on socialism given to the party
earlier that month by Sun Yat-sen. In these Sun had said that the
'Chinese Socialist Party' clearly did not understand socialism, for
if they did they would know that every socialist party has to play a
direct part in politics.[86] Chiang had toyed with the idea of a
socialist political party, but his own preference always seems to
have been for education and power through influence rather than
for direct political action.[87] Besides Chiang was under much
greater pressure from the anarchist wing of the party, which was

[84] Li Lung-Mu, 'Li Ta-chao T'ung-chih wu-ssu shih-chi Ma-k'e-ssu chu-i ssu-hsiang
ti hsuan chuan' (Comrade Li Ta-chao and the propagation of Marxism during the
May 4th period), *Li-shih yen-chiu*, 1957, no. 5, p. 4, & Wang I-t'ung, *Biographic Sketches
of 29 Scholars of the Late Manchu and Early Republican Era* (Pittsburgh, 1963, mimeo.),
p. 38.
[85] Chiang, 'Chung-kuo she-hui Tang ti-erh tz'u lien-ho-hui hou hsuan-yen' (Final
statement of the 2nd Gen. Meeting of the Chinese Socialist Party), pp. 85–85b.
[86] Sun's lectures were published in *Min-li pao*, 15–20 Oct 1912, & reissued in *TFTC*,
Dec 1912, sect. 4, p. 24.
[87] Chiang, appendix to Sung Chiao-jen's statement on Socialism, *Hung-shui-chi*, p. 49.

hostile to any dealings with parliament. This wing, led by a young medical student called Sha K'an, attacked with great violence Chiang and his concept of a legal party recognizing the state.[88] Immediately after the October meeting he and a small group established a party of their own entitled the Ch'un-tsui she-hui Tang (Pure Socialist Party) with a thoroughly anarchist programme:

1. The elimination of the classes of rich and poor.
2. The elimination of the classes of noble and humble, respect for the individual.
3. The elimination of the classes of educated and ignorant, equal education.
4. The destruction of national boundaries.
5. The destruction of the family.
6. The destruction of religion.[89]

The new party was banned by the government after only a few weeks, on the grounds—very probably true—that it was planning assassinations. After the ban, the party, which seems to have been very largely concentrated in Shanghai, continued to exist and publish its journal in the French concession there.[90]

Although Chiang K'ang-hu rejected participation in the elections, the party conference drew up a series of requests to the National Assembly most of which were merely modifications of the eight points of the party programme. Despite a franchise severely restricted by qualifications of property, education, and age, the elections of the winter of 1912–13 were probably the most free in Chinese history. They resulted in a landslide victory for the Kuomintang, an uneasy alliance between the revolutionaries and various small reformist parties. Among the victors, there were between 20 or 30 who considered themselves socialists.[91] In the spring of 1913 Chiang went to Peking to lobby these and other sympathizers for the Socialist Party proposals. But by that time the coming struggle between Yüan Shih-k'ai and the Kuomintang completely preoccupied the assembly members.

Chiang and his party took very little part in the struggle against Yüan. On May Day 1913, for instance, the Chinese Socialist

---

[88] Shih Fu, 'Cheng-fu yü she-hui Tang' (The government and the Socialist Party), *Hui-ming Lu*, 27 Aug 1913, p. 3, reprinted p. 73.

[89] Ibid. p. 4.   [90] Ibid.   [91] Chiang, 'Socialism in China', p. 19.

Party held a meeting in Shanghai addressed by a Belgian socialist on 'The Belgian Situation', while Sha K'an's Pure Socialist Party, together with two other radical groups, held a fiery mass meeting against Yüan Shih-k'ai and his misdeeds.[92] However, neutrality did not save Chiang, and the suppression of the Chinese Socialist Party began even before Yüan Shih-k'ai had goaded the southern provinces into the abortive 'second revolution'. In July 1913 the party leader in Peking was beheaded. In August the Chinese Socialist Party was banned throughout the country.[93] On 31 August Chiang was deputed by an extraordinary party meeting to go abroad to form links with other socialist parties and attend the 1914 meeting of the Socialist International.[94] As all the revolutionaries were fleeing the country, Chiang left for America. After his departure the party disappeared almost without trace. In September 1914 an anarchist wrote: 'The Chinese Socialist Party has scattered and dispersed. Of the 400,000 members there remain only 20 or 30 persons who dare to talk about socialism, and some of them are beginning to combine with us.'[95]

The reason for this sudden and total collapse was that the party did not have the revolutionary organization or ideology to sustain it in the face of the brutal oppression of Yüan Shih-k'ai and the southern warlords who took control after August 1913. The party and many other groups could only flourish as loosely organized educational associations in a relatively open society. By 1919, when mass political action became possible again, Chiang's ideas had been hopelessly outdated by internal and international developments.

The Chinese communists are right not to claim the Chinese Socialist Party as a predecessor. Chiang's party was not a political party, nor was it strictly speaking socialist. It was refused admission into the Second International until it added to its programme

---

[92] *China Republican*, 25 Apr 1913, p. 3, and Chiang, 'Chung kuo she-hui Tang tui-yu nan-fang shih-pien hsuan-yen' (Announcement on the Chinese Socialist Party and the Southern Disturbances), *Hung-shui-chi*, p. 112b.

[93] For a description see *China Republican*, 2 Aug 1913, p. 11; Chiang, *China and the Social Revolution*, pp. 30–31.

[94] Chiang, 'Chung-kuo She-hui Tang t'e-pieh lien-ho hui chu-chih hsuan-yen' (Statement of resignation at the Extraordinary General Meeting of the Chinese Socialist Party), *Hung-shui-chi*, p. 119.

[95] Paul Gunn, letter published in *Freedom*, Oct 1914. Chiang did try to establish a small socialist party in 1924, but by then his ideas were hopelessly outmoded; see Hsieh Pin, in *Min-kuo cheng-tang shih* (reprinted Taipei, 1962), p. 132.

the article, 'All organs of production and exchange should be publicly owned'.[96] Nevertheless, it was in my opinion of considerable importance in the development of socialism in China. The exiled revolutionary theorists in Tokyo had a far greater understanding of Marxist socialism than did Chiang. But they could only spread their ideas to a minute (though extremely significant) group of people. On the other hand, Chiang's naïve and muddled ideas were able to reach hundreds of thousands of Chinese. Whether or not any of these could understand the pamphlet containing parts of *The Communist Manifesto* for instance, they at least became acquainted with some of the terms involved. I am convinced that the extraordinarily rapid spread of Marxism-Leninism in China in the 1920s was helped by the fact that such terms as 'nationalization', 'communism', 'means of production', and 'class conflict' were not totally unfamiliar to large numbers of people.

If there is no organizational continuity from Chiang's party to the later mass parties, the intellectual break was not so drastic. Among *Ch'ing nien* (youth) the sons and daughters of landowners and merchants at high school and university, who formed the backbone of the Chinese Socialist Party, an interest in and a sympathy with socialism in the broad sense remained. This group was clearly predisposed towards communism and socialism at the beginning of the May Fourth period, and it was this group that launched the patriotic movement and founded the Communist Party. Vague socialist ideas may have spread to other classes in the Shanghai region from 1912, but it was not until agitation by 'youth' during the Northern Expedition of 1926 that they began to filter through to the south China peasantry. The early anarchists too with very few exceptions failed to make contact with the vast reservoir of potentially anarchist feeling among the peasants. The task of harnessing this feeling was left to the CCP and Mao Tsetung in their attempts during the Great Leap Forward of 1958 and the Great Proletarian Cultural Revolution of 1966–7—to establish the anarchist ideal of a society made up of freely federated and directly democratic communes.

[96] See J. A. Jackson, 'Letter from a Socialist', in *China Republican*, 28 Feb 1913, p. 11.

4

The Federalist Movement in China, 1920–3[*]

JEAN CHESNEAUX

FOLLOWING the first world war, when China seemed lost in anarchy, the possibility of re-establishing order by the establishment of a federal regime was seriously discussed among Westernized Chinese intellectuals, politicians, and military chiefs. This 'movement for a federation of autonomous provinces' (*lien-sheng tzu-chih yün-tung*) does not belong only to the history of lively controversy and of the discussion of ideas in China at the time of the May Fourth Movement;[1] it was expressed in practical ways, especially in the south, by initiatives tending to reinforce provincial autonomy and local particularism. Although it was an abortive episode, from 1920 to 1923, this federalist movement had considerable influence and made many converts, from Sun Yat-sen to the young Mao, from Liang Ch'i-ch'ao to Hu Shih. A study of the movement also provides the opportunity for a closer look, in the light of a concrete example, at the distinctive features of the ideological and political 'interregnum' dividing the traditional empire from the communist revolution, and Confucianism from Marxism.

What were these provinces which at the time constituted the natural framework and the political objective of the federalist movement? Far from being only arbitrary administrative divisions, they were characterized at the time of the first world war by their geographical, political, sociological, and economic cohesion.

These provinces, the outline of which on the whole dates from the beginning of the Ming dynasty (the fourteenth century), have a distinct oro-hydrographic structure, especially in central and south China; they correspond with a fluvial basin or a particular part of one, the centre of which is occupied by a rice-producing plain or a group of rice-producing plains, which are surrounded by

---

[*] Trans. of 'Le Mouvement fédèraliste en Chine, 1920–3', *Revue historique*, Oct–Dec 1966 (by permission of the author and of the Presses Universitaires de France).

[1] See below, pp. 105 & 333.

mountains or wooded hills forming the watershed between one hydrographic valley and another. Hupei corresponds to the middle Yangtze region at the confluence of the Han, Hunan is centred on Lake Tungting basin, Kiangsi on Lake Poyang basin, Szechwan on the Red Valley, Kwangtung on the lower reaches of the West River, Fukien and Chekiang on numerous little coastal streams. True, the natural framework of the northern provinces (except the horst of Shansi) or of the lower Yangtze is less well defined: and these are in fact the provinces in which the federalist movement tended to be less vigorous. But the dominant tendency is towards precise correspondence with the oro-hydrographic pattern, which favours communications by water inside the province, inter-provincial communication being more difficult. This leads to the problem of the economic cohesion of the provinces, to which we will return.[2]

Provinces are distinct politico-administrative units. The solid bureaucratic apparatus of the empire already allowed them wide powers.[3] The governor (*hsün-fu*) was assisted by ten bureaux, for military affairs, justice, education (responsible for provincial examinations for recruitment of mandarins), foreign affairs,[4] finance, &c. Provinces were military, economic (they controlled part of their own revenue), and judicial units. A law of 1907 had enlarged their administrative powers[5] and in 1908 they had been granted provincial assemblies (*tzŭ-i-chü*, consultative bureaux), responsible for making known 'public opinion' to the provincial public authorities, examining the provincial budget, and discussing plans for borrowing.[6] They were elected by vote confined to two classes—rich landowners with an income of $5,000, and holders of Confucian ranks. They thus essentially represented the gentry, the rural notables (*shen-shih*); and it was through these

[2] As far as I know, no geographer has so far made a thorough study of the physical factors involved in the division of China into provinces in modern times.
[3] Cf. H. S. Brunnert & V. V. Hagelstrom, *Present-Day Political Organization of China* (Shanghai, 1911), pp. 400–519.
[4] Although at central government level a Minister of Foreign Affairs existed from 1860, the provincial authorities retained the responsibility for foreign relations locally, in conformity with Chinese tradition.
[5] Brunnert & Hagelstrom, p. 397.
[6] *CYB*, *1912*, pp. 355–7, 363–7, 394–6 (which gives the text of the decrees relating to these assemblies). The history of the latter, from 1909 to 1923, still remains to be written; this work would involve in the first instance cataloguing the available materials, and in particular the minutes of the meetings they held.

assemblies that the gentry participated in the provincialist movement from 1920 to 1923.

The republican revolution, hostile to the despotism exercised by the Manchu provincial governors, divided their functions: a civil governor (*min-cheng chang*) became responsible for administration, a military governor (*tu-tu*) retaining only command of the troops. But it was the latter who took precedence, especially after the death of Yüan Shih-k'ai. He bore the title of *tu-chün*[7] and more directly dominated the civil bureaux, the organization of which had not changed since the empire.[8] Yüan Shih-k'ai had dissolved the provincial assemblies, but they were restored after his death. The centrifugal tendencies were therefore strengthened after the end of the empire, and the dictatorship of Yüan Shih-k'ai was unable to oppose them for long: the central administration no longer exercised more than a precarious control over the provinces.

The degree of economic cohesion of the provinces is an equally important problem but here we can consider only two main aspects of it: the economic responsibilities of the provincial public authorities, and the provincial market. It was within the framework of the provinces that, apart from a few exceptions such as the interprovincial administration of the Yellow River, the traditional economic responsibilities of the imperial state were in fact carried out. Among the provincial bureaux, there was an office of public works (dykes, roads, &c.), an office controlling grain tax, a controller of industry, and a Bureau of Mines.[9] These ancient economic responsibilities, far from declining in modern times, were enlarged with the 'movement for modernization' (*yang-wu*) of the last third of the nineteenth century. Most of the modern industrial enterprises, created by 'patronage of the mandarins and management of the merchants' (*kuan-tu shang-pan*), had been financed from provincial public funds. In Hunan, already just after the first world war, the provincial government owned not only the provincial arsenal and mint, but also the No. 1 cotton mill at Changsha, the gold mines of P'ingchiang, the tin mines of Hsinhua and Chianghua, the lead and zinc foundries at Shuik'oushan, and the porcelain factory at Liling.[10]

[7] Contraction of the terms *tu-tu* and *chiang-chün*, which the military governors had adopted between 1912 and 1914.

[8] *CYB, 1919*, pp. 306 ff.; there is no systematic study of Chinese administrative organization during the first years of the Republic.

[9] Brunnert & Hagelstrom, pp. 417–20.   [10] *Chinese Econ. B.*, 22 Nov 1922.

During the first years of the Republic, the provincial governments even started dealing directly with Western or Japanese financiers: Honan with Great Britain for the exploitation of the mines of the Peking Syndicate (9 Nov 1914), Chekiang with Great Britain for the construction of the Hangchow–Ningpo railway (19 Sept 1914), Kwangsi with France for the exploitation of the mines of the province (26 Sept 1914), Kwangtung with Japan regarding a loan to the provincial cement works at Canton (2 Apr 1917), Fengt'ien with Japan regarding a loan to the provincial bank (22 Apr 1918), and Kwangtung with Great Britain regarding the exploitation of the provincial mines (Cassel agreement at the beginning of 1920).[11]

Although we thus know a little about certain aspects of this economic administration at the provincial level, we are much less well informed on commercial activities within the province. To what extent did there exist a relatively unified provincial market, superimposed on the pattern of little local subsistence economies, but not integrated in a national market (which then scarcely existed in China)? This might very well have been so; but the question of internal commerce is one of the great gaps in our material on the economic history of modern China. One needs to examine the working of internal customs (*likin*), of which there were many posts between one province and another; it is also known that most provinces had their own public bank and issued provincial bank notes.[12] The rice trade from one province to another was strictly controlled and generally completely prohibited. In November 1919 the Chambers of Commerce and students' associations in Kiangsi protested against a plan to export rice to Japan;[13] in February 1920 the Tientsin Chamber of

[11] For agreements prior to 1919, cf. McMurray, *Treaties with and Related to China, passim.* For the Cassel agreement, *CWR*, Mar–Apr 1920, *passim.* The central government tried to take action; on 2 Feb 1920 a note from the Minister of Foreign Affairs informed the powers of his hostility to all direct financial negotiations with provincial governments (bi-monthly chronology of *TFTC*).

[12] A Hupei provincial Bank for Agriculture and Industry was founded in Nov 1919, its capital (2 m. yen) being provided by the provincial treasury and private subscriptions (*CWR*, 15 Nov 1919 & 29 Feb 1920). Here again, the central government tried to take action: on 2 Mar 1920 a presidential mandate declared that 'provincial banks have recently begun to issue bank notes, under the pretext of lack of liquid money', prohibited this practice in the future, and ordered the withdrawal of the notes already issued (bi-monthly chron. of *TFTC*). This decision had little effect.

[13] *CWR*, 29 Nov 1919.

115228   EMORY AND HENRY LIBRARY

Commerce tried in vain to get the Peking government to authorize the import of rice from Kiangsu (famine was severe in the north), for the Chambers of Commerce in this province opposed it.[14] The reality of the provincial market is again suggested, some years later, by the command to 'strengthen the economic independence of Kwangtung', formulated in 1925 by the communist unions of Canton in order to rally the merchants of the town to the boycott they had just launched against Hong Kong.[15] The success which this command met with implied that Kwangtung enjoyed real economic cohesion at that time.

The provinces are also sociological realities. This is not a matter of language; the use of the language of Peking ('Mandarin', *p'u-t'ung hua*) extends well to the south of the Yangtze, and the distribution of languages, properly so-called, which one finds in the south-east (Wu, Min, Hakka, Cantonese) does not correspond to the provincial boundaries of the region: Kiangsu, Chekiang, Fukien, Kwangtung.[16] Provincial cohesion is more a matter of social customs, although here one can only outline a situation which has not received enough attention from sociologists and ethnographers. The kind of cooking, style of classical theatre, daily customs, all help to outline the distinctive features of Hunan, Szechwan, Kwangtung. The feeling of belonging to one's 'little country' at the same time as to the great country of China, the awareness of the distinctive features of each province, were to be expressed many times during the federalist movement. In its inaugural number of 20 December 1920, the review *Hsin Anhui* (The New Anhui), inspired by left-wing intellectuals, declared:

Our province, Anhui, along the Yangtze and the Huai, is a centre of communications by road and water. Production is considerable, the people have hospitable and honest customs and practices. But we allow the bureaucrats to crush us and the militarists to plunder us.[17]

The first number of *Hsin Che-chiang*, of the same persuasion, which appeared on 1 February 1921, began: 'Chekiang is a hilly province stretching along the coast, not far from Fukien and Anhui. . . . It is

---

[14] Ibid. 14 Feb 1920.

[15] Cf. J. Chesneaux, *Le mouvement ouvrier chinois de 1919 à 1927* (Paris, 1962), p. 433.

[16] R. A. D. Forrest, *The Chinese Language* (London, 1948).

[17] *Wu-ssu shih-chi chi-k'an chieh-shao* (Introduction to the periodicals of May 4th) (hereafter *WSCC*), ii (Peking, 1959), pp. 533–4.

a meeting place of peoples and cultures, it is a very civilized part of the south-east. How beautiful is Chekiang!'[18]

This feeling of 'provinciality' is witnessed by the formation of associations of people originally from the same province when they find themselves in another part of China or abroad. Among the working class, regional associations are not uncommon; there are the *pang*, for example, among the unskilled labourers in the ports of the Yangtze.[19] When 1 May was celebrated for the first time in China on a grand scale, in 1922, a leading communist, Li Ta, called on the workers to support this manifestation of inter-national solidarity and took advantage of the opportunity to put them on their guard against provincialist tendencies in para-phrasing Marx: 'workers have no fatherland—not even a pro-vincial fatherland'.[20] The merchants, for their part, habitually met in 'provincial bureaux' or *hui-kuan*:[21] for example, at Shanghai the Cantonese Bureau (*Kwangtung hui-kuan*), which guaranteed the credit of Cantonese merchants travelling on business to Shanghai, guaranteed the custody of merchandise and offered hospitality to travellers. In Peking these regional friendly societies were par-ticularly active; they were the heirs of the 'provincial houses', where the candidates for the imperial examinations from a par-ticular province stayed when they went to the capital, until the abolition of these examinations in 1905.

Chinese students abroad regrouped themselves by province in the same way. In Japan, about 1900–10, the Hunanese had their own association and published a review with republican leanings.[22] It was the same with Szechwan students. 'Why did the Szechwan students in Japan appear particularly active?,' asks Wu Yü-ch'ang, one of the veterans of the republican movement in Szechwan, later converted to communism, in his *Memoirs*. 'Coming from the interior, they felt very strong ties with natives of the same province and tended to combine into groups. On the other hand, they delighted in discussion, they willingly adopted the role of the

[18] Ibid. p. 534.   [19] Chesneaux, *Mouvement ouvrier*, pp. 178–9.

[20] Public appeal in the special number of 1 May 1922 of the review *Hsien-ch'u.*

[21] The Western residents in China called these 'guilds': Canton guild, Ningpo guild, &c. But this term is ambiguous, for it leads to confusion with the professional guilds of the merchant-artisans (silk, bamboo, &c.).

[22] Hsüeh Chün-tu, *Huang Hsing and the Chinese Revolution* (Stanford, 1961), p. 9. The review, published in Tokyo by Huang Hsing and his friends, was called *Yü-hsüeh i-p'ien* (Translations and essays while studying abroad).

H

redressers of wrongs, and they easily got involved in fights.'[23]

In the role played by the provinces in Chinese life at the beginning of the twentieth century, these brief comments can only suggest the interest and usefulness of much more detailed study. The cohesion of the provinces seems very real, but it is not incompatible—quite the reverse—with the pan-Chinese (*ch'üan-kuo*) cohesion solidly rooted in many millennia of history, in a unique political and cultural system, in a common historical condition of which the Chinese were very much aware at the time of the republican revolution and the May Fourth Movement (1919). The scope of the latter, which involved all the provinces in a common protest against the Treaty of Versailles, is a striking manifestation of China's will for unity and of her common national consciousness; it was fundamentally a pan-Chinese movement. But the Chinese national body is not an undifferentiated mass; it is organized in provinces which have also their own individuality. Joseph Needham has expressed this idea in a vigorous metaphor: he describes the provincial structure of China as 'a geo-political muscular system hidden by the sub-cutaneous fat and the skin of constitutional and military history' (he is referring to dynastic history).[24]

The idea of reorganizing the Chinese state on a federal basis by enlarging the autonomous powers of the provinces was already in circulation among groups opposing the empire at the beginning of the twentieth century.[25] From 1900 the reformer Liang Ch'i-ch'ao declared himself to be in favour of a constitution on the Swiss model, and even envisaged extending the principle of autonomy to municipal governments. *Min-pao*, the review published in Tokyo by advanced republicans grouped round Sun Yat-sen, in its 4th number in 1906 advocated a federalist programme inspired by the example of the United States. The creation of provincial assemblies by the hard pressed Manchus, two years before the revolution, could be interpreted as a concession to their opponents. The fall of the empire gave the provinces, or

---

[23] Wu Yu-ch'ang, *La révolution de 1911* (Peking, 1963), p. 69.

[24] *Science and Civilization in China*, i. 115.

[25] There is no thorough study of the federalist movement and of provincialist politics in China during the first years of the Republic. I simply follow here the indications given by Li Chien-nung at the beginning of ch. 13 of his *Political History of Modern China* (Princeton, N.J., 1956), pp. 402–3. Li Chien-nung was in 1920–2 one of the principal propagadandists of federalist ideas and has devoted special attention to this problem in this work.

rather the gentry of the provinces, the opportunity to affirm their particularism and to play their own role in the political struggles. Immediately after the insurrection of 10 October 1911 at Wuchang, the overthrow of Manchu power originally took the form of 'declarations of independence' by the provinces *vis-à-vis* the Peking authorities: Hunan on 22 October; Kiangsi on 25 October; Kwangtung on 29 October; Shansi on the same day; Kiangsu on 3 November; Fukien on 9 November; Kwangsi on 7 November; Shantung on 12 November; Szechwan on 27 November. The initiative was taken, for the most part, by the moderate politicians of the reformist-constitutional party, supported by the gentry and the moderate bourgeoisie.[26] The declaration of independence of Shantung comprised eight articles, four of which directly concerned the problem of federalism: reorganization of the central government on federalist lines, freedom for each province to decide its own institutions and local taxes, enlargement of the powers of provincial assemblies, freedom for each province to have its own armed forces for self-defence.[27]

In the following years Chinese political activity at the provincial level in the main continued to be as vigorous as at the central level. The 'provisional Senate' of Nanking, which elected Sun Yat-sen to the provisional presidency of the Republic, was composed of delegates representing each province as such:[28] it was in reliance on the armed forces of three southern provinces favouring the Kuomintang that Sun Yat-sen launched the 'second revolution' against Yüan Shih-k'ai in June 1913; the opposition movement against Yüan Shih-k'ai at the end of 1915 began by a 'declaration of independence of Yunnan' made by General Ts'ai Ao, and this 'movement for the protection of the country' was rapidly supported by other provinces in the south. When Sun Yat-sen established a military directorate hostile to the Peking government in Canton in 1917, it was supported by six provinces in the south-west which split from the north on their own initiative.

[26] M.-C. Bergère, *La bourgeoisie chinoise et la révolution de 1911* (Paris, 1965), ch. 4, which cites numerous examples of the provincialist tendencies of the moderate bourgeoisie in the months following the republican insurrection of Oct 1911.

[27] Li Chien-nung, p. 402.

[28] Hsieh Fang-kwei ('The Provincial Self-Government Movement', *CWR*, 20 Aug 1921) compares this provisional Senate with the provisional Congress of the English colonies in America at the time of the War of Independence.

The question of the relationship between the central authority and the provinces was raised by events during the period of crisis for the Chinese state which followed the republican revolution. Political controversy over federalism was greatly stimulated. At the first parliament,[29] the Kuomintang took up a federalist position which reflected its desire to consolidate its local influence in the absence of any possibility of defeating its enemies in the struggle for the central power; and its enemies reacted by supporting centralism. The moderates of the Chin-pu-tang (Progress Party) therefore returned to the provincialist tactics which they had employed in the autumn of 1911. When parliament reassembled after the death of Yüan Shih-k'ai, these problems were again debated. At the end of the first world war power was monopolized by the politico-military clique called the Anfu clique, the heir of Yüan Shih-k'ai and his military group, *Pei-yang*. The moderates, on bad terms with the Anfu clique, rallied to the federalist cause again, for example, Hsiung Hsi-ling, a Hunanese scholar of the Hanlin Academy, connected with the constitutional-monarchists of 1900–10 and prime minister in 1913; or Chiang Tung-sun, friend of the reformer Liang Ch'i-ch'ao and promoter around 1919 of a form of 'guild socialism' inspired by English Labour.[30]

During 1911–20 federalist ideas were therefore already in the air while in practice the provinces were operating as an autonomous mechanism in Chinese politics. These first shoots of federalism, which still await detailed study, appeared, however, in two very distinct forms. The federalism of the Kuomintang was purely tactical, a temporary retreat while awaiting a political situation more favourable to national unity. But the provincialist leanings of the gentry and of the conservatives, who expressed themselves in dramatic fashion with 'declarations of independence' from autumn 1911 onwards, seem to have had deeper roots and to have reflected a more lasting preoccupation with decentralization. The distinction between these two currents was to become even more

[29] Ibid. The study of Chinese parliamentary life in the first years of the Republic has suffered discredit along with the parliament itself, which was totally deprived of real political power; the parliamentary debates were, however, the echo of currents of opinion and problems of the time, and constituted from this point of view a source too much neglected by historians.

[30] Hsieh Fang-kwei; short biography of Hsiung Hsi-lin, *CYB, 1923*, p. 815. See also above, p. 72.

pronounced as the federalist movement developed between 1920 and 1923.

In 1920 the movement was given a fresh impetus by the coincidence of two separate political phenomena: the recrudescence of the struggles between military factions, and the May Fourth Movement.

Chinese unity, already jeopardized since the death of Yüan Shih-k'ai, the defeat of his monarchist plans, and the two successive secessions of the south-west, seemed to be more and more gravely threatened in 1920. In the north the Anfu group, which had wielded power for several years with brutality but with a certain efficiency, was overthrown by a coalition of two other politico-military cliques, those of Chihli and of Manchuria. While the Anfu clique had made every effort to check the centrifugal forces,[31] the central government which succeeded them exercised merely nominal authority over the military factions in the various provinces of the north and centre. In the south, the dissident military directorate, with which Sun Yat-sen had broken in 1918, broke up and survived only as a series of provincial warring cliques. The Kwangsi group occupied Canton and pillaged this rich province; the Yunnan group coveted the riches of Szechwan. As for the conferences between the governments of the north and south which were held in 1919, they dragged on for more than a year but without results. From 1920 the federalist movement was at once a reaction against and a reflection of this general crisis of Chinese unity.

But at the same time the federalist movement itself stemmed from a very different source: the May Fourth Movement. This movement for political and cultural rebirth, which called in question the whole *ancien régime* in China, ended in defeat, at least in the short term considered politically. In spite of the vigour of the student demonstrations of May and June 1919, of the strikes and of the boycotts against Japan, neither foreign influence in China nor the political domination of the conservative cliques had been seriously threatened. The radical intelligentsia then began to consider the possibility of withdrawing to the provincial level, if possible to pursue the struggle for progress which had not been

---

[31] Cf. n. 12 above; a presidential mandate of 5 Feb 1920 had forbidden the provinces to retain the revenues of the gabelle (reserved for the servicing of loans since 1913) or to raise the price of salt (bimonthly chron. of *TFTC*).

immediately successful at the 'pan-Chinese' level. This 'tactical withdrawal' of the May Fourth Movement is seen in the founding of a series of provincial reviews of democratic and modernist inspiration: *Hsin Hupei*, founded in Shanghai in September 1920 by an 'Association of the Residents of Shanghai for the Autonomy of Hupei' (Lu-hu Hu-pei chih tzu-chih Hui); *Hsin Anhwei*, launched on 25 December 1920, also in Shanghai: *Hsin Chekiang*, launched on 1 February 1921, also in Shanghai; *Hsin Szechwan*, founded in Chungking on 1 April 1921; *Hsin Kiangsi*, founded in Nanchang on 1 May 1921; *Hsin Shantung*, founded in July 1921 in Tsinan by the General Association of Shantung Students.[32] The editorial of the first issue of *Hsin Shantung* put its position very clearly on this 'tactical withdrawal', and answered in advance the accusation of provincial particularism:

Do not criticize us for concerning ourselves solely with Shantung, and for our limited horizon. You must know, those who wish to rise up must first lower themselves, those who wish to go far must begin with what is near. On the one hand, we will build a new Shantung, on the other hand we will ally ourselves with our compatriots to build a new China. . . .[33]

In 1920, moreover, the May Fourth Movement was divided between a radical-socialist wing and a moderate wing mainly looking towards the Anglo-Saxon democracies. The federalist movement, which drew much of its inspiration from the constitution of the United States, adopted a Western standpoint. Hu Shih, the principal spokesman of the moderate modernists, who himself had strong ties with the United States, was a firm federalist.[34]

After briefly tracing the antecedents of the federalist movement,

---

[32] Vol. iii of the collective work *WSCC* contains a notice of several pages on each of these reviews and a reprint of the editorial of the first numbers. *Hsin Szechwan* constitutes a particular case. The *WSCC* catalogue cites a review of this name, published in Shanghai from March 1921 by a Lu-hu Ssu-ch'uan tzu-chih chi-ch'eng Hui (Association of the Residents of Shanghai for the Realization of Szechwan Autonomy); Wu Yu-chang, in his *Memoirs* cited below (n. 56) mentioned a review of this name founded in Chungking in April.

[33] *WSCC*, p. 483. This provincial phase of the May Fourth Movement has been completely ignored in the otherwise fundamental work of Chow Tse-tsung, *The May Fourth Movement* (Harvard, 1960).

[34] Cf. below, p. 128, his controversy with the communist Ch'en Tu-hsiu.

in outlining its history it is convenient to adopt a geographical framework imposed by the very nature of the movement.[35]

HUNAN

In Hunan[36] the federalist movement arose directly from popular hostility to the Anfu clique. The Anfu governor of the province, Chang Ching-yao, 'whose ineptitude and corruption surpassed those of his fellow warlords' (J. Ch'en), was overthrown during the summer of 1920 by several Hunan generals, among whom was T'an Yen-k'ai, a scholar from an old Hunanese family who had been elected *tu-tu* of the province after the 1911 revolution. T'an immediately proclaimed the autonomy of Hunan and its 'neutrality' between the north and the south. After some weeks he transferred his authority to his colleague General Chao Heng-t'i, who continued the same policy. Chao solemnly renounced his functions as *tu-chün*, and retained only the command of the army; but the civil governor to whom he entrusted the administration was his chief of police, Lin Chih-yu. At the beginning of 1921 Chao announced that Hunan would adopt a provincial constitution of its own, to be drafted by eleven specialists, including Wang Cheng-t'ing—a jurist who had already drafted the republican constitution of 1912—Li Chien-nung,[37] and Chiang Po-lin, a friend of Liang Ch'i-ch'ao who belonged to the 'guild-socialist' group in Shanghai. The drafting committee also benefited from the advice of the illustrious Ts'ai Yüan-p'ei, former Rector of Peking University and one of the fathers of the May Fourth Movement, who happened to be on a lecture tour in Hunan. The draft was then submitted to an Examining Committee, consisting of rural notables representing the 75 *hsien* of the province, and was amended by them. It was then ratified by the electors[38] and

---

[35] The detailed political history of the Chinese provinces in the 20th century has yet to be written; for this the Chinese daily press, and above all the local press, will be indispensable. Here I confine myself to the most outstanding episodes as outlined in the bi-monthly chronology published in *TFTC* and in the weeklies such as *CWR* or *Politique de Pékin* (*PP*).

[36] Cf. Hsieh Fang-kwei; bi-monthly chron. of *TFTC*, *passim*; *Hu-nan hsien shou-hou* (epilogue on the Hunan constitution), edited in 1954 in Taiwan by Chao Heng-t'i and published in the series *Chung-kuo hsien-tai-shih ts'ung-k'an* (Collection of modern Chinese history), i (Taipei, 1960), pp. 297–300.

[37] Li Chien-nung was editor-in-chief of the review *T'ai-p'ing-yang* of Shanghai, which very actively supported federalist ideas.

[38] The available sources do not indicate if this was by universal or restricted suffrage.

promulgated on 1 January 1922 as the 'provincial constitution of Hunan' (*Hunan-sheng hsien-fa*).

The 141 articles of this constitution,[39] grouped under thirteen headings (rights and duties of citizens, functions and powers of the province, provincial assembly, governor and cabinet, legislation, &c.), defined the competence of the provincial government very widely in relation to the central government, in the financial,[40] economic,[41] and military[42] spheres. The political system was presidential, with a governor elected by universal suffrage who nominated the members of the cabinet, and a provincial assembly endowed with legislative powers. The American influence is very clear: there was an independent judiciary, and procedures for impeachment and recall were included. Citizens also had the right of initiating laws, Swiss fashion, and of petition before the assemblies. This constitution as a whole was markedly 'Western', if not unrealistic; the real problems of China at that time were reflected in it only in respect of the unpopularity of the military,[43] or the provisions for the economic development of Hunan.[44]

Chao Heng-t'i, a more prudent warlord than the others, had succeeded in establishing a new basis for his power; in Hunan, as all over China, he now posed as a zealous defender of provincial liberties. What support did he really have? Indisputably, that of the gentry, the rural notables. The provincial assembly, which directly represented the latter, had supported the provincialist moves of T'an Yen-k'ai and Chao after the flight of the Anfu clique. Since November 1920 one of the great names among the

---

[39] Chinese text, *Chung-kuo hsien-tai-shih ts'ung-k'an*, i. 272–86; French text Sié Yng-chou, *Le féderalisme en Chine* (Paris, 1924), pp. 204–34.

[40] Art. 70, 'The provincial bank will play the part of provincial treasury and will have control of the revenue and expenses of the province'.

[41] Art. 82, 'The goods of the province will not be mortgaged or sold without the consent of the province; the natural resources of the province, whether public or private property, will not be sold to people not possessing Chinese citizenship.'

[42] Art. 89, 'The citizens of the province will maintain order and peace in the province; no troops from outside the province will be authorized to be stationed there or to pass through without the authorization of the governor and the approval of the provincial assembly.'

[43] 'The military are not eligible' (art. 31); 'the use of schools for the quartering of troops is forbidden' (art. 82).

[44] The important art. 25, which defined the 'powers of the province', included the protection and development of mines, of agriculture and forests, hydraulic works, maintenance of roads, construction of railways, telegraphs, and telephones.

Hunanese gentry, Hsiung Hsi-lin, already known for his federalist sympathies, had telegraphed from Peking to Chao urging him to put into operation as quickly as possible a regime of provincial autonomy in Hunan.[45] The gentry had also helped to draw up the provincial constitution, through the 'Examining Committee'; this was recruited from their ranks and had modified in their interests the draft prepared by the experts. One of the latter, Li Chien-nung, had openly complained of this in an article comparing the two texts.[46]

But there is no doubt that Chao's initiative also met with support from a very wide section of opinion. The modernized intelligentsia, the press, and students had played a large part in the movement of political agitation which undermined Anfu domination in Hunan in 1919 and prepared the way for its overthrow in 1920; these circles were favourable to the regime which had succeeded it. Since the departure of the Anfu clique, the students' union in Changsha had proposed to T'an Yen-kai that he should proclaim a 'Monroe doctrine for Hunan';[47] that is to say, should come out in favour of a policy of neutrality towards the north and the south. The students actively participated in discussions on the provincial constitution, recommending, for example, the inclusion in the initial draft of provision for the foundation of a Hunan university;[48] this suggestion was retained.[49] The most radical wing of the May Fourth Movement in the province shared these autonomist sympathies, which the young Mao Tse-tung, for example, did not conceal.[50]

The affair of the Changsha cotton mill in March 1921 confirms that the provincialist movement did not represent only the views of the local militarists and the gentry, but that it was supported very widely. The Anfu-dominated government had sold the cotton

[45] *CWR*, 13 Nov 1920.
[46] Li Chien-nung, 'Yu Hunan chih-hsien suo-te-ti chiao-hsun' (The lessons of the Hunan constitution), *T'ai-p'ing-yang*, June 1922. He notes, for example, that the project caused the modern professional associations to intervene as counterweights to the influence of the rural notables; this tendency has been suppressed by the Examining Committee.
[47] *CWR*, 6 Nov 1920. [48] Ibid. 16 Apr 1921.
[49] Art. 79 of the provincial constitution.
[50] One of the principal initiators of the campaign against the Anfu clique was Yi P'ei-chi, Mao's former teacher at the Hunan Normal School; he had won his students, including Mao, over to his side (Hsiao Yu, *Mao Tse-tung and I Were Beggars* (New York, 1959), p. 173). At the end of the summer of 1920 Mao was one of the 377 signatories of a petition of Hunanese personalities, asking T'an Yen-k'ai to promulgate

mill, the property of the provincial government, to some merchants of Hupei who announced their intention of replacing the Hunanese employed in the mill by Hupei workers. There was a general movement of protest expressed by a great street demonstration of 21 March 1921, in which the Chambers of Commerce, students, professional associations, and the anarchist-led union called 'Association of Workers of Hunan' (*Hunan Lao-kung-hui*) all took part; the demonstrators declared that the factory was 'the property of 30 million Hunanese' and forced the new owners to abandon their plans. Chao Heng-t'i let the demonstration take place without interference.[51]

Opinion was still more sensitive to the economic situation in the province, as this was more precarious. The administration of the Anfu clique had been deplorable and, through the provincial Bank of Hunan, they had let loose inflation on a grand scale, and this continued after their fall.[52] Chao Heng-t'i, needing resources, signed a contract at the beginning of 1921 directly with the Japanese firm of Mitsui, mortgaging the provincial mines of Shuik'oushan against a loan of 1 million *yuan* and contracting to sell the ore at a fixed rate.[53] On the other hand the autonomous militarist regime insisted in its propaganda on the idea of the 'economic development of Hunan'; several articles of the provincial constitution were devoted to this question, as we have already seen. As soon as he came to power, T'an Yen-k'ai had asked the provincial assembly to consider a plan for a provincial road network;[54] but only a detailed study of the Hunanese economy at this time would indicate whether this was a propaganda gesture, or reflected a genuine wish to form an integrated intra-provincial market.

SZECHWAN

In Szechwan also the domination of a military clique from outside the province provided the starting point of the provincialist

a provincial constitution (Jerome Ch'ên, *Mao and the Chinese Revolution* (London, 1965), p. 69).

[51] Cf. Chesneaux, *Mouvement ouvrier*, p. 243.

[52] At the end of 1920 they put into circulation 1,628,361 *yuan* in devalued provincial notes (*CWR*, 4 Dec 1920).

[53] Ibid. 26 Feb 1921.

[54] Ibid. 4 Dec 1920. These projected roads joined the main urban centres of the province: Changsha–Hsiangtan–Hengchow, Changsha–Yiyang–Hsiangte, Hsiangtan–Hsianghsiang–Hungchiang.

movement in the autumn of 1920. The *tu-chün* of Yunnan, T'ang Chi-yao, had invaded his rich northern neighbour in May 1920 and was trying to annex Szechwan to form a 'Greater Yunnan'. He was expelled in October by Generals Liu Hsiang and Hsiung K'e-wu, at the head of the provincial armies. In January 1921 Liu and Hsiung proclaimed the autonomy of Szechwan, invoking the 'will of the people', affirming the neutrality of Szechwan between north and south, and calling for the defence of the integrity of the provincial territory against all military aggression from another province; they announced the imminent drawing-up of a Szechwan constitution.[55]

As in Hunan, the left-wing intelligentsia at first participated in the autonomist movement, under the leadership of Wu Yu-ch'ang, one of the most prominent militants of the republican movement about 1905–10 and afterwards of the May Fourth Movement. Wu, who was then moving towards socialism, himself tells us that in April 1921 he founded in Chungking a 'Union for the Autonomy of Szechwan', a democratic organization with a broad popular base, which rapidly took root in more than 100 *hsien*. Its programme, publicized by the review *Hsin Szechwan* and adopted at a public gathering of several thousand people held in Chungking, comprised twelve points, among them the exercise of power by the people as a whole, equality of the sexes, respect for individual rights, promotion of industry and co-operation, obligatory work, &c. This democratic and modernist programme, in the spirit of 'May Fourth', was tinged with socialism. But, added Wu, the Szechwan militarists immediately attempted to transform the Union into an instrument to serve them; it therefore had to be dissolved.[56]

The slogan of provincial autonomy was very soon appropriated by each of the *condottiere* who contended for the province after the expulsion of the Yunnanese, in a series of confused politico-military struggles. After the eviction of Liu Hsiang and Hsiung K'e-wu, initiators of the autonomist movement, a Committee for the Preparation of a Provincial Constitution was formed in

[55] Bi-monthly chron. of *TFTC*.

[56] Wu Yu-ch'ang, 'Le chemin d'un intellectuel patriote' (memoirs published in the review *La Chine populaire* (Peking), 1962; reprinted in the *Cahiers franco-chinoise* (Paris), no. 15–16, Dec 1962). Cf. also Hao Bai, 'P' ing Ssuch'uan-sheng hsien-fa ts'ao-an' (Criticism of the proposed Szechwan provincial constitution), *T'ai-p'ing-yang*, June 1923.

August 1922 by other military chiefs, Liu Ch'eng-hsün, Teng Hsi-wu, and T'an Mao-hsing. The broad outlines were adopted in the autumn and examined by the provincial assembly. At the beginning of November the military chiefs of the province held a 'Conference for the Reconstruction of Szechwan' in the provincial capital, Chengtu. They reaffirmed the autonomy of Szechwan, at least until the reunification of China, and conferred the post of civil governor on General Liu Ch'eng-hsün, who for the last two years had gradually emerged as the most influential of the Szechwan militarists. The provincial assembly meekly confirmed this choice by 101 out of 116 votes.[57] Once again the programme of reconstruction gave much prominence to the economic development of the province: the construction of a steel-works financed by the local government, development of a road network,[58] and the formation of a provincial bank.[59]

Provincial particularism at this time seems to have been very deep-rooted in public opinion, and struck, for example, the special correspondent of the *Chicago Tribune*, who visited Szechwan on the occasion of the military conference at Chengtu.[60] The slogan 'Szechwan for the Szechwanese' was popular and even took the extreme form of attacks on the foreign steamers on the Yangtze which exported salt from the province to other regions, though other motives were involved.[61]

KWANGTUNG

In Kwangtung, too, a province with very strong particularist traditions, the autonomist movement took the form of a reaction against the domination of a military clique from the neighbouring province of Kwangsi. The chiefs of this 'Kwangsi clique', Lu

[57] *PP*, 17 Dec 1922.

[58] In Apr 1922 the provincial government had already created a road-construction service, which provided for the issue of Treasury bonds with a view to constructing five provincial roads in all main directions from Chengtu (*CWR*, 6 May 1922).

[59] From the bi-monthly chron. of *TFTC*; there is no good study of Szechwan local politics of this period.

[60] Roy C. Bennett, 'Szechwan for the Szechwanese', *CWR*, 25 Nov 1922.

[61] The *Fook Yuen*, flying the French flag and carrying salt to Ichang, going down through the gorges which mark the eastern boundary of Szechwan, had for example been shot at and had been attacked in the Chungking docks by 1,000 coolies who pillaged it; the troops of the 'autonomist' armies had let them do this. Bennett, who cites this episode, remarks that those concerned were coolies of the river junks, threatened by the competition of modern steamships. The attacks against the Yangtze steamships were therefore of 'Luddite' inspiration and were not just provincialist.

T'ung-t'ing and Mo Jung-hsin, had been associated with the dissident government established by Sun Yat-sen in Canton in 1917; after overthrowing the latter, they let their troops pillage this rich province at will. In July 1919 Cantonese public opinion clashed with them for the first time, when there was a question of making an appointment to the then vacant post of civil governor. The Cantonese proposed Wu T'ing-fang, a great name in the province;[62] the military of Kwangsi would not yield to the movement launched for this purpose by the Chambers of Commerce, students, and trade unions.[63] But in December 1920 a Cantonese army commanded by Ch'en Ch'iung-ming, former governor of the province at the time of the republican revolution, defeated the Kwangsi troops and restored Sun Yat-sen to power, in the name of the slogan *Yüeh-jen chih-Yüeh* (let the Cantonese govern Canton).

Sun and Ch'en proclaimed the provincial autonomy of Kwangtung. The drawing-up of a provincial constitution was begun, and a draft of it was published in December 1921.[64] The provincial bank, founded in July 1920 when the Kwangsi military still held the town, was reorganized with a fixed capital of 12 million *yuan*; it was the Canton government's banker and issued bank notes.[65] But the views of Sun and Ch'en on the provincial autonomy of Kwangtung were far from identical. For Ch'en it was a question of working in the interest of Kwangtung, of making it a 'model province': he was concerned only in the long term with 'cleaning up the central plain' (*cheng-ch'ing chung-yüan*), a Confucian expression which implied the restoration of central government.[66] For Sun, on the other hand, Kwangtung was a 'revolutionary base' from which to set out as soon as possible to conquer the rest of China. This duality of views was expressed in institutional terms; Sun restored to Canton the government of the Chinese Republic and had himself elected President by the parliament of 1912,

[62] Former ambassador to Washington, Minister of Foreign Affairs in the government of 1912, long-standing friend of Sun Yat-sen. In Dec 1920, along with Sun Yat-sen and Ch'en Ch'iung-ming, he signed the proclamation announcing the end of Kwangsi influence and promising provincial autonomy to Kwangtung.

[63] Chesneaux, *Mouvement ouvrier*, pp. 240–1.

[64] Cf. Chou Keng-sheng, 'Tu Kuang-tung-sheng hsien-fa ts'ao-an' (Commentary on the projected Kwangtung constitution), *TFTC*, 25 Mar 1922.

[65] *CWR*, 8 Jan 1921.

[66] Cf. Winston Hsieh, 'The Ideas and Ideals of a Warlord: Ch'en Chiung-ming', Harvard University, East Asian Research Centre, *Papers on China*, no. 16, Dec 1962.

which he convened there. Ch'en, on the other hand, directed the provincial public authorities: he was civil governor and commander-in-chief of the Kwangtung armies. The two partners at first made mutual concessions; in his inaugural speech as President of the Republic, Sun declared himself in favour of provincial autonomy,[67] while Ch'en accepted the position of Minister of War and of the Interior in the 'government of the Republic'. But relations deteriorated rapidly, and the crisis came in June 1922 over the Northern Expedition, desired by Sun, but the cost of which Ch'en and the Cantonese gentry refused to bear. Sun, expelled by Ch'en's troops, fled to Shanghai.[68] Ch'en remained in sole power and was able to devote himself to local interests, in collaboration with the merchants and the gentry; but only for some months, for Sun Yat-sen and his mercenaries returned to Canton at the beginning of 1923.

HUPEI

In Hupei the provincialist movement began in autumn 1920, when the provincial assembly sent four delegates to Peking to discuss with the new central government, successor of the Anfu clique, the granting of a statute of autonomy and the disbanding of troops.[69] The review *Hsin Hupei*, founded in Shanghai by left-wing intellectuals, natives of Hupei, in September 1920, drew up a provincialist programme which embodied both narrowly particularist preoccupations and reforming, and even socialistic, ideas.[70] In December 1920 a conflict arose over the post of civil governor. The influential circles of Wuhan—Chambers of Commerce, students, and notables—demanded that this post be conferred on Hsia Shou-kang, a member of the local gentry who had been secretary to Li Yüan-hung, former President of the Republic; 69

---

[67] 'In the future, to resolve the conflicts between the central government and the local governments, the only answer is provincial autonomy' (Sun Wen, *Tsung-li ch'üan-shu* (Complete works of Sun Yat-sen) (Taipei, 1960), p. 749).

[68] Cf. Li Chien-nung, *Polit. Hist.*; and Hsieh.

[69] *CWR*, 13 Dec 1920.

[70] Its first editorial (*WSCC*, iii. 531) says: 'Hupei is leading the Revolution [in 1911] . . . But if our province knows how to establish the Republic, it doesn't know how to fight for autonomy; it knows how to love its country, but it does not know how to save its own people.' But this editorial prescribed at the same time an eight-point programme, much influenced by May Fourth ideas: true democracy, votes for women, abolition of 'unnatural' customs (bound feet, &c.) and superstitions, collectivization of municipal land and of large industrial enterprises.

delegates from the *hsien* of the province went to Peking and got support for this. Hsia set up a preparatory committee for the establishment of an autonomous regime in the province. But he had to bow before the hostility of General Wang Ch'en-yüan, the military governor of Hupei, an Anfu clique man, and he resigned in March 1921.[71]

The separatists of Hupei then had recourse to armed insurrection against the *tu-chün* Wang and his northern troops. During the summer of 1921 a local military chief, Chiang Tso-pin, who had been Vice-Minister of War in the provincial government of Nanking in 1912, formed a dissident provincial government; he was in touch with the autonomist leaders in Hunan and was supported by local political personalities loyal to the Kuomintang, like Sun Wu, one of the leaders of the republican insurrection of Wuchang in 1911. The rebels, who launched the slogan of a provincial constitution, were successful at first. But Wu P'ei-fu, who led the Chihli clique to power at Peking in 1920, threw his armies into the 'war for the rescue of Hupei' and dispersed the federalists.[72] The idea of an autonomous Hupei was not lost sight of, particularly among the gentry. In May 1922 a member of the provincial assembly, Wang Yün-chün, brought to Peking a petition signed by forty of his colleagues, demanding the granting of a provincial constitution; Wu P'ei-fu refused.[73]

CHEKIANG

In Chekiang the autonomist movement was the direct expression of the interests of the military clique in power in the province. The local *tu-chün*, Lu Yung-hsiang, was the only one of the governors of the Anfu clique to maintain himself in power after the fall of his party in 1920. In June 1921 he proclaimed the autonomy of Chekiang. He set up a commission to draw up the provincial constitution guided by Wang Cheng-ting, who also drew up the Hunan constitution. After examination by a committee of notables representing the 30 *hsien* of the province, the draft was promulgated in September.[74] This Chekiang constitution,[75] like those of Hunan, Kwangtung, and Szechwan, was Western-

---

[71] Bi-monthly chron. of *TFTC*; *CWR, passim.*
[72] Li Chien-nung, *Polit. Hist.*; *CWR*, & *PP*, Aug 1921, p. 407.
[73] Bi-monthly chron. of *TFTC*.   [74] Ibid.
[75] English text in *Chinese Soc. & Polit. Science R.*, 1922, pp. 114 ff.

inspired. It defined the organization of provincial powers (governor and provincial assembly), and differed from similar constitutions only on particular points, for example, that military affairs did not come within provincial powers (art. 32). The international competence of the provincial government was more precisely defined than in the Hunan constitution.[76] Among the economic responsibilities of the provincial authorities, it specified not only taxation, support of the provincial bank, the promotion of industry, roads and hydraulic works, but also the development of co-operatives (art. 122).

In accordance with this constitution, the provincial assembly then elected an executive committee of the province. Lu Jung-t'ing, the military governor, obtained 107 votes, almost equal to Ts'ai Yüan-p'ei (111 votes) and Yü Hsia-ch'ing, a Shanghai financier, like many other compradors originally from Chekiang (104 votes); Wang Cheng-t'ing got 94 votes.[77]

YUNNAN

The separatist movement in Yunnan was different in two respects; it was strictly confined to its military component, without the intellectuals or civil notables seeming to take any part in it; it was also helped by outside intervention. Marshal T'ang Chi-yao, who about 1918–20 had hoped to extend his domination to Canton and to Szechwan, was pushed back within the frontiers of Yunnan in 1922; it was to consolidate his precarious power there that in June 1922 he announced his resignation from the duties of *tu chün* and published a manifesto which called for the transformation of China into a federation of autonomous provinces.[78] On 1 August he drew up a very authoritarian provincial constitution: the governor was elected by the people, but had complete power, and in particular nominated the members of the executive without reference to the elected assembly. A grand fête celebrated the abolition of the military regime and the coming into force of this constitution; T'ang appeared in civilian dress and the Chinese national anthem and the Marseillaise were played.[79] Hanoi was greatly interested in Yunnanese autonomy. In May 1922 there

---

[76] 'No law of the national government and no treaty with foreign countries which violates the provincial powers or augments its obligations will be valid without the previous consent of the province' (art. 32).

[77] *PP*, 2 Oct 1921.   [78] Ibid. 2 July 1922.   [79] *R. du Pacifique*, Nov 1922.

arrived at Kunming a 'Delegate-General of the French Minister of Foreign Affairs at Yunnan', M. Bodard, whose title and functions, though ill defined, exceeded those of a mere consul.[80] Did the Government-General of Indochina hope to encourage the establishment in Yunnan of a regime linked with France and completely separated from the rest of China? The French Far Eastern press echoed these plans,[81] but only a study of the political archives of Indo-China would reveal their real significance.

OTHER PROVINCES

In the rest of China, federalist activities were more episodic but frequent enough to confirm that it was a deep-rooted movement. Autonomist regimes had been formally proclaimed in many other provinces, even though this may often have been no more than a gesture without practical significance or an ephemeral measure.[82] In Kwangsi in the spring of 1921 the troops of Sun Yat-sen took their revenge on Lu Jung-t'ing's clique which they had already chased out of Canton the previous year; they established a pro-Kuomintang regime through alliance with a local *condottiere*, Shen Hung-ying. The provincial assembly proclaimed the autonomy of Kwangsi, and Sun Yat-sen approved this in a speech made at Nanning in November.[83] These military successes of the Cantonese troops also encouraged the neighbouring province of Kweichow to rally to the federalist idea; in April and June 1921 the civil governor, Jen Jeh-ch'eng, and the *tu-chün*, Lu T'ao, declared themselves in favour of a federation of autonomous provinces as a solution to the Chinese crisis. These ideas were echoed in the north. In July 1921 the provincial assembly of

[80] *PP*, 11 June 1922.
[81] 'We can hope that a decisive step will be taken in the political and economic understanding between the government of Indo-China and that of Marshal T'ang Chi-yao' (ibid. 8 Oct 1922). In its October 1922 number, the *R. du Pacifique* published an article by its director, the 'député d'affaires' Archimbaud ('Anarchy in China from the point of view of Indo-China'). He called for the establishment of 'energetic' regimes in the south-west provinces: 'it matters little to us if they seek to create real autonomous governments completely independent of Peking...'. 'We are thus striving to support the "Great Pacifier" [T'ang's title] by all the means in our power.' The same review in December 1922 cited a Hanoi newspaper which said: 'Indo-China must not hesitate to support financially the man who will ensure the security of her borders.'
[82] Unless otherwise indicated all this information comes from the bi-monthly chron. of *TFTC*.
[83] 'As from today, Kwangsi belongs to the people of Kwangsi; Kwangsi will be governed by the people of Kwangsi...' (*Sun Wen ...*, p. 897).

I

Shansi proposed to set up a committee with a view to drafting a provincial constitution, but as it turned out in vain.[84] In Shensi, on 21 October 1921, an 'assembly of citizens' (*kuo-min ta-hui*) was held which elected a 'Provisional Committee for Provincial Autonomy', whose president was Yü Yu-jen, a Kuomintang leader who had played an active role in provincial politics at the time of the republican revolution. Finally, the case of the north-east cannot be passed over, although it was more a question of regional separatism than of a provincialist movement properly so called. On 31 August 1922 Chang Tso-lin, master of three provinces in Manchuria, who had just been eliminated from the central government which he had controlled since the fall of the Anfu clique, promulgated 'Regulations for the maintenance of order'; the three provinces became an 'autonomous region' not only in political and financial matters, but also in military and diplomatic affairs. These regulations, which invoked 'historical and geographical causes', as in the case of Chekiang or Yunnan, reflected the efforts of a military clique, frustrated in its ambitions and seeking to consolidate its power locally. Chang Tso-lin had close relations with Japan, which again underlined the parallel with Yunnan.

In other cases it was not a question of autonomy properly so called, but of a regionalist movement which crystallized around the 'provinciality' of the senior officials. In December 1920, in Kiangsu, public opinion and the notables rebelled against the nomination as High Commissioner of the Lower Yangtze of General Wang Shih-chen, former prime minister, originally from Chihli; he was opposed with the slogan 'Kiangsu for the people of Kiangsu'. In Kiangsi a quarrel broke out at the end of 1920 between the provincial assembly and the civil governor, who was not a native of the province; his resignation was demanded.[85] Again in September-October 1922 students and businessmen went

---

[84] The *tu-chün* of Shansi, Yen Hsi-shan, represents a rather special case of *de facto* provincialism. With remarkable continuity, he succeeded in remaining in power in his province from the republican revolution till the liberation of 1949 by skilfully playing off the Peking and Nanking authorities; but he never explicitly supported federalist ideas and confined himself to the slogan, the 'model province'. Cf. D. Gillin, 'Portrait of a Warlord, Yen Hsi-shan in Shansi Province, 1911–30', *J. Asian Studies*, May 1960, an article which strangely fails to discuss Yen's fundamental attitude to the provincialist movement.

[85] *CWR*, 12 Feb 1921.

on strike against the nomination of another governor, also not a native of Kiangsi; the nominee, Li Ting-yan, had to resign.

ROLE OF THE KUOMINTANG

Were all these manifestations of a federalist spirit in the provinces only the spontaneous expression of a single historical situation and a series of parallel initiatives? Or did they arise from an organized political strategy?

During the period 1920–3 a number of attempts were made to co-ordinate the federalist movement, to give it substance at the 'pan-Chinese' level, and not only in particular provinces. The people of Hunan were very active in this. Chao Heng-t'i, in August 1921, suggested to all the provinces that a federalist conference should be held in Wuhan which would generalize the system of provincial autonomy and adapt the organization of the central government to it.[86] In the same month he intervened in favour of the federalist rebels in Hupei and asked the powers to adopt a favourable attitude.[87] During the summer of 1922 it was the provincial assembly of Hunan which proposed to the other provincial assemblies the holding of an 'interprovincial convention' at Shanghai.[88] Its members made federalist propaganda visits to other regions in China, like that of C. K. Ch'en,[89] who visited the Lower Yangtze provinces. Similar moves were made in June 1922, after the overthrow of Sun Yat-sen, by Ch'en Ch'iung-ming in Canton and T'ang Chi-yao in Yunnan. They advocated a conference at Shanghai of delegates from the provinces 'with a view to establishing a federation of provinces on the same model as the United States of America'.[90] A similar proposal had been made at the end of 1920 by the provincial assembly of Chihli,[91] and in December 1921 by a group of members of the Peking parliament.[92] Associations of private individuals also participated in this propaganda: 'the Union for the Federal Autonomy of Various Provinces', formed in Peking in November 1920 by residents of the city who were natives of Kiangsu and Hupei,[93] and the 'Society for the Promotion of Provincial Federalism',

---

[86] Chron. of *TFTC*.   [87] *CWR*, 20 Aug 1921.   [88] Ibid. 29 July 1922.
[89] *PP*, 2 Sept 1922; I have not been able to discover the characters for the name of this parliamentarian.
[90] Ibid. 2 July 1922; chron. of *TFT* (29 June 1922.
[91] Ibid. 17 Nov 1920.   [92] Ibi (23 Dec 1920.   [93] Ibid. 6 Nov 1920.

formed in Shanghai in July 1922 with the support of important political personalities such as Chang Ping-lin and Ts'ao Ya-po.[94]

But all these activities aimed especially at maintaining the movement, at broadening and co-ordinating it. There was at that time in China only one force capable of effectively directing the federalist offensive and of orienting the political life of each province for this purpose, or at least of striving towards this, and that was the Kuomintang. Did it really play this role, was it the 'leader of a clandestine orchestra' of the federalist movement?

It was no accident that Sun Yat-sen's political come-back at the end of 1920 depended on Cantonese provincialism; this idea had long been ripening in his mind[95] and was part of a larger plan; it was a matter of successively detaching from Peking a certain number of provinces by the exploitation of local autonomist movements. This plan implied also an alliance with autonomous Hunan, and in the autumn of 1920 Sun Yat-sen repeated his offers of common action to Chao Heng-t'i and his supporters;[96] the militants of the Kuomintang may even have participated actively in the autonomist movement in Hunan at the time of the fall of the Anfu clique.[97] The intervention of Sun in Kwangsi in 1921, also under the federalist banner, protected the 'revolutionary base' from attack on its flank. The Kuomintang had very probably played a part in the federalist insurrection in Hupei which broke out at the same time;[98] its leaders, Sun Wu, K'ung Keng, and Fang Kang-cheng,[99] were known for their attachment to the

---

[94] Ibid. 22 July 1922.

[95] As early as 1919, when he had taken refuge in Shanghai, he declared to a militant returning from Canada '. . . we must chase the Kwangsi clique [out of Kwantung] . . . one can't hope to improve the situation unless one puts into practice the principle that "Canton must be governed by the Cantonese"' (*Sun Wen* . . . , p. 721).

[96] In autumn 1920 he asked the Hunan provincial Assembly, then Chao Heng-t'i in person, to send the Hunan army to help the Cantonese army fight the people of Kwangsi. ('Your Excellency has already experienced Hunanese autonomy in your native country; we hope that the same system will be practised by the other provinces', ibid. pp. 855 & 888).

[97] 'Kuomintang politicians were looking for new fields of activity in the south-western provinces, for they had broken away from the Canton government. . . . As soon as Hunan was liberated from [the] hands of Peking, they flocked to Hunan and took part in agitating for self-government' (Hsieh Fang-kwei, *CWR*, 20 Aug 1921).

[98] The insurrection was led by 'the Hupeinese Kuomintang faction' (*PP*, 11 Nov 1921); its chiefs were 'mostly Kuomintang leaders' (*CWR*, 13 Aug 1921).

[99] Brief biography of Sun Wu in *CYB, 1923*, p. 835. K'ung Keng was the deputy of the leader of the rebellion, Chiang Tsuo-pin, and commanded the 'army for autonomy' (Li Chien-nung, *Polit. Hist.*, p. 406). Fang Kang-cheng, in order to support the rebels

Kuomintang. The strategic value, in the military sense, of the intervention of the Kuomintang in the federalist movement is even clearer in the case of Shensi; Sun Yat-sen, in a letter of October 1920 addressed to the *tu-chün* of this province, Hu Ching-i, underlined the political importance of this province, from the point of view of the struggle against the northern militarists:

> The problems of Canton are more or less settled since the flight of Lu and Mo. Next Kwangsi must be reformed:[100] to consolidate Kwangtung and Kwangsi, it will be necessary to put into practice government by the people (*min-chih*) . . . . We must continue to make every effort to achieve the great work of national salvation; Shensi is a strategic point, facing the northern plain; it is from this point that the southern army can enter the north. It is necessary to devote very careful attention to it.[101]

Yü Yu-jen, who launched the provincialist movement in Shensi, was a journalist, native of this province, devoted to Sun Yat-sen.[102] Many other supporters of the federalist cause were equally well known for their attachment to the Kuomintang: Ts'ao Ya-po, the Shanghai economist who played an important

who were fighting in the south of the province, formed in Hankow a 'First National Army of Hupei' (*Hu-pei kuo-min ti-i-chün*). This name is strangely similar to that adopted four years later by the armies of the 'Christian Marshal' Feng Yü-hsiang (Kuominchün) and suggests the same link with the KMT. Fang was captured and shot by the northerners in the summer (chronology of *TFTC*, 4 Oct 1921; this source calls him a 'member' of the KMT).

[100] This point in Sun's programme was to be achieved the following summer.

[101] *Sun Wen* . . . , p. 793.

[102] Yü Yu-jen, who until 1950 was to be a high official of the KMT, had been in 1915–16 one of the promoters of the anti-monarchist movement in his native province (*CYB, 1928*, p. 1187); at this time Shensi was the only northern province to participate actively in this movement and had already declared itself 'independent' on 16 May 1916 (chron. of *TFTC*). Sun Yat-sen's comment on the strategic position of Shensi, in the letter cited above, is very interesting. The search for a strongpoint in the north-west, to turn the flank of enemies who occupied the 'central plain' (*chung-yüan*) was a constant factor in the political strategy of 20th-century Chinese revolutionaries. The 'Long March' of the Chinese communists is the most spectacular expression of it; from 1935 to 1949 Yenan and Shensi were to constitute the heart of the whole Chinese revolutionary movement. But Ch'en Tu-hsiu, secretary-general of the CCP, in semi-disgrace, had already developed a 'theory of the north-west' at the 5th Party Congress in May 1927, at a time when the revolution was ebbing in the industrial towns of the east. The localization of Feng Yü-hsiang's Kuominchün was part of the same strategy and represented an attempt to relieve Canton by taking the adversaries of the southern revolutionary base in the rear. The examples just cited (1920, 1916) permit one to assign an earlier origin for this tradition of the 'north-west base'. The movement called the 'White Wolf' in 1912–14 is also part of the tradition.

part in the Wuchang insurrection of 1911 and who was in 1922 one of the founders of the Society for the Promotion of Federalism; Wang Cheng-ting, the indefatigable drafter of provincial constitutions; Hsiung K'e-wu, the promoter of Szechwanese autonomy at the end of 1920.

Hsin Anhwei, one of the reviews which enlarged the May Fourth Movement in 1920–1 in the direction of provincial federalism, was also stamped with Kuomintang ideas. Its editorial of December 1920,[103] published in Shanghai, openly invoked the 'three principles of the people'; it ended with a call to 'raise the banners of the awakening of consciousness' and of 'provincial self determination', in order to establish the principle of democracy (*min ch'üan*) and of the well-being of the people (*min sheng*) with a view to reforming and reconstructing a new Anhwei.

If the federalist movement is too complex for its origins to be attributed solely to the Kuomintang, the latter certainly played an important part in it, in particular in the autumn of 1920 and the summer of 1921. The coincidence of federalist drives at these two dates (in Hunan, Szechwan, Kwangtung, and Shensi on the one hand; in Hupei, Kwangsi, and Kweichow on the other) was not fortuitous, but was the expression of a deliberate strategy which took advantage of favourable local conditions.

FEDERALIST LITERATURE

During these years when attempts to put the principle of provincial autonomy into practice multiplied, federalist propaganda was also very active, especially among Westernized intellectuals; it provoked lively controversy and had a widespread influence on public opinion.

The main federalist organs were the great reviews of general culture published in Shanghai at the time: *Tung-fang tsa-chih* (Eastern Miscellany, from 1905), *T'ai-p'ing-yang* (Pacific Ocean, from 1917), *Kai-tsao* (Reconstruction, from 1919); these reviews were modernizing and Westernizing but they remained closer to the moderate circles influenced by the former reformer Liang Ch'i-ch'ao than to the left wing of the May Fourth Movement. In 1921 and 1922 they published a considerable number of articles and studies on the question of federalism; in September 1922 a

[103] *WSCC*, iii. 532–4.

special number of *T'ai-p'ing-yang* contained fifteen long articles and various documents.[104]

This literature favouring provincial autonomy was rather tedious and monotonous: it no longer had the vigour and freshness of the little provincial reviews published by the left-wing intellectuals at the time when the May Fourth Movement looked to such journals for a platform. The problem of provincial constitutions occupied the main place (over half the articles printed in these three reviews in 1921 and 1922), and was treated essentially from a historico-juridical angle. There were interminable discussions of the respective competence of the central power and the provincial authorities and of the structure of the latter, there were references to the German Bund of 1815, to the Swiss Confederation, to the United States of America, to Canada, to Australia, and comments on the various provincial constitutions promulgated or drafted at this time in China, but always from a technical, legal point of view rather from that of Chinese realities.

On the question of relating federalist principles to the problems of China, two themes frequently recurred: the evils of militarism, and democratic progress. It was hoped that provincial autonomy would put an end to the wars among the *tu-chün* and to their despotism. 'The members of our association support the principles of democracy, consider the autonomy of Chekiang to be a progressive step which should be championed, and oppose the cruel and domineering warlords', declared the inaugural manifesto of the review *Hsin Chekiang* on 1 February 1921.[105]

Why am I in favour of provincial autonomy? . . . I am a man of Hunan, and for ten years Hunan has suffered more calamities from civil war than any other province; the armies of the south and the north have taken up positions and fought there, everywhere and all the time; at each battle, at each action, the existence of our region is imperilled

declared Wu Yu-kan, one of the contributors to the September 1922 special number of *T'ai-p'ing-yang*.

Federalist propaganda also stressed the democratic value of the

---

[104] Most of the authors had studied in the West: Wang Shih-chieh and Chou Keng-sheng had doctorates from the University of Paris, Yang Tuan-liu a diploma from the London School of Economics; Chang Chun-mai was one of the leaders of the 'guild-socialist' group.

[105] *WSCC*, iii. 535.

solutions it advocated. This argument was developed at length by the provincial reviews founded soon after the May Fourth Movement by left-wing intellectuals,[106] but it occurred also in articles by authors who wrote in the more moderate reviews. Autonomy would permit 'giving power to the people of the province';[107] they could be given 'political education'.[108] For Wu Yu-kan, whose Hunanese profession of faith has already been cited, provincial democracy would be enriched even by the participation of professional organizations as such, which was not possible within the vast framework of China as a whole.[109]

Undoubtedly the best general outline of federalist principles is that of T'ang Te-ch'ang, in the September 1922 special number of *T'ai-p'ing-yang*.[110] 'How can the country be saved?' asks the author. His reply is: 'By a federation of autonomous provinces'. He first lists eight fundamental virtues of federalism: it is a system which permits a flexible reunification of countries which are divided; it suits large countries in which each region has special problems; it guarantees the freedom of the people against dictatorship of the central government; it develops a sense of political responsibility in the people; it brings the people closer to those who govern them; it permits small-scale experimentation with reforms and new measures, which can then be applied to the rest of the country;[111] revolts and economic disasters are confined to a single region; the costs of central government are lightened and it functions better.

Examining the concrete situation in China, he shows that it would be perfectly suited to a federal solution for five reasons:

[106] Among the eight points of the political programme of the *New Hupei* were, for example: 'The provincial Assembly should be organized by the people of the province itself' (art. 2); 'it is necessary to abolish the *tu-chüns* and the provincial presidents, and the people must set up an executive committee to deal with local affairs' (art. 4); cf. *WSCC*, iii. 532.

[107] Li Yu-chang, 'Sheng-hsien wen-t'i' (Problems of provincial constitutions), *TFTC*, 25 Nov. 1922.

[108] Yang Tuan-liu, 'Chung-kuo t'ung-i chih kuo-ch'ü hsien-tsai chi chiang-lai' (The past, present & future of Chinese unity), *T'ai-p'ing-yang*, Sept 1922.

[109] 'Lien-sheng tzu-chih yü shih-yeh-chu-i' (Provincial federalism and professionalism), ibid.

[110] *Lien-sheng tzu-chih yü hsien-tsai Chung-kuo* (The federation of autonomous provinces and contemporary China); I have not been able to trace any information on the author of this article.

[111] This point corresponds to the theory of the 'model province' (*mo-fan sheng*), which Ch'en Ch'iung-ming called for in Kwangtung or Yen Hsi-shan in Shansi.

industries still hardly developed would benefit more from a federal regime; the 400 million politically ignorant Chinese would have better opportunities for political education; each province has its own customs, and since the republican revolution has played a particular role in Chinese political life; federalism would guarantee democracy, in particular against any attempts to restore the monarchy;[112] federalism would facilitate the spread of education, the building of roads and bridges, and the development of the country.[113] Moreover, federalism seemed capable of resolving the Chinese political crisis of the 1920s; of limiting the power of military cliques and avoiding inter-provincial wars; of eliminating the *tu-chün*; of giving satisfaction to the movement of public opinion favouring federalism, especially in the southern provinces; and of re-establishing peace in the country. The author refuted a certain number of objections, some of them of a theoretical nature, but three of particular concern to China. To those who invoked the ancient Chinese tradition of centralized government, he replied that while centralization benefited the individual, federalism benefited democracy; to those who regretted that the centrifugal forces had got the upper hand since 1911 and who were anxious for Chinese unity, he replied that federalism would in reality reinforce unity by eliminating the militarists; to those who considered that the level of Chinese political consciousness was too low, lower than that of Americans at the time of Independence, he asked if they really denied China the right to democracy; it was the wars among the *tu-chün* which had discouraged the people.

As was natural, all these supporters of federalism insisted on the diversity of China, on the uniqueness of each province. 'Our country is vast, customs and traditions vary in the different regions.'[114] But this was only mentioned in passing as something

---

[112] After the republican revolution, the court continued to live in the Forbidden City in Peking and to receive a civil list from the state, according to the terms of the abdication agreement with Yüan Shih-k'ai. The possibility of a restoration could not be ruled out until 1924, when Feng Yü-hsiang, the new master of Peking, denounced this agreement and expelled the court.

[113] This concern with economic expansion was general at the time of May Fourth; cf. the movement for the 'promotion of national industries' (*t'i-ch'ang kuo-huo*). So that it was a question of achieving in the more restricted framework of the province an objective initially formulated within a 'national' or 'pan-Chinese' (*ch'üan-kuo*) framework.

[114] Manifesto of the *Hsin Anhwei*, *WSCC*, iii. 533.

taken for granted;[115] the real foundations of provincial particularism (geography, economy, customs, and history) were never
analysed in depth. The part played by the provinces in contemporary Chinese politics, in particular in 1911–12 and 1915–16,
was also never mentioned, except very discreetly. From this point
of view, the article of T'ang Te-ch'ang analysed above was quite
exceptional. The partisans of federalism willingly invoked constitutional laws and the political theory of Chinese history, and
this underlined a congenital weakness in all this literature: it was
rather abstract, rather divorced from opinion and the real conditions of Chinese politics.

THE COMMUNIST LINE

This impression is strengthened by the historical contrast which
can be demonstrated between two periods, two phases of the
federalist movement: the initial thrust in 1920–1, which has been
described above, and the propaganda effort made by *T'ai-p'ing-
yang* and *Tung-fang Tsa-chih* in 1922. This effort came about
slowly; popular enthusiasm had already evaporated, the illusions
of the left-wing intellectuals had faded, and federalism no longer
appeared as anything but an instrument which the little *tu-chün* of
the south used against the big *tu-chün* of Peking; it had failed
completely in one of its fundamental objectives—the liquidation of militarism in the provinces. In 1922 the articles in the pro-
federalist reviews were very cautious on this last point. In the
special number of *T'ai-p'ing-yang*, a single study formally con-
demned all collusion between federalists and militarists, and
declared that 'to discuss federalism with the military is to treat
with a tiger'.[116] But in general the supporters of federalism expa-
tiated on the abstract virtues of federalism; they did not pursue

---

[115] The federalist arguments almost always, even if only implicitly, relied on the
provinces as they were then constituted. Very exceptionally, some federalists proposed
an 'administrative federalism', starting from new agreements created *ex nihilo*; this
was the case of the six Peking professors who in the summer of 1922 proposed the
creation of administrative districts much larger than the provinces and published
these views in a brochure, summarized in the Sept 1922 number of *T'ai-p'ing-yang*. In
the same number Chu Hsi-tsu demanded the suppression of the provinces, which
historically were the instruments of the domination of the central power, in his opinion
since the Yuan dynasty; he demanded a constitution of thirty 'states' (*pang*) which
would be federated. But this was a lone view.

[116] Chu Tzu-tsu, 'Lien-sheng tzu-chih shang-chieh-shu' (Consultation on provincial
federalism), *T'ai-p'ing-yang*, Sept 1922.

the study of the political processes which would have enabled their system to be put into practice. They contented themselves with vague suggestions with regard to an inter-provincial Convention and the disbandment of troops, and with pious appeals to the Peking government. For example, T'ang Te-ch'ang, who wrote a vigorous and elaborate article, contented himself with proposing a 'Conference on Unity' with the participation of the south, and the adoption by the Peking parliament of a federalist constitution. The return to power of the former President Li Yüan-hung and the recall of the 'old parliament' in the capital was not in fact irrelevant to the renewal of the federalist campaign during the summer of 1922. But the originators of the movement did not seek to define the real political conditions for the transformation of China into a 'federation of autonomous provinces'; nor did they ask themselves whether the political and social forces which held power in China were capable of effectively promoting this transformation.

It was not only this lack of realism which set the Chinese communists against the supporters of the federalist movement; it was the fact that, by its social content (to which we will soon return), this movement was in the last analysis conservative. The extreme Left, no doubt, had initially shown some sympathy towards federalism. Li Ta-chao, in February 1919, had published in the Peking radical students' review *Hsin Ch'ao* (New Tide), an article entitled, 'Federalism and world organization'; in it he affirmed that the federal principle and the democratic principle were inseparable, demanded the reorganization of all great states on a federal basis, invoked the example of the cantons of the Swiss Confederation, and called for the formation of a 'world super-federation' through associating a federal Europe, a federal Asia, and a federal America.[117] It has also been noted that in 1920 the left-wing intellectuals connected with the May Fourth Movement supported the federalist line and published local reviews which strove to put into practice the democratic and modern ideas of May Fourth in the framework of the single province.

But these illusions were very rapidly dissipated. The extreme Left, having become openly communist, thereafter vigorously denounced federalist ideas. In April 1921 the communist review

---

[117] *Lien-chih-chu-i yü shih-chieh tsu-chih* (reprint in *Li Ta-chao hsüan-chi*, Selected works of Li Ta-chao) (Peking, 1959), pp. 130–4.)

of Shanghai, *Kung-ch'an Tang* (The Communist Party), published an article under the signature of P. Sheng[118] which characterized the federalist movement as a 'movement of notables' (*shen-chin yün-tung*), who sought to evict the warlords, but to their own advantage. To support federalism was to 'replace one despotism by another'; instead of putting in power a Chinese 'Third Estate', it was necessary 'to proceed immediately to the social revolution'. This article said nothing on the volte-face which this attitude of hostility towards federalism represented, and the communists maintained silence on this point. In the autumn of 1922 they actively participated in a general debate on federalism launched by the Shanghai reviews. Two successive articles were devoted to it by Ch'en Tu-hsiu, secretary-general of the Communist Party, and by Ts'ai Ho-sen, editor of the official communist weekly, *Hsiang-tao*, in its two first numbers.[119] On this occasion Ch'en Tu-hsiu engaged in a lively polemic with Hu Shih, one of the leaders of the May Fourth Movement, who two years earlier had already opposed the Marxists during the celebrated 'quarrel over isms and problems'.[120] The communists continued to insist that they were not hostile to the principle of federalism,[121] but to the use which was made of it by the reactionary social forces and especially by the militarists; in the 'federalist' provinces like Hunan, Kwangtung, or Szechwan, reactionary forces had in fact retained power, as they pointed out to Hu Shih, who maintained that federalism was the most effective weapon against militarism. A

[118] 'Tzu-chih yün-tung yü she-hui ko-ming' (The autonomist movement and the social revolution). P. Sheng was a pseudonyn used by the great writer Mao Tun, this text being one of his first political works (information given by M. Galik of Bratislava).

[119] Ch'en Tu-hsiu, 'Lien-sheng tzu-chih yü Chung-kuo cheng-hsiang' (Provincial federalism and the Chinese political situation), *Hsiang-tao* 13 Sept 1922; Ts'ai Ho-sen, 'Wu-li t'ung-i yü lien-sheng tzu-chih' (Unification by armed force and provincial autonomy), ibid., 20 Sept 1922.

[120] *TFTC* published in Sept 1922 an article by Hu Shih, 'Lien-sheng tzu-chih yü chün-fa ko-chu' (Provincial federalism and the separatism of the warlords), and reproduced at the same time the article by Ch'en Tu-hsiu which appeared in *Hsiang-tao*, no. 1. Hu Shih had already defended federalist ideas in no. 19 of the review which he managed, *Nu-li* (Effort).

[121] 'We are certainly not against the system of autonomy', Ch'en Tu-hsiu declared in the article just cited. In 1923 Mao Tse-tung was to publish in *Hsiang-tao* of 15 Aug an article denouncing the dictatorship of Chao Heng-t'i in Hunan as 'false' federalism: 'we have always taken a stand against a federation of autonomous provinces, because it is not a true federation of autonomous provinces, but an alliance of the militarists to conquer territory'.

written constitution has no efficacy in itself[122] and the provincial parliaments docilely obeyed the *tu-chün*, even when they took another title.[123] 'Autonomy! Autonomy! all the sins under Heaven are committed in thy name', concluded Ch'en Tu-hsiu.

THE ANARCHIST LINE

Did the anarchists support the federalist movement, taking on this point, as on many others, the opposite position to that of the communists? The hypothesis is worth considering even in the absence of a good general study of Chinese anarchism.[124] The decentralist tradition of Western anarchism (cf. the critics of the 'Jurassian Federation' with regard to Marx's centralism around 1870) had already prepared its Chinese disciples to support provincial federalism in their country. In fact, there were anarchists in Ch'en Ch'iung-ming's entourage,[125] and they were able to influence his provincialist conceptions. The General Association of Hunan Workers, which in 1921 supported the provincialist movement in this province, was led by anarchists.[126] The anarchist influence was very clear in the review *Hsin Shantung*, published by the students of Tsinan, and which in 1921 proposed to confine the revolutionary struggle to this province alone, in order to construct 'a workers' and peasants' Shantung'. Another anarchist review, published in 1920 at Changchow by the students of the No. 2 Normal School of Fukien, called itself simply *Tzu-chih* (Autonomy); it applied this term to all social relationships, not only to the government of the provinces ('to govern oneself and to be governed are two contradictory things').

---

[122] 'We are not like these scholars who have a superstitious faith in the constitution, in its magical virtue capable of solving difficulties and re-establishing peace' (Ch'en Tu-hsiu).

[123] 'Why do the "legally" elected members of the provincial assemblies not utilize the provincial constitutions to overthrow the warlords?' asked a writer in *Hsiang-tao* of 25 Oct 1922 ('Sheng-hsien suo-chi i-hui-ti "ch'uan" na-li chu-le?' (Where have the 'powers' conferred on the Assemblies by the provincial constitutions gone?).

[124] The little book by R. Scalapino and George T. Yu (*The Chinese Anarchist Movement*, Berkeley, 1961) is much less general than its title and confines itself to summarizing articles from two anarchist reviews of 1910.

[125] W. Hsieh (n. 65 above), p. 211.

[126] *ESCC*, iii. 166. Ch'angchou is situated in southern Fukien, a region strictly controlled in 1918–20 by Ch'en Chiung-ming, who had entrusted to his anarchist friends the control of the local bureau of education (W. Hsieh).

CONSERVATIVE BACKING

The fortunes of the federalist movement scarcely fulfilled the hopes of its supporters. The debate of autumn 1922 was plainly a last blaze, kindled by the hopes aroused by the return of the old parliament to Peking; but the movement had already lost much of its initial drive and above all its initial popularity. It had only succeeded in conferring a semblance of legitimacy on the power of certain warlords, as in Chekiang, Yunnan, Kweichow, and Hunan. In this last province, the hope and pride of the Chinese federalists in 1921, the provincial constitution had been promulgated only for the sake of form, and Chao Heng-t'i, if he continued to invoke it,[127] governed as brutally and as despotically as the other *tu-chün*: repression of workers' and students' activities, traffic in opium, exactions from the Chambers of Commerce, and priority for military expenses.[128] In Szechwan autonomy was no longer anything more than an empty catchword claimed by rival provincial military cliques in 1922–3. In Hupei federation had become merely a slogan utilized by wandering armed bands, like those which in September 1922 invaded the town of Huangmei, liberating the prisoners and exacting 20,000 *yuan* from the Chamber of Commerce.[129] In Kwangtung Ch'en Ch'iung-ming and his autonomist group held power only for a few months after their victory over Sun Yat-sen; the latter had overthrown them at the beginning of 1923, and reassumed control of his revolutionary base.

This defeat sprang first from the geographical basis of the federalist movement. The movement had only thriven to the south of the Yangtze, in those regions of China which had already put it to the test in 1911–12 with the republican revolution, in 1913 with the 'second revolution', in 1915–16 with the anti-monarchist movement, in 1917–18 with the military directorate of the southwest; but despite their dynamism and originality they had not

---

[127] "'Sheng-hsien ching" yü Chao Heng-t'i' (The sacred canon of the provincial constitution and Chao Heng-t'i); this short article, signed Tse-tung (ie. Mao Tse-tung), published 15 Aug 1923 in *Hsiang-tao*, describes Chao's efforts to organize a demonstration of popular support for the constitution, with the agreement of some Buddhist groups.

[128] Mao, in the preceding article, cited actual examples of these proceedings. On repression of workers, cf. Chesneaux, *Mouvement ouvrier*, pp. 261 & 307. On Hunan at this time, cf. Hsi-shan, 'Sheng-hsien-chih Hunan' (Hunan under the regime of the provincial constitution), *Ch'ien-feng*, 1 July 1923.

[129] *CWR*, 24 Sept 1922.

sufficient weight to give direction to the political affairs of China for any length of time.

The southern character of the federalist movement makes good sense if one examines its principal social bases, the military cliques and the gentry of rural notables. Once the illusions of left-wing intellectuals like Wu Yu-ch'ang and Mao Tse-tung or the writers of *Hsin Hupei* were dissipated, once the real popular enthusiasm, which at the end of 1920 hailed federalism as a safeguard against the military exactions which the Hunanese had just experienced with Chang Ching-yao or the Cantonese with the Kwangsi troops, had faded, the federalist movement appears to have been primarily and more lastingly a particularist movement supported by conservative social forces. There is ample evidence of this, even in default of being able to consult Chinese local documents. Federalism served the local interests of the small *tu-chün* of the south and centre; it provided political 'cover' for their defensive military strategy *vis-à-vis* the northern military groups. In reaction to this, the latter, in particular the Chihli group who had controlled the Peking government since 1920, was resolutely anti-federalist and during this period constantly opposed to the proposals for inter-provincial Conventions put forward on several occasions by the *tu-chün* of the south.[130] Considering the power relations which existed between the military group of the north and the military cliques of the southern provinces, federalism with its decentralizing solutions had no chance of being adopted throughout the country; in this respect the campaign in the federalist press in autumn 1922 was completely fruitless.

At the same time federalism corresponded with the interests and the hopes of the rural notables of the south. It was in these circles that a number of important leaders of the movement originated, like Hsiung Hsi-ling and T'an Yen-k'ai. The slogan *Yüeh-jen chih-Yüeh* (let the people of Kwangtung govern Kwangtung) and its numerous variations (the people of Szechuan, Hunan, &c.) essentially represented the ambitions of the gentry, even if, initially, it had had democratic overtones. This slogan was translated in practice into controversies over the 'provinciality' of the civil governor, for instance in Canton in 1919, in Wuhan in

[130] Thus Ts'ao K'un and Wu P'ei-fu, the Chihli chiefs, gave a negative answer on 18 July to Chao Heng-t'i's telegram proposing the federal organization of the whole of China (chron. of *TFTC*).

1920, in Nanchang in 1921. The participation of the rural notables in the provincialist movement was also expressed through the provincial assemblies, whose activity at this period has been described above, and through the delegates of the *hsien* who one sees intervening on many occasions.[131] Many modern educated intellectuals who supported federalist ideas were men connected with the gentry, men whose after all relative Westernization did not call in question the old social regime and who were therefore opposed to the revolutionary solutions recommended by the Left of 'May Fourth'. This was the case with Chang Ping-lin (a former friend of Sun Yat-sen) who at this time drifted more and more towards conservative nationalism; and this was the case with the group of Liang Ch'i-ch'ao's friends, and the reviews which they influenced, like *Kai-ts'ao* or *Tung-fang Tsa-chih*.

ATTITUDE OF THE BOURGEOISIE

What was the attitude of the bourgeoisie? It seems that at any rate they had federalist leanings. For instance, they supported campaigns demanding that the functions of civil governor should be exercised by a native of the province. In April 1922 the National Federation of the Chambers of Commerce set up a Committee of Political Studies led by Chang Ping-lin, whose report favoured federalism;[132] from March to June 1922 a Public Welfare Conference (*Kuo-shih Hui-i*) was held in Shanghai, organized by the Chambers of Commerce, the educational associations, the journalists' societies, &c.;[133] this too came out in favour of provincial federalism. Moreover, certain provincial constitutions provided a place for the bourgeoisie as such, for example that of Chekiang, of which interim provisions (art. 17) entrusted certain responsibilities to the industrial associations and the Chambers of Commerce.

The interest of the bourgeoisie in provincial autonomy was expressed in the programmes of provincial economic development several examples of which have already been given, and in various

---

[131] 69 delegates from various Hupei *hsien* made overtures to Peking in 1921 to obtain a new civil governor (n. 70 above); 75 delegates from various Hunan *hsien* examined the draft constitution of the province; 30 delegates from various Chekiang *hsien* did likewise (n. 76 above).

[132] Interview with C. K. Ch'en, member of the Hunan provincial assembly, in *PP*, 3 Sept 1922.

[133] Chron. of *TFTC*, 28 June 1922.

fiscal claims and slogans. It was the bourgeoisie, not the poor, who were concerned at seeing the taxes they contributed monopolized by the Peking government or by military cliques from another province.[134]

But these are only indications; the behaviour of the entire bourgeoisie with regard to the federalist movement is as little known and as difficult to define as its general role in Chinese politics at this time. It is, however, possible to believe that, despite its real sympathies, the bourgeoisie were unable not to be anxious about the capture of the federalist movement by the *tu-chün*, especially when the *tu-chün* mercilessly fleeced the bourgeoisie. The reversal of Kuomintang policy with regard to provincial autonomy, to which we will return, was also not without influence on the unenthusiastic attitude which the modern bourgeoisie as a whole came to take.

DECLINE OF THE MOVEMENT

Geographically confined to the southern provinces, socially heterogeneous, at least in its initial phase, the federalist movement was at the same time the expression of fundamentally divergent political tendencies. For some, the call for provincial autonomy was a purely tactical move; the aim was to establish solidly in one province, or simultaneously in several provinces, ideas, a political organization, and a programme which in the immediate future had no chance of acceptance in all China, both because of the balance of political forces and of the divided state of the country. Such were the objectives of the editors of the provincialist reviews which were the heirs of May Fourth; such it seems, was the intention of the Kuomintang in 1920–1. For others, for the gentry, for the southern *tu-chün*, doubtless for certain sections of the commercial bourgeoisie of the interior, on the contrary, it was a matter of a lasting solution for the problems of China, of a lasting provincial autonomy. They were content with only the vaguest references to the old Confucian political slogan of 'cleaning up the central plain';[135] it was essentially within the framework of the province that the governing classes sought to consolidate their

---

[134] The Canton Chambers of Commerce had been ruined by taxes imposed by the Kwangsi group, and those of Hunan by the agents of the northerner Chang Ching-yao; both of them participated actively in the autonomist movement of autumn 1920.

[135] W. Hsieh, pp. 222–7.

K

political and economic power. Between these two opposite courses, no synthesis was possible, even if the supporters of both had been able to co-operate in the initial phase of the movement. The conflict between Sun Yat-sen and Ch'en Ch'iung-ming in June 1922 was not an isolated episode, but the dramatic expression of a more general conflict of attitudes, which was decided everywhere at the expense of the left. Wu Yu-chang and his friends of the Association for the Autonomy of Szechwan had had experience of this from the spring of 1922, and more tragically still the anarchists Huang Ai and P'ang Jen-kuan, beheaded in January 1922 by Chao Heng-t'i, whose autonomist initiatives they had actively supported the preceding year.[136]

By 1923 the hour of federalism had passed. The very special circumstances which had favoured these centrifugal forces in 1920–2 no longer existed, and Chinese politics were characterized on the contrary by a growing polarization at the 'pan-Chinese' level between the revolutionaries and the counter-revolutionaries. The Peking government no longer had even the semblance of legitimacy that it still had in 1922, when President Li Yüan-hung had recalled the old parliament and reawakened the hopes of the federalists; the 'super-*tu-chün*' dominated simply by brute force, and the federalist dream seemed completely unrealizable. On the other hand, the alliance of the Communist Party and the Kuomintang favoured a regrouping of the left and of the whole national movement around Canton, where Sun Yat-sen had again returned in February 1923. But the southern President had now renounced all collaboration with the provincialist forces, with whom he had previously co-operated for tactical reasons. He called for the 'national revolution' (*kuo-min ko-ming*) and for the 'punishment of the north' (*Pei-fa*). In January 1924, at the Congress for the Reorganization of the Kuomintang, the supporters of provincial autonomy were denounced for the same reasons as the 'constitutionalists', the supporters of compromise between south and north, the supporters of government by the bourgeoisie alone, and other chimeras.[137]

---

[136] They had organized a strike in January 1922 at the Changsha cotton mill which was owned by the provincial government (Chesneaux, *Mouvement ouvrier*, p. 261).

[137] 'This school [the federalists] forgets that power in Peking today belongs not to the people but to the great militarists. . . . The suggestions of this school amount to using the power of little provincial militarists to limit the power of the central government, leaving the great militarists to control the central government in order to

THE WESTERN ORIENTATION OF THE FEDERALISTS

Viewed in the 'long' perspective of history, the federalist movement is only one manifestation, among many others, of a more general phenomenon: the existence of a provincial 'level' with a reality of its own in Chinese political and social life. It has been noted at the beginning of this study that the provinces had already played a major role at the end of the empire and during the first years of the Republic. They were to continue in this role after the setback to the federalist movement, properly so-called, in 1920–3, but always with the same ambiguity. The provinces were to serve as the arenas for the internal quarrels of the Kuomintang in 1927–37, and for the secessions and the regrouping of the 'new warlords'; but the revolutionary forces too were not to disdain to make tactical use of the movement. In 1925–6 the strike committee in Hong Kong (under communist leadership) launched the slogan 'Defence of the economic independence of Kwangtung';[138] the trade unions of Hunan (also under communist leadership) at their provincial congress in December 1926 passed a resolution on 'the industrial development' of their province.[139] Again in 1945 the communists were to accept a compromise with the Kuomintang leaving wide powers to the provincial governments,[140] thus hoping to effect in some provinces the progress they could not hope for in the whole country. From this point of view, the federalist movement of 1920–3 is not a superficial or fortuitous episode; it gave expression to the reality of the provinces as stable political,

perpetrate their crimes. What would that lead to? That the little militarists would be able to implant themselves in the provinces parallel with the great militarists, each to his own advantage. The country would be in a state of division. True autonomy cannot come to pass as long as the country as a whole has not attained independence. China has not achieved independence today, and therefore it is impossible to achieve the independence of any one of its parts. This is why the struggle for autonomy cannot be conducted in isolation from the struggle for national independence' (*Sun Chung-shan hsüan-chi* (Selected works of Sun Yat-sen) (Peking, 1956), ii. 522–3).

[138] Chesneaux, *Mouvement ouvrier*, p. 433.

[139] Cf. the translation of this text in Chesneaux, *Les syndicats chinois de 1919 à 1927* (Paris, 1965), pp. 259–60.

[140] Agreement of 10 Oct 1945 between the representatives of the Communist Party and the KMT government (Liao K'ai-lung, *From Yenan to Peking* (Peking, 1954), p. 15). According to KMT sources (*US Relations with China* (Washington, 1949), p. 579), the communist delegates would have demanded, at the time of these negotiations, the rectification of the administrative map of the provinces, taking into account the 'liberated zones' then held by their troops.

economic, and sociological entities, lastingly part of Chinese life and contemporary Chinese history.

But in the short term the federalist movement was at the same time the outcome of a series of very special circumstances: the eclipse of the central power, the disputes between the different cliques of large and small warlords, the unpopularity of civil wars and of militarism, the temporarily decentralist strategy of the Kuomintang, the innovating élan of May Fourth. Add to this the fact that the pressure of the powers on China was relaxed because of their dissensions (the break-up of the Anglo-Japanese Alliance, the setback to the Second Consortium),[141] and because the Soviet revolution posed new problems for the powers in the Far East, which to a certain extent took precedence over the problems of China.[142] But this was a very temporary conjunction of factors favouring centrifugal tendencies; from 1923 it was once more within a 'pan-Chinese' framework that the Kuomintang, allied with the communists, opposed the warlords, now openly supported by the powers.

The federalist and provincialist movement of 1920–3 was fundamentally a movement of the traditional and conservative forces of Chinese society, of the gentry of the southern and central provinces and of the local warlords, even if it benefited other supporters—in its initial phase, left-wing intellectuals, the Kuomintang, the bourgeoisie. But its historical originality was that it drew support at the same time from the 'Westernizing' tendencies which had been so strong in China since, with the Opium war, the West had proved its military and technical superiority. It reflected a desire to seek inspiration in the West, as had earlier the mandarins of the *yang-wu* movement ('to seek Chinese ends by Western means') in 1860–90, the reformers of 1898, the Chinese anarchists,

---

[141] The Second Consortium (France, Britain, Japan, USA) was established by an agreement of 15 Oct 1920 between groups of private financial concerns in each country with the approval of their governments, who guaranteed them their collective diplomatic support. Its object was the pooling and sharing of financial openings in China and the discouragement of unrestricted competition.

[142] The Western powers scarcely seem to have intervened either on one side or the other in the federalist movement. The action of France in favour of T'ang Chi-yao in Yunnan and that of Japan in favour of Chang Tso-lin in the north-east are only local exceptions of interventions confined to their respective zones of influence. The temporizing of the Anglo-Saxons in this respect is reflected, e.g. in *CWR*, 1 July 1922: 'Reunification awaits Peking's acceptance of provincial autonomy'; 4 Nov 1922: 'The drift towards federalism: a step towards China's national unity'.

and the leaders of the republican revolution of 1911, of which it seemed like a local resurgence.[143] Federalism was inspired by the Swiss model and the American model, the decentralized constitutions of which were cited as examples at the time in the columns of *T'ai-p'ing-yang*, in the proclamations of Chao Heng-t'i, and in the articles by the left-wing intellectuals. The federalists were among 'those Chinese who, since the Opium war, turned towards the West to seek the truth'.[144] Their defeat, after so many others, made more obvious the imperative need to work out original solutions for China's political problems.

[143] In many ways, in fact, the federalist movement seemed like an attempt to revive the movement of 1911–12 in the framework of the single province. In both cases, the drawing up of a constitution closely modelled on those of the West was considered an end in itself, a measure which was in itself efficacious. The men who led the federalist movement had very often already actively participated in the republican revolution in the same province: Ch'en Ch'iung-ming in Kwangtung, Hsiung K'o-wu in Szechwan, T'an Yen-k'ai in Hunan, Yü Yu-jen in Shensi, Sun Wu and Chiang Tso-p'in in Hupei. The figure of Wang Cheng-t'ing, drafter of the 1912 constitution, then of the 1921 provincial constitutions, is very characteristic of this relationship.

[144] Mao Tse-tung, *Œuvres choisies* (French ed., Peking, iv. 430). Mao names among these 'Westernizers' Hung Hsiu-ch'üan, the T'aip'ing emperor, K'ang Yu-wei, Yen Fu, translator of Spencer and John Stuart Mill, Sun Yat-sen; he ends this list at the founding of the CCP. But one can well believe that even after 1921 the 'Western model' had not lost all its prestige in Chinese opinion, and had not been totally eclipsed by the prestige of the Soviet Union: this is the case with the federalists in 1920–3; it was also to be the case with the 'Third Force' in 1940–3.

5

The 'New China' of the Kuomintang

PATRICK CAVENDISH

INTRODUCTION

IN 1928 the Kuomintang (Chinese Nationalist Party) launched the second of the three 'New Chinas' of this century in Nanking. Despite later failures which have coloured the general view of the party's history, this neglected episode deserves closer study, for some light can be shed upon the ideas and organizations of the 'awakened' Chinese midway between the creation of the Republic of China in 1912 and the inauguration of the CPR in 1949. The period of the Northern Expedition and its aftermath (1926-9) was a time of high expectations and much discussion, and it is important to know more about the Kuomintang in its most creative phase and about the problems it faced. The year 1927, in particular, has long been regarded as an important turning-point in the recent history of China' and an examination of the domestic policy and general character of the Kuomintang at the time of its advent to power will, it is hoped, illuminate its significance. This chapter will not cover the external relations of the National Revolution, which are discussed elsewhere, but it must be remembered throughout that external problems and the external stimuli to domestic political developments were of the greatest importance at all times.

The long-term objectives of Sun Yat-sen and his collaborators were to build a unified, strong, and prosperous China, mainly on the model of the West, and to evolve a just and harmonious society. Sun's political career after 1913 was not impressive and after a number of setbacks he eventually abandoned his constitutionalist position and became interested in revivifying his political party, the moribund Kuomintang. The Reorganization of the Kuomintang which took place between 1922 and 1924 was the starting-point of the party's twenty-year career as the paramount power in China. During these years Sun entered into a fruitful relationship with the USSR and accepted communists as con-current members of the Kuomintang. Thus began the collabora-tion between the Nationalists and the communists which lasted until 1927, and which was founded upon a community of basic aims between the two parties. Those basic aims were to sweep out imperialism, to eliminate militarism and introduce political demo-cracy, and to build up the 'social economy'. In Nationalist terms the aim was to set up a modern state in China. From the com-munist point of view it was to complete the bourgeois or first-stage revolution in a semi-feudal and semi-colonial country.

The background to the national-revolutionary movement was the progressive frustration of the Chinese intellectuals during the 1920s, a period in which Chinese politics and society appeared to be moving towards disintegration. The forces which had appeared on the political scene in the May Fourth period[1]—the commercial organizations, the new trades unions, but above all the students— were drawn more closely into politics. The growth of anti-imperialism, especially after 1925, played a major part in this process which eventually affected peasants and soldiers in certain parts of China. It became more and more widely accepted that an educational or a constitutional solution to China's problems was impracticable, and the attraction of a violent and comprehensive political remedy, in other words a revolution, steadily grew. With the first victories of Nationalist arms in 1926, even Hu Shih, a leading spokesman of the liberal and reformist point of view, admitted, for the moment at least, that he might have been wrong in opposing 'political' solutions.[2] This trend towards 'politics' was an aspect of the rising influence of the Nationalist and Communist Parties which, in this period, succeeded in becoming the vehicles for most of the political forces generated during the May Fourth period.

Though most of this chapter will deal with the years 1928 and 1929, the most radical phase of the revolution, from the Reorgan-ization of 1924 to the 'purge' of 1927, must also be discussed. For not only did the basic principles of the Reorganization remain the official guidelines of Kuomintang policy and organization, but the specific experiences of that period were also the background to the choices subsequently made.

[1] i.e. the period of the 1919 May Fourth Movement (see p. 333 below).
[2] Address given at Chatham House in Nov 1926 (*International Affairs*, v. 279).

THE KMT BETWEEN REORGANIZATION AND PURGE, 1924-7

Four main aspects of the reorganization concern us here. The first is the remoulding of the Kuomintang along Soviet lines into a mass and nation-wide political party with a democratic-centralist structure. Party discipline was heavily emphasized and the new discipline was often contrasted with the heroic spirit of the members of the unreformed Kuomintang, which was no longer sufficient to the needs of the revolution. On the other hand, the members were now supposed to be able to express their views through the elected hierarchy of congresses and committees. As the consensus within the party was generally tenuous, and for a number of other reasons, the structure probably did not function as intended, but it certainly did provide a means for unprecedented numbers to participate in one way or another in political activities.

The expansion of the Kuomintang was one of the most important themes in the Reorganization. The leadership's intention, in a society subject to many divisions, was to draw in all the 'awakened' and revolutionary elements regardless of class, education, or region. As an all-inclusive revolutionary party fighting for national aims the Kuomintang regarded itself as truly representative and therefore qualified to call for sacrifices from every sector of the population. Only the small but powerful 'classes' which allegedly lived off militarism and imperialism, such as the 'bureaucrats' and the compradors, were excluded from this 'United Front'.

The Kuomintang leaders now turned away from their previous preoccupation with a small leadership group and successfully enlarged the party's 'tail' in relation to its 'head', particularly in 1925 and 1926. The party's weight shifted at the same time from the overseas Chinese communities to the home country. This growth was naturally most marked in the areas under the regime's territorial control, but there was also a significant development elsewhere, especially in the bigger cities of 'warlord' China, and by 1926 the party could claim a national coverage. This can be attributed to the rise of anti-imperialism after the May 30th Incident of 1925[3] and to the greater vigour of the Nationalist movement. From a rough estimate of 'less than 50,000' members

---

[3] An incident in which police of the Shanghai International Settlement fired on anti-imperialist demonstrators, causing several deaths and many casualties.

in China just before 1924 the party grew to over 400,000 civilian members by the end of 1926, about three-quarters of this figure being within Nationalist territory. This expansion was organically connected with the rise of the mass movements, for in the areas under Nationalist control the worker and peasant elements predominated in the party membership, while in the warlord areas it was the students and teachers who were much the strongest group.[4] This contrast illustrates the importance of the intellectuals as the vanguard of the revolution and also the importance of military control for political development among the masses. It can hardly be doubted that the communists played an indispensable role in the expansion of the Kuomintang in both types of area.[5]

The mass movements,[6] the labour and peasant movements, the student and women's movements, and so forth, are the second aspect of the radical phase of the revolution which we must discuss here. 'Popular organizations' are a subject of great interest, for they provided the larger part of the motive force behind the revolution between 1925 and 1927 and they were the medium through which the Nationalist and Communist Parties worked for political and social change. Nationalists usually described these movements as devoted to the welfare of the relevant sectors of society and, of course, to the support of the regime. More substantial aims were attributed to the two most important movements. The peasant movement was entrusted with the transformation of the Chinese countryside and was allowed to build up an armed organization to combat the rural counter-revolution, which also was armed. The main political task of the labour movement was to fight imperialism at close quarters in the treaty ports. Communists

[4] The estimate for 'before 1924' is from *Chung-kuo KMT tang-yüan t'ung-chi: sheng shih fen-pu* (Membership statistics of the CKMT; provinces and cities) (1930?), introd., p. 2. The second figure is from Li Tsung-huang, *Chung-kuo KMT tang-shih* (History of the CKMT) (Nanking, 1929), pp. 442 ff. The sociological observations are based on *Chung-kuo KMT ti-erh-tz'u ch'üan-kuo tai-piao ta-hui ko sheng-ch'ü tang-wu pao-kao* (Provincial party reports to the 2nd National Congress of the CKMT), publ. by the CEC in May 1926.

[5] This is strongly suggested by some of the figures in the work last cited (esp. those for Hunan and Hankow), and by many details of KMT politics in 1924–6. See also 'Nan-ch'ang ta-shih chi' (A record of important events in Nanchang), *passim*, in *Jindaishi Ziliao* (Materials on modern history), 1957, no. 4, for a particular case.

[6] 'Mass movement(s)' is a conventional translation of *min-chung yun-tung*. Its essential meaning is 'political movements outside the party'. 'Popular organizations' is a translation of *min-chung t'uan-t'i*.

placed more emphasis on the political roles of all the movements and were naturally particularly interested in the political destiny of the labour movement. Under the concept of the United Front the various sectors of society were expected to co-operate with each other in the pursuit of national rather than particular aims. For the communists this was a strategy appropriate to a particular period of the revolution. For Nationalists the idea of social co-operation had a deep ideological foundation.

The popular organizations wielded considerable political and judicial powers, powers normally reserved to government agencies in most countries. In Wuhan the Women's Association granted divorces while the trades union pickets wielded police powers. Representatives of the popular organizations also sat on the tribunals trying counter-revolutionaries in 1927. These are merely conspicuous examples of a widespread phenomenon.[7] The wide powers of these organizations were not merely the product of the breakdown of the political order, nor were they solely occasioned by the activities of the revolutionary political parties, though this political sponsorship and leadership was extremely important. They were very largely the result of an extension of Chinese practice in unsettled or revolutionary conditions and they were by no means confined to revolutionary organizations. The functions of such bodies as chambers of commerce, merchants' corps, and military units during this period must be seen in the same context.

The most important point, however, is that Chinese revolutionaries came to regard the development of popular organizations as vital to the establishment of a new democratic order in China. The theme of developing a public spirit and a civic and national ethic had been one of the most persistent in Chinese reformist and revolutionary thought for the previous thirty years, and the mass movements now began to be regarded by the more radical spirits as a means of implementing these ideas. Above all, the mass movements and the revolutionary political parties seemed to be a possible counterweight to the all-pervading influence of military

---

[7] For the examples given see R. Y. Lo, *China's Revolution from the Inside* (New York, 1930), pp. 269 ff.; Chiang Yung-ching, *Pao-lo-ting yü Wuhan cheng-ch'üan* (Borodin and the Wuhan regime) (Taipei, 1963), pp. 101 & 141; *CWR*, 25 Feb 1927, pp. 336–42; and 'Nan-ch'ang ta-shih chi' (as cited in n. 4), p. 125. See also Teng Chung-hsia's description of the Canton Strike Committee in *Jindaishi Ziliao*, 1958, no. 5, p. 104.

organizations, which so dominated Chinese public life in this era.

Some evidence on the significance of the popular organizations can be drawn from Chiu-chiang (Kowkong), a city not far from Canton, in an area under the control of the National Revolutionary Army. Here the most absorbing problems were the suppression of banditry and disorder and the creation of a new political order in the city. Early in 1927 a local journal commented:

> Recently the attitude of the people of the *hsien* to local affairs has clearly changed and this may be a great turning-point in *hsien* affairs. Since 1916 most of the people of the *hsien* have been apathetic towards local political arrangments. Under the oppression of violent men and of dictators and in the general and hopeless turbulence the people of the *hsien* lost hope . . . suddenly forgetting where their interests lay. . . . . But now they seem to have awakened from their sleep.

Many organizations had sprung up among different sectors of the population and a party branch had also been set up in the town. The journal urged adequate public support for these developments, particularly in the matter of finance, for a return of the 'people with power', the local notables, to the control of local affairs was still to be feared.

Plans had recently been made to hand the committee controlling the local police force over to popular management. The journal commented: 'The self-governing capacity of the people of Chiu-chiang is still like a tender plant and still relies on the nourishing breezes of spring'. Having little strength of its own, it depended on the encouragement of the authorities, and the initiative for the change just referred to had come from Colonel Li of the district garrison. The citizens were regarded as still less capable of running the city government itself, which was then in the hands of a manager. The composition of the new committee was projected as follows: 3 delegates from the military and civil authorities, 2 from the local Kuomintang branch, 4 each from the peasant, labour, academic, and overseas organizations, 2 from the women's organizations, and 1 from the liberal professions.[8]

In attempting to relate such developments to the political programme of the Kuomintang the vagueness of the party's official

[8] These two paragraphs are based on *Chiu-chiang hsiang-shih hsing-ch'i-k'an* (Chiu-chiang Hsiang Weekly), esp. on the editorials in the issues for 3 Jan 1927 & 13 Dec 1926, and the latter issue p. 14.

policy on the 'constitution' of the future democratic state becomes apparent. 'Democracy' was indeed the theme of party policy and was expressed in a number of different ways, for example in the widespread use of committees in Nationalist institutions, but the shape of the new civil institutions did not begin to emerge until 1926. The institutions and symbols of the Republic, including the 'false' representative system and the national and provincial assemblies, the old political parties and cliques, and so on, were all to be rejected as bureaucratic and militaristic debris. But though the schemes for political tutelage (see p. 154) and the five-power constitution were still official policy, they were increasingly overshadowed, particularly after the launching of the Northern Expedition, by the theme of civil rights and the idea of a National Convention. The former was not merely a tactic in the struggle with the warlords but was connected with the party's policy on the mass movements. The latter, the National Convention, derived from Sun Yat-sen's attempt in the last months of his life to use the creative energies of his party and of the popular organizations to solve the country's major political problems. The calling of a Convention to represent all the progressive forces in China was frequently and authoritatively presented as the chief domestic end-product of the Expedition.[9]

In the last and most expansive phase of the Nationalist-communist front, which coincided with the first phase of the Expedition, new representative institutions became an important feature of Kuomintang policy. This development, which was encouraged by the rapid growth of the party and of the mass movements and by the need to provide a political settlement for the many provinces now in Nationalist hands, was fully supported and perhaps inspired by the communists. In October 1926 plans were made at the highest level to provide for provincial, *hsiang*, and *hsien* popular assemblies. The popular organizations were to be their electoral constituents and they were to meet annually, twice yearly, and once every quarter respectively. The project for the Hunan Provincial People's Assembly was the most advanced and was later approved by the Third Plenum of the Kuomintang

---

[9] The origins of the Convention policy are found in Sun's manifesto of 10 Nov 1924, in *Sun Chung-shan hsüan-chi* (Selected works of Sun Yat-sen) (Peking, 1962), ii. 880–3. For a statement of 1926 see, e.g. Chiang Kai-shek's 'Manifesto against Wu P'ei-fu', in *Ko-ming Wen-hsien* (Documents of the revolution), xii (Taipei, 1949).

Central Executive Committee (CEC) in March 1927. Meanwhile, to provide a basis for the National Convention, Leagues of Popular Organizations were also projected. These were to be set up from the district or municipal level up to the national level itself in a hierarchy paralleling the party's own organization. These Leagues, which were to be initiated and supervised by the party, were to include the local organizations of peasants, workers, teachers, students, liberal professions, soldiers, and women. It is worth noting here also that great interest was shown at this time in the promotion of village self-government. All these developments were to go forward under Kuomintang control, but they demonstrated the party's optimism at that moment and its high appreciation of mass organization.[10]

The development of revolutionary democracy, however, went farthest of all in Shanghai, which did not fall to the Nationalist armies until 22 March 1927. Here a true United Front had grown up with the object of hastening the end of warlord rule over the city, a front which included business leaders, communist trades union organizers, and Kuomintang veterans. The Citizens' Congress elected early in March exhibited the two leading features of revolutionary representation, the use of organizations as electoral units, and the disfranchisement of counter-revolutionaries. The aim of the Congress and its executive was stated to be the creation of a democratic city government. After the entry of Nationalist troops the National government, now located in Wuhan and dominated by radical elements, recognized the Congress and announced that the city government would be popularly elected. This development was immediately cut short, however, by Chiang Kai-shek in anticipation of the purge of 12 April. It had constituted the furthest advance made in the

---

[10] For the policies of the KMT Joint Conference of Oct 1926 see *Chung-kuo KMT chung-yang wei-yüan, ko sheng-ch'ü, t'e-pieh-shih, hai-wai tsung chih-pu tai-piao lien-hsi hui-i hsüan-yen chi chüeh-i-an* (Manifesto and resolutions of the joint conference of representatives of the central committees and the provincial, special municipal, and overseas branches of the CKMT), Nov 1926. Ch'en Tu-hsiu's view of this matter is recorded in *Hsiang-tao Chou-pao* (hereafter *HTCP*, Guide Weekly), no. 176, p. 1817. Approval of the Hunan project by the 3rd Plenum, *Kuo-wen Chou-pao* (hereafter *KWCP*, National News Weekly), iv/12 (p. 3); for identification of CP with this in particular see *Ti-i-tz'u kuo-nei ko-ming chan-cheng shih-ch'i i kung-jen yün-tung* (The labour movement during the first revolutionary civil war) (Peking, 1954), p. 364 and Ch'en Kung-po, *Kuo-min ko-ming ti wei-chi ho wo-men ti ts'o-wu* (The crisis of the national revolution and our mistakes) (1928), p. 92.

direction of extra-party representative institutions during the revolution, and it had been made on the basis of the mass movements.[11]

Propaganda and military activities, the third and fourth aspects of the reorganized Kuomintang, are related to each other as two poles of Nationalist policy, for from the end of 1923 the efficacy of propaganda was constantly extolled over that of military action. This was a fundamental point which the communists were keen to impress upon the Kuomintang leadership, which had generally been rather preoccupied with warfare. Until the beginning of 1925, indeed, communists occasionally urged the Kuomintang to give up its concern with its territory in Kwangtung altogether and to become a purely political organization relying solely on its national appeal.[12]

The Kuomintang leaders included some experienced journalists and publicists and the party had always run a number of publications, but it was not until the Reorganization that mass propaganda was given its full value as a political weapon. Kuomintang organs henceforth regarded propaganda as their most important task and applied themselves to dragging the various sectors of the population into the revolution. To this end they did all they could to hasten the abandonment of 'non-political' attitudes. Party propaganda set out to show the Kuomintang as the champion of the basic and minimum demands of each sector, and on a higher level, to arouse support for its struggle against militarism and imperialism. Meetings, posters, processions, and political drama were among the means used to bring the party's message before the people, oral propaganda being particularly important in a largely illiterate population. The most elaborate device used in this period was the propaganda train after the Soviet model, which was fitted out for use on the Hankow–Chengchow line in 1927.[13]

[11] Information on the Congress is from Tachibana Shiraki, *Shina shakai kenkyū* (Studies in Chinese society) (1936), pp. 422–4; Wuhan's recognition, from *People's Tribune* (Hankow), 26 Mar 1927, p. 1. Chiang's letter suspending the city's 'Provisional Government' is printed in Tai Wei-ch'ing, *Kuo-min Cheng-fu hsin kung-wen hsin fa-ling hui-pien* (Collected documents and enactments of the national government) (1928), i/4, p. 11. About one-third of those holding office in the Shanghai democratic movement of early 1927 are to be found on the list of those proscribed in the purge, as given in *Ko-ming Wen-hsien*, xvii. 3091–2.

[12] e.g. Ch'en Tu-hsiu, 'Hsin-hai Ko-ming yü Kuomintang' (The 1911 revolution and the KMT), in *HTCP*, no. 86, pp. 703–5 (8 Oct 1924).

[13] Shimizu Tozo described propaganda methods in Canton in his article 'Chugoku Kokumintō' (The Chinese Nationalist Party), in *Shina Kenkyū* (China studies), no. 12.

Extensive propaganda followed the Kuomintang northwards and remained a feature of Nationalist politics from that time forward. 'Never before in China has the march of an army to victory been paved with so much paper'.[14] This comment, however, should not be allowed to obscure the great importance of military activities and institutions in the revolutionary regime. The Kuomintang's preoccupation with territory and warfare continued, though it was now balanced to a greater extent by political development, and the greatest importance was attached to the military innovations made by the regime. The Whampoa Academy, founded in 1924, was an attempt to build up a politically indoctrinated and well-trained army, and party representatives and political departments made their first appearance in China. But though there were efforts to extend political training to all Nationalist units, these efforts, limited as they were, could not keep pace with the great expansion of the forces which took place during the Expedition. The system had already run into difficulties before the confusion of 1927.

The need for a war command also brought about the replacement of the army's collegiate leadership by the GHQ of Chiang Kai-shek, an organization with considerable political powers. And continuous warfare ensured an increase in the powers of military commanders everywhere. This situation was only aggravated by the established practice of assimilating erstwhile opponents and enticing hesitant enemies with financial rewards and commands in the National Revolutionary Army. The regime's strategy of fighting militarism largely through military, indeed militarist, means was a dangerous one for a party devoted to the re-establishment of civil government and to the development of political democracy.

In March 1927 Teng Yen-ta, one of the most radical of the non-communist leaders at Wuhan, spoke on this theme: 'The result of this Northern Expedition is that military influences have outpaced the development of the party, have outpaced the government, have outpaced everything. This is an extraordinary danger for our party and an extraordinary danger in the future path of the Chinese revolution.' The Wuhan leaders' talk of 'military influence'

12 (Dec 1926), pp. 258–60. The train was reported in *People's Tribune*, 19 Apr 1927, p. 2.
   14 Lo, p. 158.

was a convenient and telling way of attacking Chiang Kai-shek without mentioning his name and was partly a political tactic; but it was also more than this, for the danger was a genuine one.[15]

The army played an important part in each phase of the Chinese revolution and continues to do so, and it was not its assumption of a political role in itself which caused anxiety at this time. Military officers, such as Teng Yen-ta himself, were an important source of political leadership, and Nationalist military units, as we have seen for example from the plans for the Leagues of Popular Organizations, were also treated as political entities within the context of revolutionary democracy. While Nationalists, both before and after the purge of 1927, intended to separate military and civil administration and to free the latter from the burdens of militarism, they also intended to reduce the gap between army and people. The martial virtues of discipline, struggle, and self-sacrifice played a big part in Nationalist ideology, while militia organizations proliferated and universal military training was discussed. It was hoped that the regular soldier himself would eventually become better educated, better paid, politically conscious, and a social asset while in service and on demobilization. The army was, in short, assigned a positive role.

The danger lay in the abuse of military authority and in the divorce between politics and warfare. Under the first heading came the suspected use of military authority by Chiang Kai-shek and others to pursue policies other than those favoured by the party centre and to undermine the collective leadership. The second, the divorce between politics and warfare, was accepted as inevitable to some extent, in so far as military needs postponed reforms and entailed reliance upon otherwise unacceptable forms of authority and taxation. Chiang Kai-shek, following here the tradition of the Kuomintang, believed that political problems would sort themselves out after the end of the Expedition. At the other extreme, the communists frequently questioned the wisdom of pushing on and on without political consolidation and at increasing risk to the true objectives of the revolution.[16]

[15] Text of Teng Yen-ta's speech of 16 Mar 1927 in *KWCP*, iv. 28.

[16] Chiang Kai-shek explained his views on 14 March in a speech to his troops which displayed his hostility to the 'politicians, civilians and intellectuals' in the rear; text in *KWCP*, iv/16, pp. 7–10. Ch'en Tu-hsiu discussed the problem of 'Revolution and Military Force' in *HTCP*, no. 179, pp. 1886–7 (22 Nov 1926).

The period discussed in this section, which may be called the radical phase of the revolution, was brought to an end by the purge of April 1927. There can be no attempt to describe here in any detail the extremely complex events of the two years following, but those which were most important for Kuomintang politics after the end of the Expedition must be reviewed.

THE POLITICAL BACKGROUND, 1927–9[17]

The 'purge' began early in April in the areas centred on Shanghai and Canton and was directed against the militant mass movements as well as against the communist and pro-Wuhan elements within the Kuomintang. It took the form of a series of local conflicts between party branches and popular organizations supporting the Wuhan government and military units and other social forces supporting Chiang Kai-shek and the 'moderates'. It derived from the struggle for power at all levels within the Kuomintang regime, which had been developing over the preceding year. In essence it represented the attempt of Chiang Kai-shek and his colleagues to reply to the attack launched against them in February and March by the resurgent forces of the 'Left' within the party. The new anti-communist regime was established at Nanking on 18 April with control or influence over the south-eastern coastal provinces. Its main supports were a minority group of more conservative and nationalistic Kuomintang politicians, a large part of the Nationalist armies, and the wealth of Shanghai and Canton.

Both the Nanking and Wuhan regimes, the latter now led by Wang Ching-wei, were very insecure from the military as well as from the political points of view. The separation of the communists and the Nationalists at Wuhan in July coincided with the defeat of the Nanking armies by the north in North Kiangsu and, when Chiang Kai-shek left the political scene in August, a movement for a reunion of the majority of the anti-communist groups in the Kuomintang gained weight. Territorial rivalries between military cliques and the animosity between Wang and other politicians had destroyed this attempt at reunion by the middle of October. In November and December Chiang resumed his political life and joined with Wang in an attempt to create a new leadership coalition, but just at this juncture there occurred the Canton coup

[17] This section is based upon a full-length study of the period.

L

d'état of 17 November and the Canton Commune of 11 December. The former, a struggle for the control of Canton, created a feud between Wang Ching-wei's group and the Kwangsi clique, while the latter, a communist rising, destroyed Wang's prospects of returning to the leadership for a long time to come. This confused period was brought to an end when Chiang successfully gathered a quorum for the Fourth Plenum of the CEC in February 1928. Factional differences were papered over in order to enable the Northern Expedition to continue. Chiang's position as the 'central figure' (*chung-hsin jen-wu*) mediating between hostile factions was now established and his influence at the Centre was assured.

The latter part of 1927 was also important for the effective entry of Feng Yü-hsiang and Yen Hsi-shan into the Nationalist camp. These two had long been leading figures in the politics of north China, the former being widely regarded as a progressive and even radical warlord and the latter being credited with relatively enlightened rule in his province of Shansi. At the time of the Fourth Plenum Yen was still confined to that province, while Feng's domain included Honan, Shensi, and Kansu. Meanwhile the Kwangsi clique held Hupei, Hunan, Kwangsi, and a half-share of Kwangtung. By the summer of 1928, when the Expedition came to an end, Feng had acquired the dominant influence in Shantung and south Hopei and Yen had extended his influence over Chahar, Suiyuan, and the Tientsin–Peking region. The Nationalist regime now more than ever resembled a confederacy rather than an integrated system.

The Fourth Plenum was held at a time when the victorious conclusion of the Expedition was confidently expected. The leadership was keen to mend the damage of the previous twelve months and to revive the thoroughly disorientated Kuomintang. The plenum was very important in the development of Kuomintang policy because of this new beginning in the party and because it came at the moment when there began to be serious concern with the problems of the future Nationalist state. Most of the important themes of the Nanking regime between 1928 and 1931 can be found in its manifesto.[18]

---

[18] Documents of the 4th Plenum are printed in *KWCP*, v/6 & 7. The Manifesto is printed in *Chung-kuo KMT ti-erh-chieh Chung-yang chih-hsing wei-yuan-hui ti-wu-tz'u ch'üan-t'i hui-i chi-lu* (The record of the 5th Plenum of the CEC of the CKMT, hereafter referred to as 5th Plenum *Chi-lu*).

The compromise of February 1928 excluded Wang Ching-wei, Ch'en Kung-po, and two of their collaborators from party politics until the Third Congress should meet. Five less important followers whose presence was essential to a quorum of the CEC were allowed to continue in office. This group, together with their absent leaders, will be known here, in the context of the Kuomintang in 1928 and 1929, as the 'radicals'. They regarded themselves as the guardians of the true policies of the party as evolved by Sun Yat-sen in the last two years of his life. They claimed to stand for the principles of the Reorganization of 1924, especially for party discipline and organization and for the commitment to mass politics, and they saw themselves as standing firm between the aberration of Bolshevism and the trammels of 'backward thinking' and compromise. Wang spent the year in France, but Ch'en built up a radical group in Shanghai with its own journal. The political alignment at the Fourth Plenum was repeated at the Fifth in August, with Chiang attempting to reconcile the radicals with their bitter opponents, the Kwangsi clique and the conservative leaders. This conflict, which the radicals clearly lost, cut short the plenum and hindered the development of party policy. After the plenum the party HQ in Nanking was almost vacant and party affairs drifted while tension increased between cliques and between party branches and the authorities.[19]

A new phase began early in September with the return to China of Hu Han-min. The morale of the dominant forces in the leadership began to revive and plans for the new five-power government were pushed forward. The Nanking leaders now took action against the widespread disaffection in the party which had come into the open with the development of factional cells and opposition publications. The 'opposition' wanted more aggressive policies in domestic and foreign affairs and accused the Centre (the party HQ) of authoritarianism within the party and compromise outside it.

The political situation began to deteriorate from the end of October when the Centre decided on the rules governing elections to the Third Congress, then scheduled for 1 January 1929. Elections were to be almost entirely replaced by nominations from the Centre, on the grounds that otherwise the Congress would have

---

[19] The documents of the Plenum are printed in 5th Plenum *Chi-lu*. Ch'en Kung-po's journal was called *Ko-ming P'ing-lun* (Revolutionary Critic).

to be postponed, since few branches had yet managed to get themselves formally established after the 'party reform' of 1928. The party reform, which had begun in April, was a more systematic continuation of the party purification of 1927 and consisted in the re-registration of the entire membership and the re-establishment of the elected hierarchy from the bottom upwards. This was a very slow process and even Shanghai and Nanking only arrived at the stage of electing municipal branches at the very end of the year. Most of the provinces were far behind.

Much of the party was critical of the provisions made for the Congress and was also alarmed by the arrangements which were made for a special admission of former members of the Kuomintang and its predecessor organizations from the Hsing Chung Hui (Revive China Society) up to 1923, the year of the Reorganization. The more advanced branches feared that this might delay the evolution of branches with full status. There was, besides, widespread criticism of the readmission of elements which had stayed aloof since 1923 or earlier and were therefore regarded as unprogressive. Nevertheless, both decisions were reaffirmed on 1 November.

Trouble within the party was reflected in the appointment of a Committee of Inquiry into Party Affairs, the dispatch of two high-ranking leaders to the north to report on party reform in that area, and the convocation of a special meeting of south-eastern party leaders for the purpose of vindicating Central policy. The CEC also issued an order to party branches forbidding criticism of any of its members. Meanwhile the Centre finally decided to postpone the Congress until 15 March 1929, and early in December the rules were revised to allow elected delegations from those provincial or special municipal branches which were duly established by 15 February. In the event only four branches within China, those of Shanghai, Nanking, Canton, and Kwangtung, were able to elect their delegations. Eight other delegations were selected by a short-listing arrangement and the remainder were entirely nominated.

On 20 December a growing crisis in the party in north China came to a head when the Centre made several drastic changes in the party leadership in that region. The Peking leaders who had brought the local Kuomintang out of the warlord era were replaced by a list of an entirely different character headed by Yen

Hsi-shan and his senior subordinate, General Shang Chen. Significant changes were also made in Hopei. Having read the news in the press the ward leaders in Peking organized protests and issued a public circular. They attribute the changes made to the refusal of their leaders to compromise with feudal forces and, above all, to the reckless ambition of Hu Han-min, Tai Chi-t'ao, and Ch'en Kuo-fu, who preferred to use bad elements in order to gain control of the party.

The decisions on the Congress and the trend at the Centre had, however, done more than cause anxiety in the party. It is most likely that the radical leaders, who had much support among the rank and file, had hoped to exercise their due share of influence at the Third Congress. Now the Centre's decisions altered the outlook and, as a consequence, opposition groups began to prepare for an open conflict. By the end of the year the so-called Reorganizationist Club had emerged and, on 11 March, just before the Congress opened, a circular appeared over the names of Wang Ching-wei and his chief supporters denouncing the Congress in strong terms. By this time the Peiping and Honan branches of the Kuomintang were already in open opposition.

Meanwhile, the Third Congress applied a number of restrictive alterations to the party's constitution in order to consolidate the position of the leadership and to strengthen control throughout the party. The National Congress itself was altered from an annual to a biennial event, thus doubling the formal terms of office of the central committees, and the powers of the supervisory committees at all levels were increased. The leaders of the radicals were punished, with the exception of Wang Ching-wei who was merely 'warned', while at the same time the position of Chiang Kai-shek's supporters was confirmed.[20]

By May 1929 the radical leaders had made contact with the now disaffected generals of Feng Yü-hsiang's group and had evolved a political programme based on democratic development and a more militant foreign policy. Thus began two years of party and military strife which deeply affected the Nanking regime in its earliest period. The climax but not the conclusion of this strife came with the great war of the Central Plain of the summer and

---

[20] The proceedings of the 3rd National Congress are printed in *Chung-kuo KMT ti-san-chieh ch'üan-kuo tai-piao ta-hui hui-i-lu* (Proceedings of the 3rd National Congress of the CKMT); see esp. pp. 109–10 & 147.

autumn of 1930. During these years continuing upheaval prevented the re-establishment of democratic-centralism within the
party and of civil government outside it, and resembled a wasting
disease in the organization which had taken upon itself the building of the new state.[21]

These events may provide a key to the discussion which follows
and in which various political issues facing the party will be taken
up one by one. Like most political conflicts in the Kuomintang,
that between the Centre and the radicals in 1928 and 1929 mixed
issues of ideology and policy with those of persons and regions.
Only the former will concern us here.

THE THEORY OF POLITICAL TUTELAGE

The tutelary regime of the Kuomintang, omitted from the
manifesto of the Fourth Plenum, presumably for tactical reasons,
was ushered in by the Fifth Plenum in August 1928 and was
formally proclaimed in the 'Programme of Political Tutelage'
issued on 3 October. In June 1929 it was finally announced that
the period of political tutelage would last for a total of six years
ending in 1935.[22]

The idea of the tutelary regime was ultimately derived from the
T'ung-meng Hui (Revolutionary League) manifesto of August
1905 in which Sun Yat-sen had first defined the three periods of
what became known as the 'revolutionary process'. Sun cast the
scheme into its final and most elaborate form a year before his
death in the *Fundamentals of National Reconstruction* of April 1924.
In 1928 this work was regarded as the blueprint for the political
reconstruction of the country.[23]

The programme was slightly different from the original version
of twenty years before. The revolutionary army's task in the first
stage, the 'period of military rule', was defined as the 'propagation
of [the] ideology' as well as the elimination of obstacles to the
revolution. The transition from military to tutelary rule was to
come about as each province was pacified, but during the second

[21] The most convenient summary of the civil wars of 1929–30 is the *CYB*, ed. by
H. Woodhead.

[22] The 'Programme' is translated in Pan Wei-tung, *The Chinese Constitution* (Washington, DC, 1945), app. J.

[23] e.g. Chiang Kai-shek's speech of 16 Jan 1928 in *Chiang Tsung-t'ung yen-lun hui-pien*
(Collected speeches of President Chiang) (Taipei, 1956), ix. 47 ff. The text of the
Fundamentals is found in *Sun Chung-shan hsüan-chi*, ii. 569–71. It is trans. in Pan Wei-
tung, app. H.

of the three stages, the 'period of tutelary rule', it was the *hsien* which was to become the focus of political change. Qualified officials appointed by the government would guide the districts towards 'local self-government', that is, towards local representative government. A census, land survey, road building and police work, and above all the training of the people in the exercise of their democratic political rights were the chief tasks of this period. When local self-government was established the *hsiang* was to take on welfare and economic functions and to have direct links with the central government. On the transition from political tutelage to the third period, of constitutional rule, the *Fundamentals* were somewhat vague. The essential points were that when a majority of the provinces were entirely composed of self-governing districts an elected National Assembly would adopt a constitution already drafted by the legislative branch of the tutelary regime. Each of the approximately 1,900 *hsien* would have one elected representative in the National Assembly.

In party literature political tutelage was compared to a ladder leading up towards constitutional and democratic rule. The concept of the 'single step' from the civil war to the democratic era was rejected because the people's political experience had been so limited under centuries of autocracy. Sun, indeed, maintained towards the end of his life that the failure after 1912—the erection of a sham democratic façade and the neglect of reconstruction— had been due to a neglect of the 'revolutionary process' and a reckless advance to parliamentary government.[24] The concept of the conventional parliamentary political party was always rejected by Kuomintang writers either on the grounds of Chinese experience since 1912 or on the grounds that the parliamentary systems of the West were themselves a cover for the capitalist exploitation of the population.

In the standard interpretation the 'period of military rule' was equated with 'destruction' while tutelary rule was equated with political and economic reconstruction. Occasionally these terms were qualified by the term 'extraordinary' to underline the fact both periods were phases of the revolution. Tutelage was sometimes

[24] See, e.g. Sun's 'Chih-ting "Chien-kuo Ta-kang" Hsüan-yen' (Manifesto on the definitive enactment of the 'Fundamentals of National Reconstruction'), 1924, in *Tsung-li ch'üan-chi* (Collected works of the leader) (Shanghai, 1930), ii. 60–61. Sun's views of the 1911 revolution and its aftermath must be seen as a rationalization of his own record.

also described as educative. The concept of the transition from the first to the second stages was important in Kuomintang ideology in this early period, for the roles of party and public were interpreted in relation to this shift. The neglect of reconstruction during the war in the interests of the Expedition, moreover, focused attention even more sharply upon this transition in 1928. Unfortunately it soon became clear that not all the obstacles to the revolution had really been removed in the destructive phase, and the qualified recognition of this fact by the Centre destroyed the clarity of the scheme. In November 1928 the Central Propaganda Department discussed the question of identifying the stage then reached by the revolution by raising a number of questions. Should the party's work after the unification of the country be revolution or reform? Were destruction and reconstruction equally revolutionary in character? Should destruction be applied in the midst of reconstruction and should such destruction be the same as that appropriate to the period of military rule? No answers were supplied to these important questions.[25]

Anxious to justify the concept of tutelage, Hu Han-min, the party's leading ideologue between 1927 and 1931, maintained that it was a universal stage in national development and wrote that the scheme had the sanction both of 'the principles of progress and of the trends of the age'. Kuomintang writers often referred to the collectivist trend in contemporary world (i.e. European) politics, as well as to Chinese tradition, when explaining aspects of the Nationalist political system and the Nationalists' heavy emphasis on the state. In the early Nanking period the regime identified itself with other 'newly risen nations' and particularly with Turkey. It is not surprising to find Hu's argument supported by precedents from the 'enlightened' regimes of other one-party states, which were 'in charge of everything' and which were said to be making rapid progress. The Kuomintang, however, was the only such party, it was incorrectly claimed, which intended to hand power back to the people.[26]

---

[25] For a discussion of destruction and reconstruction, twin terms still in use in the terminology of the Chinese revolution, see Hu Han-min's speech of 18 Apr 1929 in *Ko-ming li-lun yü ko-ming kung-tso* (Theory and practice of the revolution, hereafter *Ko-ming li-lun*), pp. 276–7. The questions cited here were raised in *Chung-yang Chou-pao* (Central Weekly—hereafter *CYCP*), xxii. 1–2.

[26] Hu's claim for the modernity of the tutelage concept was made in a speech of 23 Sept 1929 in *Ko-ming li-lun*, p. 133. See also Sun Fo, 'Shih nien lai ti Chung-kuo fa-chih

The *Fundamentals* would have been more useful or perhaps more embarrassing to the Nanking leaders if Sun had clearly indicated what the party's role was to be during the tutelary period. But though the party was not referred to in the text, political tutelage was universally interpreted to mean 'party rule'. This, as Sun had pointed out, meant rule according to party principles rather than rule by party men. But, even so, it certainly meant party control, even if individual officials and civic leaders were not to be solely party members. On the principle of 'party rule' the Kuomintang was an élite temporarily exercising the political sovereignty of the people on their behalf. It was the foster-mother of the people who were, from the political point of view, infants. It was also the storehouse of political talent gathering into itself through 'the search for able men' and the 'concentration of talent' all those who were struggling for national and social ends. It was compared to the builder's shed in which the men and the materials for the building of the new China were to be collected.

Above all, the party was supposed to be the model for the nation. There were many ideas which had to be and could be tried out first within the party before being applied to the country as a whole.[27] The members' obligation for military service and the use of representative institutions within the party could be mentioned as two cases in point. The party was indeed described as the 'prototype' of the nation on the grounds that its closely-knit character, resembling 'one big family', foreshadowed the China of the future which, too, would be tightly integrated through nation-wide ties of civic discipline and national sentiment. For all these reasons, and also because of the tendency to identify party and nation, the health of the Kuomintang itself was always considered the first and most pressing political question.

In terms of the internal politics of the Kuomintang there was

kai-ko' (Changes in the laws of China in the last ten years), in *Shih nien lai ti Chung-kuo* (China in the last ten years) (1937), pp. 53 ff. For comparison with other one-party states see Hu's article on his world tour, 'Hsin yü Chiu' (The new and the old), in *Ko-ming li-lun*, pp. 101–11. The Turkish Republican Party actually experimented with allowing an opposition to exist in 1925 and 1930 and finally allowed itself to be replaced in 1950.

[27] Concepts and metaphors in this paragraph and the last, which are derived from Sun Yat-sen's writings, are found in Hu Han-min & Sun Fo, 'Hsun-cheng Ta-kang ts'ao-an' (Draft proposals for an outline of tutelary rule), in the 5th Plenum *Chi-lu*, pp. 190–3, and in the Centre's *Shih-hsing Hsun-cheng hsüan-ch'uan ta-kang* (Outlines of propaganda on realization of tutelary rule), Dec 1928, *passim*.

nothing controversial about any of the concepts described above. There was, however, serious disagreement about the ways in which these concepts were to be expressed in political institutions. The period following the end of the Expedition inevitably witnessed an agitated debate on this subject since there appeared to be a broad and largely empty canvas for the party legislators to work upon. The problems facing the party in this period can be divided roughly into two categories; the first concerning its relationship to the state and the second its leadership of the people.

THE RELATIONSHIP BETWEEN PARTY AND STATE

In theory the party was supposed to have precedence in the state, with the government coming second and the army last. The radicals complained at the Fifth Plenum that the chain of command had now been hung upside down. The army was controlling the administration which in turn was controlling the party. 'In many places the party branch has simply become the government's propaganda organ.'[28] The guiding spirit of the radical group in the party and a very large section of the rank and file at this time was the elevation of the party at the expense of its old antagonists, the civil and military authorities.

In an environment of civil war, purge, and pacification there were a number of cases in which local party branches were treated roughly by the local authorities. Party workers were prevented from carrying out their activities and were sometimes arrested. Consequently the branches' first and least controversial demand was for protection, and the Central Training Department itself called for action on this issue at the plenum. 'Now we see the provincial governments opposing or attacking as they please party personnel sent out by the centre and the military men in all provinces interfering with and directing party affairs in their areas.' Official interference in the mass movements, where these were going forward, was only another aspect of the same problem, for these movements were under the party's wing. Requests were also made for protection from 'feudal forces' in general, that is to say from the 'bad elements' in the populace. At Yencheng (Kiangsu), for example, the conversion of a local temple into a welfare centre resulted in the destruction of the local party branch.

[28] 5th Plenum *Chi-lu*, p. 82.

Similar but less serious cases were probably more frequent than appears from the sources available at present.[29]

This problem, and the radical criticism quoted above, applied to the party at levels below the Centre, for at the Centre itself it could not be doubted that the party was essentially in control. Even here, however, the character of the Central Political Council, the keystone of the political structure at the national level, drew criticism from a wider circle than the radicals. The Political Council was nominally responsible to the Standing Committee of the CEC but its frequent and well-attended sessions and its close concern with every aspect of government policy gave it increasing influence. Early in 1928, moreover, the Council had been enlarged as a means of introducing new men into the inner circle, for only a National Congress could enlarge or re-elect the CEC itself, and a Congress had not been called since 1926. Nearly one-third of its members in 1928 were not members of the CEC or the Central Supervisory Committee, and it was also admitted that the Council had been acting largely as an independent body. It was a forum for the leading administrators of the regime, including some career politicians with more background in the service of former central governments than in the Kuomintang. In these circumstances the more partisan elements in the party began to speak of a 'Northern Expedition in military affairs but a Southern Expedition in politics' and to object to the Council's anomalous status and composition in the party-state. Shortly after the Fifth Plenum all members of the central committees were admitted to the Council *ex-officio*, though the number of outsiders was also enlarged. At the Third Congress, however, in line with the general trend of policy, the problem was solved for the time being by electing a large number of new men to the CEC itself.[30]

The tension between political reliability and expertise was discussed among moderates as well as among radicals, though it was Ch'en Kung-po who summarized the Kuomintang attitude in these words: 'For most of those in the revolutionary party the

---

[29] In Chengchow the party branch was evicted from its premises and its property was auctioned (see *CYCP*, xii. 4–5). The Training Dept's motion is in 5th Plenum *Chi-lu*, p. 158; see also p. 46. The Central Propaganda Dept devoted special attention to this problem in *CYCP*, xii. 4–5 & 11. For Yencheng see *NCH*, 13 Oct 1928, p. 89 and *CYCP*, xxii. 1.

[30] Discussion of the Central Political Council at the 5th Plenum is recorded in its *Chi-lu*, pp. 77–83, 59–61, 60, & 164 ff. See also the works cited in n. 64 below.

first condition is bitter struggle, while specialist personnel and those in the arts are mostly liberal in thought and romantic in spirit.' Against the Chinese background, moreover, the tenure of official authority was regarded as an added danger. The need to give authority to outsiders in the military, diplomatic, and judicial spheres, to take three obvious examples, was therefore an issue in this early period. The party itself was probably poorly endowed with specialists of all kinds.[31]

The strong animus in the Kuomintang against 'bureaucrats' and military officers found expression in attacks upon several eminent figures during 1928, including Huang Fu and C. T. Wang, successive incumbents of the difficult post of Foreign Minister. These were merely the outstanding targets of a wider agitation. After a long period as outlaws party workers were determined to destroy the power of the civilian officials staying on from the old regime and to restrict the military officers of the new regime— often men of the old stamp in transparent disguises—to purely military roles. These desires were reflected in the branches' submissions to the Fifth Plenum. It was against this background, too, that the branches called for parity in rank and salary between party and civil officials and employees and occasionally requested priority in access to appointments.[32]

The institutional problem of the party's relations with government below the Central level was a much more important problem, however. The desire of the rank and file to exercise some control over the local administration was apparent, and most of their ideas found expression in the motions put at the Fifth Plenum by central committee members. The radicals put forward a motion proposing party control of local-government finance and the authority to ask the Centre for injunctions against any contraventions of party policy. The motion put by the Standing Committee of the CEC proposed that the party should hold direct political authority down to the district level. The national, provincial, and district party congresses were to have the rights of initiative and

---

[31] This problem was discussed by Ch'en Kung-po in his *Ko-ming ti wei-chi*, pp. 66 & 69–70.

[32] Other targets of agitation were Wang Shih-chieh and Nan Kuei-ch'ing, head of the Legislative Bureau and new Mayor of Tientsin respectively. Requests for parity in rank and salary are found in 5th Plenum *Chi-lu*, p. 332, the *Chi-lu* of the 1st Plenum of Apr 1929, pp. 34 & 37, and in the Bulletin of the Ministry for War, i. 21–23 & x. 21–22.

referendum. The district Party Congress was to have authority to select district magistrates from lists sent down by the Centre or by the province, and to dismiss magistrates if need be. The supervisory committees of the party at all levels were to be free to question, warn or impeach officials at the equivalent level and the executive and supervisory committees were to share final control over government finance. The tenor of all these proposals, therefore, was to accord a very significant political role to the party branches down to the district level.[33]

Nevertheless, the resolution which emerged from the plenum was conservative. It provided that party branches could complain against the equivalent government agency to their senior branch, which would then 'request' the equivalent senior branch of the administration to deal with the matter according to law. A parallel clause covered the administration's complaints against the party. The resolution treated the two hierarchies as equals in status and provided a barrier between them for the protection of the administration. The proposals for various forms of direct supervision and control were not adopted. This must be attributed to the policy of Chiang Kai-shek who, in his approach to the problem of party–state relations, emphasized above all the need to protect the administration from party interference.[34] Chiang's leading position in the regime at this time was unassailable and we see him following here a line with regard to party affairs which he followed consistently thereafter. The party's role below the Centre was henceforth to be restricted to 'propaganda' in the widest sense of the term.

While the enthusiasts for party control complained about their insecurity and impotence and about the survival of 'decadence', the Central leadership continually complained over the next two years about the party members' mistaken view that they could give orders to government personnel. By the end of 1930 Sun Fo was speaking of the 'yamenization' of the branches, which had degenerated, so he claimed, into negative, destructive, and secretive 'super-governments' preying on the administration and confusing the people. Until more information on the Kuomintang at the

---

[33] The ideas of the branches on this question are found in 5th Plenum *Chi-lu*, pp. 335–6. The motions of the left and of the Standing Cttee are ibid. pp. 56–57, 78, & 159–62.
[34] Chiang's proposals are printed in the *Chi-lu*, p. 163; see also pp. 56–57.

local level is collected such complaints will be difficult to interpret accurately. There is little doubt, however, that this conflict was a serious problem in the earliest years of the regime.[35]

Some particular problems of party–state relations which came up during this period may also be mentioned. In the field of foreign relations, for example, overseas party branches occasionally demanded the authority to supervise the Chinese consular and diplomatic officials operating in their area. With regard to the army there were proposals for the revival of the system of party representatives, which had been discontinued after the purge of 1927, and the more effective promotion of political training in the armed forces. By the end of 1928 these concerns were covered by the system of party branches in military units and by the newly established Inspectorate-General of Military Training. The armies of the Nanking system were now a largely separate establishment under the President and the military staff and were less subject than ever before to the kind of pervasive political influence which civilian Nationalists had tended to regard as desirable.[36]

The question of the Special Criminal Courts was more significant than either of those just mentioned. Throughout the period of the Northern Expedition revolutionary justice had been dispensed in Nationalist territory. Special laws and tribunals were directed against counter-revolutionaries and 'local bullies and bad gentry', and from 1927 such cases were dealt with by the Special Courts. These were provincial institutions run by the party. They were apparently very busy during 1928, especially with 'bully and gentry' cases.[37]

The Fourth Plenum placed great emphasis on the introduction

---

[35] Sun Fo made these complaints in a speech of 1 Dec 1930, in *Sun Che-sheng Hsiensheng yen-lun chi* (Collected speeches of Mr Sun Fo) (1933), pp. 95 ff. See also Hu Hanmin's speech of 3 Mar 1930 in *Ko-ming li-lun*, p. 184. Foreigners also frequently complained of 'Tangpu tyranny'. Note that the question of party funds, an important indication of the value placed upon the party network by the leadership, has not been discussed here. The party was, of course, a charge upon the state.

[36] Branch requests for the revival of political work and Party Representatives in the army are listed in 5th Plenum *Chi-lu*, pp. 253–4. Chiang Kai-shek's speech to political workers in the new Inspectorate-General of Military Training, dated 7 Feb 1929, in *Chiang . . . yen-lun*, ix. 165 ff., treats party and political work in the army as a thing of the past and offers various explanations for its demise. Ch'en Kung-po characteristically regarded the revival of the Party Reps as a desirable but probably hopeless project (see *Ko-ming P'ing-lun*, no. 16, p. 50).

[37] For these courts see Hsieh Chen-min, *Chung-hua Min-kuo li-fa Shih* (History of legislation under the Chinese Republic) (1948), pp. 1180–91; *CYCP*, xv. 2, and *Kiangsu Hsun-k'an* (Kiangsu Journal), no. 24/25, pp. 75–77.

of the 'rule of law', and the desire to build up a modern judiciary on Western lines combined with the end of the 'period of military rule' to make the Special Courts the subject of controversy during the year. The Centre also had its eye on the abolition of extraterritoriality and the need to show the powers that Chinese justice was up to date and effective. At the Fifth Plenum Ts'ai Yuan-p'ei, then Acting Minister of Justice, successfully argued for the abolition of the Special Courts. He pointed out that the new criminal law covered all forms of counter-revolution, that the anti-bandit laws could still be used against communists, and that the 'bully and gentry' laws had merely provided heavier penalties for essentially ordinary offences. The Special Courts were finally abolished early in 1929 at a time when the government was beginning to feel a sense of urgency on the issue of extraterritoriality. The Second Plenum (of the Third CEC) in June 1929 also gave prominence to a resolution calling for the protection of the lives and property of the people and emphasizing the sanctity of due process. Judicial reforms were to be accelerated in the interests of social stability and the ending of foreign privilege. Party branches, which had continually requested the more thoroughgoing detection and punishment of 'feudal forces', tried to obtain the revival of the Special Courts after their abolition. The Kiangsu branch, one of the strongest in the country, wrote thus to the Second Plenum: 'Though the independence of the judiciary is our aspiration, the supremacy of party authority is above all the long-standing policy of the party. It is unnecessary to state that under party rule even the judiciary cannot be independent of the party position.' A little laxity could cause disaster to the revolution. This argument did not prevail against party policy though it cannot be said that an independent judiciary was in fact achieved.[38]

The more partisan approach to party-state relations was therefore rejected on every count except at the Centre itself. The trend, indeed, was clearly in the other direction with the military authorities in particular exercising a prevailing influence over the party in many areas of China. On the other hand the constitutionalist and liberal-democratic approach was rejected also. The Fourth

[38] Ts'ai's motion is in 5th Plenum *Chi-lu*, pp. 217–18. For the resolution of the 2nd Plenum see its *Chi-lu*, p. 55. The Kiangsu submission is ibid. pp. 148–9. (But note that Kanyü and Shanghai branches suggested the restoration of the ordinary courts to the 5th Plenum, see its *Chi-lu*, pp. 339–40.)

Plenum decided to call a National Convention at the close of the Expedition, a proposal which, in the new political climate, was now generally unpopular in party circles but supported in business and military quarters. After some hesitation the idea was abandoned in the summer, but the Fifth Plenum did decide that a provisional constitution should be adopted for the period of political tutelage. This plan, too, was dropped in September when Hu Han-min returned to China, and in March 1929 the Third Congress shelved the constitutional problem by declaring Sun Yat-sen's authoritative writings to be the fundamental law of the new state. The constitutional question which did occupy the attention of the leadership towards the end of 1928 was the composition of the central government; the rights and duties of citizens remained undefined. There were indeed provisions for democratic institutions in the legislation on local government passed at this time but these innovations were only to be introduced at a later stage of the tutelary process. Despite a growing volume of legislation on particular problems the larger political context remained vague. A certain right of remonstrance was enjoyed by party organizations and by business and other public figures, and the press was largely uncontrolled. But the growing tensions sketched in a previous section only accelerated the trend towards tighter controls which was developing by the end of 1928.

THE RELATIONSHIP BETWEEN PARTY AND PEOPLE

The denial of a direct and extensive political function to the body of the Kuomintang was naturally accompanied by an increasing emphasis upon its 'educational' role among the people. This was a matter upon which there was an apparent consensus within the party. The party's duty was to 'urge on and instruct' the people in the tasks of political and economic reconstruction, an assignment which entailed 'going to the people' and 'getting close to the masses'. The specific tasks with which the branches were to concern themselves, all aspects of the local self-government policy, were defined in October 1928 as follows: the movements for literacy, afforestation, road building, and hygiene, the co-operative movement and the promotion of the *pao-chia* system of local security.[39] It must be significant that the training of the people in

[39] *Pao-chia* was the name given to the traditional system of village security and population control, based on multiples of ten families.

the exercise of their political rights was no longer among these tasks. Going beyond the tasks laid down in this statement, the fostering of national consciousness, the promotion of the 'National Goods Movement', and the creation of an 'atmosphere' favourable to the policy of military disbandment were other examples of the educational role. Another can be taken from the rent-reduction programme in Chekiang province. The party was instructed to explain to the peasants the operation of the rent laws, for it was feared that government intervention in this matter would stimulate unilateral action by tenants unless carefully explained.[40]

This case leads on to a second facet of the party's role for, in addition to acting as the tutor of the people, it was also regarded as the intermediary between them and the government. This conception derived, in Kuomintang theory, from the party's essentially representative character, its concern for popular welfare, and its special competence in social matters. Chiang Kai-shek put the concept of the intermediary at the crux of the proposals on the three-cornered relationship between party, government, and people, which he laid before the Fifth Plenum, and though the radicals disagreed with Chiang's views in other respects, their proposals, too, were based upon the same idea. By 1929 and 1930, however, the Nanking leadership was complaining that party branches were perverting this role too by presenting impracticable demands on behalf of the people, a practice which, it was said, inevitably created resentment against the regime.[41]

The idea of the intermediary was reflected in the machinery set up for the settlement of agrarian and industrial conflicts. The party joined the administration and the relevant public organizations in the work of conciliation and arbitration. In fact it appears that there were many conflicts between different social or interest groups which were reserved to the party's jurisdiction, with the administration coming in after the settlement to see to its execution. During the first half of 1929, for example, there were many conflicts between merchant organizations and anti-Japanese boycott committees which were dealt with by the Central Training

[40] For the emphasis on the educational role see Hu Han-min's speech of 3 Mar 1930, in *Ko-ming li-lun*. See also Chiang Kai-shek's speeches of 18 July & 21 Dec 1928, in *Chiang . . . yen-lun*, ix. The party branches' basic tasks were defined in *CYCP*, xxi. 1. For the particular examples cited see ibid. xviii. 2 & xiii. 1.

[41] Chiang's views in 5th Plenum *Chi-lu*, p. 163, and radical view ibid. p. 82.

M

Department.[42] There is also a hint here of the idea of the party as an 'umpire' with the function of ensuring social harmony. An umpire might have seemed unnecessary in view of the official position that classes, in the sense of social groups with well-differentiated economic interests, had not yet evolved in Chinese society. There was, however, a long history of prophylactic thinking on social questions in the Kuomintang, and the umpire can be explained in these terms. The party's path in the field of social policy was presented as a middle way between the unreasonable demands of either masters or men. This middle way would lead China safely past capitalism and communism, the twin diseases of the West which would otherwise batten on Chinese society too in due course. Ch'en Kung-po's position was unorthodox in that he admitted the existence of classes in China, but he, too, wished to eliminate them and regarded the party as the chosen instrument for the 'levelling of the classes'.[43]

The one task which above all others in the social field did occupy party branches in this period was the control of public organizations. The party's Mass Training Committees (see p. 169) and, later, its Training Departments were responsible for registering and investigating every type of union and association, for public bodies of all kinds continued to be important, particularly in Chinese urban society. There was, however, an extremely significant tension in 1928 and 1929 on the role of public organizations and on the question of the mass movements which had been so important in the preceding phase of the revolution.

Since the communists had played such an important part in the mass movements, the Kuomintang naturally regarded them with suspicion after the purge. Most of the movements were suspended during 1927, and after the Canton Commune of December 1927 their repression was renewed until they were finally suspended entirely at the time of the Fourth Plenum. Communist elements were still active in south Kiangsu and Chekiang as well as in south China throughout 1928, and fear of the Communist Party in Nationalist China's metropolitan area was a motive in Kuo-

---

[42] On conciliation and arbitration see Hsieh Chen-min, pp. 1394–404; *Erh-wu chien-tsu fa-kuei chi ch'i-t'a* (The 25 per cent rent reduction and other matters) (1932), pp. 88 ff. The *Chi-lu* of the 2nd Plenum of June 1929, pp. 156–60, lists cases of conflicts between popular organizations. For a government complaint of a party organ overstepping the mark and usurping the function of arbitration see *CYCP*, xiii, 13.

[43] Ch'en's views are given in his *Ko-ming ti wei-chi*, p. 51.

mintang policy. Kuomintang leaders were apprehensive about the mass movements and organizations because of past experience and because of the difficulty of preventing their use as covers for hostile activities. The suspension early in 1928 was opposed by the seven most powerful anti-communist trades unions in Shanghai on the grounds that healthy Nationalist organizations were the best defence against the Communist Party, and the students later echoed this view in defending their own organizations. Caution prevailed in Nanking, nevertheless, though the effectiveness of the suspension may be doubted. But, in the last resort, the need for mass or extra-party movements of some kind or another was almost universally recognized in Kuomintang circles. It was the nature and purpose of the movements which proved controversial. [44]

Once again it was the Fifth Plenum which discussed this vital problem against the background of a clamour among the party branches for the revival, expansion and definition of the mass movements. This clamour had only recently been greatly stimulated by the Tsinan Incident of 3 May in the aftermath of which the Japanese army occupied Tsinan and the railway to Tsingtao for nearly a year. The coming of peace had also stimulated hopes that the wartime neglect of social problems would now be brought to an end. From a practical point of view the movements were essential if the party was to mesh effectively with society and was to secure the wide support it needed. The two immediate threats were the authorities' plea that security demanded their suspension and the danger that all the 'outdoor' activities of the party branches would be labelled as 'communistic'. Both threats were illustrated in the case of the Peking trades unions which prospered greatly from July under the direction of the municipal branch of the Kuomintang. The military authorities complained that the unions were creating social conflicts and, on their appeal, Yen Hsi-shan closed them down on 13 August. Yen later claimed that the military situation in northern Hopei had also made this necessary. The Peking Kuomintang protested that the mass movements were authorized by the Centre—the status of the ban of early 1928 was obscure—and claimed that they were an essential

[44] Authoritative sources invariably describe the suspension of the mass movements as a decision of the 4th Plenum, though no text confirming this has been found. For the suspension of public organizations in Kiangsu see *Kiangsu Hsun-k'an*, p., 82. The Shanghai Trades Unions' petition is printed in Ma Ch'ao-chün, *Chung-kuo lao-kung yün-tung shih* (History of the labour movement in China) (Taipei, 1959), i. 790–1.

part of Kuomintang policy and had no connexion with communism. In this case the Centre was able to secure the withdrawal of Yen's order.[45]

The plea of the Peking branch was echoed by the radicals at the Fifth Plenum who commented:

> Communist methods are indeed evil, but to say that our Party must avoid saying anything said by the communists is like refusing to eat because of a hiccup. Our party naturally has its own policies and need not choose or reject them on the basis of Communist Party policies.

They accused some of their colleagues of regarding all mass movements as communistic and accused 'some of those in authority' of gradually shelving party policy in order to achieve quick gains through compromise with the old forces. Their motion on 'The Re-establishment of the Party's Foundations', which emphasized democratization both inside and outside the party, directly connected the popular organizations with the building of a democratic polity. 'The occupational organizations produced by the mass movements are the bases of democratic forces.'

The motion put by Miao Pin and General Ho Ying-ch'in, who were both very influential at this time, represented the other extreme of opinion. They argued that 'the Kuomintang is simply the expression, organization and concrete form of the will of the masses. The party's movement is the masses' movement, the two are one and the one is two.' Consequently the question whether the party wanted the masses, which, they said, had been frequently asked over the previous year or two, was superfluous. Turning to the past, they observed that the mass movements had been used by the party as a convenient cover for its advance. Unfortunately the communists had adopted the same stratagem and the movements had thereupon become an obstacle to the national revolution. Their solution was to make sure that the party was itself broad enough and to restrict popular bodies to simple forms of organization and to strictly parochial concerns. A similar view of the past history of the movements was expressed by Hu Han-min. Viewing the mass movements of the preceding period solely as a subversive weapon during the civil war, he questioned the

[45] Branches' submissions to 5th Plenum on mass movements are listed in *Chi-lu*, pp. 327–8, & see p. 79. For the Peking episode see *KWCP*, diary, 13, 15, & 18 Aug 1928, and v/27, 'Ta shih shu-p'ing', p. 11; Hatano Kenichi, *Gendai Shina no kiroku* (Records of modern China), July 1928, p. 87 & Sept 1928, p. 325.

wisdom of the Kuomintang going on to lay fires in its own rear.[46]

The orthodox view of the mass movements made a clear distinction between their tasks in the periods of destruction and reconstruction, a distinction which entailed their restriction to economic, technical, and educational roles. Their political role during the period of destruction was now interpreted in purely negative terms, as a weapon against the warlords. The positive political potentialities of the movements, which had begun to emerge in 1926 and 1927, were either ignored or denied. The second feature of the orthodox view was the absolute rejection of the class struggle, which the mass movements were now accused of having fostered. The political gap left by the reorientation of the mass movements was supposed to be filled by the local self-government programme, but this did not get under weigh in the period under review, except in a very small number of experimental villages. The only moves made by the beginning of 1930 were the passage of certain legislation, the collection of administrative information, and the reintroduction of the *pao-chia* system of local security.[47]

Moving on from the discussions of this problem, changes in the organization of the party apparatus dealing with the mass movements reveal more clearly the trend of Central policy. The Fourth Plenum had emphasized the centralization of authority in the party, and this motive, together with the view that the movements had fomented class conflict, led to the abolition of the old central departments concerned with the various sectors of society. (Organizational patterns at the Centre were mirrored throughout the party hierarchy.) These departments had played a vital part in stimulating the mass movements between 1924 and 1927. The Workers', Peasants', Youths', Merchants', and Women's Departments were now rolled into a single Committee for Mass Training. The radical group were given seats on this body at the Centre, but it did not start work for several months and the revival of the mass movements was a slow and hesitant process. From the end of May the party took steps to reform the popular organizations and to

[46] For the radicals' motion see 5th Plenum *Chi-lu*, pp. 78 & 37. For the Miao-Ho motion see ibid. pp. 126 ff. Hu used this metaphor in a speech of 22 Oct 1928 (see *Ko-ming li-lun*, p. 138).

[47] Two important articles giving the orthodox view were Hu Han-min's 'The Theory of the Kuomintang mass movements', July 1927, in *Ko-ming li-lun*, pp. 146–72, and Tai Chi-t'ao, 'Min-chung yün-tung ti kuo-ch'ü ho chiang-lai' (The past and future of the mass movements), in *Chung-yang Pan-yueh-k'an* (Central Fortnightly), i. 9.

register their members. The most interesting organizational development was proposed at the Fifth Plenum by the Standing Committee of the CEC, which suggested a fairly elaborate federal hierarchy of popular organizations as a vehicle for public opinion and a channel of communication between party and people. As with other innovations proposed, however, the plenum finally passed a non-commital resolution allowing the people to organize within the still undefined 'limits of the law'. In October the composition of the Committee was completely changed by the addition of Hu Han-min and Miao Pin, and the two generals Ho Ying-ch'in and Li Chi-shen were added to it. The radicals had not carried on routine work at the Centre for some time and Ch'en Kuo-fu, the leader of the Committee from its activation in May and a right-wing advocate of party-controlled mass organizations, also retired in October. The men just mentioned, together with Tai Chi-t'ao, now had the effective responsibility for the party's policy in this field and they formed a group which was not well disposed towards mass development.[48]

The trend towards greater control over the movements moved a stage further in April 1929 when the Committee was wound up and its functions were divided between the Central Organization and Training Departments, though, significantly, Mass Training Committees were allowed to continue in the largest cities where society was more complex. Hu Han-min later explained that this had been done because the Committee's competence had conflicted with that of the two departments. Here again there were unsuccessful protests from the branches. The Nanking branch warned the Second Plenum (June 1929) that 'The popular organizations mistakenly believe that the party is leaving the masses' and warned that these organizations were beginning to founder. But the desire to ensure stricter party control and to combat opposition currents in the Kuomintang itself had now finally resulted in the demolition of the structure built up from 1924.[49] The significance of the discouragement of mass work

---

[48] 4th Plenum decisions are recorded in *KWCP*, v. 5 & 6. For mass movement policy in 1928 see *CYCP*, xi. 15–16, xii. 15–16, & xxii. 2. This last reference gives the appointments of Oct 1928.

[49] For the winding up of the Committee see *Chi-lu* of the 1st Plenum, p. 11, and *Chi-lu* of the 2nd Plenum, p. 156. Hu explained this in Mar 1930 (see *Ko-ming li-lun*, pp. 189–90). For Nanking's warning see *Chi-lu* of 2nd Plenum, p. 143. Sub-departments survived, of course, in the remaining departments.

for the health of the party branches themselves is not hard to appreciate.

The Fourth Plenum had given great prominence to a contrast between 'mere words' and 'real work', which had the closest connexion with its policy on the mass movements. Nanking leaders constantly deplored processions, demonstrations, meetings, billsticking, and so forth, and contrasted these useless, communistic activities with the quiet and steady reconstruction work which the party and the movements ought to be undertaking. Indeed, the movements were sometimes criticized not only for not doing this work, but also for preventing it being done. The peasant and labour movements, for example, were sometimes blamed for the stagnation of agriculture and industry, a striking change from the propaganda of the previous period which invariably attributed economic difficulties to imperialism. The argument against 'mere words' was applied generally but was directed above all against the anti-imperialist movement, domestic reconstruction, as opposed to militant protest, being seen as the fundamental remedy for China's oppression by imperialism.[50]

Yet the official view was still that popular 'support and encouragement' were vital for the success of the Nationalist programme, for example in respect of foreign policy and troop disbandment. Nanking agreed with the foreigners' disparaging estimation of the strength of national and public feeling in China, as expressed in the sayings 'a five-minute fever' and 'the Chinese are good at forgetting'.[51] But were the authorities really prepared to allow the growth of the organized and trained public opinion which they professed to desire, and to set about the political mobilization of the people? Nanking failed, in fact, to reconcile its desire for public support with its insistence of the 'stabilization' of society and subordinated other considerations to the need for security. It adopted a non-dynamic approach well illustrated in a speech of Hu Han-min, made in September 1929. Commenting on a foreigner's opinion that the revolution had slackened off, he observed that 'in every newly risen nation slogans and processions

---

[50] For the application of the 'words and work' antithesis see the motion put at the 5th Plenum by Miao Pin and Ho Ying-ch'in, cited in n. 45 above. The mass movements were criticized in Chiang Kai-shek's speech of 1 Jan 1929 in *Chiang . . . yen-lun*, pp. 167–8.

[51] See the Centre's pamphlet, *T'i-ch'ang kuo-huo yün-tung hsüan-ch'uan kang-yao* (Outline of propaganda on the national goods movement) (1929), p. 1.

and so on are bound to diminish with time'. The Soviet Union, Italy, Turkey, and Germany had all been the same in this respect. 'The propaganda of the period of destruction is words and pictures, that of the period of reconstruction is figures, statistical figures.' In Hu's opinion Nationalist China in its progress from 'mere words' to 'real work' was quieter but stronger, not more slack.[52]

These words epitomize the static view which now prevailed in Nanking, for could a nationalist and state-building regime in the China of 1929 really dispense with 'words and pictures'? The tenor of Nanking's approach to the problems of reconstruction was etatist and bureaucratic; it was focused on the activities of the state and paid little attention to the wider political potentialities of the party and the movements or to the public opinion which had proved so valuable between 1919 and 1927. What mattered above all was the creation of a strong central apparatus, and the contribution which could be made by other forms of organization was recognized in theory but denied in practice. Having realized the significance of 'politics' during the seizure of power, the lesson was forgotten at the moment of success and a hiatus between politics and reconstruction was allowed to develop.

Finally, in view of the special importance of the student movement in Chinese politics under the Republic, the Nanking regime's deteriorating relationship with youth deserves special mention.[53] Here again it was the Fourth Plenum which laid out the guidelines of Kuomintang policy. Its manifesto included a section criticizing youth for joining in political and social struggles with which they were not concerned and in which they were unqualified to meddle. Adolescents, being immature, could not be entrusted with matters of national concern and should suffer adult penalties if they engaged in adult activities (i.e. politics).[54] The youth of the party's membership and of Chinese progressives in general, and the high status of intellectuals made student patriotism and radicalism a major problem for the leadership from this time forward. No fewer than one-third of the civilian members of the Kuomintang within China were under 25 at the end of 1929 and

---

[52] Hu's speech of 16 Sept 1929 in *Ko-ming li-lun*, p. 333.
[53] It would be quite wrong to assume that all Chinese students were radical in their political views or that all student radicals were radicals of the Left.
[54] For the Manifesto see n. 18 above.

more than half were under 30. The significance of this passage can be illustrated by comparing it with the mandate issued by President Hsü Shih-ch'ang on 8 May 1919 in his attempt to quell student activities. The close parallel was a bad augury for the Kuomintang.[55]

Ts'ai Yuan-p'ei, the most eminent of the Nationalist educationalists, brought up the question of the students' political activities at the Fifth Plenum and proposed the halting of the student movement. His main argument was the need to rebuild Chinese education after years of neglect and upheaval. The Shanghai Student Union, on the other hand, pointed out that students were also citizens and that 'destruction' had to be thorough before reconstruction could begin. Students could not leave the political scene and 'return to the classroom' now, and the student movement was a natural and necessary part of national politics. Furthermore, they argued, the communists would take advantage of any suspension of the movement. This point was denied by Ts'ai, who considered that the regime's control of educational institutions would prevent any revival of communist influence. The leading figures in the party, however, felt that the student movement should be allowed to survive as a broader movement of youth in general and should be keyed in with the reconstruction activities in each sector of society. There was therefore no need to take special action against the student movement.[56]

The Centre's view of the youth question was affected by the fact that it identified the party opposition with the younger members of the Kuomintang, and was also aware of the tenuous hold of Nationalist ideology on the student body as a whole. The regime was also facing a crisis in foreign relations and its failure in this sphere was undoubtedly the main source of disaffection among young nationalists. In March 1929 the Third Congress reflected the new phase in the regime's relationship with youth in the provisions for 'preparatory' and full membership of the party with lower age-limits of 16 and 20 respectively. This measure formed a contrast to the decision made three years before at the Second Congress at which the idea of a lower age-limit had been rejected,

[55] The age analysis is from *Min-kuo 18 nien Chung-kuo KMT Nien-chien* (hereafter *CKMT Nien-chien*, Yearbook of the CKMT for 1929), p. 747. Hsü's mandate is quoted in Chow Tse-tsung, *The May Fourth Movement* (Camb., Mass., 1960), p. 134.

[56] See 5th Plenum *Chi-lu*, pp. 43–44 and John Israel, *Student Nationalism in China 1927–37* (Stanford, Calif., 1966), pp. 17–28.

and the age-limit suggested had been 14 years. The Third Congress, after some debate, also restricted candidates for election to the CEC and the Central Supervisory Committees to those aged at least 30 and 36 respectively.[57] Once again an important change in the direction of policy was reflected in changes in the organization of the Kuomintang.

THE MEMBERSHIP AND SOCIAL CHARACTER OF THE
KUOMINTANG, 1928–9

As the party claimed such a vital role in the new regime, its membership is a subject of special interest. Some remarks upon this topic have been made above in connexion with the period between 1924 and 1927. The purge and confusion of 1927 do not appear to have stopped the party expanding in its new territories, for when the registration of 1928 was complete it transpired that the overall figure for all the areas occupied after October 1926 was three times as large as the figure for that month. That is to say, where there had been one member in the last phase of the 'period of secrecy', there were three in the earliest phase of tutelage.

This did not apply to those areas which had already been occupied by the time of the last count in October 1926 (i.e. Kwangtung, Kwangsi, Hunan, Hupei, Canton, and Hankow). In these areas taken as a whole there was an enormous reduction in membership over the next two years, and it is significant of the change which came over Kuomintang politics after 1927 that the party contracted to such an extent in the areas where the revolution had gone farthest. In 1929 the party's strength in these areas stood very close to the figures reported to the Second Congress three years before in January 1926. Despite this northward shift, however, Kwangtung and Canton still accounted for 29 per cent of the party's fully enrolled strength at the end of 1929.[58]

[57] These innovations and the discussion of them are recorded in the official record of the 3rd Congress, *Chung-kuo KMT ti-san-tz'u ch'üan-kuo tai-piao ta-hui hui-i-lu* (Proc. of the 3rd national congress of the CKMT), pp. 109–10.

[58] The sources of these figures are the first two works cited in n. 3 above. The relevant figures are: territories occupied after Oct 1926—from 66,814 in that month to 128,796 in Oct 1929; territories already held—130,000 in Jan 1926, 362,590 in Oct 1926, and 122,899 in Oct 1929. Kwangsi's figures for 1926 seem implausibly large. These calculations do not reflect the further extensive growth of party membership in Wuhan's jurisdiction in 1927, as recorded in *People's Tribune*.

One of the more striking facts to emerge from these figures is the stagnation or contraction of Kuomintang membership in the major cities. The Shanghai branch, with 6,204 registered in 1929, was little stronger than it had been at the time of the Second Congress. The Canton membership dropped from 12,381 in October 1926 to 10,277 in October 1929. In Peking, beset by party troubles, the old figure of 4,000 was down to 1,770. In view of the part these cities had played in the history of the national-revolutionary movement and the generally urban character of the Kuomintang, the party's failure to grow in them when they came under its control is especially significant. The growth that took place between 1927 and 1929 in north and east China took place outside the great revolutionary centres.

The overall figure for the civilian membership within China at the end of 1929 was 266,338, but the civilian membership itself constituted only 49 per cent of the whole body of the Kuomintang; 280,000 members were registered in military branches. Before 1928 such branches had been set up and large numbers of the regime's troops enrolled in the party, but military branches were now established on a much more systematic basis in the armies of the Nanking military system. By the end of 1929 military members slightly outnumbered their civilian counterparts.

Soldiers were therefore the largest single bloc in the Kuomintang after 1928 and their proportionate weight in the party increased slightly during the 1930s.[59] To turn to the civilian membership, it is interesting to find both the radicals at the Fifth Plenum and the Centre during the same period drawing attention to the question of the party's composition. The radicals considered the first figures from the Nanking and Shanghai registrations 'alarming'. In their view the number of applications was extremely small but, more important, they alleged that about one-half of those registered in Nanking were party or government functionaries of one kind or another and about three-quarters of those in Shanghai were functionaries or police. Young people and students had not come forward, not to mention the labouring masses. Behind this complaint lay the populist views of Ch'en Kung-po, who considered that the party should ideally consist of peasants,

[59] The total figures of party membership for 1929 are given in *CKMT Nien-chien*; figures for the first half of the 1930s in Yang Yu-chiung, *Chung-kuo cheng-tang shih* (History of Chinese political parties) (1936), p. 200.

workers and petty bourgeoisie in the proportions of 50, 30, and 20 respectively.[60]

The Central Organization Department, run at that time by Ch'en Kuo-fu, agreed with the radicals that these figures were unsatisfactory and issued an announcement containing this passage:

> The significance of this registration is to examine the components of the total party membership. The calculation of the forces of the revolution is of the greatest importance for the way ahead, but the result of a survey of partial registration is that military and political circles seem to predominate. . . . Students come next and peasant and worker elements are the least numerous, and this certainly departs too far from the party's principle of emphasizing the peasants and workers.

The responsible organs were instructed to put out propaganda before registration and to help peasants and workers through the procedures.[61]

From the evidence available most of these undesirable characteristics seem to have persisted. Figures on the occupations of members in three of the largest cities (Shanghai, Nanking, and Hankow) in 1928 and a national statistical table of October 1929 are available. These figures are crude but reveal that students and teachers formed about one-third of the party's civilian membership over the whole country and between one-third and one-quarter of the membership in the two cities of Nanking and Shanghai. The party did indeed consider the teachers particularly important for the expansion of the party's influence. Functionaries of all kinds formed about one-fifth of the national membership and predominated in Nanking itself, which was clearly a special case. Industry and commerce were poorly represented with only one-tenth each of the national membership, but were much better represented in Shanghai and Hankow, and were reported to predominate in the small Tientsin branch. The agricultural sector of society occupied a conspicuously unimportant position, with only one-tenth of the total.[62] The figures on the chief cities mentioned,

[60] The radical view is recorded in 5th Plenum *Chi-lu*, pp. 80–81; Ch'en Kung-po, *Chung-kuo KMT so tai-piao-ti shih shenmo?* (What does the CKMT represent?) (Shanghai, 1928), p. 96.

[61] *CYCP*, x. 1.

[62] Figures for Nanking, Shanghai, and Hankow for the latter part of 1928 are given in *CYCP*, xv. 2–3 & xxi. 1. Tientsin is mentioned ibid. xxii. 2. The national figures for Oct 1929 are found in *CKMT Nien-chien*. The information from these crude sources can be expressed as percentages of the relevant total as follows:

which accounted for about a seventh of the party, are defective enough, but virtually no detailed information at all on the party outside these areas has been found. The impression remains that it was largely confined to the cities and the district seats.[63] In the continuing strength of the teacher and student element the social character of the Kuomintang in 1929 bore some resemblance to its composition before 1927 in the areas then beyond its control. The functionaries of all kinds were naturally a newer component. The party was still very restricted both in its absolute size and in its composition. It is probable that the large military element constituted the most important 'downward' penetration of the party in terms of social class and by virtue of the army's presence in the countryside.[64]

POLICIES OF THE NEW STATE

To conclude this survey of the new regime in its earliest period the leading policies of the state must be reviewed. By considering the nature of the problems tackled by the Nanking Centre the

	Shanghai	*Nanking*	*Hankow*	*National* (*Oct 1929*)
Education (students & teachers)	29	26	10	32
Civil service, law enforcement, party officials, &c.	15	61	32	21
Industry	27	negl.	40	10
Commerce	13	negl.	7	8
Agriculture	negl.	negl.	negl.	10
Professions, &c.	?	4	7	2
'No occupation'	—	8	—	negl.

Note that there was a large number of 'not knowns' in the national figures. The term used to distinguish categories is *chieh* (sector), a vertical term opposed to 'class'. The total for the national count was 271,671.

[63] The great strength of the educational and functionary element in the party tends to confirm this impression. The only description of the KMT outside the large cities which had been found is contained in a very discouraging report on the party in N. Kiangsu in Dec 1928, in *CYCP*, xxx. 1–2. The inspectors suggested that this was not an exceptionally backward area as far as party work was concerned.

[64] From 1929 recruitment into the party became more systematic under the new rules for probationary admission introduced by the 3rd Congress. Admission was more closely controlled from the centre and attention was paid to the social composition of new intakes. For an example of recruitment after 1929 see details of a 3-month drive to recruit 10,000 new members of specified occupation in Canton, beginning on 1 June 1930, in *CYCP*, cix.

debates and disputes discussed in earlier sections can be seen in a wider perspective.

Of all the areas of policy the revision of the 'Unequal Treaties' was the most urgent in party ideology and opinion, but since the Fourth Plenum internal issues had been given, in effect, a disguised priority. This concluding review will be confined to matters of internal policy.

The Kuomintang ideal was a 'modern state' with a powerful 'omni-competent' government backed by a sound citizenry and able to take its place among the advanced nation-states of the world. The government was to be uncorrupt, efficient, specialized, and unitary, and capable of taking on economic, social, and defensive functions. A strong 'Centre' was the first aim of the Nanking leaders, an aim which was pursued with such single-mindedness that it was allowed to obscure other elements in the political structure of the country.

All factions intended the state to take a leading role in the economy, in agriculture as well as in industry, foreign trade, and communications. The state would tolerate capitalism where expedient but would move in to provide what was lacking, while at the same time protecting the country from foreign exploitation. During the period we are discussing, however, the state was too weak to do much constructive work in this field. Of all the areas of the economy communications were considered the most vital for economic and military reasons and also for the political reintegration of the country. For it was unification which, above all, was the preoccupation of the Nationalist leaders.

The Northern Expedition had been fought for national unification but had itself led to a strengthening of military influences on Chinese politics, and the close connexion between military influences and regionalism had been clear since 1916. It was illustrated once again in this period in the Branch Political Councils. Provision for these bodies with general political powers in areas cut off from the revolutionary base in Kwangtung had been made since 1926. Early in 1928 Branch Councils were set up for all of Nanking's chief military supporters: Feng Yü-hsiang controlled one Branch in Kaifeng, Yen Hsi-shan another in Taiyuan, Li Chi-shen another in Canton, and Li Tsung-jen a fourth in Wuhan. These councils had overall political control of groups of neighbouring provinces but were, nominally at least, subject to central veto. At the end of the Expedition a strong current in the Kuomintang was opposed to the continuation of the Branches because of the desire for unity and the general disapproval of military commanders exercising political powers. Many submissions to the Fifth Plenum called for their abolition and this was also the chief point of contention between the radical and the more conservative delegates. Chiang Kai-shek and his closer collaborators were also undoubtedly opposed to the existence of the Branches on principle but arranged a compromise by which they should continue to the end of the year. They were finally wound up in March 1929. At the same time, however, Nanking allowed Manchuria, which it treated with extreme caution, to retain a regional political organization in Mukden.

The Branch Political Councils, super-provincial governments in effect, were particularly anomalous in that the Kuomintang's policy of integration was biased against the province itself as a political unit. The *Fundamentals of National Reconstruction* emphasized the Centre and the districts and aimed at reducing the province to a mere link between them, the ideal being to develop direct communication between the top and the bottom. The provinces were held to have battened on both the Centre and the districts and were regarded as having been associated with militarist and bureaucratic politics under the Republic. In 1929 and 1930 schemes for reducing their size and increasing their number were mooted at the Centre, though no plans of this sort were ever realized. [65]

The key policy for bringing about unification in 1928 and 1929 was the 'disbandment and reorganization' of the country's armies. This was indeed regarded as the crux of the entire strategy in the opening phase of reconstruction. Military expenditures were so huge that something had to be done to reduce China's swollen armies, then estimated at well over 2 million men. In January 1929 the Finance Minister calculated that military expenditures would consume 78 per cent of the central revenue left over after the service of foreign debts and the expenses of the revenue services

[65] The Branch Political Councils are discussed by Ch'ien Tuan-sheng & others in *Min-kuo cheng-chih shih* (History of political institutions under the republic) (1946), p. 166 and by Ch'en Chih-mai, 'Kuomintang ti Cheng-chih Wei-yuan-hui' (The political council in the KMT), in *She-hui K'o-hsueh* (Social Science), ii/4 (1937). For the Branch Council problem at the 5th Plenum see the *Chi-lu*, pp. 333–5 and Hatano, *Gendai Shina no kiroku*, Aug 1928, p. 136.

themselves.[66] Nor was it merely a question of fiscal and economic effects, for the political implications were just as serious. Chinese armies, including most of those in the Nationalist establishment, lived off the areas in which they were stationed and tended to exercise local or regional political influence, if not power. Finance and administration could not be reformed or brought under control until the armies were thinned out and reorganized.

The elaboration of policy on this issue was undertaken by the leading commanders and also, though unofficially, by the country's financial and commercial leaders who had been interested in this problem for many years. The six commanders, the four mentioned in connexion with the Branch Councils together with Chiang Kai-shek and Admiral Yang Shu-chuang, discussed the questions of large-scale demobilization and the building up of a national army. The Fifth Plenum merely ratified the principles; a 'truly national army', a national defence plan, the introduction of conscription, the extension of central appointments, interchangeability of units and personnel, and the limitation of military funds to 50 per cent of the national budget. The aim was to break down all systems based upon regions or persons. Military colonization on the borders and the creation of an organized labour force out of the disbanded men, who should soon have totalled over 1 million men, were also integral parts of the plan.[67]

The first stage of disbandment was described as voluntary and was carried out by the commanders on their own initiative. The general principle was the proportional reduction of the various Army Groups in order to preserve their relative balance. From January 1929 and the establishment of the Commission for the Disbandment and Reorganization of the National Army the policy moved into a more systematic and enforceable phase with the setting up of disbandment districts and inspectors. A loan was floated at the same time and six months were allowed for a reduction to a figure of 800,000 men. Care had been taken to associate publicly every military leader in the formation of an enforceable policy. Even Manchuria was represented in the Commission. But

[66] T. V. Soong's motion on finance at the Disbandment Conference, 11 Jan 1929, in *Ko-ming Wen-hsien*, xxiv. 4870. The sources for the disbandment policy are scattered. Many of the important documents of 1929 are collected ibid. xxiv. And see *Kuo-min Ko-ming Chün Chan-shih* (Military history of the national revolutionary army), pt. 4.

[67] 5th Plenum *Chi-lu*, pp 25–27.

the policy, which now became known as 'peaceful unification', was immediately jeopardized by the short war along the Yangtze between the Kwangsi clique and Chiang Kai-shek's armies in April 1929. Feng Yü-hsiang broke with Nanking in May and most of his group finally declared against Nanking in September. Yen Hsi-shan moved into opposition from the end of the year. In the course of the conflicts of 1929 and 1930 the Centre was able to extend its power into parts of central and north China and along the south coast. But though the disbandment policy was renewed in June 1929 with new funds and personnel and a bigger field for direct action, the policy never developed. According to one source there were actually 2,599,000 men under arms by September 1930, probably more than there had been at the end of the Expedition.[68] Since warfare had long since replaced agreement as the Centre's method of disbandment, the Commission was terminated at the end of 1930.

The military situation and the relationship between Nanking and the great regional cliques naturally determined the degree to which the Centre was able to effect reintegration. This could be measured perhaps by the attendance of only five south-eastern provinces at the first National Administrative Conference in November 1928. The best measure, however, is the extent of the reach of the national treasury. Early in 1928 the Finance Minister was only able to call on three provinces, Kiangsu, Chekiang, and Anhwei, for payment of central tax revenues collected in the provinces. Anhwei, however, was unable to make any contribution in any case. Kwangtung, previously a very important source of National Government finance, had stopped payments to the Centre in October 1927 and was very much opposed to resuming them. By January 1929 the Minister could still call on only four provinces, the three mentioned above, together with Kiangsi. A few months later he visited Hankow and Wuchow in the wake of the victorious Central or pro-Nanking forces, presumably to insist on the payments due to the Centre. By March 1930 he was able to report that Hupei, Hunan, and, later, Kwangtung, Kwangsi, Shantung, and Honan had been drawn into the Ministry's system. All these provinces except Kwangtung had been acquired in the wars and struggles with the Kwangsi and Feng groups. But these wars had at the same time sapped the Minister's financial plans

[68] *CYB 1931*, p. 437.

N

and forced him unwillingly to float large numbers of internal government loans. Fukien was the only other province he claimed at this time, and the rest of China, except for the Maritime Customs Service, was beyond his reach.[69] The relative fiscal value of the provinces is not clear, but it is reasonable to think that Kiangsu, Chekiang, and Kwangtung accounted for most of the sums paid in. It is probable, too, that most of the government loans floated between 1927 and 1930 were subscribed to in the Kiangnan area. Nanking was a good choice of capital from this as well as from a military point of view.

Despite the narrow limits of the Centre's effective powers, as opposed to its influence, the border areas were an aspect of the integration or unification policy which attracted an extraordinary amount of attention at this time. The economic and strategic significance of these areas was constantly underlined and the pressures of imperialism were believed to be insistent there, a point of view confirmed by the Sino-Soviet conflict over the Chinese Eastern Railway in the autumn of 1929. Both economic and military considerations were behind the widely discussed idea of settling large-scale colonies of demobilized soldiers along the borders. Schemes of this kind were an invariable part of any discussion of disbandment which, in turn, was the most prominent public issue in 1928. Here again the poverty and impotence of the state prevented action. Conditions in the border areas were, besides, particularly unfavourable at the time. Nanking's intention of integrating these areas was reflected in the creation of several new border provinces, and it was expected that Tibet and Mongolia would follow suit in due course. It is clear that Mongolia included Outer as well as Inner Mongolia. The nationalistic aspect of Nanking's border policy was underlined when the First Plenum (April 1929), in dealing with the resolution on the borders, deleted from the draft the words 'towards self-government and self-determination' which had followed the opening reference to Sun Yat-sen's ideal of helping the weaker peoples.[70]

This interest in the Border Areas leads back to the question of

---

[69] This information on finance is from T. V. Soong's successive statements; for early 1928 see 5th Plenum *Chi-lu*, p. 260. For Jan 1929 see *Ko-ming Wen-hsien*, xxiv. 4871. For Soong's report of March 1930 see *CYB 1931*, pp. 336 ff. On Kwangtung see *NCH*, 4 Aug 1928.

[70] For the new border provinces see below, p. 309. The resolution of Apr 1929 is in 1st Plenum *Chi-lu*, p. 38.

national defence, a very important facet of Nanking's policy. China's armies did not constitute a national defence force since they were so much inferior to any possible foreign enemy, and the policy of disbandment and reorganization was intended to be the first step in the building of a national army. After the Tsinan Incident the government was widely criticized for its 'weakness'. Nationalist opinion was largely in favour of early retaliation against Japan and the unilateral denunciation of the Unequal Treaties, but Nanking policy was completely opposed to both these responses. To deal with this problem the Centre advocated a long-term process of military and economic reconstruction to enable China to retaliate effectively at some date in the future, and it wished to avoid courting disaster by premature action. Chiang Kai-shek, who was already identified with this strategy, believed that it was better to study the way in which Japan had been able to oppress China than to be pushed along by 'useless anger'.[71]

Small beginnings were made in the military field in this period. In August 1928 Chiang spoke of his hopes for 60,000 tons of naval construction over the next decade, and there were also plans to develop an air force. During the autumn the Western press was stirred by news of the arrival in China of German 'industrial experts', who now began to play an important part in Nanking's military programme. An approach was also made to Britain for the loan of naval instructors. Such contacts were made easier when the Treaty Powers lifted the arms embargo of 1919 in April 1929. (This had been designed to deny weapons and military advice to rival militarists and so restrain the civil warfare of the Peiyang era.) Both government and public opinion habitually linked anti-imperialism with rearmament, and government policy in this field had public support, though its corollary, namely great caution in foreign relations, was unpopular. The extended comparison to Meiji Japan which Chiang made in his longest discussion of this problem gives a clue to his outlook. Its wider implications indicate why many Nationalists felt out of sympathy with the Centre.[72]

[71] Speech of 1 Jan 1929 in *Ko-ming Wen-hsien*, xxiv. 4842 (and see also his speeches of 10 Dec 1928 & 14 Jan 1929).
[72] Chiang's speech of 1 Jan 1929 as just cited. For rearmament see *CWR*, 25 Aug 1928, p. 43 (naval), RIIA, *Survey of International Affairs 1928*, p. 396, and F. F. Liu, *A Military History of Modern China* (Princeton, 1956), which devotes some attention to the German mission.

CONCLUSION

The object of this chapter has been to present the policy and character of the Kuomintang in the period in which it first achieved its aim of dominating the politics of China. Our view has been restricted to the formative phase of the Nanking regime, and has not covered the Nanking decade as a whole, which is still a largely uncharted field. During this formative phase the capacities of the Kuomintang were stretched to the utmost, and its limitations and the immensity of the tasks confronting it ensured it a turbulent beginning. The problems faced by the regime in 1928 were indeed formidable and many of them have continued to vex its more vigorous and much better prepared successor.

By 1930 the unpopularity and scant success of the Kuomintang was troubling Hu Han-min, who gave warning that the party's period of tutelage, scheduled to end in 1934, would flash by unless the party became more effective. A sense of urgency was already evident by June 1929 for the Second Plenum attached time-limits for the carrying out of all its important decisions. There is no doubt that its anxiety was well founded.

All sides in the Kuomintang were agreed that the failings of the party were partly to blame for its difficulties. The radicals complained of the corrupting effects of power and territory upon the leaders; the leaders spoke of the ideological confusion and indiscipline of the members and of the residual effects of the communist infection. Ideological confusion was indeed a widely recognized feature of the party, which embraced a broad spectrum of opinion on every important issue. Similarly, factionalism was a marked feature of the Kuomintang. Some factions displayed ideological features or disagreed with others over questions of policy, but many reflected rather the various types of informal relationship which characterized Chinese politics.

The most important development within the Kuomintang in this period was a loss of sympathy between the central leadership and more radical nationalist opinion. Nanking failed to find a useful role for the party, especially by discouraging the mass movements. Even as an auxiliary agency for the promotion of local reform it is doubtful if the party received sufficient funds, protection, and guidance for the task. For the implementation of its programme the Centre preferred to fall back upon the more conventional means of the civil and military bureaucracies and upon the manipulation of existing types of authority. The general policy of compromise in the interests of a distant day of reckoning conflicted so much with Nationalist feeling that restrictive measures had to be applied in order to protect the position of the leading group. There were, no doubt, many other reasons for the trend towards greater autocracy within the party.

The avenue of revolutionary democratic development along the lines which had begun to form by 1927 was closed off. The possibility of a populist and radical national-socialist regime based upon the urban literate elements and the 'minor townsfolk', if such a possibility ever really existed, was not realized either: nor was the aspiration, widely held in the Kuomintang, for strong agrarian support based upon owner-cultivators. The avenue of constitutional or liberal democracy was also closed, at least until the party opposition forced the Centre in November 1930 to make some moves towards the drafting of a constitution. The Japanese pressure after September 1931 gave an added stimulus to this aspect of the Kuomintang programme.

The party's tutelage programme, with its emphasis on the districts and its realization of the need for a dynamic interference in local political life, showed an advance over the more superficial political programmes of the early Republic. It was, however, a programme which required conviction, trained and devoted personnel, and an efficient organization, as well as economic backing, in order to succeed. The tentative beginnings made during the Nanking decade in this important field did not enjoy these benefits. Here, too, the static and bureaucratic approach of the Nanking Centre was a handicap, for by dividing off 'words' and 'work', the significance of political mobilization as the accompaniment, rather than the sequel, to the reconstruction of the country was overlooked. The party's self-appointed task was not merely to reflect popular opinion in the manner of the political parties of 1912, but to arouse it. This was a task requiring a close and continuous attention to mass politics in some form or another.

Finally, it seems more accurate to see the crisis of the National Revolution not as a single traumatic episode in 1927, for the revolutionary movement was by no means synonymous with the communist movement, but as a continuing crisis with a second stage during the years 1928 and 1929. During this second stage a lasting choice between the populist and the etatist strands in Chinese nationalism was made.

February 1967

6

The Chinese Army

JOHN GITTINGS

There can be no salvation for China until the military is brought under proper control. . . . .
Proper control of the military may not mean instant realization of orderly government, but
orderly government is dependent on proper control of the military. China has suffered at
the hands of the militarists in the recent past and still suffers today. She will continue to
suffer unless a future regime is able to dominate instead of being dominated by the mili-
tarists.[1]

THESE words were written by the leading Chinese political
scientist, Ch'ien Tuan-sheng, just over a year before the communist victory of 1949. His remarks had particular relevance for
the Nationalist army, which had shown itself to be incapable of
achieving unity and cohesion even at such a time of dire emergency. They also reflected China's recent experience of endemic
warlordism, which had largely contributed to the failure of the
Republic and of its democratic experiment, and had badly
inhibited effective resistance against the Japanese. Yet although it
is the Nationalist army and the warlords whom Ch'ien's remarks
bring immediately to mind, his warning was not without relevance
to the Chinese communists as well. It is true that their army was a
relatively homogeneous body, with a long tradition of obedience to
party control and unified leadership. But this tradition might still
be dissipated once they were victorious, if the army failed to adapt
to peacetime conditions, or to adjust to the very different kind of
role which would then be required of it. Looking back on the last
seventeen years (in 1966) it is a considerable achievement that

---

[1] Ch'ien Tuan-sheng, 'The Role of the Military in Chinese Government', *Pacific
Affairs*, Sept 1948, p. 251. Cf. also the following remarks by Franz Michael, written
in 1946 ('Chinese Military Tradition', *Far Eastern Survey*, 13 & 27 Mar 1946, p. 87):
'The military unity sought by them [the present Chinese leaders] is not only a matter
of party politics. It depends on a political and social system in which a centralized
program of taxation will replace a local gentry leadership. The restoration of civilian
control over the army will also depend not only on an active participation of the people
in government but on improvements within the military leadership—on the choice of
men of higher education and integrity. Then alone can the Chinese army change from
a dominant factor in the political scene to a tool and servant of the people.'

since 1949 the PLA has, by and large, emerged successfully from this very necessary process of adaptation and adjustment. Although the process is still incomplete, and although many difficulties have arisen and continue to arise, China has at least not been 'dominated by the militarists' since 1949, and is unlikely to be so in the future.[2] This is the theme of this chapter: the way in which the PLA has been transformed from a revolutionary army to an established army of national defence, the difficulties which this transformation has created, especially in the PLA's political and social roles, and the implications of this upon China's military strategy.

CHINA'S MILITARY GEOGRAPHY

The geophysical, political, and economic features of China combine to lend themselves to military regionalism. The sheer size of the country presents a problem which is aggravated by the lack of good communication from north to south. The best lines of communications lie from east to west, along the three major river systems of the Yellow River, the Yangtze, and the West River. Broadly speaking, communication laterally along each river system is infinitely easier than vertically between one and the other. The Hwaiyang mountains seal off Hupeh and the central Yangtze from the Yellow River plain of north China. South China and the West River basin is even more effectively sealed off from the Yangtze region by the Nanling mountains. As one geographer has written, 'the basis of the regional division [of China] is broadly physiographical, i.e. great river basins, plateaux and inland drainage basins. Each region . . . is large; some are immense and are capable of almost infinite sub-division.[3] The relative ease with which China could be divided into lateral sections, as contrasted with the comparative difficulty of maintaining vertical cohesion, goes a long way towards explaining the phenomenon of political division into north and south which China experienced during the Six Dynasties period, during the later half of the Sung dynasty, and for other briefer periods. An important sub-division is the Red Basin of Szechwan, which enabled the Nationalist government to hold out against the Japanese during the anti-Japanese war.

---

[2] For a discussion of the army's role in the Cultural Revolution see below, pp. 220–3.

[3] T. R. Tregear, *A Geography of China* (London 1965), p. 206.

Other sub-divisions with significant political consequences in recent years are the entire north-east, adequately joined to China proper by only a narrow strip of coastal plain at Shanhaikuan, the loess region of north China centred on Shensi province, where the Chinese communists made their base after the Long March, and the southern coast area of the Liang-kuang (Kwangsi and Kwangtung provinces) where the Nationalists made their last stand in 1949. The Mongolian plateau, the Sinkiang basin, and the Tibetan highlands also lend themselves to major sub-divisions, and raise strategic problems from a military point of view of vast magnitude.[4]

The economic and political consequences of China's geographical diversity follow naturally. Centralized supply of food and provisions to military units far from the capital is cumbrous and awkward to arrange. They must therefore be principally supplied from within their own regions unless they are to be inadequately supplied and potentially dissident or ineffective. This may lead to dissent between military leaders and provincial officials on whom the burden of supply will fall. Alternatively, the military leaders may themselves be allowed to levy taxes in order to support their armies. This expedient may solve the supply problem at the price of putting excessive political power into regional military hands. This was the case with the new provincial armies of Li Hung-chang and Tseng Kuo-fan in the 1850s onwards, the forerunners of Yüan Shih-k'ai's New Armies and indirectly of the warlords.

The political consequences are twofold. First, China's geography makes for lack of mobility. There is a tendency for armies to assume the static character of a garrison force, increasingly identified with the region in which they are garrisoned, and reluctant to move outside it. This kind of reluctance greatly impeded Nationalist resistance first against the Japanese, and later against the communists in the civil war. Static disposition of a supposedly national army also encourages inefficiency and corruption among units who have grown comfortable and idle in their garrisons. Secondly, the geographical facts of life make centralized

[4] On Chinese military geography see further E. F. Carlson, *The Chinese Army* (New York, 1940), pp. 6–12. For general descriptions of Chinese geography, see Tregear; see also Theodore Shabad, *China's Changing Map* (London, 1956).

political control of regional units at the same time more important and more difficult to achieve. Even the most impressive system of control on paper may turn out to be grossly defective in practice.

There arises out of these circumstances an inherent contradiction within the handling by the central government of its armed forces. The unresolved question is whether to have a weak army which poses no threat to political stability, or a strong army which does so. The point of equilibrium, at which the army is both strong and receptive to central control, is in practice difficult to arrive at. The methods employed to exercise control themselves may tend to diminish military efficiency and to impair the army's strategic value. A relaxation of control may improve this value, but at the price of diminished political stability. This process is illustrated very clearly by the decline of the Ch'ing dynasty's military apparatus in the first half of the nineteenth century, and by the emergence of the new regional armies in the latter half of that century.

CH'ING MILITARY POLICY

The eight Manchu Banners were the élite fighting force of the Manchus, and were largely responsible for the overthrow of the Ming rulers and the establishment of the new Manchu 'Ch'ing' dynasty in 1644. Originally modelled upon the *wei* garrison system which the Ming dynasty had employed to pacify Manchuria, each Banner was under the separate command of a *Beile* or Manchu imperial prince. It was exclusively responsible in the area under its control for civil administration, taxation, and military service. Once the new dynasty had been established, however, the Ch'ing emperors consistently sought to curtail the Banners' power. Three of the eight Banners had already passed under the emperor's control by the time that the Ch'ing dynasty was inaugurated. The remaining five were taken away from *Beile* control by the Yung Cheng emperor (1723–35). The Banners were garrisoned at key strategic points throughout China, on the frontiers, around Peking in Chihli province, on important waterways (the Yangtze, Grand Canal, &c.), and in provinces of particular strategic significance (Szechwan, Shensi, &c.). They were no longer allowed to control civil administration, and were now a purely military force. Nor was the civil administration itself allowed to control them; a complex system of checks and balances ensured that military and civil powers were evenly matched. The same balancing formula was applied to the division between Manchu and Chinese officials. Thus the Banners both counterbalanced and were counter-balanced by the Chinese 'Green Standard' provincial forces. The Banners were commanded by the Manchu Tartar general, who himself served to keep the power of the provincial governor in check. Members of the Banners were awarded special grants of land and other privileges. They were, however, debarred from seeking employment outside the service. The inevitable con-sequence was that the number of Banner dependants increased as time went on, and their land and pensions became inadequate to support them. By the nineteenth century many Bannermen were said to be reduced to the status of beggars. Hence the isolation of the Banner system as an élite fighting force encouraged its own ossification and decline. The counterbalancing formula also applied within the Banner system itself. Each Banner garrison was 'made up of a mixture of units from different banners, served by their respective banner administrations', writes Franz Michael. 'Even the Manchus' own security force was thus held down by administrative safeguards that could not but hamper its military effectiveness'.[5]

The last military campaign in which the Banners played a prominent part was the Sinkiang campaign of 1755-9. From then on, increasing use was made of the 'Green Standards' or Chinese provincial troops, until they too underwent a process of disintegra-tion similar to that of the Manchu Banners. The Green Standard, it has been written, 'was a great constabulary rather than a combat army'.[6] They were employed in crime prevention and assisted in the transportation of bullion, grain, prisoners, and mail. They were stationed in small units throughout China and were under the control of the Ministry of Defence in Peking. By the time of the T'aip'ing rebellion the Green Standards in turn had degenerated. They were poorly equipped and poorly paid. Their officers embezzled the funds, and padded the pay-rolls, so that by the

---

[5] In his introd. to Stanley Spector, *Li Hung-chang and the Huai Army* (Seattle, 1964), p. xxxii.

[6] Ralph L. Powell, *The Rise of Chinese Military Power, 1895–1912* (Princeton, 1955), p. 13. See further ibid. ch. 1, 'The Chinese Armies Prior to 1895', pp. 3–50, on the Banners and Green Standards. See also Hsieh Pao-chao, *The Government of China, 1644–1911* (Baltimore, 1923); Franz Michael, *The Origin of Manchu Rule in China* (Baltimore, 1942).

beginning of the nineteenth century their real strength may have been less than half that recorded in the books. Training was superficial and based on classical military texts. Discipline was often lax, so that soldiers became virtually indistinguishable from bandits.

While the decline of the Banners and Green Standards partly reflected the more general decline in administrative efficiency of the Ch'ing emperors, it was also an almost inevitable consequence of Ch'ing military policy, which was more concerned to render its armed forces harmless to itself than to maintain them as an efficient fighting force. Besides, until Western powers began to knock at the gates of Canton, no foreign threat existed with which to galvanize the throne into overhauling its military machine. The Banners were deployed as a form of regional internal defence; the Green Standards performed the same function at a local level. The combination of external Western aggression and endemic internal rebellion in the mid-nineteenth century proved too much for the existing military structure.

RISE OF THE WARLORDS

In order to stem the T'aip'ing rebellion, the imperial court was reluctantly forced to sanction the creation of regional armies in the affected areas; Tseng Kuo-fan's Hunan Army (1853), Tso Tsung-t'ang's Ch'u Army (1860), and Li Hung-chang's Anhwei Army (1862). For the first time provincial officials were allowed to raise troops within their own province and to control them without any effective counterbalance from Peking. Personal loyalty was generated as much between the soldier and his general as between the soldier and the emperor. Previously military authority had been the exclusive monopoly of the central government; now it was passing into the hands of the provincial gentry. Furthermore, since Peking persisted in its unwillingness to fund the army adequately, its commanders were often allowed to hold concurrent provincial civil office, and to milk provincial taxes and other sources of revenue.[7]

---

[7] It is not intended to suggest that the powerful provincial armies formed in this period represented, at the time, a threat to the government in Peking, nor that their commanders nourished political ambitions at the expense of the central authorities. As Prof. Mary Wright has observed, 'the leaders of the Hsiang [Hunan] and other new armies were literati, men who had a profound interest in the preservation and strengthening of the existing state'. Professor Wright nevertheless concludes that

Although the picture is complicated by a constant process of disbandment and re-formation, the regional armies of Tseng, Li, and others provided the essential nucleus for the new-style armies or *lu-chün* which emerged at the end of the nineteenth century, and which themselves were the forerunners of the warlord armies of the Republic. Attempts by the throne to resuscitate the Green Standards as an effective counterbalance and to maintain control of the new armies, were generally unsuccessful. Perhaps of greater importance, the officer élite which staffed the new-style armies, many of whom went on to become fully-fledged warlords, originated in the regional armies. Thus Yüan Shih-k'ai, first President of the Republic of 1912 and the foremost military leader, served as a young man with the Anhwei Army of Li Hung-chang, to whom he was linked by family connexions. A complex network of relationships, formed in the new armies before the Republic, joined nearly all of the leaders of the military cliques which helped bring about the Republic's disintegration between 1915 and 1927.

The 1911 revolution itself was very largely the creation of the new armies, and its success mainly determined by the new military class led by Yüan Shih-k'ai. Revolutionary propaganda among the new armies in the south was an important factor, but the decisive factor was Yüan's Peiyang group of armies in the north, which gave him the authority with which to mediate between the throne and the revolutionaries, to secure the dynasty's abdication, and to assume the presidency himself. The Peiyang Army was hardly disaffected at all by revolutionary propaganda, but it nourished entirely non-revolutionary grievances against the throne (over attempts to revive the Banners, inadequate pay, &c.). The foundation of the new Republic rested therefore upon an ambiguous basis; it was avowedly a political revolution, but its course had been largely decided by military leaders who were interested in power rather than reform. This ambiguity became painfully apparent by 1913, with the collapse of the first parliament, the abortive second revolution, and Yüan's steady progress towards the assumption of dictatorial powers. The military grouping on which his authority ultimately depended was itself highly fissionable;

'Certainly the shift of military power to the new armies was potentially dangerous to the central government . . . , and it cannot be denied that they contained the seeds of warlordism' (Mary C. Wright, *The Last Stand of Chinese Conservatism* (New York, 1966), pp. 199, 220–1).

his death in 1915 ushered in a decade of virtual political interregnum in which military cliques proliferated, supported at times by competing foreign powers, and political authority became increasingly fragmented into regional or even provincial military kingdoms.

THE NATIONALIST ARMY

The Nationalist army originated as a small and well-knit revolutionary army, with the Whampoa Military Academy as its central core. A system of political education and control on Soviet lines operated in very much the same way as it subsequently did in the communist army. But unlike the communist army, the KMT's national-revolutionary army never went through the slow process of organic growth which alone could preserve qualitative homogeneity during quantitative expansion. The Northern Expedition of 1926–7 was mounted by a coalition of armies, the KMT core plus its allies. After the success of the Expedition, only one out of the four Army Groups which made up the Nationalist army was chiefly composed of KMT units. The Second was Feng Yü-hsiang's Kuominchün, the Third was Yen Hsi-shan's Shansi Army, and the Fourth was controlled by the Kwangsi group led by Li Tsung-jen. In addition, the Manchurian Army under Chang Hsüeh-liang was still very largely intact and independent of the central government. Within three years of the Northern Expedition, all of these units had rebelled against the central government, although unsuccessfully. The growth of Japanese aggression in Manchuria helped to bring about unity, forcing the Manchurian army closer to the central government. By the mid-1930s unity appeared at long last to have been achieved. But it was an artificial unity which was based upon compromise and upon the need to come together against a common enemy. It had not been organically achieved, and this being so, it necessitated the use by Chiang Kai-shek of the familiar divide-and-rule tactics. F. F. Liu, author of the standard work on this period, has written that

In the ministry of war, whether it was deliberately planned or not, an intricate system of checks and balances seems to have existed. A minister's power could be balanced by vice-ministers and strategically placed bureau chiefs who could be counted on to keep an eagle eye on the minister's loyalty to the ruling interest. . . . The whole military organization suffered from the fear, weakness, and indecision of its central administration.

And he concludes that 'in the hands of the president alone rested the one opportunity of ultimate military coordination'.[8] This concentration of power was essential for unity but destructive of efficiency. It led to the blind overruling of better-informed subordinates, about which American advisers so frequently complained both in the war against Japan and in the civil war. This led in turn to lack of initiative and factionalism at lower levels. The origins of the Nationalist army as a coalition of convenience were never entirely shaken off. There are numerous examples where government forces from different factions failed to aid each other. Strong armies were featherbedded by their provincial leaders while weak armies were annihilated next door. Rivalry in particular between the KMT core and the Kwangsi clique was a constant factor, emerging into the open in the last year of civil war, when Li Tsung-jen's last-ditch stand along the Yangtze was fatally hamstrung by lack of support from the Chiang-controlled air force and navy.

Two major *lacunae* in particular arise directly from the disparate origins of the Nationalist army. First was its inability to demobilize a chronic excess of manpower. Attempts to do this had led to the rebellions of 1929–30. Although these were defeated, Chiang was never strong enough to demobilize those whom he had beaten. Japanese aggression provided a convenient reason to defer demobilization indefinitely. But throughout the anti-Japanese and civil wars, the Nationalist army was too large for the job; quality was sacrificed for quantity—another frequent complaint of American advisers. Thus in 1946 at the start of the civil war, the Nationalist army was believed (no accurate figures were ever available) to number some 5 million men. Only $1\frac{1}{2}$ million—less than a third —could be considered as first-line troops. Until the autumn of 1948, less than a year before the final communist victory, this meaningless numerical superiority over the communist army was maintained.

Secondly, the Soviet system of political departments and political commissars which had been followed in the National Revolutionary Army before 1927 seems to have disappeared in the

---

[8] *A Military History of Modern China, 1924–49* (Princeton, 1956), pp. 69–70.

wake of the Northern Expedition. This may have partly been a result of the purge in 1927 of the communists, many of whom had great influence in the political structure. It is also clear that the political network could not keep pace with rapid KMT expansion, nor could it be extended into the allied armies of the coalition. Furthermore, it appears to have been a casualty of the deliberate switch-over from 1928 onwards from the Soviet military model to that of Germany. German technical assistance and instructors began to mould the Nationalist army, and increasing numbers of Chinese officers went to study at military academies in Germany. As F. F. Liu writes, 'The outlook of the early Whampoa days drifted towards a pattern more closely resembling the orthodox plan of Western military schools'.[9] KMT party branches were widespread in the army, but their purpose was to control the military leadership rather than to educate and inspire the rank and file. This was perhaps the most significant area of difference between the Nationalist and communist armies.

ORIGINS OF THE COMMUNIST ARMY

The CCP was founded in 1921, at a time when the mutual rivalries of China's provincial warlords were at their peak. The party allied itself with the KMT led by Sun Yat-sen, which itself was in the process of building up sufficient military power with which to challenge the warlords' rule. In 1926 the KMT armies and their allies, now led by Chiang Kai-shek after the death of Sun Yat-sen in 1925, launched the Northern Expedition against the warlord cliques and achieved a greater measure of national unity than at any time since 1915. In 1927 Chiang Kai-shek, supported by the right wing of the KMT, conducted a bloody purge of his party's left wing and of the Communist Party.[10]

The lesson of this period of 'United Front' with the KMT was a simple but hard one. No political party could effectively survive in China without military backing. After a series of abortive attempts to capture towns or to organize urban risings, the CCP's centre of gravity shifted to the countryside, where it was to remain for the next twenty years. At first, in the southern province of Kiangsi, where from 1930–4 the CCP organized a Soviet Republic and held out against repeated Nationalist 'pacification campaigns', then during the 'Long March' to Shensi in the north (1934–6), and

[9] Liu, p. 83.   [10] See above, pp. 149 ff.

finally during the anti-Japanese war (1937–45), by the end of which communist areas in north and central China controlled some 100 million of the population,[11] communist political power depended in the last analysis upon their military strength. Political power, as Mao Tse-tung had said, 'grows out of the barrel of the gun'.

By the end of the anti-Japanese war, the communist army had expanded from approximately 80,000 in 1937 to 900,000 in 1945.[12] Communist territorial holdings in north China and Manchuria put them in a powerful bargaining position during the subsequent peace talks with the KMT, and when these broke down, enabled them to emerge victorious from the civil war which followed (1946–9).

Very little work has yet been done on the political and social roles and the essential structure of the communist Red Army[13] in the Kiangsi Soviet period. A mass of relevant material waits to be examined in the Ch'en Ch'eng papers and other primary sources. By the time of the anti-Japanese war, we can single out three distinctive features of the communist army which contributed materially to its success. These were the political control and education system, its social policies towards the civilian population, and its reliance upon popular mobilization. All three features had been present in varying degrees during the Kiangsi Soviet, and had been formulated even earlier by Mao Tse-tung in 1928–9. How far and how consistently they were put into practice is another matter. Official communist history claims that during the period of the three 'Left' lines, i.e. while Mao himself was not as yet undisputed leader of the CCP, his theories on 'people's war' were not fully implemented. In particular, the people's militia and the political structure were allowed to lapse.[14] While this may well be

[11] See below, p. 226.

[12] For statistics of communist military strength during the anti-Japanese war see Gittings, *The Role of the Chinese Army* (London, 1967), p. 303.

[13] The communist army was officially known as the Red Army during the Kiangsi Soviet and the Long March. From 1937 until the end of the anti-Japanese war it was identified by its two components as officially recognized in the United Front with the KMT, i.e. the Eighth Route Army in north China and the New Fourth Army in central China. In 1946 at the start of the civil war it adopted the title of People's Liberation Army, by which it has since been known.

[14] See the claim in *Liberation Army Daily*, editorial, 1 July 1958, 'Hold aloft the banner of the party committee system', that the 'system of party leadership' was abolished by the 'third Leftist line' during the later stage of the second revolutionary war (trans. in *SCMP*, no. 1881). See also criticism of the military policies of the three

o

an exaggeration, it is reasonable to suppose that in its early days, and under pressure first of KMT encirclement and then of the Long March, there were defects in the army's approach to these matters. It was not until the process of consolidation in Shensi under the United Front had begun that the revolutionary model for the army was constructed in all its details. It is perhaps significant that post-liberation panegyrics on the glorious revolutionary history of the PLA hark back almost without exception to the anti-Japanese war and no earlier. The Long March is cited as an example of heroism and struggle and of Mao Tse-tung's inspired leadership, without special emphasis on the army as such. Similarly, accounts of the Kiangsi Soviet period use the army's record in order to illustrate extraneous themes rather than to glorify the army itself and its leadership.

The crucial formative period of the communist army was therefore essentially that of the anti-Japanese war. This is not necessarily to say that without the stimulus of Japanese aggression the CCP would never have been able to reach the take-off point for expansion and consolidation, nor that it was of decisive importance in contributing to their ultimate victory. There is no doubt that resistance against Japan provided a common cause with which the CCP and the civilian population could jointly identify, or that the KMT–CCP United Front, which created a breathing-space for the communists in Shensi, stemmed directly from the outbreak of formal war with Japan in 1937. But the take-off point might well have been reached, although admittedly under much more difficult conditions, even if the circumstances had been different. It was primarily the rectification of the party under Maoist leadership, the sinification of Marxism to a more specific Chinese form, and the adoption of popular social and economic policies, including those of the army, which provided the essential basis on which the communists were able to build. It is probable that some such process of rectification and readjustment would have occurred in any case, once the Yenan regime had been established and Mao's undisputed leadership of the CCP had allowed him for the first time to put his theories fully into practice. It is also probable that the political and economic decline of the Nationalist government

<hr />

'Left' lines in Mao Tse-tung, 'Resolution on certain questions in the history of our party' (adopted by the enlarged 7th plenary session of the 6th CCP central committee, 20 Apr 1945) (*Selected Works*, iii (Peking, 1965), pp. 205–8).

would have continued, although at a slower pace, thus generating popular resentment and unrest which favoured the communist cause.

Nevertheless, regardless of what might have occurred, it is a fact that the moulding of the army's revolutionary blueprint took place very largely during the anti-Japanese war. The vital time-span can indeed be narrowed even further, to the 'hard years' of KMT blockade and constant Japanese pressure which followed the communists' Hundred Regiments' offensive of autumn 1940, and which were not relaxed until mid-1944, when Japan once more turned her attention to the KMT in central China. It was during these years that the main lines of the army's social and economic policies were established, that the militia and People's Self-Defence Corps were put on a sound footing, and that the system of political education and control was radically overhauled.

During this period of revolution, the CCP went a long way towards reconciling the three basic contradictions which had traditionally weakened and at times crippled Chinese military policy.

(a) MILITARY AND POLITICAL UNITY

The failure of the democratic experiments of the Republic and the growth of the provincial warlords was primarily due to the lack of unity between China's political and military leadership. The history of the CCP, however, shows a remarkable lack of military-political conflict. (This occurred only at times of great stress, for example, immediately after the purge of 1927 and during the 'Long March'.) The system of dual party and military command was applied to the Red Army from its outset, with political groups and commissars down to company level. It was revived and strengthened during the rectification movement of 1942 onwards. Perhaps more important, in the circumstances of resistance against the Japanese and of civil war, military and political objectives tended to coincide, thus helping to eliminate potential conflict. Furthermore, almost all the top CCP leaders held concurrently military and political positions. The year 1942 also saw the introduction of a movement for 'military democracy' among the army rank and file, whose object was to improve relations between officers and men, and to create a larger measure of political awareness at basic levels.

(b) MILITARY AND POPULAR UNITY

In imperial China the military was widely held in disfavour. There was a saying that 'good iron is not used to make nails; good men are not used to make soldiers'. The warlord and KMT armies did little to change this attitude. By contrast, the CCP made consistent attempts to promote good relations between army and people. Theft, rape, looting, enforced conscription, &c., were not only prohibited in theory but to a large extent in practice (though there were, of course, exceptions). This policy was not only desirable but vital to the continued existence of the CCP. The communist armies depended for support and for recruits upon popular goodwill. They were not garrison armies; they lived on and in the countryside. Peasant opposition would make their situation untenable. The army must live among the people, in Mao's simile, 'as the fish swim in water'. During the worst years of the anti-Japanese war, regular army units turned from fighting to the fields 'with a hoe in one hand and a gun in the other', and were exhorted to make themselves economically self-sufficient. Special procedures were also created to ensure that civilian grievances against the army were remedied.

(c) POPULAR MOBILIZATION

Another characteristic of imperial and Nationalist China was a reluctance to put arms in the hands of the peasantry. Such arms had a habit of being turned against their donors. In the early days of the CCP there was a similar reluctance. But during the anti-Japanese war, popular guerrilla and militia forces played an increasingly important role in regional defence.

Regular army units were subject to transfer from one communist area to another. But within each area a local guerrilla force was organized to a strength of as much as 50 per cent of the regular forces. In addition, an armed militia force of approximately 5 per cent of the population was responsible for internal security, sabotage and local defence against the Japanese. This was supplemented by the People's Self-Defence Corps—numbering some 10 per cent of the population, which was primarily a civil defence organization. These popular organizations also provided a reservoir of manpower for the regular army.[15]

[15] For more detailed discussion of the military–political and military–popular

LIBERATION AND AFTER

Thus in 1949, when the Chinese communists came to power, their military machine was in much better shape and more firmly under their control than those of most other revolutionary movements. Its loyalty to the Communist Party and the machinery for enforcing it had been tested by twenty years of civil war. It was a homogeneous body with traditions and a mystique of its own, and it could draw upon a considerable reserve of popular goodwill and support. Nevertheless, by the very act of victory, it entered upon a new phase and a new role in which it had little or no experience. By exchanging its revolutionary role for one of national defence, it severed the most important bond of unity with the Communist Party and with the people—the sense of common identity and struggle which had permeated the communist areas and linked army, party, and people together in the revolutionary period. It was not simply a question of how the army would adapt to its new role as guardian of China's national defence; it was also a question of how the party leadership itself would view the army's status and position in the People's Republic.

One of the special features of China since 1949 is the way in which policies once formulated are applied across the board to all sectors of society and at all levels of organization. It is therefore extremely difficult to talk about the Communist Party's policy towards the army—or towards any other professional group in China—in isolation from its nation-wide policy at any particular time. The structure of the policy-making hierarchy is a vertical one, with the central committee at its apex. Any decision of the central committee which is remotely relevant to society at large— and there are very few which are not—will be passed down through the usual channels to the General Political Department of the PLA for implementation. This would apply equally to, for instance, a decision to promote the study of the works of Chairman Mao, and to a decision to promote a movement for the destruction of flies, sparrows, and other pests.

It is therefore more than usually fruitless to talk about 'military policy' in a vacuum. One can only talk about military policy as a component part of the totality of policy formulation. This

relationships, and of popular mobilization, during the anti-Japanese war, see Gittings, pp. 48–61, 111–16.

indeed is the key to our understanding of the role of the PLA, as its story since 1949 is to a large extent the story of the way in which its own priorities, demands, and requirements have at some times coincided with overall policy and at other times have conflicted with it. There are also occasions when military considerations play the decisive part in the formulation of overall policy. On other occasions, military considerations appear to have been devalued or even shelved.

Bearing this in mind, we can identify two basic sets of policies which have affected the PLA's role since 1949. The first set of policies places top priority upon politico-military goals, either internally, or more usually in foreign policy. This was the situation during the Korean war, when all other aspects of Chinese policy were subordinated to the needs of the Korean front. The second and more frequent set of policies places the higher priority on domestic politico-economic goals. This was the case during the Great Leap Forward, when the PLA's requirements were subordinated almost entirely to those of the great economic and social revolution which swept the Chinese countryside. There are also periods of relative equilibrium when overall policy is neither dominated by military requirements nor does it conflict with them to any significant degree.

Against this variable background of the changing status of the armed forces on the ladder of policy priorities, we can set the permanent factors which affect the role of the PLA in China. Firstly, its internal health in terms of morale and relations between enlisted men and officers, which affects its performance and loyalty to the government. Secondly, its relations with the Communist Party, both between its personnel and those of the party, and in its understanding of and support for particular party policies. Thirdly, its relations with the civilian population, the strain which it throws upon civilian resources, or the way in which such strain is alleviated; and the social popularity which it enjoys or the hostility or apathy which it arouses. These are the permanent factors which, as has been pointed out, are inherent in the role of any Chinese army.[16]

---

[16] It should be added that the interrelationship of the above-mentioned permanent factors and variable background raises some problems. One would assume, for instance that relations between the army and the people were good during the Korean war and bad in subsequent years, since little criticism is voiced of them until the war is

It may therefore be useful to look first of all at the way in which military policy has intermeshed with national policy since 1949, and the difficulties which this has created. Secondly, we shall consider the exact relations between the army and the people, within the army itself, and between the army and party. Or to use the short-hand phrases employed in Chinese: army–people, officer–men, and army–party relations.

THE PLA AND NATIONAL POLICY

If a graph were constructed of the PLA's position in the order of priorities since 1949, it would show a series of waves—a short dip during the first half of 1950, when plans were begun for its participation in production work and for partial demobilization, followed by a swift rise to an all-time high priority peak during the Korean war. The line descends very gradually and almost imperceptibly in 1954–5, the period when the army was being reorganized along the Soviet model, although its needs were no longer of such paramount importance as during the Korean war. From 1956 to 1959 the line descends at an increasingly sharper angle, as ever more demands are made upon it for participation in non-military tasks, and its professional status comes under critical scrutiny. The period 1958–9 sees an all-time low, with the PLA heavily criticized for alleged 'deviations', and the Minister of Defence himself dismissed for 'right opportunism' in September of 1959. Since 1959, under the new Minister Lin Piao, the graph has shown a steady improvement, until by 1964 the entire Chinese nation was exhorted to 'learn from the achievements of the PLA'. Political control of the PLA, and its participation in non-military tasks, continued to be insisted upon, yet these demands on it were harmonized with its own requirements in such a way as to avoid excessive strain between the two. By 1964 the graph could be said to have reached a temporary state of equilibrium, although by 1965–6 it was again starting to show signs of imbalance.

To recapitulate the course of events outlined above in more detail: After liberation in the autumn of 1949, the new government

over. But one must take into account the shift in policy priorities. During the war, the PLA's behaviour towards civilians was regarded with much greater tolerance because its role was valued so highly. After the war its role became subject to successive devaluation until it was the target of persistent criticism. Yet its actual behaviour over the entire period had not necessarily altered as drastically as might be supposed.

of the CPR was faced with a major problem of reconverting the economic and social fabric of China to a peacetime footing. This problem had been accentuated by the very speed of the PLA's success in winning the civil war over the previous three years. Victory had come far more quickly than the communist leadership had anticipated. As late as the summer of 1948, Mao Tse-tung and his colleagues still thought the civil war would last until at least 1951. They did not expect the Nationalist armies to collapse with such demoralizing speed as they did during the following autumn and winter of 1948–9. This collapse had two important consequences; first, the communists gained possession of the overwhelming part of the Chinese mainland with such rapidity that they were hard put to it to find the necessary personnel and administration with which to govern their newly acquired responsibilities. Secondly, because such a large proportion of the Nationalist armies surrendered or were captured without a fight, and were therefore incorporated into the PLA, the PLA's size attained vast dimensions—some 5 million by 1950, of whom well over half had defected from the KMT in the last year and a half.[17] To put it crudely, fewer soldiers had been killed than expected; the problem of resettlement and of demobilization was that much greater.

The top priority for 1950, repeatedly emphasized in government statements, was therefore 'national reconstruction'. Already in December 1949 the PLA had been ordered to devote as much of its manpower as possible to productive work—reclaiming land, building irrigation dykes, laying roads and railway tracks, whatever work suited the needs of the locality and the skills of the military units stationed there. It was also decided to make plans for large-scale demobilization, although their implementation was not felt to be feasible until 1951. For the time being, the great majority of military and civil government employees, whether communist or ex-Nationalist, were to be kept on an official payroll which now totalled 9 million employees, rather than risk social upheaval and mass unemployment by their dismissal. But by June

[17] PLA strength increased from 1,278,000 in June 1946 to 1,950,000 (June 1947), 2,800,000 (June 1948), 4,000,000 (June 1949), 5,000,000 (June 1950). According to PLA claims, a total of 4,586,750 KMT troops were captured during the civil war and a further 1,773,490 surrendered or changed sides. Over 75 per cent of these KMT losses occurred in the final years 1948–50. The figures may be inflated, but they probably convey the right order of magnitude (Chang Chün-ying, *Ko-ming yü fan-ko-ming ti chüeh-chan* (Peking, 1961), p. 113; see also Gittings, Table 2, p. 304).

1950, plans for demobilization of PLA men had been speeded up. Mao Tse-tung told the central committee that the PLA should demobilize 'part of its troops' in that same year. The 'main forces' of the PLA were to be kept under arms to carry out the unfinished military business still on hand—the suppression of bandits and other forms of armed opposition still at large on the mainland, the occupation of Tibet, and the liberation of Taiwan.[18] By the 'main forces', Mao probably meant the regular or first-line PLA units totalling some $2\frac{1}{2}$ million. As many again were therefore scheduled for demobilization.

These plans were brought almost to a sharp halt by the Korean war and China's intervention. Production work by the PLA was virtually suspended throughout China, except for the north-west province of Sinkiang where a special Production Corps of semi-demobilized soldiers was engaged in reclamation of barren land. Elsewhere production became at best a 'spare-time activity' performed in token quantities for the sake of good public relations. Demobilization was halted, and some troops who had already been released from service were recalled. Although demobilization of those no longer capable of service was apparently resumed in the next year, the Chinese People's Volunteers in Korea required the raising of replacements, and I have estimated elsewhere that during the course of the Korean war between $1\frac{1}{2}$ and 2 million soldiers were recruited for service either in the PLA or CPV.[19]

The effects of the Korean war upon the PLA can hardly be exaggerated, both with regard to its modernization and professionalization, and to its relations with the party and with the civilian population'.[20]

As far as the PLA was concerned, the Korean war helped to

---

[18] Mao Tse-tung, 'The struggle for a basic turn for the better in the financial and economic situation of the state', 6 June 1950, NCNA (London), Spec. Suppl. 50, 16 June 1950.

[19] Gittings, ch. 6.

[20] Nor have I space to consider the wider consequences of the war upon China's domestic and foreign policy. One can only suggest that in domestic politics, the war brought about a rapid intensification of land reform, and contributed largely to the series of oppressive campaigns against political nonconformity in China—the 'suppression of counter-revolutionaries', the '3 & 5-antis', and the like (see also below, pp. 272 f.). In foreign policy, the war drove China closer into the arms of the Soviet Union, widened the chasm between China and the West, destroyed all hope of better understanding between China and the US, and by preventing the return of Formosa to Chinese hands helped to create a permanent block to the normalization of China's position in Asia,

raise its status once again, and to ensure that the modernization of China's armed forces, which had been endorsed in principle in the Common Programme announced at the formation of the People's Republic, would begin to take effect. The Korean war was directly responsible for the re-equipment of the PLA with modern weapons systems, for the wide range of military training colleges which were hastily set up or expanded to meet the need for qualified officers and n.c.o.s, for changes towards a more complex staff structure with centralized control in Peking—in short, for the creation of a more sophisticated and professional PLA, adequately equipped with Soviet arms and modelled on the pattern of the Soviet Red Army. In 1954 a number of reforms were introduced which broke completely with the past. An annual draft system was put into effect, bringing in between 500,000 and 700,000 recruits a year for an average of three years' service, so that once the system had completed its first rotation, as much as three-fifths of the PLA was composed of short-term conscripts.[21] A fully articulated system of ranks and insignia was instituted for the officers, with all the epaulettes, badges, and other paraphernalia which distinguishes a regular army. In 1955 military awards were bestowed on those senior officers who had been singled out for meritorious service during the revolution. A new disciplinary code was promulgated which stressed loyalty and unquestioning obedience rather than the old revolutionary concept of 'military democracy'. Some veteran elements in the PLA opposed these innovations on the grounds that they were incompatible with its traditions, but others, especially the new generation of young officers who had been trained during the Korean war in the new military academies, appear to have welcomed the privileges and *esprit de corps* of a modern-style army.

But the PLA'S enhanced status during the Korean war helped to bring about its own reversal as China returned to peacetime conditions when the war was over. In the first place, the PLA's modernization and re-styling had been closely associated with the Soviet Union, which provided the necessary aid and advice. This meant that the position of the PLA would in future be vulnerable

---

[21] The terms of service were army—3 yrs; air force—4 yrs; navy—5 yrs. In 1965, these were extended by one year each, except for the special arms and the public security forces of the army (extended by 2 years), and the shore arms of the navy (remained the same).

to any political changes resulting from a deterioration in Sino-Soviet relations, since it would to some extent be regarded as pro-Soviet and as a partly Soviet creation. Secondly, during the Korean war the PLA had necessarily lost some of its popular character, and this was further dissipated by the trend towards professionalization.

From 1956 onwards, therefore, a number of different pressures combined to bring about a devaluation of the PLA's role, and to increase criticism of it by the party leadership. There was the simple fact that under peacetime conditions military requirements were accorded a lower priority. For instance military expenditure had more than doubled between 1950 and 1955. By 1958 it had fallen again by almost one-quarter.[22] There was the growing alienation between army and party, and also the deteriorating relations with the civilian population. Professionalization, combined with the new disciplinary code and the replacement of revolutionary veterans by conscript soldiers, had led to some estrangement between officers and rank and file. The policy of taking the Soviet army as the 'model' for the PLA had also been carried to excess. In many cases, the form but not the substance of the Soviet model appears to have been copied, so that bureaucracy and stereotyped manœuvres led to inferior leadership and loss of efficiency.

The seriousness of these developments should not however be exaggerated. It is very doubtful whether army–party and army–people relations deteriorated to such an extent as was later alleged, or whether the Soviet model proved so totally inappropriate as was later claimed. More important perhaps was the fact that the form which the army was assuming, that of a regular professional army concerned exclusively with national defence, jarred with the basic concept to which China's veteran leadership still clung of what a communist army should be like. This was part of the whole trend in the late 1950s away from the mechanical application of foreign experience back to specifically Chinese and 'revolutionary' models. It was the same dynamic which powered the Great Leap

[22] Military budgetary expenditure rose from 2,827 m. *yuan* in 1950 to 6,500 m. in 1955, when it represented just under 25 per cent of total expenditure. By 1958 it had fallen to 5,000 m. or 15·1 per cent. It rose again to 5,826 m. in 1960, but continued to decline as compared to total expenditure (8·3 per cent). No figures are available since 1960. It is probable that expenditure on nuclear weapons development is totally excluded from these figures. See further Gittings, *Chinese Army*, Table 7, p. 309.

Forward. The PLA was also affected by changes in strategic planning brought about by loss of confidence in the Soviet Union as the Sino-Soviet rift deepened.

At first the Chinese leadership attempted to solve the difficulties which had arisen in the PLA by the wholesale application of measures which had proved effective in the revolutionary period. It was made to take part in production on a massive scale, to practise all kinds of economies, both trivial and fundamental, often at the expense of military efficiency. 'Military democracy' was revived and almost carried to excess, with officers going to the ranks and humbling themselves before the rank and file in a way which was no doubt good for the soldiers' morale but probably bad for their own. When the Great Leap was launched in the autumn of 1958, the 'Everyone a Soldier' movement was also launched as part of it, with a quite unrealistic target of enrolling every able-bodied man and woman into the militia, arming them and training them.

Most of these reforms and innovations seem only to have worsened the situation, creating the very antagonism between army and party which they were intended to prevent. This was not so much the fault of the reforms themselves as of the headlong pace and indiscriminate way in which they were carried out. These were of course the same defects which brought the whole of the Great Leap Forward grinding to a halt.

In September 1959 the Minister of Defence, P'eng Teh-huai, was dismissed together with a handful of his senior staff. He is believed to have both opposed the measures enacted against the PLA and favoured closer co-operation with the Soviet Union in the military sphere. Negotiations designed to secure Soviet aid for China's nuclear weapons programme had broken down shortly before, and P'eng may have been held responsible for their failure. It was now clear that China would have to 'go it alone' in defence. Her strategic arrangements since then have centred on three objectives; first, to acquire her own independent nuclear capability, secondly, to build up the militia, although on a less ambitious scale than originally envisaged, and thirdly to restore the PLA's morale and political reliability.

This last has been achieved by essentially the same policy as had been tried before, but it is now applied with more intelligence. For the PLA, as well as for the rest of Chinese society, it is a case of 'back to the revolution', and the old customs and traditions of the revolutionary struggle have been revived. The policy appears to have been successful primarily for two reasons: first because measures are no longer taken to excess—army production work, for instance, has fallen steadily year by year; and secondly because a major effort has been made to secure the individual loyalty and commitment to the regime and its policies of the rank and file soldier at the basic company level.

The party organization at the basic company level has been completely overhauled. In 1960 it was discovered that 60 per cent of the companies within the PLA had no company party branch and a similar number of platoons had no party cell. These have now been re-established. The Soldiers' Committee—a democratically elected body which had been popular during the revolution but had later been allowed to lapse—was also revived. The role at company level of the Young Communist League in acting as a political 'spearhead' was also re-defined. And the post of Company Political Commissar, with special responsibilities for political education and ideological work, was also restored. The company was now seen as the most sensitive link in the political chain which leads from the Military Affairs Committee of the central committee right down to the individual soldier, and whose party branch and personnel must be kept in good health.

The content of political education has also been enlarged to include almost every aspect, however trivial, of the average soldier's life. It is almost impossible to exaggerate the variety of subjects, ranging from the most important to the most mundane, which are now embraced under the heading of political education. It may include the way in which a cook prepares the meals for a company mess, as well as the way to educate the rank and file to the significance of the latest polemic against Khrushchevite revisionism. The *Selected Works* of Chairman Mao, especially the fourth volume which deals with the civil war period, are studied intensively, both privately and in classes throughout the PLA.[23]

Mao's works are the canon or bible in which guidance may be

---

[23] The choice of the fourth volume is of particular interest, since it underlines the way in which the Chinese leadership sees a direct analogy between its position in the civil war, when it 'relied upon its own resources' and fought the KMT with no outside help, and today, when once again self-reliance is the key-note of Chinese economic and foreign policies, and China stands in splendid isolation with both major powers as potential enemies.

sought and found for every problem whether trivial or important. The revolutionary period is the historical myth, whose story provides countless object lessons in how to maintain revolutionary standards today. If young soldiers are tempted to forget the need for vigilance or to relax in the more comfortable conditions of peacetime, they are reminded of the 'bitterness of things past' by veterans who remember the hard days before 1949 better than they do.

This return to the revolutionary model, or the socialist education movement as it is known, far from being confined to the army in China today, is standard procedure for every segment of Chinese society.[24] It is part of the struggle to combat 'revisionism' at home, to encourage the emergence of 'revolutionary successors', and to substitute an indigenous model and pattern of behaviour instead of the foreign models—especially those of the Soviet Union —which were absorbed in the 1950s. Its application to the army is, however, of special interest, because one would have expected a modernized and professional army to be less receptive to the moral exhortations and emphasis on doctrinal purity embodied in the socialist education movement. Far from this being so, from 1960 onwards, the army appears to have been used as a test-bed in which the revolutionary model was intensively applied before being more generally practised among the people at large. Here again there is an analogy with the revolutionary period, when the Red Army was itself perhaps the most important engine of social change.

The party's success in strengthening its control over the army and in raising the PLA's level of political awareness was impressive. By February 1963, after two and a half years of intensive work, new regulations on political control were introduced which raised the status of the political commissar and relegated that of the military commander to little more than an executive officer without powers of decision-making.[25] The fact that these new regulations could be introduced without apparent dissent from the officer corps suggests that the party already had the latter well under control. Final proof of the rehabilitation of the PLA in the

[24] See also below, pp. 270, 279 ff.
[25] See *Liberation Army Daily*, 8 May 1963, editorial, 'Raise aloft the great red banner of the thought of Mao Tse-tung, resolutely implement regulations governing PLA political work', 10 May 1963 (*SCMP* 2984).

party's favour came in February 1964, when the entire Chinese nation was exhorted to 'learn from the experience of the PLA in political and ideological work'. Movements such as the 'Five-Good' emulation contest for the individual soldier, and the parallel 'Four-Good' campaign for army companies were extended into civilian life.[26] Army cadres and demobilized army officers were detached to take up positions in industry and commerce, bringing the PLA's 'revolutionary style of work' to bear upon sensitive sectors of the country's economy.

Yet although the party strengthened its control over the PLA to an unparalleled extent, it also took care not to infringe upon its prestige. The party had evidently learnt from the mistakes made in 1956–9 when it first attempted to 'rectify' the 'deviations' to which it objected in the PLA. It no longer expected the army to take part in a variety of mass campaigns without regard for their effect on efficiency or their intrinsic value. Army participation in production work, for instance, declined from 59 million man-days in 1959—or nearly a month per soldier—to $5\frac{1}{2}$ million— about two days per soldier—in 1964. Frugality and economy in personal life among the army continued to be urged, but the sort of major cuts in the PLA's budget and equipment which were imposed in 1957–8 were no longer inflicted. The army was no longer openly criticized for unsatisfactory behaviour; on the contrary, it was praised to the skies and offered as a model sector of society.

If this account of the PLA were to stop short at 1964, its rehabilitation over the previous four years under the leadership of Marshal Lin Piao might almost be regarded as an unqualified success story. But there have been increasing signs since 1964 of a recurrence of party dissatisfaction with the PLA, and of opposition within the PLA to the new anti-revisionist militancy of the party leadership. Party leaders have denounced 'the revisionist military line', and have criticized 'those whose heads are crammed full of foreign doctrines'. The charge that bourgeois elements within the PLA are opposed to party leadership has been revived. In June 1965 it was decided to abolish formal ranks within the PLA, and

---

[26] The 'Five-Good' movement of 1958 called for good performance in study, care of weapons, practice of economy and production and physical training; the goal of the 'Four-Good' movement of 1961 was to be good in political thought, in working style, in military training, and in management of living.

to revert to the single and functional distinction of revolutionary days whereby there were only two ranks—'Commanders' (officers) and 'Fighters' (rank and file). It was explained that this would help to 'eliminate certain objective factors contributing to breed class consciousness and ideas to gain fame and wealth'.[27] By the beginning of 1966 it was acknowledged that 'the question of whether the gun will direct the Party or the Party will direct the gun' had still to be finally settled.[28] The militia, which itself had made a comeback of sorts in 1964–5, and had been praised as the spearhead of the class struggle, also came in for criticism. 'Class enemies' and 'bourgeois tendencies' were said to be at large within its ranks.[29]

A full explanation of this decline in army–party relations must take into account the general increase in the quantity and intensity of anti-revisionist class struggle throughout all sectors of Chinese society since 1963–4. In this respect, the army has fared no worse in the class struggle, and if anything, the tone of party criticism against it is relatively mild, as compared with that of criticism against 'poisonous weeds of revisionism' in literature and art. Indeed, the use of the official army newspaper as the leading vehicle for attacks against literary revisionism suggests a continuing degree of confidence in the army itself. The charges of military revisionism are also much milder than the similar accusations of 'deviations' which were levelled against the army in 1956–9.

The causes of continuing army–party tension arise out of the nature of the relationship itself, as well as out of specific disagreements over policy. First, there is a built-in instability factor in the continual struggle by the party to maintain control over the army. We have seen that this struggle produces a series of oscillations, with relatively rare periods of equilibrium. The equilibrium was temporarily reached by the movement of 1960–4 for intensive political control and education, but this movement contained in itself the seeds of disequilibrium. First, because it restored the

---

[27] The military rank system was abolished by decision of the State Council as from 1 June 1965. See *Liberation Army Daily*, 25 May 1965, editorial, 'An important measure for promoting further the revolutionization of our army', NCNA (Peking), 24 May 1965. Distinguishing insignia, uniforms and epaulettes were also abolished.

[28] Hsiao Hua, director of Gen. Political Dept, report of Jan 1966 to PLA political conference, NCNA, 24 Jan 1966, trans. in BBC, *Summary of World Broadcasts*, pt 3, no. 2071.

[29] Hsu Li-ch'ing, deputy director of Gen. Political Dept, quoted in *New York Times*, 13 Apr 1966.

army's self-confidence to a point, symbolized by the 'Learn from the Army' campaign of 1964, where such self-confidence could easily degenerate into over-confidence and impatience with party interference. Significantly, it is since the 'Learn from the Army' campaign that criticism of the army has been revived, and the first charge which was levelled against it was one of arrogance and complacency in the wake of the campaign. Thus the army Chief of Staff complained that 'acclamations from the outside have promoted self-assurance, complacency and stagnancy among some of our comrades'.[30] Secondly, the very intensity of the political-control and education campaigns tends in time to produce an unfavourable reaction, if carried to excess, leading to the attitude criticized in January 1966 by the army's Political Department Director, that 'military affairs and politics should be given first place in turn'.[31] There are some indications that the innumerable emulation campaigns and movements to study Mao's writings which have been launched in the army during 1965–6 have become counter-productive.

We are now in a position to look back at the three distinctive features of the revolutionary army which were referred to earlier, namely the army–people, officer–men, and army–party relations, and to see how far they have survived since Liberation.

(a) ARMY–PEOPLE RELATIONS

Of the three relations, this has probably been the most harmonious since Liberation. The PLA enjoyed considerable prestige at the time of victory, which was soon enhanced by its performance in the Korean war. Some local difficulties arose during this period, when the Korean front was of paramount importance, over compulsory requisition of land, army monopoly of transport, and other such privileges. These were later solved during the 1957–8 'rectification' movement, and probably never reached serious proportions. Army help in production work may have been at times more of a hindrance than a help, but it was well-intentioned and met with popular approval. Of more fundamental importance was the simple fact that China was unified and that her army was well paid and fed, and under central control. At one stroke the

[30] Quoted on Peking radio, 31 Dec 1964 (BBC, *Summary of World Broadcasts*, pt 3, no. 1778).
[31] As n. 28.

P

basic cause of popular fear and hostility towards the military was thus removed. Observers in China report that admiration for the PLA is genuine, and that it is regarded as a great honour to have a son or relation serving in its ranks. There is no reason to doubt that the army is free of the stigma attached to it in pre-communist China.

(b) OFFICER–MEN RELATIONS

No serious breakdown appears to have occurred in this relationship either. During the Korean war and period of modernization, discipline and rank differentials followed conventional Western (and Soviet) lines. During the subsequent period of 'rectification', it was alleged that this had led to 'warlordism' and other highhanded behaviour on the part of officers towards men. While there was clearly some truth in these charges, one must remember that they are made from a standpoint based upon the revolutionary principles of 'military democracy', and that what was regarded as 'warlordism' in the PLA might pass for common practice in a western army. Since that time, officer privileges have been reduced and democratic machinery re-established throughout the PLA. This may not be to the liking of all officers, but it is presumably popular among the rank and file. There is certainly no indication of major difficulties in this relationship.

(c) ARMY–PARTY RELATIONS

Until 1949 the majority of leading PLA officers had served at one time or another both as political cadres and as military commanders. Since the very nature of the war fought by the PLA and the tactics which it employed were semi-political, the dividing line between the military and political functions was in any case often blurred. After 1949 the development of specialized military training in the new academies, and the growth of the new technical service arms—navy, air force, engineers, artillery, air defence, &c. —as well as the increasing complexity of staff headquarters, led to the birth of a new generation of essentially specialist officers. In addition, many leading officers who before had combined military and political functions, as well as frequently holding office in the local civil administration, now developed specialized interests. Thus it is not surprising that in the mid-1950s there was a certain amount of bipolarization in the PLA's officer corps between the 'professional' or 'modernizing' element and the 'political' or 'guerrilla-type' element.

These at any rate are the labels used by some Western analysts who have discussed the resultant tension and clash of interest between these two groups in some detail.[32] Yet three important provisos have to be made if the distinction between these two groups is not to be exaggerated. First, that there was never at any time a 'split' between the two groups of the kind which Pekinologists and Kremlinologists are prone to infer too readily when examining a closed system like that of communist China from afar; secondly, that at no stage did the party lose control of the army, nor was there an overt challenge to party leadership; thirdly, that it is very difficult to identify individuals as belonging to one or other group, and that many individual officers themselves probably subscribed to both 'modernizing' and 'political' arguments. In other words, the increasing technical complexity and professionalization of the PLA's role did not so much create divisions between individuals as divided loyalties within individuals; and the contradictions created by such divided loyalties reflect the basic contradiction inherent in the PLA's role since 1949, i.e. between its political role as the servant and military arm of the party, and its strategic role as the defender and guarantor of China's national security.

We know of only two instances since 1949 where a particular faction associated with the PLA opposed party policy to the point of open dissent and rupture. The first was the Kao–Jao conspiracy in 1953, when Kao Kang, the chairman of the North-east People's Government and concurrently commander of the North-east Military Region, together with Jao Shu-shih, Political Commissar of the East China Military Region, were said to have organized an 'anti-party alliance' against the leadership in Peking. Even this incident is a doubtful candidate for inclusion as a case of military dissension. Although Kao Kang was accused of having 'tried' to enlist army support, there is no evidence that he was successful. All the evidence suggests that three basic issues were involved in the Kao–Jao affair; an attempt by Kao to defend regional authority

[32] For a successful attempt to distinguish different strands of thought in the PLA, see Ellis Joffe, *Party and Army: Professionalism and Political Control in the Chinese Officer Corps, 1949–64* (Camb., Mass., 1965). A less happy attempt to distinguish by name between differing factions is made in Alice Langley Hsieh, *Communist China's Strategy in the Nuclear Era* (Englewood Cliffs, NJ, 1962).

in the north-east against the centralizing policies of the government in Peking, a fundamental dispute over economic policy, and personal rivalry between Kao and Liu Shao-ch'i. None of these issues directly concerned the PLA.[33]

The second apparent challenge within the PLA leadership to the party occurred in 1959, when the then Minister of Defence, P'eng Teh-huai, was dismissed along with five or six of his colleagues. Here again the evidence clearly indicates that P'eng was not opposed to the party as such; indeed both he and those dismissed with him were loyal party members of many decades standing. They objected specifically to certain trends in the Great Leap Forward, such as the expansion of the People's Militia and the campaign for PLA participation in production, which they felt were at variance with their other responsibilities. What was more significant, P'eng had been responsible for the abortive negotiations with the Soviet Union which took place in 1958–9 over the possibility of Soviet nuclear aid to China, and his dismissal may well have been partly designed to make him the scapegoat for the failure of these negotiations. Other than these two incidents of Kao Kang and P'eng Teh-huai, our knowledge of the command structure in the upper echelons of the PLA—which is admittedly somewhat defective—does not suggest that there have been any purges, splits, divisions, or other dramatic conflicts of the kind so beloved by Peking—and Kremlinologists.

On the contrary, the Chinese PLA leadership is distinguished by the way in which the great majority of its members have held responsible office without interruption since 1949, in many cases without even moving from their original assignment. Most of the leading officers of all the specialized service arms and of most of the thirteen military regions display the same lack of mobility in their careers since 1949. If it had not been for the unsettling effect of the Korean war, when entire PLA armies and their commands were transferred to Korea, the degree of mobility among the PLA leadership might have been even less. Furthermore, there is no particular attempt to ensure that officers do not serve in the provinces of their origin, nor apparently is there any objection to

[33] On the Kao Kang case see further Harold C. Hinton, *The 'Unprincipled Dispute' within the Chinese Communist Top Leadership* (US Information Agency, July 1955); Peter S. H. Tang, 'Power Struggle in the Chinese Communist Party; the Kao–Jao Purge', *Problems of Communism*, Nov–Dec 1955.

provincial military staffs remaining at their posts for years on end without being reshuffled or re-posted, although one would have thought that a fear of provincial cliques would have led to more frequent leadership transfers. Even more remarkable is the ease with which civilian government was established in the five years after Liberation in 1949–54. In 1950 two out of the six regions into which China was then divided (north-west and south-west) were almost entirely under PLA control, operating through the regional and provincial 'Military and Administrative Committees', and two more (central-south and east) were partially under military control. Only in north and north-east China, where communist control was well established, was the PLA not dominant. Yet by 1954, when the first National People's Council was held and the constitution proclaimed, local government had been transferred without apparent difficulty from military to civilian hands. Once again the Kao Kang case was the only possible exception.

There are three explanations for the relative ease with which the Chinese party ensured the continued loyalty of the upper echelons of army leadership. First was the way in which China's intervention in the Korean war and the subsequent modernization of the PLA almost monopolized the army leadership's attention for the first seven or eight years after Liberation. Second was the system of party control through the party committee and political department. Third and most important was the fact that at least 80 per cent of the top 100 or so military leaders of the PLA are 'revolutionary veterans', whose service dates back to the Kiangsi Soviet period in the early 1930s or earlier, comrades-in-arms of Mao Tse-tung and indeed of almost all the present civilian and party leaders. It has been this element of continuity with the revolutionary traditions of the past which, more than anything else, has so far prevented the emergence of a 'military faction' in the top leadership, in spite of the essential contradiction between socio-political and military priorities in the PLA today. On the other hand, the existence of this contradiction does appear to have led to divided loyalties among those officers in executive positions on the PLA General Headquarters in Peking who have to reconcile the conflicting demands of their party loyalties and their military functions. Significantly, most of the leading officers who have fallen from favour in the PLA come from precisely this sector of military leadership—the Chief of Staff and the directors of PLA

General Headquarters, who have at one and the same time to keep the army in fighting trim, and to implement the party's policies on economy, participation in production, and other such campaigns.[34]

CONCLUSION

It would therefore appear that the CPR has achieved at least a qualified success in the handling of its armed forces. The proof of this is mainly negative; there has been no overt challenge to the party by the PLA; the PLA has not incurred popular hostility, nor has there been any marked degree of intra-army discord.

This success is based upon the translation of the revolutionary model, after some trial and error (notably during the Great Leap Forward) to modern conditions. Those elements of the model—intensive participation in production &c.—which are no longer so relevant have been discreetly played down since 1960. Meanwhile the essence of the model, the political and education structure, has been increasingly emphasized. But it is also clear that this success has been achieved at a certain price.

First, the constant emphasis upon political control and education, if carried to excess, may bring about a reaction against itself. This occurred in 1958–9, at the height of the army's rectification campaign. A similar process could begin to be detected at the time of writing in 1966. This counter-productive tendency is a feature of all mass campaigns, and not solely of those directed towards the army, but its implications may be more serious within the army than in civilian life.

Secondly, success has been achieved at the price of what may in retrospect be seen to have been an excessive reliance upon the senior revolutionary generation. Even among this generation, signs of a conflict of loyalty between political and military functions can be detected, especially at the executive level of leadership. This conflict may become much more pronounced when a more junior generation of officers comes to assume control. It would be a mistake to regard this second generation as a potential movement of 'Young Turks'. Yet the fact remains that they have less in common with the original revolutionary model, and that

---

[34] The Chief of Staff and the directors of the Political, Training, and Rear Services Depts (Huang K'o-ch'eng, T'an Cheng, Hsiao K'o, Hung Hsueh-chih), were all dismissed around the time of P'eng Teh-huai's removal from the Ministry of Defence.

as a class they have apparently been so far excluded from holding the most crucial category of office.

Finally, the party has to some extent maintained its grip on the PLA at the expense of purely military efficiency. It would be absurd to claim that the army is not an efficient fighting machine for normal defensive purposes, or that its position is in any sense analogous to that of the Manchu Banners or Green Standards. Yet in creating the kind of army which is responsive to political control, the party has in effect placed definite limitations on the uses to which that army can be put.

In terms of its capability and training, the PLA is essentially a defensive force. This is not to underestimate its capacity to mount limited operations beyond the Chinese frontier very successfully. But its capacity for sustained hostile action abroad is not very large. It lacks sufficient transport to move its troops outside China, it has an exiguous offensive bomber force in the air, nor has any attempt been made to construct a navy capable of deepsea operations. The whole content of Chinese military strategy since 1949 has been consistently a defensive one. This is reflected in both the PLA's equipment and training, and in the way in which it is motivated. It is told by the party that its role is to defend Chinese soil against imperialist aggression, and told in some detail the form which such aggression will take—a nuclear attack by the United States followed up by conventional invasion. That is its first task. Its second task is to maintain law and order at home and to co-operate with the civilian authorities. Finally, it is told that the means it must employ in the case of defence against imperialist aggression are essentially those which were employed during China's revolutionary struggle. There is no evidence at all —even in the secret documents recently published by the United States[35]—that the PLA is educated to regard offensive military action of its own as on the agenda.

An army whose role is defined in these defensive terms is more likely to be receptive to central control than one which is encouraged to believe that it has a special role to play in China's destiny by expansion overseas. If the Chinese leadership had decided to build up an army which was not simply modernized for defence but also modernized in a way capable of major offensive action, it

[35] The *Kung-tso T'ung-hsun* (PLA Political Work Bulletins) available for first half of 1961 from the Library of Congress.

is doubtful whether such a military force would remain effectively under political control. By encouraging an aggressive ethos in the PLA, the party would also encourage it to defy its own authority.

This is not to say that the Chinese leadership is only deterred from pursuing a policy of military expansion by fear that its armed forces would assume too much power and independence. On the contrary, the defensive nature of Chinese military strategy is entirely credible in itself as a deliberate policy based upon considerations of national interest and security. But the converse may be true: that a weakening of political control would lead to demands from within the PLA for a more powerful offensive capability. There have in the past been signs of PLA resentment at the relatively low proportion of the national budget assigned to military expenditure. The expansion of the militia—to some extent at the expense of the regular army—and the wholesale rejection of Soviet techniques, was also questioned by some quarters in the PLA. The time may again be coming when the PLA will claim a greater share of the budget. In particular, it may demand more expenditure upon the development of a modernized offensive capability, and correspondingly less upon the current programme of nuclear defence.

Paradoxically, therefore, the revolutionary model of the present Chinese leadership, as far as military policy is concerned, results in a PLA which is orientated mainly towards defence. A 'revisionist' approach might result in a more outward-looking and potentially dangerous military policy, in which the voice of the PLA was more influential. In a certain sense it is as much in the interests of the outside world as of China herself that politics should remain in command of the PLA.

THE PLA AND THE CULTURAL REVOLUTION

The Cultural Revolution has placed the PLA in a more difficult situation, and has submitted its loyalty and cohesion to greater strain, than any previous event in its history. Signs of serious dissension have appeared within the PLA leadership, and there is even some evidence of incipient military regionalism in the more remote Chinese provinces, notably in Tibet, Sinkiang, Inner Mongolia, and Szechwan. Although in the earlier stages of the Cultural Revolution the PLA appeared to be united behind Mao, there came a time when this could no longer be taken for granted.

These developments do not invalidate the conclusion reached in the previous pages that party policy towards the PLA in recent years has been generally successful. They point rather to the way in which the Cultural Revolution has undermined the basis for, and upset the pattern of, the harmonious adjustment of conflicting interests in Chinese society, including the relationship between party and military authorities. When in the early months of 1967 the PLA was called upon to intervene physically in the Cultural Revolution, and when the Revolution was extended to its own ranks, it became clear that verbal loyalty to the thought of Mao Tse-tung could not automatically be translated into action. Indecision and perplexity rather than either outright commitment or opposition has marked much of the behaviour of the PLA, and the precarious balance between military and political priorities has been seriously upset.

Throughout 1966, as long as the PLA was not required to take action, its verbal support for Mao could be relied upon. This was guaranteed by the leading role of Lin Piao as Mao's 'close comrade-in-arms', and at lower levels by the pro-Maoist indoctrination which had been so intensively carried out in previous years. PLA support for Mao was further assured by the prestige and respect paid to it during the Cultural Revolution, and by its exemption from the actual process of Cultural Revolution within its own ranks. After the dismissal of the Chief of Staff Lo Jui-ch'ing (whose name was linked with the disgraced Peking First Secretary P'eng Chen) there was no suggestion that further revisionist elements awaited exposure within the PLA leadership.

The crucial turning-point came in January 1967, when almost simultaneously the PLA was called upon to intervene on behalf of the 'revolutionary rebels' in the Cultural Revolution, and to accept the control of the Maoist Cultural Revolution Group in hunting out deviationists within its own ranks. Meanwhile in some provinces and regions, anti-Mao opposition from party leaders appeared to find allies among local military leaders. There is no evidence of a concerted challenge to Mao's authority on the part of the PLA, but rather of isolated resistance, or more commonly of confusion and of reluctance to prosecute the revolution to the extreme and disruptive limits favoured by the Maoist faction.

It is possible that Lin Piao himself was unhappy about Mao's decision to order the PLA to intervene. Certainly, local PLA leaders showed no great anxiety to do so, and PLA intervention, usually of only a symbolic nature, was reported in less than half of the Chinese provinces. Nor was it always entirely clear on whose side the PLA was intervening, although it always professed to be pro-Mao.

The PLA, like the rest of the Chinese nation, has suffered from the Cultural Revolution's shattering revelation that support for the party is not synonymous with support for Chairman Mao. The effect of this revelation is possibly more damaging for the PLA than for other sections of society, since it strikes at the very roots of the entire system of political control and education. This system operated on the assumption that there existed a centralized party hierarchy operating through a vertical pattern of command on a united and nation-wide basis. The thought of Mao Tse-tung was the official party doctrine, not a separate source of authority. Loyalty to the actual party authorities in deed was as important as loyalty to the principles of Maoism in thought. In the last analysis, the army was controlled by the party committees at the regional, provincial, and lower levels, and this control had in fact been intensified in recent years.

The Cultural Revolution converted the party's greatest asset—its all-pervasive and decentralized (although obedient to central authority) control of Chinese society, including the PLA—into a major liability. Factions in the party leadership were duplicated at lower levels, and as the Cultural Revolution developed it increasingly assumed the form of a struggle between Mao and the party itself. Thus when the PLA was called upon to intervene, there was a considerable doubt as to which side should be favoured. Loyalty to Mao, the fountain-head of the PLA's inspirational doctrine, conflicted with obedience to local party authorities, often under attack by the 'revolutionary rebels' as anti-Maoists, who in many cases held concurrent posts in the military party committees.

Another casualty of the PLA's intervention in the Cultural Revolution was the concept of 'army–people' unity. Hitherto the sanction of PLA force had been held in reserve by the authorities as far as possible. Even during the hard years after the Great Leap Forward, when there was fairly widespread social unrest, it appears that the PLA had been used sparingly and with deliberate caution. The task of maintaining law and order usually fell upon the police and the militia rather than upon the regular army. The PLA's intervention in the Cultural Revolution appears to have aroused considerable popular resentment, which was being officially acknowledged by April 1967. It was admitted that the PLA had in some instances given support 'incorrectly' and that it must observe 'modesty' in its behaviour. On more than one occasion PLA units were required to make a public self-criticism of the mistakes they had made during the process of intervention.

Until recently, as has been shown, the PLA had been exempted from the more 'revolutionary' measures which had earlier been imposed upon it during the Great Leap Forward. As the Cultural Revolution grew in intensity, however, demands for such measures were revived, although it seems unlikely that they were actually satisfied to any great degree. These demands included massive participation in agriculture, wholesale expansion of the militia, an accelerated officers-to-the-ranks programme, even stiffer doses of 'Mao-study', and finally the carrying-out of a genuine 'Cultural Revolution' within the PLA's own ranks. These demands, especially the last, appear to have led to a split within the PLA's own Cultural Revolution Group, which was reorganized in January 1967, and in the highest military leadership. The veteran Marshal Ho Lung, and possibly other members of the party Military Affairs Committee, as well as Chu Teh himself, have been denounced as anti-Maoist. It should be added that these demands have so far apparently been successfully resisted, perhaps because it is realized that to press them too hard would cause major disaffection.

This picture of growing disunity and confusion within the PLA is to some extent offset by the added prestige and authority which it has acquired during the Cultural Revolution. The three-way alliances (between the PLA, revolutionary rebels, and cadres) have given the PLA a decisive say in a number of local administrations. In other places the PLA may, by the mere threat of intervention, be able to arbitrate with authority between rival factions. There is no indication, however, that the PLA is particularly anxious to accept the implication of its enhanced political power. In view of the social and political confusion in China today, one might have expected the PLA to yield to temptation, and to intervene on its own account to impose a decisive solution. In the great majority of other countries in the world, the army would have done so long ago. It is not impossible that if the Cultural Revolution continues, the temptation will prove too strong to resist, but so far there is no sign of it.

The Cultural Revolution has undoubtedly loosened, even if it has not yet destroyed, the bonds of political obedience which have made the PLA such a successful and docile instrument of policy over past decades. The fact that the PLA, contrary to many predictions in the West, has not yet 'taken over', testifies to the continuing strength of the tradition of loyalty to the party leadership and to Mao. But unless the gap between the party and Mao can be bridged very soon, the pressures upon the PLA may prove too strong to be contained by tradition. A third possibility is that the PLA's irresoluteness and divided loyalties will impose a stalemate in large areas of the country, since neither side will be able to count on its unqualified support. This would be a temporary solution to the Cultural Revolution, but not necessarily one with which the Maoist faction would be content. It would also tend to weaken central military and political authority, a development which would threaten the country's future stability, especially in the event of Mao's death. Much will now depend upon whether Mao is prepared to moderate the pace of the Cultural Revolution, and if so whether it is not too late for divided loyalties to be repaired. The Cultural Revolution has had no lack of success in creating or revealing contradictions, in the PLA as elsewhere. The question remains whether they can be resolved.

July 1967

7

The Role of Law in the Changing Society

SYBILLE VAN DER SPRENKEL

In the legal sphere as in others the Chinese had been trying for half a century to modernize, but little of lasting value had been accomplished for the country as a whole before 1949. Since then the newly introduced legal system, which is subject to further modification as circumstances may demand, has been made one instrument (among others) for carrying through social change over the whole area of China. I propose here to look at legal and other developments and try to see how the operation of law has affected and been affected by changes in society generally, and how much has been left to law—both in comparison with other agencies and in comparison with the part traditionally assigned to it in China.

Any attempt to analyse another social system objectively, without judging it in the light of values which are not its own, is liable to appear as uncritical. There is a danger of feeling that terms like 'democracy', 'religion', 'economics', or 'law' have been pre-empted for the forms of these institutions which have developed in our own countries and therefore a tendency to judge as failures institutions which do not conform to our idea of them. It may be that there *are* universally valid grounds for preferring particular forms of institutions to others, but we are not entitled to assume this from the outset. It is unhelpful to approach the study of contemporary China (or other countries) with such preconceptions: the Chinese have not set themselves the goal of reproducing our institutions—of many of which (and this includes our legal system) they are very critical. Perhaps it may be well also to point out here what should become apparent later—namely, that all that has happened so far represents instalments of an incomplete story in which the actors themselves intend to introduce further changes. However, we cannot wait until institutions reach their final form (if that ever happens) to come to terms intellectually with what is going on, and this must be the justification for this (in some senses) premature attempt.

While the communist achievement of power in 1949 was a highly significant watershed in that it created the first really favourable opportunity for effective nation-wide social reconstruction, it should be noted that regions which had previously been under communist control (altogether something between a quarter and a third of the country in 1945, but scattered interstitial areas, essentially rural, rather than a compact and balanced territory) had long been subject to the sort of legal system now generally introduced, and the practical 'laboratory' experience gained in those regions went some way to facilitate its introduction after 1949 as the system for the whole country.

The completeness (subject to the qualifications above) of the societal transformation which has happened since 1949, to which I shall devote most of this chapter, should not make us forget how much searching went on in the previous period. Much was consciously attempted and there was some accomplishment; some of the groping and partial innovations moreover had consequences —virtually irreversible—beyond those foreseen. What has happened since, however, represents a new start at reconstruction for the whole country and not a culmination of gradual reform.

In considering Chinese society in the half-century 'interregnum' period before 1949, one has to keep in mind several separate chains of events which represent different levels of social activity. Of these, one can distinguish first the on-going functioning of life processes as the generations succeeded one another in carrying on traditional occupations and ritual, generally according to existing familiar patterns, but subject to voluntary and involuntary modification as changing conditions offered new ways of pursuing old values or made old ways progressively more difficult to follow, or as the absorption of Western ideas—by a minority—made old practices unacceptable to them.[1] Beneath the umbrella of government and officialdom—which offered less and less cover as time went on—such activities were usually small in scale and always characterized by particularism, that is, local or particular group loyalties. Meanwhile on another level, the level of thinking, an articulate minority engaged in the analysis of the problems facing

[1] Marion J. Levy has analysed in detail the impact of these new influences in *The Family Revolution in Modern China* (Camb., Mass., 1949).

China and the search for remedies for the various ills from which she was suffering. These included the patriots, reformers, radicals, and revolutionaries (not mutually-exclusive categories) who thought in broader, more inclusive terms of country or state, the Chinese race, culture, or even nation, but the diversity of their ideas kept them divided among themselves and prevented them from winning the necessary wide support, and they lacked effective means to translate their programmes into action. Then, at the level of action, attempted innovation can be classified broadly into three types: first, innovating activity undertaken on private or sectional initiative (not always Chinese) and as a rule functionally specific—industrial and commercial enterprises, for example, educational institutions, transport and communications, and so on; second, relatively cohesive social movements, usually with an egalitarian (therefore universalistic) tinge—like those in support of the use of the vernacular language for scholarly and official purposes, of nationalism, and of the rights of women and of labour; and third, public or government-sponsored innovations such as constitutional changes and legislation, which seem *prima facie* as though they ought to have been pervasive in their effects on society, but which rarely were. The dividing lines between the different levels and types of activity were not of course clear-cut: social movements drew some of their inspiration from thinkers, while the difficulty one has in classifying the military is itself significant—partly traditional in character, partly innovative of both sectional and public types, it tended to fill any vacuum.

The general trend of all these developments during the 'interregnum' was towards increasing social disintegration. Innovations were not entirely abortive. They gave rise to new social classes (as Jerome Ch'ên noted)[2]—new types of intellectuals, businessmen and soldiers. Cultural and social attitudes were in some cases lastingly affected, though less so outside the major urban centres.[3] Social

---

[2] See above, p. 20.

[3] Jerome Ch'ên has mentioned (p. 18–20 above) the culturally-alienated returned students. Another example of change that was lasting but not pervasive was that in 'the position of women' in certain circles. For a minority of women emancipation had gone a long way even before 1949. Subject to overall limiting economic conditions, the shortage of trained manpower and the availability of servants eased the entry into careers for women. My observation in 1948 was that exceptional women rose (on the staff of universities or in hospital administration, for example) to positions it would have been difficult to reach in England. Women also played a significant part, of course, in radical political and social movements in the early decades of this century.

organization was sometimes reshaped in response to changed conditions, as for example the change in size and function of marketing areas as a consequence of new methods of transportation.[4] In
general, however, the changes remained unincorporated pockets
or excrescences, never co-ordinated because by this time society
itself lacked co-ordination. Progress was achieved in some directions, but at the cost of loss of social cohesion. New communications disrupted local economic systems and distorted existing communities. The concentration of commerce and industry in the
coastal cities disturbed the old pattern of rural-urban interdependence. The effect of introducing modern education for some
without diffusing it generally through society (besides creating
aspirations that could not be satisfied in existing conditions in
China) was to widen the gap between different sections of the
community: without functional interdependence, there was no
community of ideas between them—hence no possibility of meaningful communication. Nor did the innovations generate any new
source of social cohesion or mechanism of articulation. Political
changes had only ripple effects outward from the centre: they
did not reach the agrarian hinterland. One observes a paradox in
the rise of a sentiment of nationalism in a period of waning internal
cohesiveness within the entity which was supposed to be the object
of the sentiment; besides pride in a past the country was powerless
to live up to in the present, only external factors gave reality to the
'nation' and no new forces generated within proved strong enough
to articulate the whole. Even the colloquial language (*pai-hua*)
movement remained a matter of the style in which intellectuals
wrote—it was not taken advantage of fully to lead into a common realm of discourse shared by all. On the theories of Durkheim
and Tönnies one might postulate the development of a legal system to compensate for the loss of other sources of cohesion,
but in China the legal system did not develop this integrative
power.

The strand of legal development in fact illustrates what has
been said of uncoordinated progress.

Until the end of the nineteenth century the formal legal system
had barely developed beyond being a system for maintaining
order and punishing crime. Nor did any section of the old society

[4] See G. W. Skinner, 'Marketing and Social Structure in Rural China', *J. Asian Studies*, Nov 1964, Feb & May 1965.

have much interest in seeing its role expanded. Dependence was placed instead on the norms of traditional morality, on customary procedures for handling transactions, and on informal techniques of conciliation, mediation, and arbitration within and between virtually self-governing communities and corporations—in village, clan, and guild.[5]

In the last years of the Ch'ing dynasty, however, the interest in constitutional and other reforms (reinforced by the desire to bring the system of extra-territoriality to an end) directed attention to the need to overhaul the legal system if China was not to lag behind other countries, and a beginning was made in introducing new codes and new procedures. In 1902 the throne ordered that persons experienced in Western criminal and commercial law should be appointed to a committee for the compilation of laws, and in 1904 the committee, under the direction of Shen Chia-pen and Wu T'ing-fang, started work.[6] The old Board of Punishments became the Ministry of Justice. Laws on commercial practice and the reorganization of the courts followed the revision of the criminal code. The Supreme Court was given new powers and in its deliberations set about adapting the principles of Western law to Chinese needs. A kind of 'reception' of continental law was under way, and the work of jurists of this time represents a considerable feat of scholarship in assimilating conceptions that were quite unfamiliar—like the principle of causation or the rejection of analogical application.[7] The power of legislation and the intention to protect rights were written into successive constitutions;[8] academic courses in law were introduced in the universities, and private practice was opened to the profession. With some interruptions, this work continued, reaching a peak in the years after 1928 when the courts were again reorganized under the judicial *Yüan*, new social policies found expression in legislation, and a

---

[5] See J. Escarra, *Le droit chinois* (Peking & Paris, 1936); S. van der Sprenkel, *Legal Institutions in Manchu China* (London, 1962); J. A. Cohen, 'Chinese Mediation on the Eve of Modernization', *Cal. Law R.*, Aug 1966.

[6] For details of the relevant memorials, edicts, and biographies, see M. J. Meijer, *The Introduction of Modern Criminal Law in China* (Batavia, 1950).

[7] See M. H. van der Valk, *Interpretations of the Supreme Court at Peking* . . . (Batavia, 1949); J. Escarra, *Recueil des sommaires de la jurisprudence de la Cour Suprême de la République Chinoise, 1912–28* (Shanghai, 1924).

[8] See Franklin W. Houn, *The Central Government of China, 1912–28* (Madison, Wis., 1957).

survey of customary law by provinces was undertaken with a view to comprehensive codification.[9]

In content, the legislation of the period is impressive: it was effective powers of applying it that were lacking. It never had deep roots in actual practice. In so far as law happened to coincide with customary or moral norms (either traditional or what resulted from the piecemeal social advance described above), it was likely to be observed, but this did not amount to legal enforcement. The marriage and family law contained in the Civil Code of 1931, for example, gave expression to new values—of individualism and the raised status and greater independence of women —and where these were accepted, it would be observed; but in rural areas where ideas were slow to change, it had little effect because the administration did not penetrate deeply enough to supervise its enforcement.[10] Factory laws, admirable in intention, were never followed up with a system of inspection, so were never enforceable. The function of substantive law here can perhaps be said to have been to give clarity and public expression to newly emerging moral principles and aspirations: perhaps this may have contributed a little to their fulfilment, probably not very much.

On the conduct of the courts the evidence is somewhat conflicting. From the statistics of cases entering court (in yearbooks) it appears that sections of the business community had been converted to the view that there was advantage to be gained by taking civil cases to law. These no doubt represented only an 'advanced' minority in the cities, while the rest of society clung to the idea that courts were something to be avoided at all costs. Franz Michael speaks of the high standard of procedure observed by courts he visited in the years 1934–7, but also refers to frequent cases of arrest and execution of bandits and robbers which occurred without the slightest reference to court procedure, or any reaction on the part of the Chinese public to demand that there

[9] *Min shang shih hsi-kuan t'iao-ch'a pao-kao lu* (Nanking, 1930). (German trans., E. J. M. Kroker: *Die amtliche Sammlung chinesischer Rechtsgewohnheiten . . . Untersuchungsbericht über Gewohnheiten in Zivil- und Handelssachen* (Bergen-Enkheim bei Frankfurt a M., 1965).

[10] The difficulties of accommodating into family law and criminal law all the consequences of recognizing the principle of the equality of the sexes, and the chain of modifications in the old kinship system this would require, are described in Van der Valk, *Conservatism in Modern Chinese Family Law* (Leyden, 1956), p. 19.

should be, though there was plenty of discussion in the journals about citizens' rights under law.[11]

Whatever conclusion one comes to about the exact measure of progress achieved in this field, the fact remains that China never had time to consolidate any gains: they were destined to become casualties in the cataclysm that followed—the anti-Japanese war, and subsequent hyperinflation and deterioration in governmental standards. (I can speak from my own observations in 1948.)

It would be a mistake to think of constitutionally-guaranteed liberties as having been established in this period and then swept away in 1949. The fact is that in spite of sincere efforts, and even some success on the level of scholarship, such things had never been created in China. In the decades before 1949 liberty was enjoyed by default, as it were: without effective legal guarantee and ever less protected by the customary safeguards—a situation which could, and did, easily degenerate into licence (as among gangs, for example, in Shanghai), improper exactions (of war-lords, corrupt officials, &c.) or terror (employed against suspected communist sympathizers). However good the system may have looked on paper, law in practice offered little or nothing in the way of remedies. A legal system must be enmeshed in other institutions if it is to operate: law courts and judges need both financial and moral support and can, like other institutions, be reduced to disorder in a state of social chaos.

It would be agreed, I think, by anyone who knew China at first-hand in 1948 (and perhaps this needs to be stressed if attitudes within China to changes introduced there since are to be understood, and if changes in China are to be compared with changes contemplated or going on elsewhere), that the processes of disintegration had reached a point at which there was no section of society which had as its interest the preservation of the existing state of affairs. By no means all Chinese were in favour of the sort of change they expected the communists to introduce, but all, whether they were peasants, intellectuals, businessmen, urban workers, or unemployed, were by 1948 suffering frustration and/or misery, and all shared at least in the knowledge that some (large-scale) changes had to be introduced. This psychological attitude constitutes one factor in the situation.

[11] 'The Role of Law in Traditional, Nationalist and Communist China', *CQ* 1, ix (1962), p. 134. On informal tribunals under the KMT, see above, p. 142.

Following the victory of the PLA in 1949 and the establishment of the CPR, what has been attempted in China is the total transformation of society on the basis of a comprehensive social theory. The revolution meant a shift in power from those who previously exercised it on the basis of wealth, influence, naked might or social prestige to the Communist Party, which claimed to represent the working class—an alliance of peasants and workers. Having achieved political power through military victory, this had to be translated into social and economic policies to make the power effective.

It will be understood from what has been said in this and other chapters of disintegration and failure that there was no ready-made instrument available for their purpose. The government machinery by which policies were to be given effect has had to be created *pari passu* with the working out of policy and the intermeshing of measures to implement it, and both have had to be tested and modified with experience. The Common Programme, adopted by the People's Political Consultative Conference in the autumn of 1949 (summoned as being broadly representative of a wide spectrum of the population) served as a provisional constitution, and from then on they have continued to improvise. In all this law has had its part.

To put it very briefly: the Common Programme announced the establishment of the CPR which should carry out the people's democratic dictatorship (led by the working class and uniting all 'democratic classes' and all ethnic groups), which would set itself the task of developing the economy, transforming it from an agrarian into a modern one in which agriculture and industry formed a balanced whole. It set out a scheme for elected People's Congresses at various levels up to the All-China People's Congress at the summit, and for the practice of democratic centralism by the organs of state power. It detailed interim arrangements to meet the situation until elections could be held, considerable powers being left for the time to be exercised by military government.[12] It proclaimed people's rights to freedom of thought, speech, association, domicile, religious belief, &c.; equality of women with men in respect of various rights, and equality of different nationalities (i.e. peoples within China of different ethnic origin).

Law is mentioned at various points in the Common Programme.

[12] See above, p. 204.

People enjoy rights to elect and to be elected according to law (art. 4) or may be deprived of political rights according to law (art. 7). It is the duty of every national to abide by the law (art. 8) besides observing labour discipline, protecting public property, paying taxes, &c. By article 17 all existing laws, decrees, and judicial systems were abolished: in their place 'Laws and decrees protecting the people shall be enacted and the people's judicial system shall be established'. The next two articles I shall quote in full:[13]

Art. 18. All state organs of the People's Republic of China must enforce a revolutionary working-style, embodying honesty, simplicity and service to the people: They must severely punish corruption, forbid extravagance and oppose bureaucratic working-style which alienates the masses of the people.

Art. 19. People's supervisory organs shall be set up in the People's Governments of county and municipal level and above, to supervise the performance of duties by the state organs of various levels and by public functionaries of all types, and to propose that disciplinary action be taken against state organs and public functionaries who violate the law or are negligent in the performance of their duties.

The people or people's organisations shall have the right to file charges with the people's supervisory organs or people's judicial organs against any state organs or any public functionaries that violate the law or are negligent in the performance of their duties.

What 'law' means in communist thinking will be considered later. We have here at least a programme which allows a place for law: no arbitrary dictatorship seems to be intended, though familiarity with the provisions of earlier constitutions would make one cautious of building too much on expressed intentions unless their authors possessed both the determination and the power to give them effect.

Starting only with this programme, some practical experience gained in the old scattered border regions and liberated areas (areas in communist control before 1949), and a readiness, as they put it, to learn from other countries which had advanced farther on the road to socialism, the new government abolished overnight all that was already in existence as being useless and inimical to their purposes. What they have set up in its place has evolved gradually and has undergone progressive changes as

[13] A. P. Blaustein, ed., *Fundamental Legal Documents of Communist China* (S. Hackensack, NJ, 1962), pp. 41–42.

developments have occurred in other spheres. As each new policy is adopted and each campaign gets under way, the legal system has its part to play and is developed in the process. Law has to keep pace with social development; whether this is economic planning, the Great Leap, or collectivization, the law (as a system of rules, procedures, and a profession) has to be adapted to the needs of the changed situation.

Before going on to specifically legal development, it may be well to consider very briefly the rest of the societal transformation which is the context of legal development.

In the matter of values (to which, of course, the content of the new law is related) there has been a deliberately fostered shift— away from the former system based on the observance of the proprieties due to status and hierarchy, the maintenance of harmony by compromise, and narrow group loyalties, to a new ethic in which the ingredients are social justice, revolutionary fervour and struggle, service to the people, loyalty to the whole national community and even to the revolutionary movement beyond it, and readiness to make sacrifices for the sake of the future. Their opposites—individualism (equated with selfishness), conservative attitudes, complacency, apathy, and private enjoyment in the present—are disapproved of. The young are brought up with these new ideals, and their seniors have been re-educated to accept them by repeated campaigns of mass persuasion and small group discussion, the total effect being something like a continuing process of religious conversion on a national scale. Conservatism does not have to be continuously relearnt; enthusiasm for change has to be constantly reawakened if some are not to become satisfied and complacent before the social transformation desired by China's present leaders is accomplished.

At the same time changes have been going on which have resulted in a more tightly articulated social structure. In the first place there has been an increase in the 'density' and comprehensiveness of formal social organization. Besides the political hierarchy of people's congresses, there are new forms of agricultural and industrial organization—the communes, factories (with which are associated housing, welfare, and recreation for their workers), and communication enterprises—all of which fit into a series of hierarchies headed by the appropriate government ministry or planning authority. There are the 'mass organizations'

—such as trade unions, peasant associations, professional associations, and women's organizations—which operate at local, provincial, and national levels. And there are local community organizations—neighbourhood groups and street committees. People are organized at work and at home to take active part in what is going on: various forms of social pressure ensure that no one shall stand aside (if they tried to, they would be visited by neighbours or colleagues and talked to), with the result that strands of organization bind the Chinese population—horizontally and vertically—to an extent unknown before. Only the bonds of kinship and the old ties of locality (and the latter will have been replaced by new ones) have diminished in importance—because people have moved to new areas, or as interest has shifted to other organizations. Besides the organization for the masses, there is the organization of the élite, the Communist Party, which, organized locally and nationally, pervades the structures of other organizations: it claims to exercise the function of leadership, and has, for the sixteen years it has held power, managed to contain the internal conflicts that must arise over the massive policy decisions that have to be taken, so that, though other citizens may consider members at times guilty of over-zealousness, it has succeeded through these years in giving to the public an appearance of a cohesive, disciplined body, and it can be seen by the outsider to have an articulating function throughout the country, penetrating everywhere.[14]

These organizations, plus the new mechanical mass media, offer a multiplicity of channels of communication which are exploited to the full. A succession of campaigns and movements have one after the other claimed public attention, and, reinforced by nation-wide small-group discussion, have created a virtually universal awareness of government policies—of the link between problems to be solved and practical measures to be taken to solve them, and of the part of the citizen in the whole activity (not, of course as an individual but in his or her capacity as member of

[14] This was written early in 1966. It remains to be seen whether the conflicts recently brought out into the open can be reconciled to maintain cohesion. This is not, of course, meant to imply that there were no serious disagreements within the party in the first seventeen years: we know that there were. But 1966 was the first time that the mass of the people were involved in the issues, or that there was any doubt that the party was the body responsible for leading the country through the process of transformation.

various groups, teams, or organizations). The experience of having all shared in these intensive campaigns, and more particularly the widespread study of Marxist and Maoist classics, has given the entire nation a shared repertory of topics and terms—an esoteric vocabulary to the outsider—which has gone a long way to create a new sense of community. Millions of people have entered together into a new world of ideas and the effect of having shared this common experience is to make meaningful communication possible. Some of this growth may be seen as the indirect result of specific policies directed to other ends. Deliberate attempts have been made besides to create greater cultural homogeneity by reducing existing gaps, for example between town and country, between workers engaged in management and on the shop-floor, and by eliminating the old distinctions which arose out of the former system of property ownership.

This is not necessarily to suggest that there is universal social harmony or that all share identical views on policies adopted, or that local differences of custom have all disappeared, but merely that the new organizational forms and community of ideas have resulted in a social structure with a degree of articulation unknown in China before, the lack of which hampered previous attempts at reform. Chairman Mao emphasized appeal to reason and persuasion as a method of handling 'contradictions among the people' and policies have—at least in these first years—in fact been designed and presented in such a way as to win and keep the support of those who might have been expected to oppose them, e.g. the constructive role offered to 'national capitalists'.[15] By these means the proportion of those who do not share in the general consensus has been kept as small as possible (which is relevant to the actual amount of legal coercion needed). A stage may be reached at which this consensus may be self-destructive, e.g. the processes of differentiation that follow from industrialization may lead to new divergences and disagreements about subsequent goals. However, in the early stages it can be said that these developments have operated to produce a more cohesive

[15] Chinese entrepreneurs shared the communists' antipathy for foreign imperialists, of course, if not for capitalism itself. In the early stages of reconstruction and transformation, when the paramount need was to restore the economy and raise production, they were encouraged to continue in their business, and they basked in approval of their patriotic activity at first as private owners, later under joint public-private ownership.

society than China has known for more than a century. The last seventeen years have seen the arrest and reversal of the disintegration process and in its place concentration of energies on the reconstruction and reintegration of society on the scale of the national community. While power of actual decision may be delegated and actually exercised locally, particularism and sectional divisions have given way to overall co-ordination, directed from the centre, that penetrates social life at all levels.[16]

All this gives part of the answer to the question raised earlier about the effectiveness of law. The new cohesiveness of society gives the regime much greater capacity to give effect to measures once decided on and finally enacted.[17] The history of recent decades seems to show that in China law—at least as considered under this aspect—has been the beneficiary rather than the provider of social cohesion.

THE LEGAL SYSTEM SINCE 1949

Before looking at what has been done concretely, it may be helpful to say something about the underlying theory.

The Marxist view of law is that a country's legal system is part of the coercive apparatus of the state and an instrument in the hands of the ruling class by which that class asserts its interests. There is no law, it is said, which is not the law of a dominant class. On these grounds, in the early days after the Russian revolution the attempt was made to dispense with law altogether. However, experience of doing without suggested that it could be usefully turned to new purposes, and (some oscillations of policy apart) the idea of a special form of 'socialist legality' developed.[18] The Chinese communists accepted these views and showed themselves ready to build on Russian experience in this area as in other fields:

---

[16] Revelations during the Proletarian Cultural Revolution show that disagreements have indeed arisen. It is too early to say whether the recently achieved cohesion can be restored. When writing in 1966, I fear that I underestimated new particularisms based on party associations and regions.

[17] The way the regime deliberately undertook campaigns of persuasion and re-education to secure compliance through understanding of the new marriage law as a democratic reform and not just an administrative measure is described by van der Valk, *Conservatism*, ch. 1. The introduction of effective registration of marriages is one way in which more efficient administration has contributed to make its enforcement more possible.

[18] On the notion of 'socialist legality' see H. J. Berman, *Justice in Russia* (London 1951).

in the past, they said, law had been a tool in the hands of the exploiters and oppressors—in a socialist state it would be part of the apparatus by means of which the people's democratic dictatorship and socialist transformation of the economy and social structure would be carried through, its tasks changing in successive phases of development. It is said to be a weapon in the continuing class struggle and offers a way of dealing with 'contradictions which exist between ourselves and the enemy' and 'among the people'. Together with the other organs of state power, the legal system should be concerned: to protect the revolution against subversion; with the execution of policy (in this closely associated also with the Communist Party which is the moulding and guiding force of policy); with the supervision of policy according to the principle of socialist legality and the protection of the new order and the system of rights created. (For this last point, the system of property relations is crucial and will be considered later.)

An article in *Cheng-fa Yen-chiu* (1955) speaks of law as having three basic functions. The first is punitive, using force to restrain counter-revolutionary and *déclassé* elements left over from the old society, and also in relation to individual backward elements from among the workers; the second, to further the successful fulfilment of state plans, development of the movement towards co-operatives (later communes), and to ensure the correct use and essential limitation of private capital existing in the country; and thirdly, the education of the masses in the spirit and the principles of socialism. The idea of the educational function of law crops up frequently, and I shall refer to it again. In regard to procedure, the choice among different possible courses of action seems often to be determined by consideration of the social-educational effect.

Translating these theories into action has involved development in a number of different directions: the formulating of a body of substantive law—family law, land law, labour law, &c.—expressing the content of new policies; setting up a system of courts, offices, and procedures and meshing these with other agencies like security, police, and procuratorate which share some of the powers and duties of law enforcement and supervision, and with the rest of the institutional framework; the recruitment and training of personnel to carry out the routine business of adjudication and enforcement; the gradual emergence of a profession with its own expertise and understanding of the technical legal aspects of relating socialist principles to the requirements of Chinese society, as they already exist or as they develop as time goes on. And they had to overcome the distaste for all law of the Chinese public.

As mentioned, the intention of the Common Programme was to sweep away all existing legal machinery—rules, courts, and profession. To fill the vacuum in the first days when the new regime was short of reliable trained personnel in all fields (and previously trained lawyers were not considered reliable), as a first step, a system of rather simple, untechnical 'People's Courts' was set up, staffed by cadres with revolutionary experience or (mostly young) intellectuals who joined the Communist Party after the liberation of the cities—none of whom had specialized legal training. They gave *ad hoc* decisions based on the facts of the case, such new laws and regulations as had been promulgated or, in their absence, on socialist principles or common sense. In so far as they were handling civil matters (what would later be classed as 'contradictions among the people') these courts in the main proved efficient and workmanlike; the decisions they gave were not always radical (e.g. in dealing with the divorce cases that flooded in after the promulgation of the new marriage law); and reports[19] of the way they worked with quiet concern for ordinary people, plus respect for facts and honesty (in sharp contrast with most previous experience) helped to win confidence for the new regime. On the criminal side, the major preoccupation at this time was the campaign for the suppression of counter-revolutionaries (later to be described as 'contradictions between ourselves and the enemy'), of which more must be said later.[20]

[19] I am drawing here on my own recollection of what happened in the early days in the Peking–Tientsin area. A number of cases—e.g. claims for compensation for wrongful dismissal months or years earlier—were brought by staff previously employed by foreigners or wealthy Chinese businessmen and were decided with an impartiality which surprised the defendants—when decisions in a contrary sense might have seemed an easy way of winning popular favour. See H. McAleavy, in *Am. J. Comp. Law* (1962), pp. 52–65; also P. Townsend, *China Phoenix* (1955), pp. 322–7.

[20] The large public accusation meetings (held at the time of the Korean war), at which Procurators denounced counter-revolutionaries and traitors, and the public were encouraged to show their feelings against them, were clearly staged for political-educative effect. The cases selected for this treatment were never in any doubt. The records of the accused would have secured conviction in any court, but the regime wished to secure publicity for these cases for other reasons. While the atmosphere was the reverse of what we associate with judicial proceedings, this was not simply lynch law. The accusation meeting's recommendation was forwarded to the courts.

Some of the former judges and court employees were retained—presumably because not enough substitutes were available immediately—and the proportion was probably higher in central and south China (liberated later) than in the north. Some of these must have been slow to change their ways and many came under criticism in 1952 at the time of the judicial reform campaign.

To meet the long-term need for trained legal personnel, several different methods have been adopted. The chief avenues are the law departments of institutions of higher learning (4- or 5-year courses) and short courses of 6 months or 1 year for cadres who already have some practical experience of legal work. They are then assigned to work in courts for one year, after which they are appointed judges or recorders according to ability. Links were established with the legal profession in other socialist countries, and socialist lawyers (from countries other than socialist ones) were invited to visit China. With Russian jurists as advisers, Russian judicial experience was studied and drawn on extensively. 'To begin with the socialist civil law is the Soviet civil law. It is the first civil law in the history of mankind which can handle people's internal contradictions.'[21]

There has been much discussion within the nascent profession—at specially-summoned conferences, in journals, and with visiting socialist lawyers from other countries (not only socialist countries)—on particular problems as they arise in China. As each stage in social and political development is reached and as successive campaigns have been launched, there have been exhortations from government and party leaders for the legal profession to strengthen itself so that it would be capable of playing its part, and discussion within the profession as to how this should be done, so the professional discussions reflect changes in general policies. As time has gone on (and latterly, of course, without Russian assistance) the debates have become increasingly concerned with actual Chinese experience and as to how the principles of Mao's thinking should be applied to concretely developing situations.[22]

[21] Inst. of Civil Law, Central Political-Judicial Cadres' School, *Basic Problems in the Civil Law of the People's Republic of China* (hereafter *Civil Law Lectures*) (Peking, 1958; JPRS trans. 4879).

[22] This can be documented in the periodic reports on work of the courts. A good example is a speech by Kao Ke-lin, Vice-President of Supreme People's Court, on the work of Supreme Court since 1955 to the 1st session of 2nd NCP, 24 Apr 1959 (*CB* 569).

The interrelatedness of different developments significant for our theme may be illustrated by campaigns which took place shortly before the launching of the first five-year plan in 1953. The Economy Check-up Committee revealed laxness in the application of the laws. Two necessary preliminaries before economic planning could be expected to be effective were shown to be the raising of efficiency among party and other cadres and the elimination of some occupational vices in industrial-commercial circles. So there were launched the 'San Fan' and 'Wu Fan' movements— the first was aimed at eliminating bureaucracy, waste, and corruption on the part of cadres, and the second was directed against businessmen guilty of bribery, tax evasion, deception in fulfilling government orders, stealing state property and theft of state secrets (improper use of official information). The courts, as then operating, were not considered adequate for the task, and by order of the Council of Government Administration, special tribunals were set up 'under the leadership of the courts'. These tribunals, composed of persons prominent in different local organizations—trade unions, womens' organizations, and the like —dealt with a mass of cases in which behaviour in varying degrees anti-social was exposed; they operated with some jurisprudentially unconventional categories—'law-abiding', 'fairly law-abiding', &c.; and they did a great deal to publicize the higher standards of probity now required. They could recommend a range of punishments from fines to death, and could order the restitution of illegal gains or the payment of compensation, but the execution of their decisions was entrusted to the courts.

All this directed attention to the need for judicial reform, which now followed. Representatives of local mass organizations were invited to large meetings to carry through the reform of *their* courts (the 'mass line' in judicial work). Cases previously dealt with were submitted for re-examination, and it was shown that in their decisions, judges had not been giving full effect to government policies: by being too lenient to those guilty of corrupt practices, the public economy was being damaged and the welfare of all was being sacrificed. After summing up[23] on a national scale, the results of this were increased effectiveness of the courts, financial gain to the state, and greater familiarity with, and presumably trust

[23] This summing up and generalization of experience is a standard feature at the end of campaigns—probably of educative as well as administrative benefit.

in, legal procedure on the part of influential members of the public. From whom, it may be supposed, it communicated itself to the rest.

It is possible and may be helpful, perhaps, to think of legal development up to 1965 as falling into three rather clear phases—the first, the years before the launching of the first five-year plan, during which certain fairly basic principles of social justice were enacted, and courts and judgments were rather untechnical; this ended with the judicial reform of 1952 already referred to. Then in the years 1953–7 more trained personnel were available and there was more reliance on, and confidence in, legal machinery;[24] the constitution of 1954 was promulgated, the courts, according to annual reports, were working more satisfactorily, and articles appeared in the press about citizens' constitutional rights.[25] Then came the anti-rightist campaign of 1958 when some of the outstanding jurists were denounced, particularly for advocating the independence of the judiciary.[26] After this there was some administrative reorganization involving more co-ordination at the local level of the different agencies concerned with political and judicial work, since when courts and party have worked more closely together. (During the 'Great Leap' the courts were urged to speed up their handling of cases—though there were warnings that they should not sacrifice quality to quantity.) Since collectivization the number of civil suits is said to have declined in rural areas.[27]

In regard to substantive law, i.e. the content of legal rules, the policy has been to proceed slowly. Certain fundamental and organic laws setting out the structure and powers of government bodies, courts, &c. were promulgated at a fairly early stage, the Common Programme serving as provisional constitution for the early years of reconstruction until the constitution and accom-

[24] e.g. the decision of 16 Nov 1956 to transfer to the courts (from Public Security in urban areas and from government organs in the countryside) responsibility for surveillance of counter-revolutionaries. Previously the courts were not sound in structure and not able to shoulder the task, but conditions had changed, according to an article in *Shih-shih shou-tse*, 10 Dec 1956.

[25] The citizen's right of removal, for example, was defended in *Hunan-pao* (Changsha), 6 Oct 1956 (*SCMP* 1464)—on the ground that otherwise the individual would suffer and society would not be benefited. A case is reported from Canton of a court finding a cadre guilty of overstepping his duties and infringing citizenship rights. 17 Nov 1956 (*SCMP* 1422).

[26] See e.g. *PD* editorial of 20 Dec 1957, 'Political and law departments must be thoroughly reorganized' (*SCMP* 1687).

[27] Wang Shu-wen, 'The Movement for People's Communes and Political and Legal Work', *Cheng Fa Yen-chiu* (*CFYC*), Dec 1958.

panying organic laws were adopted by the first National People's Congress in September 1954. On certain other matters, like marriage and organization of trade unions, new laws were formulated and announced as early as 1950. For the rest, policy as it unfolds is usually translated by gradual stages, through a series of resolutions, decrees, regulations, and statutes—a method which has the advantage of giving scope for a certain amount of experimentation before a satisfactory general standard is arrived at, when at last the law on that particular subject is finalized and promulgated; but it must also have had the disadvantage of uncertainty and a lack of clarity (and this might be important when decisions have to be made as to what constitutes infringement or what is to be included in the category of counter-revolutionary). A Russian observer described the process in an article published in 1957: 'After working out the primary variations of many laws, a mass discussion took place, and later taking into consideration valuable comments made during the discussion, the laws were worked into final shape and published.'[28]

Thus the initiation of important policies like collectivization of agriculture and the introduction of the communes rested on resolutions of the central committee of the CCP (11 October 1955 and 29 August 1958 respectively) while tentative regulations for one commune in Suiping *hsien*, Honan, were published in the *People's Daily* in full 'as reference materials for all other parts of the country'.[29] On the other hand, penalties for corruption (1952) or undermining the monetary system (1951) and regulations for surveillance of counter-revolutionary elements were incorporated in statutes adopted by the State Administrative Council, the reason for giving these statutory form immediately being, perhaps, that the latter could more easily be made both specific in content and general in application. There are as yet no comprehensive codes—civil, criminal, or procedural—though Tung Pi-wu, President of the Supreme Court, urged the need for completion of the work in 1956[30]—and the lack of them has been adversely commented on (e.g. at the time of the 'Hundred Flowers' the criticism was made that it was impossible not to fall foul of the law because

[28] 'Achievements in the Field of Legislation', *Druzhba* (Friendship, 8 Aug 1957).

[29] *PD*, 7 Aug 1958. All these resolutions are translated in Blaustein. Interestingly, a *PD* editorial ('On the 3-level ownership system') of Dec 1960 still quotes the text of the party resolutions as authority for what has been done (*SCMP* 2408).

[30] Speech at 8th Congress of CCP, 19 Sept 1956.

of the mutual contradictoriness of various laws). However, flexibility in the introductory stages of applying new policies has frequently been remarked on by outside observers as a strong point in the Chinese communists' technique of implementing policy. This is how it is reflected in their legal practice—in sharp contrast (and perhaps deliberately so) to the methods of the 1920s and 1930s, when unrealistic statutes were promulgated without regard to the feasibility of implementing them and they remained dead letters, bearing no relation to the realities of actual situations on which they therefore failed to impinge. It is perhaps worth remarking that, apart from the autonomy allowed to minority peoples 'living in compact communities' if laws (e.g. the marriage law) offend their own customs, once laws have been enacted they are uniform for the whole country, the size and local variations of which are no doubt reasons for some experimentation until more experience has been gained. (In contrast to the United States, for example, which does not have uniform criminal laws, marriage and divorce laws in all states.)

The constitution of 1954 was a landmark.[31] It set out the basic principles and detailed structure of the state from top to bottom, also the fundamental rights and duties of citizens. It signalized the achievement of unified, effective control over the whole country and a measure of political development and stability which could by this time be validated and consolidated by giving it public expression in law, though it showed less immutability than is usually associated with constitutions.

The CPR is described in the constitution as a people's democratic state in which all power belongs to the people, and much of the lengthy document is devoted to setting out the system of people's congresses and the administrative structure through which power is to be exercised. Article 4 indicates that the constitution is the framework within which change will take place—'by means of . . . socialist transformation [it] ensures the gradual abolition of systems of exploitation and the building of socialist society' and, as one might expect, there are no mechanisms—like House of Lords or Supreme Court veto powers—calculated to

---

[31] Eng. trans. in Blaustein, pp. 1–53. The provisions of the constitution have not always been adhered to in practice. There has, for example, been no meeting of the National People's Congress (NPC) since Dec 1964. See Richard Harris, 'Chinese in Search of Party Legality', *The Times*, 9 Aug 1967.

delay change. Types of ownership, and the rights and obligations attaching to each type, are given in some detail—a significant feature. (I shall refer to these again later.) Section VI (arts. 73–84) deals with the people's courts and People's Procuratorate[32] (roughly the equivalent of criminal investigation and the public prosecutor), and article 78 provides, without further specification, that 'in administering justice, the people's courts are independent, subject only to the law'.

Adopted the day after the constitution (together with the law on local People's Congresses and People's Councils) was the Organic Law of the People's Courts and that of People's Procuratorates. The first of these spells out in detail the system which, with minor changes, has been in force since for courts of various levels—basic courts, intermediate courts, higher courts, and supreme court— their composition, their double responsibility to senior courts and to People's Congresses of corresponding levels, their powers of jurisdiction, rights of parties, &c. Article 6 of the Organic Law of the Procuratorates provides that these bodies exercise functions and powers independently and are not subject to interference by local organs of state. It must be added in parenthesis that the co-ordination and specification of the respective duties of the courts, procuratorates and public security offices (known collectively as *kung-chien-fa*) have been revised as time has gone on, the public security bureau (which has been the one most closely linked with the Communist Party) gradually gaining in importance over the other two.[33]

Some of the procedures introduced represent practices that had been attempted before but had never taken firm root, some are completely new in Chinese experience and must have required some effort to master. It is provided that trials should be public unless there are special reasons (such as military security being involved) and that they should be conducted through their successive stages according to detailed procedural regulations. A distinction is made between civil and criminal cases. Judges are elected by corresponding people's councils and their work is supervised by higher courts and procuratorates. In courts of first instance only, lay assessors (*jen min shen pan*) (who receive compensation for lack

[32] This, of course, was copied from USSR, the Soviets having continued Russian continental tradition.

[33] See A. Doak Barnett, *Cadres, Bureaucracy and Political Power in Communist China* (New York, 1967), p. 195.

R

of earnings) sit with judges, who act as a 'college', and there are also committees (in which procurators may participate) attached to the courts whose function it is to discuss cases of special difficulty, and to standardize or generalize judicial experience. Rules of evidence have been adopted and determination of guilt (in criminal cases) depends on the evidence.

The object of trial is said to be twofold—to reach a judgment based on the law and the facts, and secondly, to achieve the most satisfactory social-educative result. Much attention seems to be paid throughout to the educational aspect of the proceedings (and officials of the courts give public lectures to explain law in relation to actual situations). Since 1956 professional lawyers have been attached to courts to advise individuals on the laws and in criminal cases can act as defence counsel, but they are supposed to act in the interest of society as well as the accused.[34] Ensuring the accused the right of defence is said to be one of the ways people's democratic legality secures expression; and the chairman of the court has the duty to explain to parties their rights, e.g. to make additions to an appeal or to present new evidence. On the other hand, 'the subjective rights of all citizens collectively' are also safeguarded: the masses have the right to appeal against a verdict they consider wrong. Moreover, higher courts exercise supervision over lower, and courts and procuratorates exercise mutual supervision: verdicts are subject to review if any of these are dissatisfied.

An unusual principle which pervades the judicial apparatus is that known as judicial supervision, established by the law on organization of the people's courts. Besides the actual trial of cases, the courts have the duty to study all that is going on in their area in order to eliminate contravention of the laws. During the time of the intensified co-operativization campaign, for example, it is reported that they studied the local situation in order to understand (*a*) which elements were sabotaging the process, and by what means, and (*b*) the changes in peasant relationships. Thus they were able both to help the Party in carrying out the policy

[34] A good deal of advisory work seems to be done by the lawyers' offices attached to the courts. These lawyers are members of a lawyers' association; there are, of course, no private lawyers. I was told in 1964 that the fee for defence was paid by the accused and that it was low; if the lawyers' income from fees was not enough for daily life, it would be supplemented from public sources. The accused can, if he wishes, conduct his own defence, or it may be undertaken by a kinsman or organization. I was told that it was rare to avail oneself of the services of a lawyer.

and to observe legality in rendering decisions.[35] The courts are, in fact, a source of information on the actual effect of policy as implemented and one link in the chain of communication 'from the masses to the masses'.[36]

We have here evidence of a link which has become more significant as time has gone on, between the courts and the Communist Party. This is not surprising perhaps in the dynamic situation existing during the period of revolutionary transformation in view of the fact that both are concerned with policy—the party in its formulation and implementation, the courts with its interpretation.

The position occupied by the CCP until 1966 was probably unique. The party publicly adopted a constitution in 1956 in which it charged itself with the role of 'leader and core in every aspect of the country's life'. Among the tasks laid on local party organizations are these:

To lead the masses of the people to take an active part in the political life of the country

to lead the masses to give full play to their creative ability, to strengthen labour discipline, to ensure fulfilment of the production and work plans.

. . . to expose and eliminate shortcomings . . . and to wage struggles against the violation of laws and discipline . . .

Provision is also made for examining and dealing with cases of violation of party discipline and of state laws and decrees by party members.[37]

In view of the party's comprehensive and pervasive responsibility for policy fulfilment it was almost inevitable that it should be involved in judicial work. It is clear that a court's interpretation of 'law' (i.e. all the resolutions, decrees, &c. that serve as law) in its decisions will be affected by its understanding of the programmes and policies to which these give effect. The judges in

---

[35] V. E. Chugunov, *Criminal Court Procedures in the Chinese People's Republic* (Moscow, 1959; *SBTS* 458), p. 14.

[36] Before convocation of 34th session of the 1st NPC, a number of deputies visited different areas to inspect the work of the People's Courts and reached an understanding of conditions in this field. They also brought up valuable views 'which we shall solemnly study for the improvement of our work', according to a report by Tung Pi-wu to the NPC, June 1956, on the work of the courts in previous years (*CB* 394).

[37] Blaustein (pp. 55–96) translates the party constitution. See particularly pp. 61, 89, 91. On punishments for lapse of party discipline, see also Doak Barnett, p. 196.

courts at all levels, like everyone else, will have taken part in small group discussions of the issues and problems with which any particular policy is intended to deal, and many of them will have participated in discussions within the Communist Party. When a doubtful case arises in court, the proper channel of consultation through which guidance should be obtained (according to the organic law), would, of course, be the superior courts which presumably possess, and would thereby develop, greater expertise. It seems, however, that the course increasingly adopted in recent years has been to consult the secretary of the local party branch.[38] If in course of time the party ceases to be the chief instrument of popular will, whatever organization displaces it will presumably inherit this function and the courts will be expected to back up the new source of policy.

LAW IN RELATION TO PROPERTY

In Marxist thinking the system of property ownership is the crucial determinant of a society's structure. And it is one of the functions of law, as part of the machinery by which state policy is enforced, first to act continuously to bring about the desired ownership system (i.e. one in consonance with socialist values) by establishing legitimate forms of ownership and by the systematic and orderly transformation of existing forms into desirable ones; secondly, to uphold the ownership system by providing legal protection of property rights, not in an absolute sense but in accordance with public interest.

As is well known, and in self-conscious and explicit contradiction to both their Chinese predecessors and 'Western liberal' attitudes, they regard as immoral the vesting of permanent ownership of expanding wealth—and in particular the ownership of socially-used means of production—in private hands, so the general aim of policy in this case has been the gradual transformation of private property (with exceptions to be noted) into collective and state property. An independent worker's means of production (e.g. a craftsman's tools) are not included in this prohibition. Nor are the 'means of life'—broadly, income from labour, savings, and consumer capital: the house one lives in and the bicycle one rides may be privately owned. But private

---

[38] J. A. Cohen (see n. 46), p. 485, says that the party is more significant in legal process in China than in Russia.

ownership, wherever it exists, is always subject to restriction in amount, in time, or in kind, in accordance with regulations currently in force. (Private savings, encouraged presumably because of the need for capital investment and to avoid inflation and protected under article 11 of the constitution, could become a problem in future.)

The forms of ownership for the means of production legally recognized (according to the constitution) are the following:

i. State ownership, that is, by all the people, e.g. of heavy industry, railways, port facilities.

ii. Collective ownership [by co-operatives, communes, &c.] e.g. of agricultural land, marketing facilities, agricultural equipment and produce.

iii. Individual ownership, e.g. tools of a craftsman working on his own.

iv. Capitalist ownership—the restricted rights of existing owners of enterprises [for as long as this type of ownership lasted].

Two forms of co-ownership are provided:

i. Common ownership of things which can, for purposes of disposal be divided (e.g. in regulations for co-operatives, all property of peasant households, other than means of life, which were privately owned should constitute the common property of the household). This applies particularly to marriage and divorce settlements, regardless of what was contributed by each partner.

ii. Co-ownership by shares, of things which cannot be divided, according to which individuals have the right to withdraw, sell, or transfer their own share, but co-owners have preferential rights of purchase (as perhaps craftsmen working in co-operatives, wishing to transfer).

While the actual allocation of property between these types is regarded as being in flux (and one does not need to remind the reader of all the changes there have been through land reform, co-operatives, communes, &c.), the distribution in existence at any time is subject to legal protection and remedy for infringement of rights. According to the 1957 textbook, the purpose of this protection was said to be: in the case of state and collective ownership, to ensure the growth of socialist economy and the consolidation and development of socialist public ownership; in the case of individual owners, to 'help him increase production, improve methods, and take the path of co-operativization on the basis of the principle of willingness'; in the case of the capitalist, it was said to be to 'implement the policy of utilization, restriction and transformation, gradually to replace capitalist ownership by the system of ownership by all the people'. With regard to the protection of the means of life, it was said to be 'for the benefit of the citizen's material and cultural life, and the constant improvement of people's life on the basis of developing production'.

Rights of ownership, as in other civil law systems, imply rights of possession, use, and disposition, but these are not unlimited: they must be exercised in conformity with the norms of law in force and with the assumption of the appropriate legal duties, which vary as between the different types of ownership. In regard to the right of use, socialist principles of mutual assistance and co-operation are to be observed, e.g. in allowing others access across property. If the state needs to use property in the public interest (e.g. for the erection of electric power or telecommunication poles), it does not usually pay compensation unless great damage is caused. In case of a conflict of interest between a co-operative (now teams, &c.) and the state planning authority. there is said to be protection from coercion, though this, one would think, might be difficult to assert. State organs or enterprises (category (i) of the four listed above) enjoy only somewhat restricted rights of disposition over their assets.

Legal remedies are provided for the protection of property rights. Actions may be brought into court (1) to determine ownership of disputed property; (2) to restore property to its rightful owner; (3) to remove interference with legitimate use and disposition (e.g. cutting off water supply, piling of rubbish); (4) for compensation for loss or damage; or for restitution of undue enrichment. These were said, in 1957, to be 'frequently used in our judicial practice'. Frictions may still occur, but such cases could be expected to decrease afer the organization of communes, (and the number of civil actions is reported to have decreased) if only because of the reduction in the number of 'juristic persons'. Commune organization may also facilitate administrative (in place of judicial) adjustment of conflicts, and presumably Mediation Committees play their part. (The principle of 'fair exchange' in price fixing was of course one practical way of recognizing property rights.)

It is expected that changes in actual ownership will be carried out in the light of actual conditions and practical experience, and *pari passu* with other material and technological change, the aim of policy being always to bring about the distribution of resources which will ensure their utilization in the interests of the people. In China since 1949, the public interest has broadly been equated with expanding production and preventing the re-emergence of 'capitalism', that is, exploitative relationships. The aim is to carry through the changes on the basis of the principles of fair exchange and willingness, i.e. by persuasion rather than coercion.

About the application of these policies, two things are to be noted: first a distinction between 'transitional' and later periods (though what must be remarked is that no sharp break in policy is contemplated between the two); secondly, a difference from Western thinking in the matter of the balance between protection of public and private interests.

During the transitional period, a gradual transformation of ownership was to be expected as collectivization proceeded, but the communists have emphasized that this is a process that will continue indefinitely. If the emergence of capitalism is to be avoided, it must be a continuing object of policy to prevent wealth from accumulating in private hands (by pursuing appropriate investment and interest policies and mechanisms like credit co-operatives, which therefore form part of the climate of ideas in which law will be applied and rights protected).

Whereas in the West the assertion and legal protection of rights has been primarily concerned with private rights (though this principle has become eroded somewhat as the state has undertaken more responsibility for social welfare), this is not the case in China. People as individuals—even the word 'individual' it will be remembered, has pejorative overtones—are believed to have most to gain by the extension and protection of rights of public (state) and collective ownership over the means of production. This is not to say that the individual is of no account: marriage and inheritance settlements respect the rights of individuals, and it may perhaps be mentioned that the principle of co-ownership is a way of protecting individuals who would formerly have had no rights. But it is a matter of a different order of priorities. We hear of 'protection of socialist public property and citizens' property from wilful damage', for example, in that order. It is thought that material and cultural life will improve as more assets are brought within the sphere of public and collective ownership. Only the latter get *unconditional* legal protection; private ownership receives protection according to the statutory decrees in force at any given time.

This is not to be taken to mean that the trend of transformation is always simply in the direction of transfer to progressively *larger* collectivities, as can be demonstrated by what happened in the matter of property ownership when the communes were re-organized. As contrasted with the concentration of ownership and authority of the first days of the communes, since the reorganisation, the three-tier system of economic organization and political authority is mirrored by a three-tier system of ownership. As ownership confers rights of disposition and use, it was deemed to be correct to vest ownership in the group making use of resources for purposes of production. Ownership is thus closely linked with the functions of management and accountability. In 1960 it was the middle tier, the production brigade (*ta tui*), as the central link in a chain of tasks, that was considered the most suitable basic unit of ownership, while the commune above and the production team below both enjoyed 'partial ownership'.[39] This, it was said, would strengthen the material basis of both commune and team, facilitate leadership in organizing co-ordinated operation and support the distribution system. By 1962, the emphasis had swung to the production team (*hsiao tui*) as the basic unit.[40] Thus, the ownership of land was from this time vested in the production team which worked it; similarly with agricultural implements, machinery, workshops, and animal farms for which the unit of management is the team. The brigade owns large-scale and medium-scale agricultural equipment unsuitable for dispersed use, and besides acts as an intermediary and supervisor in guiding teams to use their resources for production in accordance with

[39] 'The Three-level Ownership System with the Production Brigade as the Basic Level . . .', *PD* editorial, 21 Dec 1960 (*SCMP* 2403).

[40] Kuan Huai, 'A tentative Discussion on ownership based on production teams in rural people's communes', in *CFTC*, i (1963), pp. 15–20.

state requirements, and in seeing that government bulk-purchase quotas are fulfilled—and no doubt in the allocation of funds between consumption and investment. Meanwhile the commune itself is the owner of the means of production for basic construction, large-scale agricultural machinery, means of transport, forest and mountain land, and enterprises which it continues to run with the agreement of the commune representative council and the approval of the *hsien* people's committee. (The onus seems to be on the commune to justify retaining ownership of these.) As well as the direction of these changes, perhaps one should again note the flexibility which the possibility of absorbing this kind of change into the legal order affords to the implementation of policy. When this allocation was adopted, it was expressly stated to be the correct one at the stage of economic and social development then reached.

There have also been oscillations in regard to the technical ownership of the privately-owned plots, *tzŭ-liu ti*. In view of the fact that they are not a chief means of production and are worked by the 'owner' without exploitation of others' labour, and that it is in the public interest that this should be so, in the early days of the co-operatives they were treated as private property (and could be inherited). Since 1956, however, they have been regarded as 'private property for public use'.

Consideration of ownership rights leads on to two related topics: inheritance and contracts. Both are the subject of fairly detailed studies by lawyers in the west and are not very controversial, so I shall pass over them lightly.

On the first it may be said that the principle seems to be that things that may be privately owned may be inherited, but in China succession is always limited succession. (The interesting question of whose claims are entertained—beyond the fact that there is no longer discrimination against females—need not detain us here.)[41]

The system of civil law adopted by the CPR provides theoretic- ally for several different kinds of contract indicating the rights and duties of parties.[42] In practice, '[t]ransfer of goods within the state sector does not involve change of title; it can be done by an

[41] On this whole subject see van der Valk, in Z. Szirmai, ed., *Law in Eastern Europe*, v: *The Law of Inheritance in E. Europe and China* (Leyden, 1961).
[42] *Civil Law Lectures*, chs 13–20.

administrative order. But a transfer of goods from one sector to another involves alienation of ownership. Contract in this case becomes indispensable.'[43] Contracts, *ho-t'ung*, are negotiated between industrial enterprises, communes (and units within communes), municipalities, and various agencies of the Ministry of Commerce; they signify the entry into relationship and acceptance of obligations subject to agreed penalties. They are perhaps most properly to be regarded as part of the machinery of economic planning; any accounting units are potential contracting parties. The state plan for distribution of goods carries legal force[44] but contracts are not, I was told, drawn up by lawyers, nor is it legal machinery that enforces them.

They are broadly of two kinds. The first, *kung-ying ho-t'ung*, are for the supply of industrial products on specified terms. The second, *kou-hsiao chieh-ho ho-t'ung*,[45] are two-way exchange agreements, reached by a long and dynamic process of negotiation, by which the supplier agrees to provide the purchaser with a specified product in return for the means of production needed to produce it.

An important function of these agreements appears to be the formalizing of obligations so that workers can be exhorted to achieve targets set for their production unit. Differences prior to reaching agreement or arising out of them later because of non-fulfilment are subject to discussion and adjustment between bodies higher in the administrative hierarchies (assisted one might suppose by related party organs). The specified penalties are by no means always enforced, though there is apparently some extra sanction in the scrutiny of past performance in regard to contract obligations, for example, before loans are granted for purchase of agricultural products.

Perhaps it may be said that, above a certain size and level of technical complexity, economic activity in any country—whether of the 'free market' type or centrally planned—has need of a mechanism for creating *ad hoc* relationships entailing obligations

---

[43] Gene T. Hsiao, 'The Role of Economic Contracts in Communist China', *Cal. Law R.*, liii (1965), 1029–90. Reprinted Berkeley Chinese Series no. 187, p. 1042. See also Richard M. Pfeffer, 'The Institution of Contracts in the Chinese People's Republic', *CQ* (1963), no. 14, pp. 153–7; no. 15, pp. 115–39.

[44] *Civil Law Lectures*, pp. 241–2.

[45] Hsiao (p. 1053) has some interesting comments on the way these marry Marxist dialectic with concrete Chinese actuality.

which can be enforced by legal judgement or some other way. The Chinese, having apparently rejected the Russian expedient of a central agency for arbitration of economic questions, seem to have preferred to draw on their own tradition where it was serviceable: particularly in techniques of negotiation, mediation, and compromise backed by pragmatic (and now reinforced by economic) sanctions.

CRIMINAL LAW[46] AND DISPUTE SETTLEMENT

The view taken of the criminal law is that it plays only an auxiliary role in the effort to build socialism, its tasks and form changing in line with change and development of the political and economic situations. While socialist economic and cultural construction are themselves the foundation and guarantee for the eventual elimination of crimes,[47] the criminal law is a necessary means in the transition to socialism. Its aims are said to be to punish criminals, to educate citizens to observe law, and so to protect and promote the accomplishment of socialist construction and socialist transformation. No one is punished without the attempt also being made to educate and reform him: the system is oriented to the future, not the past.

The criteria of what constitutes a crime are laid down as being offences (1) which constitute a danger to society, (2) which deserve punishment (as being a violation of any law, resolution, order, &c.), and (3) committed with intention or fault. Of the substantive law, I have already spoken of its inclusiveness and flexibility, and therefore its uncertainty and vagueness, especially where different policy objectives conflict. The aims of criminal procedure are to decide: (1) if a crime has been committed; (2) whether the person accused is guilty or not; (3) if so, of what crime he should be convicted; and (4) what punishment he should be given.[48]

As mentioned above, legal safeguards include provision of defence counsel and possibility of appeal. Cohen mentions cases,

---

[46] The fullest treatment of this so far is by J. A. Cohen, 'The Criminal Process in the People's Republic of China: an Introduction', *Harvard Law R.*, Jan 1966, pp. 469–533.

[47] I was told on a housing estate on the outskirts of Shanghai that it was a fact that fewer inter-personal quarrels—one cause of crime in old China—arose as living and housing standards improved.

[48] See *Lectures on the General Principles of Criminal Law in the PRC* (Peking, 1957) (SBTS 463), s. 2, 'The Tasks of Criminal Law'.

which occurred in the 'middle period', when defence lawyers argued spiritedly for mitigation or conviction for a lesser crime than the indictment, but their functions appear later to have become attenuated. There is no presumption of innocence, and refusal to confess entails more severe punishment, so accused persons do not always avail themselves of the appeal procedure. Since the functions of the procuracy were reduced in 1958, mutual surveillance as between different offices seems not to operate, and checks against improper arrest, for example, are operated only internally by different offices of the police. Errors by legal officers are subject to internal check by their own superiors, not publicly, though a person wrongly convicted has the right to apology or compensation.[49]

The sanctions which can be imposed by the courts comprise: (1) reprimand or criticism-education; (2) control (or surveillance), whereby the person punished is subject to labour reform under the control of state organs[50] or mass supervision; (3) detention— imprisonment for the period of not more than six months; (4) imprisonment for a given period with labour reform;[51] (5) life imprisonment; (6) death sentence—suspended for 2 years (giving a chance to the convict to repent and reform); (7) death; (8) fine; (9) confiscation of property; (10) loss of political rights. The last three are accessory punishments, and it is particularly stressed that a fine cannot be substituted for imprisonment, as in bourgeois societies.

It would be unrealistic to look at sanctions only as they are imposed by the courts, since there are besides a range of sanctions which can be imposed on ordinary members of the public by Security (*Kung An Pu*) police, or local neighbourhood com-

---

[49] Cohen's view (p. 531) is that as compared with the USSR, the Chinese communists have put more reliance on persuasion, and on social and administrative pressures to secure conformity, but that, when the criminal process is invoked, the accused receives less protection from legal procedure than was the case in Russia at a comparable stage.

[50] *Chi-kuan kuan-chih* (organ surveillance) was introduced after the 'San Fan' movement. The person would be retained in his post, given only essential living supplies and deprived of political rights while under supervision—usually a period of 1–2 years. See *Wen-hui pao* (Hong Kong), 27 Mar 1952 (*CB* 306).

[51] Labour re-education (*lao-tung kai-tsao*) in corrective labour institutions was said to be intended (1950) as a means of 'punishing counter-revolutionaries and other criminal offenders and educating them into new persons in the process of work'. For the conditions attaching to it, see Blaustein, pp. 240–65. See also Rickett, *Prisoners of Liberation* (1957) and Aisin Goro Pu Yi, *From Emperor to Citizen* (1964).

mittees, &c., ranging upwards from criticism-education to rehabilitation through labour, while members of the Communist Party and personnel in state administrative organs are subject to disciplinary measures which derive from their status in them and are defined in the constitution or regulations of these bodies. One reads of cases in which an official has been dismissed from office and/or expelled from the Communist Party, and then, after these hearings, handed over to the law. Conversely, acquittal by a law court may not clear a person completely. In practice, the courts are only part of the official sanctioning apparatus.[52]

A large part of the work of the procuratorial and judicial organs has been concerned with what is described as the 'suppression of counter-revolutionaries', that is, opponents of the regime, under the 'Statute on Punishment for Counter-revolutionary Activity' of 20 May 1951[53] (arts 16 and 18 of which allow analogical and retroactive application). In the early days after 1949, until about 1955, these were mostly recalcitrant landlords and former KMT agents who did not give themselves up. They might be treated with leniency if they voluntarily confessed and repented of past misdeeds (art. 14), and if they were doing socially useful work, this was often taken into consideration. In later years it was claimed that agents had infiltrated from Taiwan. Latterly they have represented the ineducable conservative opposition. At any time of intense political activity, there will be a proportion of people whose thinking lags behind; these must as far as possible be dealt with by persuasion, but—so the thinking goes—if any deliberately break the law, attempt acts of sabotage, or commit personal violence for a political motive, they must be dealt with by the criminal law. Counter-revolutionary *crimes* must be dealt with by courts; this represents the courts' part in the handling of 'contradictions between ourselves and the enemy'; hence the rather unlegal tone of reports of courts 'striking blows at the enemy'.

This question needs more thorough examination than I have been able to give it here. However, reading reports of a good many cases that have appeared in the press suggests that many persons accused of being counter-revolutionary could simply have been dealt with as criminals. They had records of crimes that would have secured conviction in any country. The Chinese have chosen

---

[52] See Cohen, pp. 488–92. [53] Blaustein, pp. 215 ff.

to emphasize the political aspect. Likewise, they have chosen to treat as sabotage what might have been dealt with as cases of trespass, negligence or causing wilful damage. This seems to be another aspect of linking political with legal—the legal part in a propaganda campaign.

On the actual working of the courts, whether as agencies of law enforcement or for resolution of inter-personal or inter-organizational conflicts (i.e. assertion of rights), there is very little information to go on.[54] Both these functions moreover are shared with other institutions. Just as law courts are only part of the coercive apparatus of the people's democratic dictatorship (and there are besides administrative sanctions, re-education agencies, &c.), so settlement of disputes is provided for formally by other machinery than courts.

As mentioned above, the procedure usually adopted to settle an argument arising out of non-fulfilment of contract (between one enterprise and another, or between commune and municipality) is by arbitration between higher levels of the respective administrative hierarchies. Perhaps this is covered by the provision that 'civil rights are further protected by administrative procedures. . . . The people's government . . . reconciles disputes between a higher organ and lower organisations.'[55] In 1964 I was told that the courts would not receive such cases.

The all-China Federation of Labour drafted provisional rules for settling labour disputes (which were to be worked out in detail by local People's Governments to suit local circumstances), according to which the Labour Bureau of the People's Government should be the organ for mediation and arbitration in all disputes.[56] If both parties themselves, and then higher levels of the trade union and management, have failed to reach agreement, the dispute should be taken to the Arbitration Committee of the Labour Bureau. Appeal against an award of this committee might be lodged with the People's Court.

[54] Visitors to China who have seen courts at work have usually been favourably impressed, but there have been few such reports in recent years. On the volume of work, reports from People's Courts to People's Congresses give statistics usually under the heads of civil and criminal cases dealt with, letters from the public disposed of, and public calls received; also some information on fluctuations in the different types of case.

[55] *Civil Law Lectures*, pp. 63–64.

[56] See Blaustein, pp. 501–6, 'Provisional rules of procedure for settling labour disputes'.

Production disputes in rural areas seem to have constituted a problem for a time. A report from Chekiang speaks of conflict over scarce resources arising from a selfish mentality and habits formed under long years of individual operation and small property.[57] Disputes in the Tientsin area arising from the expansion of the irrigated area beyond the capacity of local water resources were reported at about the same time.[58] Cadres were encouraged 'to intervene fearlessly and, after studying conditions, to offer solutions based on mutual concessions and bearing in mind over-all interests'.

In the early days mediation offices were attached to the courts in the larger towns. They gave way to lawyers' offices at the courts, which are said to dispose of many incipient disputes by supplying information about the law, and to semi-formal neighbourhood mediation committees (*tiao chu wei yuan hui*). There is no obligation to approach these in preference to the courts, but they are said to be specially useful for dealing with cases of marital disharmony or cases involving juveniles. The *Kwang-ming jih-pao* (Kuangming Daily) summarized a correspondence on People's Mediation Committees in 1956 showing that there was some controversy about them.[59] They were advocated on the grounds (1) that people were used to the idea: such mediation was part of Chinese tradition; (2) that matters could be dealt with before they reached large proportions, informally and without delay; and (3) that the committee could act as a channel of communication between the court and the public. In the towns they seem to have been accepted more readily, but in country districts opponents (11 out of 30 correspondents) argued that they were a waste of time and that disputes that arose over work, pay, or benefits could be better handled by leaders of production. A report by the Vice-President of the Supreme Court speaks of judges of basic-level people's courts 'familiarizing themselves with agricultural and industrial production in order to live together with workers and peasants . . . and be able to guide the work of Mediation Committees'.[60]

In 1956 Tung Pi-wu, President of the Supreme Court, spoke of embodying in the new legal system whatever was beneficial to the

[57] Report of Chekiang Higher Court to People's Congress, 22 Dec 1956 (*SCMP* 1465).
[58] *PD*, 17 June 1957 (*SCMP* 1561).   [59] *SCMP* 1391.
[60] To the NPC, 24 Apr 1959 (*CB* 569).

people in the old.[61] It seems as if some inheritance has after all been accepted from traditional Chinese practice in the area in which it was strongest.

CONCLUSION

It was inevitable that in attempting such a broad survey the treatment must at many points remain superficial. All these questions deserve much more thorough examination and fuller documentation than I have been able to give here. I shall, nevertheless, attempt some tentative conclusions.

In a country in which law and law courts had never been regarded highly, and while themselves rejecting the innovation of their predecessors in government, the leaders who came to power in 1949 have set out to create a legal system as one of the instruments by which to implement their policies, and at the same time to win for it the confidence of the mass of the people. With these ends in view they have devoted a considerable amount of attention to legal development; they have gone some way gradually to develop a body of substantive laws embodying new policies; they have set up an apparatus of courts for trying civil and criminal cases which bears no relation to courts of previous regimes; they have organized the systematic professional training of the body of men and women engaged in the work; they have set up research institutes and technical journals; and at the same time they have sought to remove public prejudice by making the mass of the people aware of the new developments and by encouraging them to take part in the work. Results summed up in a sentence have been arrived at only after intense and widespread activity. As was to be expected, the system has gone through successive phases of development. There have been changes in the nature of the work performed and types of case dealt with *pari passu* with other social development. While the regular reports from the courts are at pains to point out their shortcomings and slowness in eradicating age-old attitudes towards law, the statistics of cases, &c. dealt with and the reports of greater efficiency (measured by the number of cases calling for reinvestigation and revision) give evidence of some success in this field. Legal machinery has no doubt benefited from the general

[61] 19 Oct 1956 (*SCMP* 1375).

raising in standards of conscientiousness and honesty in the public service.

Besides owing a debt to the USSR and other socialist juris-prudence, in the notion of socialist legality, for example, and in procedures of investigation and trial, some features of the new system represent a development of old Chinese techniques—like low-level adjudication of disputes by informal or semi-formal agencies, extra-judicial arbitration by administrative organs, and sanctioning by extra-judicial bodies.

What they have never attempted is to make a sharp distinction between political or administrative work on one side and legal-judicial on the other. The idea of the separation of powers is rejected as a bourgeois notion. Law is an adjunct of policy, and the conjunction is signalized in a constantly recurring expression —*cheng-fa*—in phrases like political-legal work, political-legal cadres, and political-legal research.

The legal system may be observed to be performing (but not to have a monopoly of) tasks expected of it in other modern societies: the demarcation of changes in the content of relationships by means of a variety of forms of what we may loosely call legislation; as a source of decisions in doubtful cases arising from these, and punishing those guilty of infringement of legal norms or endanger-ing society. It does now possess the power to reinforce the new value system and is particularly effective in reinforcing the tran-sition from private to public and from particularistic to univer-salistic values. Some tasks laid on the law by the Chinese them-selves appear mutually incompatible unless understood in the light of these values—e.g. the protection of private rights has a place, but, in case of a conflict between the two, comes second to public rights.

Since 1949 the legal and judicial apparatus has been used to reinforce the dynamic aspects of society, or as Tung Pi-wu put it in a report to the National People's Congress in 1956, 'to establish a revolutionary order'. It provides an extra corrective to ensure that policies adopted are carried out as intended, and policy has more often than not been dynamic. There are, however, some examples of its use for the protection of the existing social order, for example of capitalists' or peasants' property. It has not acted as a brake on progress—this would understandably have low priority in a revolutionary situation after centuries of stability

s

now regarded as evil and decades when the central government did not have effective power to introduce change. Nor has it served (at least in public; in private advice to the Communist Party the courts may try to serve this function) as a mechanism for the mutual adjustment of conflicting objectives of policy. The law as such does not offer any check to the introduction of ill-considered policy.

One may question whether law itself adds much (as much perhaps as Chinese as well as others may desire to see) to the individual citizen's personal sense of confidence and security (though it could be argued that other aspects of the dynamism which the legal system serves do in other ways secure these things —the opportunity of work, welfare, &c.). It seems to be taken for granted that the interest of each is identical with the interest of the people as a whole or, as remarked above, that in case of conflict the collective takes priority over the individual. For a time this may have been a defensible position, following decades when the exercise of individual rights was achieved in the context of suffering of helpless masses of people.

There may be some sources of weakness inherent in some other features; for example, judicial decisions the world over have a prescriptive (i.e. educative) effect as a by-product; that is, people tend to take note of them in their future conduct. But it may be that there is an inherent incompatibility between the roles of judicial arbiter and *conscious* educator. The sports referee steps out of that role when he becomes the coach. Again the criteria of justification may depend on the stage of social transformation reached, and as a method this may at some stage fall into disuse, whether or not theory catches up with practice.

Another long-term disadvantage from the point of view of technical and legal development may lie in the retention of extra-judicial mediation procedures, though these can be justified on a number of grounds, and the advantages and disadvantages may be delicately balanced. But if the effect is to reduce the number of civil cases reaching the courts to a point at which the latter become exclusively associated in the public mind with criminal cases, the newly-created confidence in the courts might ebb away. If, besides this, a serious proportion of the sanctioning that goes on should be by official bodies other than courts, the most technically perfect court cannot be expected to retain respect. Such exercise of power subject only to administrative, not judicial, restraint may be justified on grounds of security in an emergency situation or time of revolutionary transformation. As a regular procedure it would be difficult to defend.

Societies vary in the proportion of societal tasks that are placed on the legal system; as the system gains experience and strength, more may be placed on it. While in China it may be difficult to distinguish technical legal development at the upper and lower extremes where law, security and politics tend to intermingle, it appears that in the middle levels of the judicial hierarchy—that of the intermediate courts—the experience of these years may have given rise to a store of technical expertise, representing a real gain of which more use might be made in the future.

We are speaking at an interim stage of a country still undergoing revolutionary transformation. A Belgian jurist[62] has compared the constructive legal task in China in these years to what faced France in the years following 1789. Perhaps we may say that, while the part assigned to law was not what we in the West would require of it, much of what was set out in the Common Programme in this regard has been achieved and may be the foundation for further advance. What we are now seeing perhaps is how much there was to do.

POSTSCRIPT

The reader will wish to know how the legal/judicial system has been affected by the Proletarian Cultural Revolution, in the course of which for nearly two years now all existing structures have again been called in question.

In March 1968 it is still too early to say what the total effect of this upheaval will be and what organizational forms will eventually be established in China in consequence. The fact that most available reports of what has been happening emanate from press and radio which are under the control of the (Maoist) Cultural Revolution group must make one cautious about drawing final conclusions. However, certain things can be said.

While revolutionary change is still the watchword and this upsurge in fact represents a swing farther to the left (that is towards collective and away from individual values), for a time

[62] René Dekkers, 'La vie juridique', in Inst. Solvay, *La régime et les institutions de la république populaire chinoise* (Brussels, 1960).

at least the Communist Party has ceased to be the generally recognized vanguard, inspiration, and arbiter of revolutionary change in China and to constitute a hierarchy of power parallel to or overlapping with the administration. In January 1967, by which time first the youth of the country, then the workers and then the peasants had all been roused to revolt against existing authorities (including authority in the Communist Party), new structures called 'three-way revolutionary alliances' and made up of 'revolutionary masses, revolutionary cadres, and the PLA' emerged to take the lead in the current transformation.

In one province and municipality after another, as conditions permitted, Provincial and Municipal Revolutionary Committees have been set up and now exercise executive power under the Revolutionary Great Alliance at the centre (that is, the Communist Party central committee, the State Council, the Central Military Affairs Commission, and the Central Cultural Revolution Group of the party). The constitution of 1954 is not referred to but is presumably regarded as suspended. Government and non-governmental organizations have carried out their own internal reorganization and set up their own revolutionary committees. Among them, the Chinese Academy of Sciences set up its revolutionary committee, and now has an Institute of Jurisprudence of Mao Tse-tung's Thought.[63]

Government organs at municipal, borough (*ch'u*), and *hsien* levels have been required to carry through 'struggle-criticism-transformation tasks' so that they could strengthen and maintain the dictatorship of the proletariat. From reports of struggle at moments of local crisis, it appears that there have been sharp clashes of loyalties among the staff at these offices, which have been in part the arena in which the struggle has taken place and in part the apparatus by means of which it has been conducted *vis-à-vis* the public. The *Kung-Chien-Fa* (Public Security, Procuratorate, and courts, but Security is named as the mainstay of the three) were in the thick of the conflict at Wuhan in August 1967.[64] There were reports of revolutionary masses struggling against those who had manipulated the *Kung-Chien-Fa*, and of hoodwinked comrades of the Municipal Court and Security realizing how they had been misled and calling a public meeting to clarify their stand to the masses.

The Proletarian Cultural Revolution is represented as a new and heightened form of class struggle in which—following familiar lines—legal/judicial apparatus has its part to play. The Shanghai Municipal Revolutionary Committee, for example, called on the organs of proletarian dictatorship to heighten their revolutionary vigilance and in course of mass criticism and repudiation to deal heavy blows at class enemies, who are portrayed as those with an interest in disturbing social order and stirring up crime.[65] 'The criminal activities of a small number of criminal elements meet the needs of the handful of persons in authority with no concern for the public interest.' The courts and public security are said to be waging war against crime as part of the class struggle to wrest control of the younger generation.[66] As before, it has been stated that the emphasis should be on education, with punishment only as a supplementary measure: attacks should be concentrated on swindlers, robbers, murderers, those whose crimes are serious and who refuse to repent after admonition, those who vacillate politically, particularly landlords, rich peasants, counter-revolutionaries, and bad elements who engage in acts of hooliganism and robbery.

As has happened in the past, mass denunciation has been used for maximum political-educational effect, the attempt always being made to equate dissolute living with the demand for privilege, social disturbance with support for the 'bourgeois road' faction, and common crime with political undependability. Again a moral conversion on a mass scale is being attempted, and the vigilance of the Public Security combined with the threat of mass denunciation must constitute a powerful sanction. It is clear that in many cases it would have been possible to prosecute according to normal procedure, but instead of a simple indictment for improper use of public funds under the law against corruption (or a new law if that was not sufficiently inclusive), the opportunity has been taken to discredit by means of a mass denunciation the whole way of thinking and living of a person who could have committed such an act at a time when the country was in economic difficulties—which may be good for morals but bad for law. Public

[65] BBC *Summary* FE 2538, 9 Aug 1967.
[66] Article in *Wen-hui pao* (Shanghai), Aug 1967 (BBC *Summary*, 6 Aug 1967).

trials have been reported from many large cities—Shanghai, Changsha, Tsinan, Tsingtao, &c.—and some, attended by enormous crowds, have been used as oath-taking rallies in support of Public Security to show that the revolutionary mass organizations are supporting the dictatorship of the proletariat and all that it stands for. Where sentences have been passed at mass trials,[67] it is stated that this has been done with the approval of the courts or of the political/judicial committee of the revolutionary committee; or the cases have been handed over to the courts for sentencing. The evidence of the way they are dealt with will need to be studied. Laws against corruption, crimes of violence, and the rest exist: it remains to be seen how they are applied, and this will depend to some extent on the character and temper of the staff in office at the time.

One must note that, just as judges had been accused in previous anti-Rightist campaigns of being too tender to individual interests in their sentencing, so as the Cultural Revolution has reached its 'criticism and repudiation' stage, one of the crimes for which 'those in authority . . .' have been denounced (i.e. Liu Hsiao-ch'i, Teng Hsiao-p'ing, T'ao Ch'u and those who supported them all over China) has been that of doing their best to secure the reversal of verdicts—in the interests of individuals and against the public interest, understood. The 'wind of reversing verdicts' has been put alongside the 'wind of individual farming' as equally obnoxious and leading similarly to the restoration of capitalism. There have also been some complaints of unjustifiable arrests having been made. Such disclosures serve to underline the disadvantage inherent in the legal/judicial system being made subservient to politics.

Throughout the country wherever the struggle has been most acute the body which has replaced the Communist Party as the source of political wisdom for consultation and guidance is the politically educated and reliable PLA. In Canton at the time of the national day celebrations and the commodities fair in October 1967, the Public Security was called on to be vigilant against all enemies (from agents of Chiang Kai-shek to rich peasants, Rightists, counter-revolutionaries and bad elements) under the leadership of the military control group of the municipal bureau. This is not a

---

[67] After the Wuhan incident of 20 July 1967 a public trial was held which resulted in a collective sentence, details of which I have not seen. See *SCMP*.

matter of calling in the military for police purposes but a shift in the locus of political control.

To conclude, it seems that trends that were already discernible have continued and that patterns that had become familiar in previous campaigns have been repeated, but with significant variations in both organizational links and tone. In the atmosphere of heightened political struggle the legal/judicial apparatus—particularly public security and courts—have been used wherever possible to reinforce political action. As before, the order it stands for is revolutionary order. One shift noticeable so far has been that the pervasive influence of the Communist Party has been—temporarily at least replaced by that of the politically reliable army. Besides this, only the key in which the work is performed has sharpened: where before one heard of the people's democratic dictatorship (in which there was room for all supporters of the People's Republic) we now hear of proletarian dictatorship. The aim is clearly a shift to the left in values and greater intolerance of deviation from these standards: it remains to be seen whether the share in enforcement entrusted to the criminal law will in fact be greater than before.

8

The Performance of the Cadres

JAMES MACDONALD

THIS chapter discusses the performance that is expected of
cadres in China, and describes some of the actual complaints
made against cadres in the period from 1963 to early 1966
(i.e. before the division in the top ranks of the CCP developed in
public). Nearly all of the evidence came from the *People's Daily*,
but concentration on it is thought justifiable because that journal
is required reading for members of the party, and until 1966
provided evidence that it was not the exclusive organ of a faction
of the central committee. There is in fact an advantage to be
gained from relying on the *People's Daily* since what is published
there requires integration with the formal position of the party.

A deficiency of this method of proceeding is that it precludes
taking much account of activities which were not officially
publicized: for example, the 'clean-up' movement of 1963–6 in
city and country, aimed specifically at cadres, was generally
known throughout China to be proceeding, but was only very
briefly and scantily mentioned, as far as I can tell, in publications
allowed to leave China. In the absence of substantial new sources
of information, however, it is difficult to give an account of such
movements anyway.

To begin with, some discussion of the use of the word 'cadre'
should be undertaken. Basically, in its present use it seems to
mean 'official'. Office-holders who in most other countries would
be called 'officials' are known in China as 'cadres'. A distinction
has to be made at once between party cadres and non-party
cadres, i.e. whether the office is held inside the party or outside.
Inside the party, members, elected officers and appointed officers
of committees are cadres. Cadres within and without the party
all seem to have ranks, with different groupings (such as what
might be called the 'civil service', the military, the academic
profession, industry, and the mass organizations) all having their

own tables of rankings. But none has been published. One authority lists a 'civil service' of 32 ranks, with the Chairman of the Republic at grade 1. Graduates are said to enter this scale at grade 21. Another authority says that 'state' cadres go no further down the list than grade 24 in the cities and 26 in the country. However, below the state cadres there are in the country local cadres, for example in the communes, where only one or two state cadres may be found.[1]

The position is thus one of considerable complication. For general purposes, it is useful to think of officials of all organizations as cadres. But as the Chinese word for 'official' is now only used as a term of abuse, and implies attitudes contrary to those required of a cadre, so that for a cadre to be accused of acting like an official is a grave accusation, the distinguishing features of the cadre must be sought outside of a bureacratic structure. The cadre is a new type of official.

The core of the newness can be indicated shortly. But the complex of qualities making up a good cadre were not defined at one point in time. They grew up, so to speak, with the Chinese revolution. It is true that one could point to Mao Tse-tung's 1938 report to the sixth plenary session of the sixth central committee, where he enumerates the criteria by which a cadre should be judged: whether he is resolute in carrying out the party line, keeps to party discipline, has close ties with the masses, has the ability to find his bearings independently, and is active, hardworking and unselfish.[2] But this is lacking in the suggestion of all-out commitment to the revolutionary dynamic which is now identified with Mao. The revolutionary dynamic is the quality which is the core of the new 'official', the cadre, and is in contradiction not only with the old 'officialdom', but with the institutional implications of anything which replaces it, including the cadre structure, except as the institution may be self-adapting through the self-adaptation of the people involved. The performance of the

---

[1] Precise information on this subject is hard to find. The general listing is in *Staffing Procedure and Problems in Communist China*, by the Sub-Committee on National Security Staffing and Operations to the Committee on Government Operations, US Senate (Washington, 1963). The nature of cadres, including the distinction between state and local cadres, is discussed by A. Doak Barnett in *Cadres, Bureaucracy and Political Power in Communist China* (New York, 1967), pp. 38 ff. & *passim*.

[2] Mao Tse-tung, *Selected Works* (Peking, 1961–6), ii: 'The role of the Chinese Communist Party in the national war', p. 202.

activities listed by Mao itself depends on commitment to the cause in this way. It may be thought that this is too obvious to mention: but it was not too obvious to mention inside China in 1964, and indeed was fundamental to the socialist education campaign which began there in 1963 and continued till 1966. For the cadre, correct commitment to the cause consists in being a permanent revolutionary: in a conception of the revolution as an ongoing activity continually presenting new tasks to the revolutionaries, who have continually to strive for new awareness in order to cope with those tasks. Hence derive such slogans as 'Be a revolutionary for a life-time, study the works of Chairman Mao for a life-time', 'Live to old age, study to old age, reform to old age'.[3] An Tzu-wen, director of the Organization Department of the central committee, said in September 1964: 'Some cadres were active as good cadres during the period of New Democratic Revolution. But at the new stage of the revolution . . . they fell behind the development of the situation. Such cadres, if they do not intensify ideological remolding . . . will no longer be good cadres and will be unable to become good successors.'[4] A further gloss on this is to be found in an article of 20 August 1964 on Youth League cadres by Lu Chin-tung, secretary of the secretariat of the central committee of the Communist Youth League. He says: 'Generally speaking, the ideological consciousness of a revolutionary is always such that it does not meet entirely the demands of the revolutionary struggle which he carries on to realize his ideals.'[5] Ideally, therefore the cadre is engaged in continual ideological remoulding.

His purpose is thereby to serve the interests of the revolution and the people. A central committee party organization handbook of 1958 says that a 'cadre is someone who can be high or low, an official or a citizen, who can lead the masses or accept leadership from the masses: cadres of party and state are advanced elements recruited from the people to lead them in revolution and reconstruction and to serve as the servitors of the people: they are not a permanent profession nor a special class.'[6]

[3] These slogans were frequently given in the *PD* and the *Liberation Army Daily* and other publications in these years.   [4] *Red Flag*, nos 17 & 18, 23 Sept 1964 (SCMM 438).
[5] *China Youth*, no. 16, 20 Aug 1964: 'League cadres must set an example of revolutionization for the youths' (SCMM 438).
[6] *Questions on Organization Work in the Party* (Peking, 1959, in Chinese) by the Research Office of the Organization Dept, CCPCC, Oct 1958 (JPRS 7273), ch. II, answer to question 7.

The party has prescribed numerous forms of activity to try to guarantee the 'revolutionization' of cadres, many of them to be found in the works of Mao. All communists set store by systematic education, but few face the same problems as the Chinese communists, with their enormous peasant population and their largely peasant-made revolution. Mao has always seemed convinced that the right revolutionary outlook could be achieved through education. In 1928, on the Chingk'ang mountains, he admitted that the class basis of his fighting force was hopelessly adulterated, saying that the only solution was 'to intensify political training'.[7] In this way even those coming from mercenary armies came to realize that they were 'fighting for themselves, for the working-class and the peasantry' and so could 'endure the hardships of the bitter struggle without complaint'.[8]

In 1929, in his resolution for the Ninth Party Congress of the party organization of the Fourth Red Army, Mao traced the incorrect ideas in the party organization in the army to a faulty class stand-point but said also that the party's failure to wage a 'concerted and determined struggle' against incorrect ideas and 'to educate the members in the party's correct line' was an important contributory cause. His own constantly reiterated remedy for his list of incorrect ideas was political education.[9]

Political education did not, however, exist in a vacuum. For Mao it had immediate organizational implications: the strengthening of the party. This he also stated in 1928:

The Party representative is particularly important at company level. . . . He has to see that the soldiers' committee carries out political training, to guide the work of the mass movements, and to serve concurrently as the secretary of the Party branch. Facts have shown that the better the company Party representative, the sounder the company, and that the company commander can hardly play this important political role.[10]

These two basic, linked ideas were carried forward when Mao Tse-tung reached a position to influence the programmes of the whole party. The large-scale programme of rectification adopted

---

[7] Mao, *Selected Works*, i, 'Struggle in the Chingkang mountains', p. 81.
[8] Ibid.
[9] Ibid. 'On correcting mistaken ideas in the party', pp. 105 ff.
[10] Ibid. 'Struggle in the Chingkang mountains', pp. 81–82.

for the party in 1942 gave first place to the education of cadres, and required guiding organs to attend to the matter energetically.[11] The methods of political education gave priority to education in post, requiring 90 per cent of it to be done there, and 10 per cent to be done in full-time schools;[12] i.e. education was to be a part of normal life.

Other essential aspects of cadre performance were now isolated. One was personal activism—summed up in the slogans 'Investigate and research', 'Seek the truth from the facts', and 'No investigation, no right to speak'. Mao's reports of some of his own investigations were used as texts.[13] This was doubly important in a party which had suffered so long from dogmatism, and in a country weighed down with the tradition of the man in his study knowing everything, and with all-pervasive backwardness.

Another was the practice of the 'mass line', in which the personal behaviour of the basic-level cadres was crucial. This involved the cadre in constant two-way activity—he passed up the unsystematized ideas which he gathered from those about him and passed them back down once they had been concentrated and systematized, in a ceaseless cycle. Thus was to be guaranteed both leadership by the masses and also the constant raising of their level of political consciousness.

Another was identification with the workers and peasants. In 1940 Mao said

the Chinese revolution is essentially a peasant revolution . . . meetings, work, classes, newspaper publication, the writing of books, theatrical performances—everything is done up in the hills and all essentially for the sake of the peasants. And essentially it is the peasants who provide everything that sustains the resistance to Japan and keeps us going.[14]

In the party rectification of 1942, one of the questions put forward was *whom* revolutionary writing was to serve; the answer: the workers, peasants, and soldiers.[15] Intellectuals were told to remodel themselves through physical labour.[16] Already in 1939, in commemoration of Norman Bethune, Mao had emphasized

---

[11] See resolution of the CC in *Mao's China*, trans. Boyd Compton (Washington, 1952), p. 80.   [12] Ibid. pp. 80–81.
[13] Mao, *Selected Works*, iii, 'Preface and postscript to rural surveys', p. 11.
[14] Ibid. ii: 'On New Democracy', p. 366.
[15] Ibid. iii: 'Concluding address to the Yenan Forum on Literature and Art', p. 84.
[16] Ibid. 'Rectify the party's style of work', p. 40.

the need for selfless devotion;[17] and in 1941 the proper attitude to the people: '. . . the masses are the real heroes, while we ourselves are often childish and ignorant. . . .'[18]

Another was the need for professional qualification. A good illustration of the variety of the needs which had arisen already during Yenan days is to be found in a resoluton of the Politbureau of February 1942, on the subject of cadre-training, which was to include the following types of work: military, political, cultural, educational, propaganda, organization, popular movements, the liquidation of traitors, finance, economics, money, medicine, and sanitation.[19]

These requirements may be briefly summed up. Correct political standpoint is basic and governs all actions. This demands continual political education, which in turn must be organized by a strong party branch. Professional education is also necessary and must be undertaken simultaneously, although political education is the leading factor. Education must be undertaken in an active manner. To correct knowledge and to ensure the correct application of policy there must be constant close contact with the masses. All must understand that they are the servants of the masses. Unity with them can be ensured only by being among them and actually physically working with them.

Just as the struggle to obtain power required a transitional strategy for the CCP, so since 1949 all other phases of development have required their own transitional strategies, and in the process some of the criteria for cadres have attained special prominence and taken on new significance. If the cadre had been crucial for the earlier phase, how much more so did he afterwards become. But the prospects for satisfactory cadre performance at once diminished.

The first need was for a much larger party, and this diluted its quality. Without the tempering struggles of the anti-Japanese and the civil wars, authority increasingly passed to persons less and less qualified by personal experience to lead. Soon the majority had joined the party after it attained power.

A second group of obstacles was created by the early decision to industrialize by means of centralized five-year planning. On

[17] Ibid. ii, 'In memory of Norman Bethune', p. 338.
[18] Ibid. iii, 'Preface and postscript to rural surveys', p. 12.
[19] *Mao's China*, pp. 81–82.

the one hand existing technical personnel still had to some extent to be used in leadership positions. On the other a great number of new technical cadres had to be produced, whose qualifications were, in the event, exclusively (and then often unsatisfactorily) technical, because of the urgency of the need and the fact that the teaching material was exclusively of Soviet origin.[20] Such cadres were often selected because of mere suitability for training, and this put class standpoint in question.[21] There was thus a trend away from the immersion in basic-level Chinese conditions which characterized the party reorganization of the early 1940s.

This trend affected even political teaching material, both in civilian life and in the armed services. The works of foreign communist authorities had a large place in such courses.[22] The thought of Mao Tse-tung was not mentioned in the new party constitution of 1956, although it had been introduced into that adopted in 1945. In the forces, some teachers opposed the teaching of Mao's works because they were not part of the Marxist-Leninist canon.[23]

The supremacy and clarity of the 'correct' political standpoint thereby suffered, without the need for technical cadres even being met. To make matters worse, that need increased. From 1955 to 1957 socialist co-operatives were set up in the countryside and these large-scale units called for large numbers of cadres with appropriate qualification.[24] In 1957, the end of the first five-year plan was accompanied by the decentralization of much economic activity and the proliferation of local industry was encouraged. The need for technical qualification could not be met.[25]

---

[20] See Chang Chung-lin, Director of Planning of the Min. of Higher Education, 'Strive to improve the low quality of higher education', in S. Fraser, *Chinese Communist Education* (Nashville, Tenn., 1965), pp. 209 ff.

[21] Ibid.

[22] *Mao's China*, p. xlix, which mentions, *int. al.*, 12 out of 13 essential books trans. from the Russian.

[23] See the resolution of the enlarged meeting of the Military Affairs Commission of the CCP, pt 1, para. B8 in J. Chester Cheng, ed., *The Politics of the Chinese Red Army* (Stanford, Calif., 1966), p. 72.

[24] *Jenmin Chiaoyü* (People's Education), no. 8, 1958, Chan Cho, 'The needs and training of agricultural technical cadres' (JPRS 17, 183), which quotes a preliminary estimate of Szechwan's needs as 10,000 or more senior (excluding farm machinery experts), 70,000 intermediate, and 900,000 elementary agricultural technical personnel.

[25] See, e.g., ibid. no. 9, 1958, Chan Cho, 'How to cultivate technical cadres for local industries' (JPRS 17, 183).

The reaction of the authorities was twofold. They introduced a demand for 'red and expert' cadres, and also instituted a system of physical labour at the bottom levels as part of the permanent ideological remoulding of cadres.

The qualities of *ts'ai* (basically 'talent') and *te* (basically 'virtue'), which are given as 'ability' and 'political integrity' in the official English version of Mao's 1938 discussion of cadres,[26] are obvious precursors of 'red and expert'. The 1958 organization handbook discusses the relationship between them. It describes 'virtue' as having a firm proletarian standpoint, being loyal to socialist and communist enterprises and wholeheartedly serving the people. 'Talent' is defined as ability, i.e. having a definite understanding of policy and theoretical knowledge. 'Virtue' is, however, said to be basic. If a cadre has the virtue of serving the people wholeheartedly, it will be possible for him incessantly to enhance his talent and his own efforts. But without 'a proletarian stand, one cannot be loyal to socialism and communism, and even with talent one cannot serve the people. (As for the reactionaries, the greater their talent, the more detrimental they will be.) The demands of 'redness' and 'expertness' are said to be basically the same as this, but to represent a higher demand, in keeping with the stage of socialist construction.[27]

In the stage of the socialist revolution, says the handbook, the ideological reform of intellectuals becomes more urgent, although many do not realize it. Some say 'specialize first and become red later' or 'be specialized but not red'. Consequently a sharp struggle has to be waged against the denial of political leadership and ideological reform. Nor is it only the intellectuals, but also the broad masses of cadres who must become 'red and expert'. As Liu Shao-chi had said to the second session of the Eighth Party Congress, 'being red and expert is the way forward for party cadres at all levels'. 'Redness' meant having a firm proletarian standpoint, a communist world outlook, the proletarian ideology and working style, and the Marxist-Leninist method of thinking. 'Redness' had to guide the quality of being specialized, but there was no limit to either: each cadre had to be thoroughly red and profoundly specialized. Each should have his own 'specialization' plan.[28]

[26] As for n. 2.   [27] As for n. 6—ch. II, answer to question no. 9.
[28] Ibid.

The second great principle now again brought forward, and developed in a new way, was that of cadres engaging in physical labour. This was required of cadres on all levels by both party and state. The handbook said that only thus could leadership be improved, relations between cadres and masses established, and officiousness eradicated. It was essential for leading personnel on all levels, and all other cadres too. All except the sick and the aged were to perform manual labour for at least one month a year. Leadership cadres must appear as common labourers in order to help them understand and solve problems. It would also help them to improve their leadership—to overcome 'the three styles' of bureaucratism, factionalism, and subjectivism, and 'the five airs'—'officiousness, plushness, senility, arrogance, and effeminacy'—and to be closer to the masses.[29]

There was still another point, however; this was the indispensability of cadres, having basic-level experience before they could assume leadership. Leadership cadres required a certain theoretical level as well—but basic-level experience was the first demand.[30]

So, in 1957, the great 'downward placement' movement took place, whereby large numbers of cadres were sent out into the countryside and 'red and expert' schools, of varying sorts and sizes, were widely set up. In spirit this was something of a return to the Yenan period when the need to fulfil immediate tasks did not permit the acquisition of a high level of skill and the better part of leadership qualities lay in finding one's orientation within the larger political framework and doing one's best. Emphasis on direct leadership was restored and the union of both physical and mental labour sought in cadre work.

However, the burdens which the Great Leap threw on to its cadres were enormous, and correctness of political orientation could not in fact make up for other deficiencies. It is even far from clear that the political orientation of cadres was in fact 'correct'.

The party expansion had been so rapid, the work requiring to be done so demanding, the use of foreign experience and teaching materials so extensive, that members of the party could not have been prepared for their work, and the conditions of the Great Leap gave them little opportunity to acquire the tempering that a cadre needs in order to perform adequately the quite

[29] As for n. 6—ch. II, answer to question no. 8.   [30] Ibid.

subtle work of representing the views of the lower levels and propagating the policies arrived at at the upper levels. Merely advising them to avoid getting above the level of consciousness of the masses could not prevent this.[31]

This view is supported by the events of the immediate post-Leap period. Cadres were criticized for being too 'over-eager',[32] which can only mean that they did not 'unite with the masses' in their work. In 1961 a major rectification movement was undertaken to correct this deviation and reassert the primacy of the mass line.[33]

A most important statement on the movement was made by Liu Shao-ch'i on the occasion of the party's 40th anniversary, in July 1961. Liu stated the main purpose of the campaign to be 'to help all Party cadres further to understand and grasp the objective laws of China's socialist construction'. Both party members and cadres were to

study conscientiously the basic Marxist-Leninist principles of socialist revolution and socialist construction, study the theoretical and practical problems of China's socialist construction as elucidated by Comrade Mao Tse-tung on the basis of Marxist-Leninist principles, study the general line and the various specific policies of socialist construction as formulated by the Central Committee of the Party, and study the experience in socialist construction of the Soviet Union and other fraternal countries.

Success depended on the understanding of Chinese conditions. Study must be diligent and at the same time practical—it had to be based on meticulous investigation of the environment.[34]

This was further elaborated in an article in *Red Flag* at the same time. It asserted the need to 'seek truth from facts', which could only be done by conscientious investigation of objective conditions. As Mao Tse-tung had said, 'All conclusions must be reached after the situation has been investigated, and not before.'[35] Such

---

[31] See, e.g. Hsü Li-chün, 'Have we already reached the stage of communism?', *Red Flag*, 16 Nov 1958, quoted in R. R. Bowie & J. K. Fairbank, *Communist China 1955–9* (Camb., Mass., 1962), p. 479.

[32] Bowie & Fairbank, the 'Wuhan resolution' of the CCPCC, p. 492.

[33] The campaign was introduced over a period, following the 9th Plenum of the central committee in Jan 1961. The keynote was sounded by Liu Shao-ch'i, in July, in his *Address at the Meeting in Celebration of the 40th Anniversary of the Founding of the Communist Party of China* (Peking, FLP, 1961, in Engl.).

[34] Ibid. [35] *Red Flag*, no. 13, 1961, 'Carry forward the party's fine tradition.'

T

investigation could not be divorced from the principle of the mass line, which demanded the adoption of a modest and prudent attitude, and opposition to arrogance, impetuosity, complacency, and over-confidence. The party member and cadre had first to be the pupil of the masses. No matter what their work or position or how meritorious their deeds, they must be on a footing of equality with the people, behave like ordinary labourers, share the rough and the smooth with the masses, and be at one with them. Party organizations at all levels were to regard the work of educating cadres as an immediate task of great importance.[36]

Two points emerge from these statements. The first is that the thought of Mao Tse-tung was not given supremacy. This is particularly interesting in view of the facts, already pointed out that before 1958 the work of party-building certainly could not have been carried out so as to give thorough training to new members and cadres, and that the borrowing of material from the USSR had to some extent displaced the study of Mao, a process assisted by the failure of the 1956 party constitution to mention Mao's thought. The 'new course' of 1961 once more demoted Mao. The fact that study was now to be so important was certainly the assertion of one of his principles, and his slogan 'Seek the truth from the facts' was used in the process. The accent on revolutionary initiative is clearly missing, however. After all, this was what the rectification was about: over-active cadres. It aimed, at best, to ensure the derivation of initiative from the concrete circumstances, including the state of consciousness of 'the masses'.

But Mao, although not at the centre of national affairs any more, was still chairman of the party, and in public great deference was still paid to him. One thing which he could fairly claim about the disorganization of the period was that according to his long-standing views work could only be done correctly with the correct political orientation, and that this orientation could only be guaranteed by a strong party organization. What this meant precisely can be seen from the work which was now undertaken in the armed forces. There, too, the thought of Mao had previously been demoted when the army had been remodelled from 1955 on, on Soviet lines. But because of the removal of P'eng

[36] *Red Flag*, no. 13, 1961, 'Carry forward the party's fine tradition.'

Te-huai from his command, the army had to come in for some special attention. When examination revealed a great falling off in party and cadre work, a correspondingly more thorough rehabilitation was called for.

In 1960 no less than three enlarged meetings of the CCP Military Affairs Commission were held. The third of these resolved on the complete rebuilding of political work in the armed forces.[37] This resolution was not merely important for the forces, however On 21 December 1960 the central authorities ratified and endorsed it as suitable for political work generally. They ordered it to be distributed to party organizations, government organs, schools, and enterprises down to the local committee level. It is not fanciful, therefore, to look at this document for an expression of what the central authorities sought in political work in the country as a whole, and for a developed statement of the role of the cadre. Indeed, its provisions were given general effect in official policies over the next few years.

Basically, the resolution established certain ideal activities and prescribed the organizational means for achieving them. The primary activity was naturally education, conducted in accordance with the 'four firsts' invented by Lin Piao: first, education had to be directed at the individual man; in it political work came first; in political work, ideology came first; and in that, living ideology as opposed to text-book ideology came first. The fundamental requirement was the widespread study of the works of Mao, especially Book IV, which had then recently been published.

The main strength of organization was expected to come from the rebuilding of party committees at company level and in particular from the collective leadership of the committees. Concurrently recruitment of new party and Youth League members was to be stepped up.

A separate section of the resolution was devoted to the political directors, who were assigned to the companies to conduct party and mass work. These were to be chosen from those company and platoon cadres or technical cadres at the primary level who had had practical training and were experienced in political work. They had to be outstanding party members with a high class awareness, a good ideological quality, a strong desire to make themselves a good example, close ties with the masses, a given

[37] General reference as n. 23.

standard of political knowledge, and the ability for political work.

The work of such a director required a good deal of energy. He had to be a model in his ideological, working, and ethical behaviour. In his work he was to rely upon the party and the Youth League to keep in touch with the masses. He was to take the lead in the development of thought and in using persuasion as a means of education, in verifying the facts to get at the truth, and in enforcing orders swiftly and vigorously. He had to visit platoons and squads frequently to listen to the opinions of soldiers, to carry on individual interviews, and to get to know the names, background, and personalities of the members of each company. In respect of the problems of the rank and file he was to obtain information quickly and clearly, to transmit it rapidly and accurately, and to deal with it properly and expeditiously.

His second task was to be equally active in transmitting the policies of the party and the resolutions of the party branch. He was to explain the purpose and significance of major tasks while they were being performed and to point out favourable and unfavourable aspects of policies and methods. He had to try and stimulate the masses to debate and argue, and to transform the intentions of the leadership into the action of the masses. Special attention was to be paid to backward and delinquent soldiers, in accordance with the principles of the correct handling of contradictions among the people. (There was to be no beating, or use of coercive power or other 'rough' methods.)

The last method specifically recommended was to publicize good, advanced ideas, good persons, and good things; to criticize erroneous thoughts and other bad tendencies; and to intensify the combat nature of ideological work.

In addition to political committees and political directors, cadres in general were dealt with, under the heading 'Build a cadre force which is not only red but also expert.' This section reproduced certain ideas with which we are familiar. The first problem raised was that of new cadres who had grown up under conditions of peace and so lacked experience, and whose ideology was not fully 'proletarianized'. In future cadre policy would pay special attention to these points (among others):

1. Political requirements, including special attention to behaviour in practical struggles and political movements, as well as technical and educational qualifications.

2. Recruiting 'nucleus cadres'—party branch secretaries and party committee secretaries.

3. Drawing primary cadres from soldiers of workers or peasant origin.

4. Boldly promoting suitably experienced young cadres.

5. Giving special training in preparation for positions of importance.

6. Educating and reforming promptly rank and file political cadres with ideological shortcomings (those incompetent and refusing to learn after repeated help to be replaced).

7. Those who became cadres immediately after being students to become soldiers; after training they were again to become cadres but would continue their reform.

8. Cadres all to have the chance to study in rotation at academies and schools for periods of six months to a year; curricula to be realistic and useful, daily classes allowing time for self-study, both teachers and pupils learning to rouse 'the masses'.

9. Cadres in active service to continue military, political, cultural, and professional studies, these not to exceed one-third of the cadre's working hours in the year.

These were high demands and, as events showed, much more easily made of a captive audience of soldiers than of the 'broad masses' of the cadres at large.

As regards the civilian sector, the cadre-rectification campaign was called off at the plenum of the central committee in September 1962.[38] In the following May a new all-embracing educational campaign was directed at the party and the nation, based on the 'three great revolutionary movements'—the class struggle, the production struggle, and scientific experimentation. This was accompanied by attempts to extend and consolidate the system of cadre physical labour which had been introduced in 1957.

However, there was now in the situation a new element, the consequences of which were eventually to be regarded by Mao and his supporters as calamitous. This new element is now widely known as 'economism'. It meant that productive work was directly linked with material incentive, for example in agriculture by the cultivation of private plots and the reinstatement of free rural markets in some products, and in industry by the use of part of

---

[38] The communiqué of the 10th Plenum of the CCPCC (*San Lian Shu Tien*, Hong Kong, Oct 1962) emphasized party solidarity and the class struggle.

retained profits for bonus and welfare funds.[39] This principle conflicted with the expectations of 1958—that the introduction of 'socialist relations of production' would release vast latent energies in the masses which had been repressed in 'capitalist relations of production'—and also with the principle of ceaseless, selfless political leadership. The role of the cadre becomes unclear. If he receives rewards proportionate to his efforts he becomes a kind of manager. This is likely to bureaucratize him and rob him of his revolutionary role. If he does not receive such rewards, but acts in a spirit of self-sacrifice, the rationale of that sacrifice is made more difficult for him to accept and he is likely to become demoralized.

This contradiction lay beneath the *People's Daily's* discussion of cadre behaviour from 1963 to 1966, although it emerged with clarity only towards the end, as the 'national survival' element in economic work became less important. The discussion did not take place in a vacuum. In the background was a growing concern with ideological questions in at least one major section of the leadership. This concern had two prime elements: the development of the polemic with the USSR, and an attempt to combat real and prospective 'revisionism' within China. The struggle over revisionism was the common root of both. It was central to the 1963 socialist education campaign. It was part of the 'Learn from the PLA' campaign which began in February 1964 and was directly injected into the organizational life of many economic ministries in March 1964. It showed itself shortly afterwards in the campaign against Yang Hsien-chen, former Director of the Higher Party school, for propounding a principle alleged to conduce to the theory of peaceful coexistence. It was central to the movement of the middle of that year which tried to guarantee an un-revisionist succession to the existing generation of revolutionary leaders but was also extended to rectify aberrations on the part of those leaders. Perhaps its clearest statement was in the Ninth Comment of the Central Committee of the CCP, published in July 1964, on the Open Letter of the Central Committee of the CPSU of the previous year. In that Comment was the assertion that primary organs of the CCP had degenerated and were seeking protectors and agents in the higher ranks of the party.

---

[39] See Franz Schurmann, 'China's "New Economic Policy"—Transition or Beginning', *CQ*, no. 17, 1964.

It is against this background that the various items of news and editorial discussion of cadre performance must be interpreted. Nevertheless, the total supremacy of this ideological line is not categorically asserted until 1966. Until then its assertion is sporadic and the opposition inherent in the basic contradiction persists. Even the reinstitution in 1964 of the old Peasants' Associations, in the form of Poor and Lower Middle Peasants' Associations, clearly intended as a vehicle for promoting the special interests of those elements of rural society, was not attended by an overt national campaign with that promotion as its object.

To use terms employed earlier in this chapter, what seems to be happening is the gradual reiteration of the need for each cadre to possess a 'revolutionary core'. A reason for the gradualism naturally suggests itself: the need to avoid disruption of economic work. At what stage one could isolate within the party hard-line 'ideologues' and 'economists' is a difficult question. Both sides had identical interests to push as well as divergent ones. Both had good reason to oppose much of the cadre deficiency that was being exposed. The depth of the divergence could easily remain hidden.

Before October 1965 one might see these deficiencies as falling into five groups, all bearing on each other and none really distinct. First are those concerned with the need for cadres to take part in manual labour. Second are a large group concerned with the ways in which cadres act when taking part in manual labour and the effect on it of their ways of performing their normal cadre work. Third may be isolated specific complaints about party work. Fourth comes some discussion apparently intended to improve the professional quality of cadre performance. Fifth, one might isolate discussion directed at ideological shortcomings.

As to the first group, on the question of participation in physical work, there is remarkably widespread evidence of cadres not taking part in it at all. Take, for example, the continual need to send cadres out of the central offices. This should have been a matter of routine. Yet in February 1963 we find the Canton provincial committee announcing that 30,000 cadres should go down to the front-line of production to work with basic-level cadres. Among the officers listed as taking part were a vice-governor of the province, the first secretary of the provincial party secretariat, and secretaries of district and *hsien* party committees. A short time later the Canton committee selected a district party secretary who was said to be able to link closely with the working people and urged all the party members and cadres of the province, especially the leading cadres, to imitate his way of going deep into the country and making himself like one of the family with the masses.[40]

On 2 June 1963 the *People's Daily* repeated the fundamental necessity of cadres taking part in physical labour, and cited an example which was afterwards turned into one of the great models of recent years. This was the celebrated *Ta Chai* (Great Camp) production brigade. Among the lessons to be drawn from it was the cautionary one of how it had been dogged by failure as long as its cadres departed from their pre-1949 attitudes of working with the people and became divorced from physical production. Cadres of both party and state were urged to put into effect sincerely the policy for cadre work.

In the same month the CCP itself commended a special district of Fukien where 80 per cent of the cadres, including those of provincial, special district, *hsien*, and commune level, had 'taken off their shoes and gone into the paddy fields'. At the lower level of the production brigades, 95 per cent of the cadres, it was said, normally worked with the members. One *hsien* was specially mentioned because 13 out of 16 of its party committee members, and 28 out of 34 important commune members, laboured with production teams. From another *hsien* it was reported that in future assessment of cadres their performance of, and leadership in, manual work would be important.[41]

Other examples of cadre practice of manual work could be cited from Kirin, Hopei, Shantung, Shansi, Shensi, Chekiang, and Kiangsi. In 1964 the same needs asserted themselves, with further indications that labour participation by cadres was still sporadic and unsystematic. In March it was reported that over 7,000 cadres had been sent from central government organs to spend a whole year in factories, mines, or communes, and the parent institutions were required to make plans for the successive detachment of cadres requiring such 'tempering'. In Tientsin in the same month a vice-governor of the province, the Mayor of the city, leading members of the provincial and city party committees

[40] *PD*, 12 June 1963.   [41] Ibid.

and over 26,000 cadres took part in street-sweeping to promote a hygiene campaign.

However, it appeared by the middle of the year that the whole theory required restatement, and this it received in the campaign to bring on revolutionary successors. Here the keynote was again that young cadres especially needed 'steeling' by work in the basic-level units. They were to be singled out regularly by rota from all government organs, and those coming directly from schools were to be sent there first, to gain practical experience and 'be tempered in struggle'. Not only the young were involved, however; the same requirements were imposed on the old cadres and leading cadres had to set the example. Those who did not do so could not become qualified to lead the socialist revolution.[42]

Closely linked with failure of cadres at all levels to undertake manual labour was an inadequate performance by many who did take part. One complaint was of lack of system. *Ta Chai* set a good example by preventing their cadres from merely putting in an appearance at the basic levels and working half-heartedly, clocking up work-points which they had not really earned. During the summer of 1963 one *hsien* set up special rules for harvest work. The *hsien* party secretary and magistrate had to put in at least 7–10 days, the *hsien* party committee departmental directors, the *hsien* People's Council office directors, the commune party secretaries and directors at least 10–15 days, the ordinary cadres of those levels at least 20 days, and the cadres of the lower levels as many days as the commune members.[43]

The experience of *An* Mountain district, in Liaoning, is worthy of remark. Comprising two municipalities and two *hsien*, the district had no less than 993 backward production teams. In 1963 a drive to get leading cadres at all levels, and other cadres like accountants and wireless operators, into the fields led to immediate improvement in some teams. All the cadres had to work with plans and targets and use labour record books. There were regular appraisals and the results were published. One of the *hsien* introduced fixed inspections on the 1st of June, August, and October.[44]

[42] *Red Flag*, no. 14 of 31 July 1964 (SCMM 433) editorial & ibid. joint issue 17/18 Sept 1964 (SCMM 438).
[43] *PD*, 14 June 1963.   [44] *PD*, 15 June 1963.

Such encouragement of systematic participation in labour was common. But of itself it was only a step towards actually making that labour useful. A substantial number of items dealt with this aspect of things. In industry it was particularly important. A hemp-spinning factory in Harbin organized a display of skills by cadres, the date of the display being fixed in advance to force them to prepare beforehand. Of 126 cadres taking part, 112 demonstrated ability to perform jobs independently at a satisfactory standard.[45] In a chemical plant in Shanghai 50 young cadres were said to have found work on the factory floor dirty and tiring, but to have reformed under the guidance of cadres who were promoted factory workers.[46] In a machine factory in Shansi the cadres were required to put in one day a week on the shop floor. Some of them merely walked around making observations, and put on 'cadre airs', with the result that the workmen refused to talk to them.[47]

Later in 1964 the experience of a Chungking water-wheel engine factory was widely commended. In order to prevent cadres from talking and looking on they invented the 'three fixeds, one deputize' system whereby each cadre had a fixed job, time, and place, and had to work up enough skill to be able to deputize for a skilled worker.[48]

In agriculture the problem was no less. By mid-1965 it still had not been settled. On 21 May the rule was put forward that at the production-brigade level cadres should take part in labour for at least 120 days in the year, and those of production teams for more than that. A few days later it was advised that plans be drawn up and then agreed in discussion 'with the masses'. In August that year a lengthy report from a *hsien* in Shansi repeated the necessity for rural cadres to work regularly and seriously, for their work to be inspected and publicly appraised, and for each cadre to have a work-record book and to be subject to work-point assessment.

The performance of manual labour was not, however, the only example of unsatisfactory working style. The problem was what Chou En-lai, in his report on government work to the Third National People's Congress in December 1964, called a tendency to act like 'bureaucratic overlords'. A whole group of complaints

[45] *PD*, 28 July 1964.   [46] *PD*, 29 July 1964.
[47] *PD*, 7 Sept 1964.   [48] *PD*, 22 Sept 1964.

was associated with typical bureaucratic malfunction. Much of this is reminiscent of complaints made in most countries, although it usually went further than the simple excoriation of excessive numbers of civil servants and their love of forms which preoccupy the leader-writers in the West. In August 1963, for example, after a series of cognate reports, the 'five fewers' and 'five into the fields' methods were recommended. These called for fewer forms, telephone calls, reports, meetings, and conversations between visiting and local cadres, and advocated five pieces of work which could be taken from office to field. In April 1964 the same problem was again under discussion. One Fukien *hsien* stopped its departments from 'wildly' calling meetings, allotting duties, and demanding reports.[49] Next month another *hsien*, in Liaoning, required its leading members to go to the places where work was actually being done in order to pass on information, and to gather it, rather than work by telephone.[50] In June next year, however, the same problem was still being discussed.[51]

Working from offices alone had other undesirable effects. One quoted from the *Southern Daily*, in March 1964, spoke of many decisions of leading organs simply not being put into effect. They were said to stop short at meetings, or the making of formal arrangements and regulations.[52] A discussion on 21 June 1965 spoke of the requirements of the upper levels obstructing the lower cadres in their work. The duty of the upper levels was to make things convenient for the lower levels, not to keep asking for things to be done so that a thousand threads all led to the same needle.

One way of overcoming such attitudes was for cadres to make themselves one with the basic-level cadres and the masses, for example by putting into effect the 'three togethers' policy—working, eating, and living at the basic-levels. The party secretary, magistrate, and other leading cadres of one *hsien* in Hopei were said to have done this so successfully that they were known to the working people as 'old' this or 'old' that.

Another was by returning to a plain style of living and working. An example to follow was *Ch'i*-side *hsien*, in an old revolutionary area in Shantung, which was described on 21 June 1963. The offices at the *hsien*, district, and commune level were plainly

---

49 *PD*, 3 Apr 1964.   50 *PD*, 7 May 1964.
51 *PD*, 21 June 1965.   52 *PD*, 13 Mar 1964.

furnished, which saved money for developing production. The *hsien* leading cadres mended their own clothes and repaired their own shoes, they carried water and coal, and needed no special attention. At all levels when cadres went into the city or down to the fields they carried their own luggage and took dry rations with them.

The third group of comments on cadre behaviour concerns the performance of party branches. In one way or another, all complaints concern party work, but there were a number of news items and discussions directly relating to it. As should be expected, particularly from the Military Affairs Commission's resolution, any complaint could in the last analysis be traced to a faulty party branch. It is thus no surprise to find the Mayor of Shanghai, K'o Ch'ing-shih, helping on the agricultural production drive of spring 1963, with the assertion that one of the basic principles for success was a solid party branch. Party secretaries of various levels were commonly selected for imitation, and the importance of the party secretary's personal performance emphasised. On 16 July 1963 the *People's Daily* reproduced from the *Chekiang Daily* a substantial article stating that whether a commune was run well was decided by whether the production brigades and teams were run well; this in turn was decided by the performance of the party branch; which depended in the first place upon the branch secretary. He must lead both in political and production work, and must strive to become a skilled worker and a labour model.

Their example of such a man—the secretary of 'Well Top' production brigade—is worth recording. He took the lead in labour, and production increased yearly. He always put the public interest first, so that his nickname was 'the selfless cadre'. He hated the class enemy: when the 'landlords' invited him to drink with them, not only did he not go, but he called a meeting of the other cadres to warn them against going. Lastly, he implemented the party line, by relying on the poor and lower-middle peasants, and uniting with the middle peasants. To achieve this red and expert standard, said the *People's Daily* next day, one must unceasingly work and study, and regularly and systematically take part in production.

The same was true in industry. On 18 March 1964 the experience of a 'five-good' workshop in a Peking iron and steel works provided an example of how essential was a good party branch, with a committee the members of which would lead in politics and production.

The prospective, or actual, deterioration of party secretaries was instanced in August 1965, in a lengthy review of the experience of the Shansi *hsien* 'First of the month'. On one occasion the cadres had been shown an exhibition of one commune where all shared 'bitter and sweet together', and another, where the party secretary of a production brigade had fallen off in quality when he became divorced from manual work. Commented some of the party branch secretaries, 'During the land reform we struggled against the landlords because they didn't work and exploited us. Now that we have changed and become cadres it will be really dangerous if we too don't like working.'[53]

The fourth and fifth groups of attitudes, comments, and complaints concerned with cadre performance are those associated with professional and 'economist' qualities, and those with ideological questions. The two are variously present from 1963 to 1966—they can be seen in many of the examples given already. But at first they are not clearly isolable as contradictory. Indeed, the three great revolutionary movements of 1963, the class struggle, the production struggle, and scientific investigation, appear to promote them in association. Another slogan being used at the same time—the unity of leadership, specialists, and masses—aims at the same thing. As time passes, however, a degree of polarization appears to take place. The case of the *Ta Chai* brigade was publicized in 1963 because there what solved problems was essentially the self-sacrificing devotion of the party secretary. But those were problems particularly susceptible to the application of plain intelligence and raw energy. These qualities were doubtless in great demand in many rural areas. But were they equally appropriate in all? It sometimes seemed, for example, that attack on excessive numbers of meetings was an attack on crude mass-mobilization methods. This came through strongly in a discussion in April 1964 on the proper adjustment of the work and leisure of both workers and peasants. A Fukien commune was praised for its work in this field, and the way it reduced the number of its meetings and took its problems into the fields to find solutions. The cadres here were commended for having 'warm hearts and cool heads'.[54] From time to time thereafter further attention was paid to the question of ensuring adequate leisure time. One detailed article appeared on 19 June 1965, dealing with the Hofei Iron Press Machine factory, in Anhwei. There the struggle for adequate leisure time had to combat a general 'extra shift' mentality on the part of the cadres. One way used to overcome this 'superstitious' use of overtime was to put on a demonstration of new production techniques. Another was to give more attention to the preparation of work plans, the better to balance requirements and more efficiently use technical resources. One other method was to reduce substantially the number of meetings, which were criticized as having fatigued everybody with their long and repetitive content. Now the cadres were said to prepare meetings more thoroughly, so that, though fewer, they were more useful. It seems likely, however, that running meetings in this way made them into occasions for the passing on of information, and took away from the lower levels some opportunity of taking part in organization.[55]

The ideologues would naturally not object to cadres displaying 'cool heads', nor their advocating improved techniques. Equally, one of Mao's early requirements of cadres was the adequate preparation of meetings so that they achieved their objects.

At the same time there was danger in emphasizing coolness and technique, and the possible manipulation of the masses, in a general situation in which on the one hand there was still a shortage of expertise in the modern sector of the economy and on the other that economy still depended to an overwhelming degree on manual labour in agriculture. As we have seen, for long the emphasis of the ideologues was on identifying cadres with workers through manual labour and on continual correction through this process. Success, however, appeared to be lacking. The basic nature of the difficulty was well illustrated in an editorial of 29 July 1963, which called labour-participation a 'deep ideological revolution'. Even the cadres who came from the working people, it said, had felt the influence of several thousand years of despising physical labour: after becoming cadres they thought manual work was not appropriate for their status. This even included veteran party members and cadres.

The relation of this to the 'class struggle' in the countryside doubtless provided real cause for alarm. The story of the 'Well

[55] *PD*, 12 Aug 1965.

Top' production brigade secretary provided dramatic evidence of this . In his area the 'landlords' were so resurgent that they were openly plying the cadres with liquor, and apparently to some effect, since the other cadres had to be warned against these tactics. Small wonder, then, that An Tzu-wen remarked in September 1964, during the campaign for training revolutionary successors, that some cadres who had been worthy during the new democratic phase of development were proving unsatisfactory for the socialist construction phase. One article in *Red Flag* of 31 July 1964 had already spoken of the 'usurpation of political leadership of some basic-level units'. According to An, 'Only those who really act according to Marxism-Leninism and Mao Tse-tung's thought . . . are good cadres.' Through all the efforts to train the successors, and to retrain the existing leaders, emerged the old problem: to ensure the correct political standpoint.

Whatever the 'four clean-ups' might have been achieving, however, less and less, did it seem that exhortation to take part properly in collective manual work provided a solution. It was easy to talk about but hard to arrange. And here the basic contradiction forced its way through. At the lowest level in the countryside the two duties of the cadre could be considered to be complementary, in that leadership duties need not entail complete detachment from physical labour. Nevertheless there was some conflict, to judge from the steady complaints about cadres within the communes not working in the fields. Properly selfless service led to the cadres' standard of living being depressed while that of the members of the commune might be rising—most likely through private plot production. Even if, as suggested in the *People's Daily* on 21 May 1965, the commune members took steps to see that the cadres' standard of living did not drop below that of members of the commune as a whole, this might not adequately recompense the cadre for his extra work and study, nor compensate him for not giving his time to maximizing his income.

Once, in fact, the question of adequacy of recompense arose, revolutionary principles were hard to maintain. It was little help for the *People's Daily* to tell cadres that the reason for doing well both their official duties and manual labour was not to earn work-points but to serve the revolution. The gift of work-points to maintain an average standard contrasted the principles of cadre work and other work so as to expose the different values of each.

Could cadres and masses coexist indefinitely with different principles of action? The difference was emphasized by the suggestion that important cadres, whose work prevented their undertaking supplementary private production, should be considered for supplementary work-points, i.e. they should be compensated for doing their cadre work when instead they might have been working their own ground.

Even basic organizational principles were apparently little understood. On 19 June 1965 some cadres were said to have no idea of what the principle of democratic centralism meant. Some acted on any suggestion that came from the people. Others, on the contrary, thought that a cadre was 'head of the household' and that what he said should 'go'.

To make matters worse, there was little leadership from higher levels.

The plain message of the ideological complaints was that revolutionary momentum had been lost. Without doubt, different interpretations of what this meant existed, and opinions differed as to what remedies should be taken. A distinct stiffening of attitude now entered the discussion, however. On 13 October 1965 the *People's Daily* stated that there was an evident need to 'revolutionize' the *hsien*-level cadres. It admitted great deficiencies in its previous handling of the leadership problems of the *hsien*, and its reporting of conditions in them. Development was said to be uneven. Where leadership was good, so was the *hsien*; where it was bad, the *hsien* was bad too: the fault was that the leadership was not revolutionary.

However, it was not ready to prescribe the remedies. How to make the *hsien* revolutionary and how to promote correct methods of leadership was recognized as a very complex question, and a general discussion, with contributions from all sides, was called for.

Over the next few months about half a page was devoted to this discussion twice weekly—in all 54 such discussions were published. Although this campaign was only one of a number being promoted at the same time, it was obviously important since it dealt with the leadership activities of *hsien* where some 80 per cent of the population lived. As the *People's Daily* said on 18 October—all the party's policies had to be put into effect through the *hsien* committees. It drew the profoundly important conclusion that where the leadership had been poor, party work had gradually fallen off and capitalist thinking had spread in the party and among the cadres and the masses.

Among the various complaints which appeared, the following illustrate the basic deficiencies that were being exposed. Some were new, but most had appeared before. *Hsien* committees were warned against thinking that because they were engaged every day in the work of the revolution they did not need 'revolutionizing': a revolutionary could not be satisfied with the appearance of things, nor be afraid to take responsibility.[56] Preoccupation with stability prevented some leaders from being truly revolutionary: by comparing their results with those of the past, of the period of small-producer economy, they became satisfied and stopped seeking still better results—mere improvement over the previous year was good enough for them.[57] Another piece of advice was not to act the official but to be the people's labourer: some *hsien* officials acted as though the lower levels had to serve the upper levels; they only held meetings, or went to the basic level to look around; the workers called them 'birds' because they flitted from place to place.[58] Some *hsien* committes only saw themselves as leading a small peasant economy—some even had that mentality themselves. Others were 'meeting fanatics'. Others could not work without a secretary—they fell into a 'lazy style'. The combination of these two failings 'institutionalized' the *hsien* committee and made it impossible for it to lead.[59] The need for direct contact with 'the masses' was brought out when a *hsien* in Kansu province was reported to have tried to revolutionize itself but 'behind closed doors', so that it achieved nothing; it was only when the movement was taken down to the lower levels that anything got done.[60]

For those with ears to hear, the new call was sounded more clearly with an astonishing report on 8 November 1965, from Chekiang, of a meeting of representatives of poor and lower-middle peasants, who put forward no less than 5,103 criticisms. The call was less in the number of the complaints than in their nature, which 'revealed' three main areas of weakness in cadres: they were deficient in supporting class-struggle in the villages and pushing the socialist revolution through to the end; they were not sufficiently earnest in promoting the party's policies; they lacked class

---

[56] *PD*, 22 Oct 1965. [57] *PD*, 25 Oct 1965. [58] *PD*, 29 Oct 1965.
[59] *PD*, 1 Nov 1965. [60] *PD*, 5 Nov 1965.

U

outlook and so did not have the interests of the peasants at heart.

Inefficiency at *hsien* level was attacked by one *hsien* party secretary who reported that he had seriously criticized a production brigade in public on the basis of information from the *hsien* agricultural office. Although he had checked it with the office beforehand, the information was mistaken and he had been forced to make a public apology.[61] Also attacked was the bureaucratic mentality, which was said to make for bad relations with the masses, and opened the way to ideological degeneration, and 'peaceful change'.[62]

Criticism was also levelled at 'middle-of-the-road' cadres who were satisfied with the formal discharge of their responsibilities: as long as things got a bit better each year, some results being better than theirs, and some being not so good, things were fine; they themselves thought that by working in the country all the year round, doing the people's work and eating the same food as the people, they were doing their duty; but this attitude concealed individualism in its fear of difficulties and danger, and lack of daring to seek greater progress.[63] Individualism was also found among cadres in Canton, criticized for attending to production without attending to politics; this led to the abandonment of class struggle, and an incorrect style of work, which prevented cadres from taking the lead.[64] A different form of individualism was described in Kansu, where members of a *hsien* committee concentrated on their own activities and did not co-ordinate with each other, with the result that the lower levels got no positive leadership.[65]

A remedy was now offered—to arm their minds with the thought of Mao. The offer was at first somewhat lacking in dynamism. In Anhwei province the thought of Mao Tse-tung was said to be being studied by every level of cadre to develop leadership methods combining energy with steadiness: success in leadership techniques was said to lie in the combination of these two factors.[66] But soon the dynamic element began to grow stronger. On 30 December the *People's Daily* reported that a thought revolution had begun on the finance and trade 'front' (which was also being discussed in special columns of correspondence

[61] *PD*, 8 Nov 1965.   [62] *PD*, 12 Nov 1965.
[63] *PD*, 19 Nov 1965.   [64] *PD*, 14 Dec 1965.
[65] *PD*, 20 Dec 1965.   [66] *PD*, 27 Dec 1965.

in that newspaper, simultaneously with the columns on the *hsien*). There leading cadres, setting the example, were 'actively studying and actively using' the thought of Mao Tse-tung. The No. 4 Department Store in Shanghai was quoted as an example of how thrusting politics in the foreground made their work better and better: they were able to do this because they had a revolutionary leadership core.

In the new year, 1966, more general lessons began to be drawn. The New Year's Day editorial included a statement that the broad mass of cadres needed still better leadership and organization; they were urged to increase the use made of the thought of Mao Tse-tung, and to study still further the methods of the PLA. That day's column on the revolutionizing of the *hsien* party committees went considerably further, recalling the statements of mid-1964, with its assertion that both new and old cadres 'must be re-educated'. Some comrades took the view that the only matter in question was methods of leadership—that everybody knew for whom they were working and that they wanted to organize the work of the revolution properly. In fact, however, they were still unclear about whom to serve—they might know the answer verbally, but their practical activities did not serve the people with one heart and mind. The *hsien* where over 5,000 criticisms had been made by poor and lower-middle peasants was an example—the *hsien* committee did not have the peasants in their hearts and lacked class standpoint. The questions of whom to serve and how to serve them could not be separated: after solving the problem of whom to serve, the question of how to do it was naturally not difficult to solve.

On the same day the *Workers' Daily* called for the revolutionizing of enterprises, and required every level of leading cadre to revolutionize their own thinking first. The *Liberation Army Newspaper* also called for further implementation of Lin Piao's 'five principles', the first of which was the promotion and use of the thought of Mao.

A comparison with the work of the army was drawn on 14 January, when it was pointed out that Mao's party-building and army-building principle of establishing party branches at the company level was equally suitable for work among the workers and peasants and the fields of education and trade. All basic-level units were to establish and support a sound party organization and to have an appropriate number of robust party members. The army were said to have taken in another 900,000 new party members in the previous year. The basic-level organizations, if they now had no, or too few, party members were to follow a policy of taking in new members so as to carry out the party's core functions.

The sheer difficulty of doing the job of the leading cadre at the basic level was pointed up a few days later when the *hsien* party secretaries were urged to learn the job of those of the production brigades whose job was said to be the most difficult and whose responsibilities the heaviest. It was they who had to turn the party policies into action, and put into practice and bring to completion every one of the party's tasks. No matter whether it was as worker, peasant, trader, educationalist, or in the military, in agriculture, forestry, the side occupations, herding or fishing— they took the responsibility for all the tasks and all the plans, and one by one put into practice each task which was passed down. The production-brigade secretary was like the sluice-gate of a reservoir —all the tasks of all the offices of all the departments at the higher levels flowed into the reservoir and became duties for the brigade secretary. The leaders of the brigades and teams were the direct leaders, organizers, and educators of the masses, whose needs and complaints they had in addition to reflect upwards. Few cadres could sustain this load. At meetings they were unable to communicate to the masses even the least enthusiasm. The masses said 'The commune talks about policies, the brigade talks about principles, the team talks about half the matter—the members don't understand what it is all about.'[67]

Thus the point seemed to be emerging that the cadres, and especially the party cadres, and perhaps the party as a whole, were being viewed much as the armed forces had been viewed in 1959–60, and were being found wanting in much the same way. The revolutionary spirit needed refurbishing if not recreating, and the principal remedies were party reconstruction and the study of Mao. Interspersed with calls for specific measures of leadership or production management, calls to all cadres, but especially leading cadres from *hsien* to provincial level, to take the lead in revolutionizing their own thought and put politics in command, began to be made in various parts of the country. The

[67] *PD*, 17 Jan 1966 (SCMP 3649).

Peking party committee led off, followed by the top committees of Shanghai, Chekiang, Hopei, Anhwei, Yunnan, Shantung, Szechwan, Sinkiang, Tibet, Hunan, Kiangsi, and Heilungkiang.

While this new wave of study of the thought of Mao was getting up, it was channelled in a new direction with the selection of a model for imitation—a *hsien* party committee secretary from Kansu province, named Chiao Yü-lu, who died in 1964. His life story was given a full page in the *People's Daily* of 7 February, and from then onward followed a spate of calls from all over the country to study and imitate him. Various committees and work bureaux of the central committee, the six national regional party bureaux, provincial and autonomous region committees, national organizations like the Youth League, the trades unions, the Federation of Democratic Women, the PLA and twenty departments of the State Council, all took part within a few days.

Chiao was a perfect subject for the cadre campaign. Like many other heroes, he had sacrificed his health in the interests of others and had had eventually to be ordered away from his work to hospital, where he had died not long afterwards. His post had been in a permanent disaster area, where regular floods and sand storms, coupled with salty ground, compelled it to rely on subsidies. In two years Chiao had changed this in many parts of the *hsien* by an outstanding display of 'revolutionary' activity. Starting from the need to transform the thinking of the leadership at each level, he had personally sought out the true situation by visiting nearly every village in the *hsien* (which had a population of over 360,000 people). He went out in all kinds of bad weather to discover the ill effects it had. He also visited the poor in their homes and made himself the son of the people. He had worked at their sides and got as dirty as them. By making plans for keeping down sand hills, draining flood water, and digging below salt deposits, he helped several brigades to become grain-selling instead of grain-importing teams before his two years were up, and had made plans to rehabilitate the others. His death occurred just as these plans were reaching their high point, and he died expressing regret that he had been unable to fulfil the tasks which the party had allotted to him. After his death two volumes were found under his pillow—one was a selection of works from Mao Tse-tung, and the other was Liu Shao-ch'i on the cultivation of a Communist Party member. In the many stories which now began to be told of Chiao his key method of work was portrayed as the active method inculcated by Mao Tse-tung—he studied the facts, then studied the works of Mao, then found his course of action by applying the one to the other. It was thus that he was offered as a model—as Chairman Mao's good student, and as a leader with a strong flavour of the Yenan period about him.

The wheel that had begun to turn in 1960 with the rehabilitation of political work in the army had now come full-circle. The fighting leader, with a correct political orientation, responsive to all changes of circumstances, closely linked to the people, recognizing his dependence on them—the man on whom the campaign crowned by the achievement of power in 1949 was said to have been based—was projected once again as the ideal type for leadership in socialist construction as much as formerly in the new democratic revolution. Over the next few weeks the tide of the study of Mao rose still higher, and then changed into the floods of the Great Proletarian Cultural Revolution, by which all cadres were required to be baptized into a condition of permanent self-revolutionization as a necessary condition of the march towards socialism and communism.

9

The Frontier Regions in China's Recent International Politics

GEORGE MOSELEY

THE Western powers and Japan intruded upon China not only along her Pacific littoral but also across her land frontiers. Accustomed to the idea that the sea itself constituted a barrier, nineteenth-century China had no real defence against the maritime powers. Once these powers established themselves along the coast, however, their naval might could no longer afford them the absolute supremacy which they had enjoyed at sea. Situated amidst dense Chinese populations, the treaty ports were ultimately doomed by the rise of Chinese nationalism.

Whereas China's maritime marches constituted an ethnic as well as a geographic frontier, her land frontiers were indeterminate. They had the aspect of a zone rather than of a line, and this zone was composed of ethnically distinct regions over which China exercised suzerain, but not sovereign, powers. In approaching these frontiers the Western powers and Japan did not possess the same preponderance of arms that they did along the coast, but penetration was made easier by the fact that the frontier peoples they encountered were not under direct Chinese administration.

Under the Ch'ing empire, the areas inhabited by these frontier peoples fell into three main categories: vassal states, imperial dependencies, and native districts. While the Ch'ing court had a special relationship with each type of frontier region, these relationships had certain features in common. In each case a lesser sovereign was recognized by a great sovereign: the emperor of China invested the local ruler with legitimacy, the investiture being manifested by a seal of office.

Far from being empty ritual, investiture by the emperor of China had real political meaning. Prior to the arrival of the

Europeans, Chinese power was politically decisive throughout a large area peripheral to China. Within this frontier region, no rule was legitimate which did not have imperial sanction. The Ch'ing empire was capable of deploying armies to put down usurpers, or to unseat rulers who had become disloyal. An imperial decision to support one faction or another could determine the outcome of the struggle which often attended succession to office in these frontier states. Flaunting of the imperial will by a local ruler invited political intrigue between the Ch'ing court and his political opponents. In arrogating to itself the role of political arbiter, the Ch'ing dynasty sought to safeguard its own security by maintaining a tranquil state of affairs on its frontiers.

The rulers in the frontier regions on China's periphery were permitted to govern their own people without reference to Chinese administrative procedures and institutions. This deference to local customs was in recognition of the fact that, from the Confucian point of view, these non-Chinese peoples were not yet prepared to accept the bureaucratic system of government which prevailed in China Proper. It was expected that, in time, these frontier peoples would become Chinese by adopting Chinese ways, at which point Chinese administration—a precious thing which had to be earned—could be extended to them. It was in this way that the Chinese state, over a period of several millennia, had expanded from its original centre in the middle Yellow River valley, and it was expected that this process would continue. The administrative autonomy enjoyed by the frontier dependencies of the Ch'ing empire was not inconsistent with the idea that they were intrinsically part of China.

Summing up his description of the various parts of the empire, a prominent Chinese historian has said: 'Spread out like stars in the sky, or pieces on a chess board, they reached the sea in the east, Persia in the west, Malaya in the south, and the Hsing-ling mountains in the north [Siberia], making up a great East Asian country [*tung-ya ta kuo*].[1] All modern governments of China—the Republican and communist as well as the Ch'ing—have to some extent held to this position, even though these frontier regions have had no status in the 'international' law of the Western powers. In her 'search for a political form' China has looked for a system of

[1] Hsiao I-shan, *Ch'ing-tai t'ung-shih* (General history of the Ch'ing dynasty) (Shanghai, 1928), ii. 157.

government which would take into account the special relationships existing between the Chinese core area and the non-Chinese parts of the empire—the vassal states, the imperial dependencies, and the native districts.

Severely shaken as it was by the encroachment of foreign states in its frontier regions, the Ch'ing dynasty did not seek a new basis for its relations with its dependencies to take the place of the Confucian system. On the contrary, it attempted, at first, to fit its relations with the Western powers into the imperial system. After 1860, when the Ch'ing court was obliged to recognize these powers on a basis of equality, it gradually allowed and finally encouraged Chinese colonization of the frontier regions, in many cases suppressing the local autonomy which the non-Chinese peoples in these regions had previously enjoyed. This was a policy of using Chinese imperialism to counter foreign imperialism; this same policy was pursued during the period of Republican rule on the mainland (1911–49). If the Ch'ing dynasty clung to an outmoded ideology, this ideology at least had the merit of once having been effective. The situation under the Republic was worse. The various strong men who held sway in different parts of China during this period had no workable intellectual system to draw upon, for the dominant ideology of the time was nationalism, a negative one from the standpoint of frontier affairs. The ideology which the Chinese communists took over from Stalin, on the other hand, did provide a systematic theory for the management of a multi-national empire, and this was one of the reasons it had appealed to Sun Yat-sen. One element which each of these periods—late Ch'ing, Republican, and communist—have in common is the interaction between frontier affairs and foreign affairs which characterized them all. Only in the last few years has a sharp distinction been made between the two.

COMPOSITION OF FRONTIER REGIONS

At the height of Ch'ing power, just as China was coming into contact with aggressive European imperialism, the dependencies of the empire consisted of Mongolia, Chinese Turkestan, Tsinghai, and Tibet. Together, these areas comprised China's northern and western marches. Imperial relations with the nomadic peoples who inhabited them were handled by the *Li Fan Yüan*, or Frontier

Control Bureau.[2] The *Li Fan Yüan* was an administrative office newly created by the Manchus. It grew out of a Mongol Affairs Office (*Meng-ku Yamen*) which had been set up by the Manchus before their entry into China, a fact which indicates the importance of the Manchu–Mongol relationship in this early period. When relations developed in the seventeenth century between the Russian and Chinese empires across this same frontier (*fan*) they were also put under the *Li Fan Yüan*.

For the management of its relations with tributary states, on the other hand, the Ch'ing court perpetuated an office in use in Ming (1368–1644) times, that of the *Chu K'o Ssu* (Reception Department) in the Board of Ceremonies (*Li Pu*), and Ch'ing relations with the European maritime powers were initially entrusted to this same office.[3] The principal tributary states of the Chinese empire at the time of the Opium war were Korea, the Ryukyu Islands, Annam, Burma, and Siam. With the exception of the Ryukyu Islands and Siam, the tribute missions from these states travelled overland to China.

The institution of *t'u-ssu* (native chiefs) inherited by the Ch'ing was a creation of the Mongols, who were also responsible for making the province the territorial unit of Chinese administration. The *t'u-ssu* system was employed for the administration of native (that is, non-Chinese) districts in the south-western provinces of Yunnan, Kwangsi, Kweichow, and Szechwan. The principal native tribes coming under *t'u-ssu* administration were the Miao (Kweichow and Kwangsi), Shan (Yunnan), and Lolo (Szechwan). They inhabited mountainous regions and malarial lowlands which were generally unattractive to the Chinese who began colonizing the far south-west during the Ming period. While the Manchus were never as partial to the *t'u-ssu* as they were to the Mongol princes and Tibetan lamas, it was not until the middle of the nineteenth century that the restrictions on Chinese emigration to these districts were removed and the position of the *t'u-ssu* themselves gradually undermined. Ch'ing repression combined with Anglo-French aggressiveness on the southern frontier made the *t'u-ssu* areas especially sensitive to the fortunes of China's foreign policy.[4]

[2] See J. K. Fairbank, 'On the Ch'ing Tributary System', *Harvard-Yenching Inst. Studies*, vol. xix.

[3] Ibid.

[4] Chang Hsia-min, *Pien-chiang wen-t'i yü pien-chiang chien-she* (Frontier problems and frontier organization) (Taipei, 1958), pp. 69–70.

Taken together, the vassal states, imperial dependencies, native districts, and also the imperial domains in Manchuria, described China's frontier regions. It was in these land frontiers, as well as along the coast, that the Ch'ing dynasty confronted the imperialism of the Western powers and Japan. These frontiers had remained ethnically distinct from the Chinese core area because their climate and topography were inhospitable to the agricultural system upon which the Chinese bureaucratic state depended. Communist China has at its disposal the technology required for the colonization of these areas, but it was during the later Ch'ing period that China was forced to accept linear frontiers to delimit what was 'Chinese' from what was 'foreign'. There was the danger that in the process China would lose these frontier regions which, commanding the several land routes into China proper, were vital to the security of the state.

The importance of this frontier zone could not have been better understood than it was by the Manchus, who themselves had usurped China's seat of empire from a position on the frontier. No sooner had the Manchus consolidated their position in China Proper than the Russians, from their position in Siberia, began to probe the northern periphery of the empire. The Manchus replied by eliminating from Mongolia the threat of the Dzungars (western Mongols), with whom the Russians may have considered allying themselves, and by then meeting the Russians at Nerchinsk. There, on the Shilka river east of Lake Baikal, China signed her first treaty with a Western power. It was an unequal treaty, but unequal from the point of view of the Russians, who were compelled to dismantle their frontier posts and to leave the entire Amur basin in the hands of the Manchus. Maintaining their position of strength, the Manchus next met the Russians at Kiakhta, south of Lake Baikal, in 1727. The treaty signed there regulated Russian trade with the Ch'ing empire carried on at Ma-mai Ch'eng, the Chinese town opposite Kiakhta. The treaty also delimited the Mongolian sector of the frontier between the two states. The Manchus succeeded, too, in maintaining their position in the northern part of Chinese Turkestan (*T'ien-shan pei-lu*, or Dzungaria), which had been pacified by the Ch'ien-lung emperor in the middle of the eighteenth century, although at an early date the Manchus lost control of the Kazakhs in the Semi-rech'ye region east of Lake Balkhash. In a series of treaties signed with the Russians at Ili and Tarbagatai in the first half of the nineteenth century, the frontier was delimited and an agreement reached concerning the trade to be carried on in this sector. Subsequent Russian dissatisfaction with their commercial opportunities in Chinese Turkestan was one reason for their intervention in Ili later in the century.

Partly as a side effect of its pacification of the Dzungars, the Ch'ing established its ascendancy in Tibet where the Dzungars had attempted to impose themselves. As a result of a series of expeditions to Tibet during the eighteenth century the Ch'ing succeeded in expelling the Dzungars and in establishing the Dalai Lama as the temporal ruler of Tibet. Perhaps the most spectacular feat of the Manchus in reducing the imperial dependencies to submission was their twin-pronged attack of 1792 which traversed the Himalayas to chastize the Gurkhas, who had invaded Tibet, and drive them back to Nepal.

By the beginning of the nineteenth century, however, the Ch'ing dynasty was on the defensive throughout its peripheral territories. From her position in India, Great Britain stripped away the Tibetan dependencies along the 1,500-mile arc of the Himalayas through Ladakh, Nepal, Sikkim, Bhutan, and Assam. In 1817 a British Resident took up his post in Khatmandu; the other states followed one by one.[5]

In the south, where the frontier zone intrudes upon China proper, Britain and France began their race, through Burma and Indochina respectively, for a commercial route to Szechwan. Lower Burma was annexed to British India and Cochinchina ceded to France in the same year, 1862. It was again in the same year, 1868, that François Garnier followed the Mekong into south China while a British expedition explored the Irrawaddy route via Bhamo. In 1873 a Chinese army under Ts'en Yü-ying, with French weapons, suppressed the Panthay (Moslem) rebellion in Yunnan led by the self-styled Sultan Suleiman, who in the previous year had sent a mission to London to solicit British support. In 1874 France secured a *de facto* protectorate over Annam, and in the following year the murder of a British subject, A. R. Margary, on the Burma–Yunnan frontier, gave Britain the opportunity of advancing new demands on the Ch'ing court.

[5] For the period of European encroachment I have relied mainly on H. B. Morse, *The International Relations of the Chinese Empire* (London, 1910–18).

Despite a military defeat at Langson in 1885, the French were able to secure in that year a treaty with China which ended, in a way satisfactory to France, her undeclared war with China. The effect of the Tientsin peace treaty was to open up the Red River route for the French penetration of Yunnan and to recognize the French protectorate over Annam and Tonking. One year later, in 1886, the British annexed upper Burma.

By the 1876 treaty of Kianghua, said to have been modelled after the 1862 treaty of Saigon by which France grabbed Cochin-china, Japan obtained the 'independence' of Korea, and several Korean ports were opened for trade.[6] As in many other instances of Ch'ing reluctance to assume responsibility for the defence of its client states against Western encroachment, the Manchus did not respond to the pleas of the Ryukyu Islands for help, and in 1879 they became a Japanese district. Following her defeat by Japan in Korea and Manchuria in 1894–5, China was obliged to cede Formosa and the Pescadores and to recognize the complete 'independence' of Korea. The 'Chinese family of nations' was a thing of the past.

All the nations tributary to China had now fallen to the Western powers except Siam which, having unilaterally abrogated her tributary relationship in 1882, had succeeded in maintaining her independence. It was now the turn of the imperial dependencies. The maritime powers had acquired positions on the continent by means of their seizure of China's tributary states. Great Britain was ready to force the 'opening' of Tibet from her string of protectorates along the Himalayas, while in Burma she readied herself for the commercial exploitation of Yunnan and all south-west China. The French, already proceeding with the economic penetration of Yunnan, dreamed of annexing south-west China and adding it to their Indochinese realm. The Japanese only awaited a favourable opportunity to annex Korea outright, the more purposefully to proceed with the penetration of Manchuria; the Russians were already busily engaged in Manchuria, having stripped away the Ch'ing possessions north of the Amur and east of the Ussuri. In the Mongolian sector the Russians were preparing to make use of Buryat Mongols from Siberia for the undermining of Ch'ing influence in Mongolia and, secondarily, in Tibet.

[6] Li Chien-nung, *The Political History of China, 1840–1928* (Princeton, NJ, 1956), p. 129.

Events had taken an even more sinister turn in the far north-west of the Ch'ing empire. For ten years, from 1871 to 1881, the Russians actually occupied the Ili valley, taking advantage of a great Moslem revolt which by 1866 had eliminated Manchu control from all of Chinese Turkestan. Much to the surprise of the Russians and the British (the latter had supported the cause of the rebel chief, Yakub Beg, who operated from Kashgar), the Ch'ing mounted a great expedition under Tso Tsung-t'ang which gradually reasserted imperial authority north and south of the T'ien Shan, obliging the Russians to withdraw from Ili in 1881.[7]

THREATENED DISMEMBERMENT

The threatened dismemberment of China is generally thought to have been ushered in by the Ch'ing defeat at the hands of the Japanese in 1894–5. It was at this time that the intense rivalry among the Western powers and Japan for spheres of influence in China began. This contest, which did violence to the most-favoured-nation principle and to Chinese sensibilities, led to the American 'open-door' notes and to the Boxer rebellion. By this time, however, the Chinese empire, having been divested of its vassal states, was already but a shadow of its former self. Japan's defeat of China was thus the culmination of one process, the destruction of the tribute system, and the inauguration of another, the threatened dismemberment of China proper. Both were reflected in the treaty of Shimonoseki, which on the one hand removed all ambiguity from Korea's independent status *vis-à-vis* China and, on the other, ceded Taiwan, a part of China proper, to Japan.

China's defeat by Japan also, as Jerome Ch'ên has pointed out,[8] brought about an awakening of Chinese nationalism. This awakening had been foreshadowed in the 1860 treaty of Peking, which forced the Ch'ing court to recognize the Western powers on a basis of equality. No longer could they be regarded as tributary states; no longer, therefore, could the idea of a Middle

---

[7] A major policy question surrounded the dispatch of the expedition to Ili: should China try to maintain her position in the imperial dependencies or devote all her limited resources to meeting the challenge of the maritime powers in the coastal provinces? This dispute is the subject of *The Ili Crisis* (Oxford, 1965), by Immanuel C. Y. Hsu who, in my opinion, draws the wrong conclusion—namely that China could not afford to protect her land frontiers.

[8] See above, p. 8.

Kingdom be logically sustained. After the 1860 treaty the Western powers were permitted to station diplomatic representatives in Peking. To cope with this new situation, the Manchus established a Foreign Affairs Office (*Tsungli Yamen*) and gradually posted their own diplomats abroad.

With the recognition of other states, states which (except for Russia) had the special quality of being *nation*-states, as China's equals, and with the encroachment on the part of these states on China proper, the concept of Han Chinese assumes an *ethnic* in addition to its usual *cultural* connotation. It was as a cultural entity, embodied in a bureaucratic state, that the Chinese—i.e. the Han Chinese—had been so successful in incorporating ethnically and linguistically diverse peoples. The creed of nationalism, together with foreign imperialism, had rendered obsolete this traditional Han Chinese concept. And it was of no immediate advantage to China that the nationalism and the colonialism of their adversaries were mutually contradictory. For the moment, it seemed obvious that only as a nation-state could China become powerful enough to withstand the challenge of the Western powers, as Japan had done. This implied a policy of Han Chinese imperialism to counter Western and Japanese imperialism in those frontier regions of the empire which had not already been lost. The contest between these two imperialisms was to decide where the boundary between the two would be drawn.

The scrapping of the earlier Ch'ing device of isolating the different parts of the empire from one another was implicit in the establishment of Sinkiang as a province in 1884, following its pacification by Tso Tsung-t'ang. After the turn of the century the Ch'ing government went further by opening Inner Mongolia and Manchuria to Chinese colonization. Emigration to Inner Mongolia was facilitated by the completion of the Chinese-built Peking–Kalgan–Suiyüan railway in 1909. Railways already existed between China proper and Manchuria, which was reorganized into three provinces in 1907, the year in which Russia and Japan agreed on their respective spheres of influence in Manchuria and Inner Mongolia. As the homeland of the Manchus which the Ch'ing court had sought to maintain as a special preserve, the opening of Manchuria is especially noteworthy as an indication of the straits in which the dynasty now found itself. In 1910, on the eve of the Manchu collapse, imperial armies were dispatched to Tibet and Outer Mongolia, where the situation had been disturbed by the Younghusband expedition of 1904 and the Russian revolution of 1905 respectively.

The connexion between China proper (*pen-pu*) and the imperial dependencies (*fan-pu*) which the Ch'ing court had struggled so tenaciously to preserve was all but completely severed by the Chinese revolution of 1911. The Mongols and Tibetans had recognized the overlordship of the Manchu sovereign rather than that of China as such. To some extent, indeed, the Ch'ing dynasty rested on an anti-Chinese alliance between the Manchus and the non-Chinese peoples of the empire, notably the Mongols. The brake which the Manchu dynasty had placed on Chinese imperialism was greatly appreciated by the other peoples of the empire, just as British and French protection was appreciated by the minority peoples of Burma and Vietnam.

Mongolia declared her independence in December 1911, actually a month before the proclamation of the Chinese Republic. In 1913 the Dalai Lama declared the independence of Tibet and concluded a pact with the Living Buddha at Urga (Ulan Bator). At the Simla conference in 1914 Great Britain sought unsuccessfully to gain Chinese recognition of Tibet's independence, and in the following year a Sino-Russian-Mongolian agreement was signed recognizing the autonomy of Outer Mongolia. Although neither Sinkiang nor Manchuria ever became independent officially, the central government exercised no authority in either region between 1911 and the end of the second world war, and very little between 1945 and 1949. The authority of Chang Tso-lin and his son in Manchuria was superseded only by the Japanese-created 'Manchukuo', while in Sinkiang the personal rule of Yang Tseng-hsin was followed, after a brief interregnum, by the Soviet-sponsored rule of Sheng Shih-ts'ai.

Thus the establishment of the Chinese Republic only hastened the dismemberment of the larger China which had been constituted under the empire. In its powerlessness, the Republic sought to prevent the complete loss of the non-Chinese parts of the Ch'ing domains by resting its claim to authority on the idea of a free and natural union of the five peoples of China—the Chinese, the Manchus, the Tibetans, the Mongols, and the Mohammedans (*Han, Man, Tsang, Meng, Hui*)—symbolized by the five bars of the new national flag. Chiang Kai-shek recognized the futility of this device by discarding the five-barred flag in 1928, following the victory of the Northern Expedition, and substituting for it a flag dominated by a white sun, symbolizing the central authority of the KMT. In the critical situation in which China now found herself it was deemed wiser to promote the national unity of the Han Chinese at the expense of the border-lands than to endanger that unity by appealing to the nebulous idea of a union of five peoples. Once this decision had been reached, the KMT sought to enlarge as much as possible the area under Han Chinese control at the expense of Tibet and Outer Mongolia, now treated as sovereign states, though not formally recognized as such, by Great Britain and the Soviet Union respectively.

In 1928 the half-Tibetan, half-Mongol region of Tsinghai came under direct Chinese administration, as did the new province of Sikang, established in the same year. By creating Sikang the government in Nanking simply detached eastern Tibet, sometimes referred to as the Chamdo region, from Tibet proper. On the northern frontier nearest Peking, the KMT placed Inner Mongolia under Chinese provincial administration with the establishment of Jehol, Chahar, and Suiyüan provinces. These had already evolved as special districts during the period of warlord rule preceding the Northern Expedition. Changes had already been made in the far north-west, too, where the Altai district, which would have otherwise fallen to Outer Mongolia, was attached to Sinkiang in 1919. Another Turkic region of the Ch'ing empire, however, became isolated from China by the emergence of an independent Outer Mongolia: this was Tannu Tuva, which became a republic of the Soviet Union in 1928. In the reorganized KMT administration of the post-1928 period, what remained of frontier—that is, non-Han Chinese affairs—could be handled by a Mongolian and Tibetan Affairs Committee in the Administrative *Yüan*.[9]

In the south-west, the KMT accelerated the process of dissolving the *t'u-ssu* local governments which had commenced under the Ch'ing dynasty. By 1931 the *t'u-ssu* system had disappeared. The 'indigenous' peoples of the south-west had inhabited the Yangtze basin in ancient times, where they coexisted with the early Chinese. Driven before the Han Chinese advance, the remnants of these peoples took refuge on the Yunnan–Kweichow plateau,

[9] These developments are detailed in Chang, pp. 51 ff.

W

which afforded them some natural protection. The *t'u-ssu* system had helped them to preserve themselves, their lands, and their institutions in the face of Han Chinese colonization. They clearly had a special claim to national minority status. The elimination of the *t'u-ssu* system was a logical corollary of the equality of all citizens (i.e., no protection for minorities) proclaimed by the KMT.

KMT nationality policy was elaborated by the Third National Party Congress of 1929 which blamed the Manchus and the warlords for all the misunderstandings which existed among China's nationalities. It promised to right the wrongs of the past and to create a united nation (*Chung-hua min-kuo*) on the basis of the free association of China's five peoples who, because of the facts of geography and history, were really one nation (*Kuo-tsu*);[10] in effect, it sought to deny the existence of national minorities in China. In subsequent years, this position was rationalized by scholars sympathetic with the KMT. According to one:

Heretofore it has been widely believed that China is a multi-national state . . . , comprising large groups, namely, Han, Man, Meng, Hui, Tsang, and small ones, such as Miao, Yao, and Lolo. This is a mistake. . . . Due to a thousand years' interaction and Han influence there has developed a great Chinese nation (*Chung-hua min-tsu*).[11]

To the extent that the non-Han peoples of China were still minorities, it was asserted, they were geographic rather than ethnic minorities.[12] This academic discussion gave a certain intellectual veneer to the well-known view of Chiang Kai-shek that China was not composed of different nationalities but only of several 'clans' of a single nation.

The practical effect of KMT policy, coupled with foreign encroachment, was to reduce China to China proper, virtually eliminating the frontier zone. By the early 1930s the imperialists were at the gates of China proper. Following the establishment of 'Manchukuo' the Japanese invaded Chahar and Suiyüan in

[10] These developments are detailed in Chang, pp. 53 ff.

[11] Ch'en Chia-wu, 'Lun min-tsu yü tsung-tsu' (Concerning nations and clans), *Pien-cheng kung-lun* (Frontier affairs) (Chungking), iii (1944), p. 1.

[12] Ma Ch'ang-shou, 'Shao-shu min-tsu wen t'i' (The problem of national minorities), *Min-tsu-hsüeh yen-chiu chi-k'an* (Ethnological research), (Chungking), vi (1948), pp. 8–23.

1936–7 and later established an 'autonomous' regime there under a Mongol collaborator, Te Wang. Simultaneously, a detachment of Soviet troops was positioned at Hami, in the extreme east of Sinkiang, thereby controlling all access to the province. Just at that moment the Chinese communists arrived in Shensi, at the end of their Long March, and began propagandizing among the Mongols and the Chinese Moslems, promising them future autonomy in exchange for their immediate co-operation in the anti-Japanese United Front. Finally, the Japanese occupation of Indochina obliged the KMT to destroy the French-built Hanoi–Kunming railway in order to deny the Japanese use of this important link with south-west China.

Had there been no second world war, it is conceivable that the detachment of the entire frontier zone of China could have become permanent, but the Japanese invasion of China Proper and the emergence of a group of powers allied with Nationalist China in her struggle against Japan meant that China would once again, with the defeat of Japan, be able to advance her claims to the border regions. By raising a border issue with British Burma during the war the Chinese Nationalists made it clear that China's national crisis had not caused them to lose sight of old frontier questions. There was one contingency, however, which the KMT wartime strategy could not take account of, and that was the question of the Soviet attitude towards China's northern frontier zone following the cessation of hostilities.

The Soviet Union's eleventh-hour entry into the war against Japan enabled her to take up a strategic position in Manchuria and Inner Mongolia from which to influence the course of events in China; in Sinkiang she looked after her vital interests by means of the control she exercised over an anti-Chinese rebellion of Turkic peoples which controlled the Ili valley and most of Dzungaria. To any Chinese well read in the history of his country the threat posed by the Red Army situated beyond the Great Wall must have seemed reminiscent of past occasions when barbarian horsemen had paused to collect their forces before descending upon China Proper.

The interests of the Soviet Union in China's Inner Asian frontier zone were, apparently, not very different from those which she pursued in eastern Europe. She sought to extend her influence, both territorially and economically, by installing governments subservient to her interests. Soviet concern about the small states peripheral to her was, then, rather like the traditional Chinese view of her *fan-pu*. What is unique about the post-second world war situation in Manchuria, Mongolia, and Sinkiang is that the similar frontier concerns of the Soviet Union and China overlapped in the same region. This clash of interests extended to Korea. While the Soviet Union stripped the Japanese-built industrial plants in Manchuria and eastern Inner Mongolia and transported this booty back to the USSR, just as she was doing in eastern Europe, she forced the Nationalist government of Chiang Kai-shek to agree in 1945 to a plebiscite in Outer Mongolia which, held in 1946, established a Mongolian People's Republic completely separate from China.

Most provisions of the 1945 Sino-Soviet treaty concerning the inner Asian frontiers, including the one pertaining to the complete independence of Outer Mongolia, were reaffirmed in the treaty concluded between Mao and Stalin in 1950. The Russians were confirmed in their rights to participate in the management of the Manchurian rail network, to make use of Port Arthur, and to share in the exploitation of Sinkiang's mineral resources.[13] Despite these concessions, however, the Chinese People's Republic was in a much stronger position with respect to securing China's rights in her northern frontier region than would have been the case with a Chinese Nationalist regime. The Chinese communists succeeded in establishing control in northern Sinkiang, which had long been a Soviet sphere of influence,[14] and by 1954 Khrushchev had agreed to the termination of all special rights in China which the Soviet Union had been granted under the 1950 treaty.

If a KMT victory in the Chinese civil war might have resulted in the loss of parts of the northern borderlands other than Outer Mongolia, it would also have meant the exclusion of China from North Korea and North Vietnam. The first would have remained an exclusively Russian sphere of influence, while in Vietnam Ho Chi Minh would almost certainly have been defeated by the French. Ho's fear lest the Chinese Nationalist army which had

[13] Howard L. Boorman, 'The Borderlands and the Sino-Soviet Alliance', in Boorman & others, *Moscow-Peking Axis* (New York, 1957).

[14] George Moseley, *A Sino-Soviet Cultural Frontier: The Ili Kazakh Autonomous Chou* (Camb., Mass., 1966).

occupied North Vietnam on behalf of the allies in 1945 might remain indefinitely was one reason for his acceptance of the return of French military forces in 1946, for only in this way could he be certain that the Yunnanese army would retire to China. But it was Chinese communist military support which, from 1949 on, enabled him finally to defeat the French.

Soviet support for the Chinese communists in Manchuria in 1945 had scarcely been less important than the aid subsequently extended by the Chinese communists to the Viet Minh. Japanese units north of the Great Wall had surrendered to the Red Army. A large part of their equipment was thereafter turned over to the Chinese communists, who were already in control of much of the Manchurian countryside. They also controlled the rural areas of north China, but the Japanese surrender in the principal cities south of the Great Wall was taken by United States forces dispatched to China for that purpose. The Chinese communists' strongest base was therefore north of the Great Wall. When Chiang Kai-shek failed in his attempt to eliminate this base, the outcome of the civil war was virtually decided. The cities of north China which had been turned over to the KMT soon fell to the communists. The subsequent course of the civil war had the character of a barbarian invasion, in the sense of a descent into central and south China from Manchuria and the north China plain. The KMT continues to regard it in this light, interpreting the Chinese communist movement as but a creature of the Russians.

Like the Ming followers who fled before the Manchu invasion, the KMT faithful sought refuge in Burma as well as Formosa; a few trickled into Laos or trekked across the Tibetan plateau to Kashmir. Behind them, the new regime was making a tremendous effort to reassert Chinese authority throughout the traditional empire, exclusive of Outer Mongolia. During 1950 the People's Liberation Army was engaged in Tibet in addition to the obligations it was discharging in Korea and Vietnam; an invasion of Taiwan seemed to be in the offing. From the core area which was all that remained of China at the time of the Marco Polo Bridge incident of 1937, the Chinese communists, taking immediate advantage of the momentum afforded by their victory in China proper, were thrusting out in all directions in order to drive the foreigners as far as possible away from the Middle Kingdom and reinstitute an order in Asia which would allow China once again to be the arbiter of men's destinies in her part of the world.

POLICY TOWARDS NATIONAL MINORITIES

The 'liberation' of China extended only to 'the sacred frontiers of the motherland' (a phrase frequently used in the literature of the period). There was no uncertainty about where, in a general sense, these frontiers lay. With the exception of Outer Mongolia, they embraced all the frontier dependencies of the Ch'ing empire, including Tibet, as well as all of Manchuria and China proper, including Taiwan. The former vassal states were outside these frontiers. They had either already attained, or were in the process of attaining, full independence. As soon as it was feasible to do so, the CPR established normal diplomatic relations with all her immediate neighbours:

Soviet Union North Korea Outer Mongolia	October 1949
Burma India	December 1949
Pakistan Afghanistan North Vietnam	January 1950
Nepal	1955
Laos	1962

The foreign relations of Bhutan and Sikkim are under the control of New Delhi, although no Chinese Government conceded India's right to exercise this control. By formally recognizing the independent governments of all the states contiguous to China, the CPR endorsed its inherited frontiers as China's outer limit.

The communists also recognized a delimitation between the areas of the CPR inhabited by Han and non-Han peoples. The latter, embracing fully half of the total area of the country, covered most of China's frontier zone. Called 'frontier' peoples (*min tsu*) by the KMT and minority peoples[15] (*hsiao shu*) by the

---

[15] Sometimes referred to as national minorities.

communists, these non-Han peoples had occupied the *fan-pu* and *t'u-ssu* areas of the Ch'ing empire. Under the CPR, which employed Stalin's definition of 'nation', some fifty different national minorities were identified, including some which had not previously been administratively differentiated from the Han Chinese. As envisaged in the Common Programme of 1949, autonomous areas were established for each national minority. By 1956 this process was well advanced.

The Sinkiang Uighur Autonomous Region (SUAR) was established in 1955, following the creation in the previous year of autonomous *chou* (prefectures) for the principal non-Uighur ethnic groups in the province—the Mongols on the frontier with the Mongolian People's Republic (MPR) and the Kazakhs, Kirghiz, and Tajiks on the Soviet frontier, where they looked across at their fellow nationals organized in constituent republics of the USSR. The enormous expanse of the Inner Mongolia Autonomous Region (IMAR), established in 1947, had been brought more firmly under the control of the CCP. In the southwest, Yunnan and Kweichow were covered with autonomous *chou* and autonomous *hsien*, while in Kwangsi steps were being taken towards the establishment of a provincial-sized autonomous region for the Chuang people (established in 1958). In Manchuria an autonomous *chou* had been established for China's Korean minority; it bordered the Soviet Union as well as the Korean People's Republic. And in 1955 a Preparatory Committee for the Tibet Autonomous Region had been established under the chairmanship of the Dalai Lama. Although the Ninghsia Hui Autonomous Region was not established until 1958, most of China's Moslems who lived in compact communities had been organized into autonomous regions earlier. Altogether in 1956 there were 74 autonomous areas at the *hsien* level and above. These gave precise administrative form to the frontier zone between the Han Chinese core area and the independent states contiguous to China.

The formal distinctions drawn between the foreign and domestic spheres and between the national minority and the Han Chinese spheres produced three separate fields of action for Chinese communist policies. Such a division was in keeping with Marxist-Leninist theory and conformed, in the main, with Soviet practice. Moreover, it suited the requirements of the Chinese revolution, which was being consolidated in the Han Chinese sphere, established in the national minority sphere, and projected into the foreign sphere. This configuration placed China's frontier zone in a middle position in the spectrum of the CPR's overall policies.

As Paul Linebarger once remarked: 'From Han [times] down to the present, the border areas have been centers of Chinese strategic thinking.'[16] This concern with a frontier zone was different from the style of Tsarist imperialism. The comparatively recent advance of Russian power into Siberia and Central Asia had been based on territorial acquisition. The Cossack lines were gradually extended, with new forts being erected to mark the line of imperial control. In this fashion, one after another of the tribal lands of Siberia and the Moslem principalities of Central Asia were brought within a Russian sphere of influence militarily defined. The interests of imperial China, on the other hand, were relatively constant and limited: she sought to maintain the tranquillity of a frontier zone inhabited by peoples with whom the Chinese had long been in contact.

In European Russia the empire included peoples, such as the Ukrainians and the Poles, who were at least as advanced as the Russians themselves. Furthermore, their populations were quite large. At the time of the October revolution, in fact, the Russians accounted for less than 50 per cent of the population of the empire; in China in 1949, the Han Chinese made up 95 per cent of population of the country. The different compositions of the Russian and Chinese empires, and the different conceptions of the Russians and Chinese with respect to their frontiers, explains in large measure the dissimilar ways in which Marxist-Leninist theory on the national question was applied in the two cases.[17]

After coming to power, the Bolsheviks hoped that other states,

---

[16] P. M. A. Linebarger & others, *Far Eastern Governments and Politics* (Princeton, NJ, 1954), p. 75.

[17] Some of these differences are dealt with in Chang Chih-i, *Chung-kuo ko-ming ti min-tsu wen-t'i ho min-tsu cheng-ts'e chiang-hua (t'i-kang)* (A discussion of the national question in the Chinese revolution and of actual nationalities policy (draft)) (Peking, 1956), which has been translated in George Moseley, ed., *The Party and the National Question in China* (Camb., Mass., 1966). It should also be mentioned that, according to Marxist-Leninist theory, China was not an imperialist country, as was Russia, but rather an oppressed, semi-colonial country. It does not appear, however, that this doctrinal fine point contributed as much to the differences in Soviet and Chinese communist national minority policy as did the real differences mentioned above.

not previously part of the Russian empire, could be brought into the Soviet sphere as republics of the USSR. Persia and Afghanistan looked particularly tempting. Soviet extension was a task specifically assigned to the new Kazakh SSR, which declared in a public document:

We wish to point out the special task which results from the location of the Kirghiz [Kazakh] republic. Being situated in the Asian borderland, and having close contact with the peoples of the East, we, the Kirghiz [Kazakhs], will be the instrument for spreading the revolutionary influences of Russia in the East. . . . In joining the ranks of the Russian Soviet Federation, the Kirghiz [Kazakh] Soviet Socialist Republic hopes to become the school of revolution for the entire East. . . .[18]

This mode of territorial extension was implicitly rejected by the Chinese communists when they chose the autonomous area rather than the federated republic as the administrative unit of their national minority programme. The autonomous areas of China are inalienable parts of a unitary state, whereas the Soviet republics had the formal right of secession. The state structure of the CPR did not invite the adherence of other states, as did the state structure of the Soviet Union in the days when Stalin was Commissar of Nationalities.

The thrust of Chinese communist policy in the frontier zone has aimed at full integration in the national minority sphere and at reasserting Chinese influence in the adjacent foreign sphere, occupied in part by former vassals of the empire. In the words of Robert Scalapino, China has been engaged in 'moving the buffer zone which was once *inside* her boundaries to encompass states adjacent to her.'[19] Geographical and historical factors, together with trans-frontier ties of race, language, and religion, have placed the frontier regions of the CPR in a special position with respect

[18] 'Declaration of the First Congress of the Soviets of the Kirghiz [Kazakh] Autonomous Soviet Socialist Republic to all Autonomous Republics and Oblasts of the Russian Soviet Federation, October 4, 1920', in X. J. Eudin & Robert C. North, *Soviet Russia and the East, 1920–1927: A Documentary Survey* (Stanford, Calif., 1957), p. 53. The governor of Sinkiang, Yang Tseng-hsin, interpreted the Soviet attitude at the time as proof that Moscow meant to subvert Moslem regions of China adjacent to the Kazakh SSR.

[19] R. A. Scalapino, 'Tradition and Transition in the Asian Policy of Communist China', in Edward Szczepanik, ed., *Economic and Social Problems of the Far East* (Hong Kong, 1962), p. 267. This theme is taken up by C. P. FitzGerald in his interesting Chatham House Essay, *The Chinese View of their Place in the World* (London, 1964).

to the conduct of communist China's foreign policy. While it is not possible, from the outside, to investigate the formulation of this policy, the following examples of the involvement of the frontier zone in China's international relations suggest that the foreign and national minority policies of the CPR are related.[20]

NATIONAL MINORITIES AND FOREIGN POLICY

China's Mongol, Turkic, and Tibetan peoples have been especially important as intermediaries in the foreign policy of the CPR. In the early 1930s, when Chinese communist policy had favoured the establishment of republics on the Soviet model, a federal China had been envisioned which would incorporate a Chinese republic together with republics for each of these three peoples; today they constitute the major autonomous units of the CPR. Each of these peoples spans the frontier, extending into areas which are now parts of adjacent states.

The MPR established its first consulate abroad at Huhehot, the capital of the IMAR (in 1957). Huhehot also has a branch of the Sino-Mongol Friendship Association. The MPR and the IMAR are linked by a trans-Mongolia railway, completed in 1956, which connects Peking with the trans-Siberian railway at Irkutsk. This line was used in 1961 by a special IMAR delegation which attended celebrations of the fortieth anniversary of the victory of the (Outer) Mongolian people's revolution. It is noteworthy that a Kazakh from the Altai district of Sinkiang joined the delegation, for the MPR includes a Kazakh minority in territory adjacent to Sinkiang. The daily newspaper of Inner Mongolia (*Nei-Meng -ku jih-pao*) always carries a good deal of material concerning the friendship between the peoples of the IMAR and the MPR. This was particularly so at the time a delegation from Ulan Bator visited Huhehot in 1957 to participate in the celebration of the tenth anniversary of the founding of the IMAR. Later in the same year an agreement was reached which provided for use of adjacent grazing areas of the MPR by herders of the IMAR.

As in Sinkiang, an indicator of the state of Sino-Soviet relations in Mongolia has been the issue of language reform. It became

---

[20] These examples have been taken mainly from the clipping files of Chinese communist newspapers held by the Union Research Institute, Hong Kong. This chapter does not take account of developments during China's Cultural Revolution, in the course of which there has been a notable deterioration in Peking's relations with certain of her neighbours, and especially Burma.

known in 1955–6 that the Chinese communists intended to replace the traditional Mongol script with the Cyrillic alphabet, which the Russians had earlier introduced in the MPR. In 1958, however, the Chinese announced that the Latin alphabet, rather than Cyrillic, would be used. This was in line with a new programme for the reform of the written languages of all the peoples of China, including the Han. But the programme was short-lived, and what has actually happened in the IMAR is that the Chinese have encouraged the continued use of the traditional script. If this was a gesture calculated to please the Mongols of the IMAR, it also suggests that the Chinese still hope to regain influence among the Mongols of the MPR.

In the past few years the MPR has taken the Chinese communists to task for attacking the Soviet leadership; it has also criticized the CPR for its treatment of national minorities. While there have been instances of Mongols quitting the IMAR for a new life in the MPR, it is probable that these accusations of the MPR derive more from its reliance on the Soviet news agencies than from dissatisfaction with CPR policy specifically in the IMAR.

The issues of revisionism and of national-minority policy have been much more important in Sinkiang than in the IMAR. In Sinkiang, moreover, these two questions have been closely connected. In 1963, 50,000 people—mainly Kazakhs—of Sinkiang's Turkic population fled across the border to the Kazakh SSR. This was the culmination of Sino-Soviet friction in Sinkiang which had been produced by the CPR's determination to exclude Soviet influence from this border region. Soon thereafter the several Soviet consulates in Sinkiang, including the consulate-general in Urumchi, were closed down under Chinese pressure, while the Soviet press began to castigate the CPR's national minority policy. Unfavourable comments made by refugees from Sinkiang were frequently quoted; the crowning invective used on the Soviet side was the labelling of people's communes for the minority groups in Sinkiang as 'concentration camps'.

The Chinese, for their part, accused the recalcitrant Uighurs and Kazakhs, who had demanded Soviet-style republics, of 'Khrushchev revisionism'. The label of 'revisionist' became simply a euphemism for pro-Soviet, and a great many non-Han people in Sinkiang were guilty of this 'error'. The language issue has raged furiously in Sinkiang, too. As in the IMAR, the Chinese initially planned to make Cyrillic the standard vehicle for the writing of the national minority languages of the SUAR, the most important of which, apart from Mongol (Khalkha), are Uighur, Kazakh, and Kirghiz. This was dropped in favour of the Latin alphabet in 1958. In contrast to the IMAR case, where the traditional Mongol script was ultimately retained, the mainly Islamic peoples of the SUAR have been denied the right to retain the Arabic alphabet which had previously been in use. The Chinese communists are apparently more worried about outside influence in Sinkiang than in Inner Mongolia. In recent years Sino-Soviet trade across this frontier has dwindled, while the Sino-Soviet rail link through Sinkiang, scheduled to be opened in 1962, has never been completed.

Notwithstanding their various language-reform schemes, the Chinese communists have apparently not interfered with the use of the traditional script in Tibet, which is, as a result of vastly expanded printing facilities, more widely used than ever before. This suggests that the CPR does not wish to antagonize the Tibetans unnecessarily; it also suggests that use of the traditional Tibetan writing may be considered useful in promoting Chinese communist influence in the Himalayan states of Ladakh, Nepal, Sikkim, and Bhutan, which are largely Tibetan in race and culture. Construction of the Nepal–Tibet highway, agreed upon in 1961, is probably more indicative of the trend in this area than is the Sino-Nepalese accord of August 1962 which, presumably aimed at the Khamba (east Tibetan) rebels operating from the Mustang area of Nepal, restricted the movement of tribespeople across the frontier.

The 'question of Tibet', which arose in the United Nations after China's suppression of the 1959 Tibetan revolt, has probably had more influence on the CPR's international relations than any other situation arising in a national minority area. It poisoned China's relations with India, which gave sanctuary to the Dalai Lama, and became a test of the attitude of many other states towards China. Nepal, which sympathized as much with the plight of the Nagas in India as with that of the Tibetans in China, was one of the states which held the 'correct' view: namely, that Tibetan affairs were a purely domestic concern of the CPR. The Philippines and Malaya, which at different times raised the

Tibetan issue in the United Nations, were bitterly attacked by the Chinese communists. The 1962 fighting between Indian and Chinese troops added fuel to these flames, bringing the Soviet Union in on India's side. By 1964, with the Soviet Union deeply involved in a military aid programme to India, Peking charged that *Pravda* was 'singing a duet' with the Indian news agencies in 'spreading slander about Chinese maps showing Nepalese territory as Chinese.'

Compared with China's major frontier regions of Inner Mongolia, Sinkiang, and Tibet, her southern frontier region has been relatively tranquil. With the exception of the fiercely independent Lolo, most of the national minorities in the south, formerly under *t'u-ssu* administration, have assimilated much more readily to Han Chinese ways than have the Mongol, Turkic, and Tibetan peoples of the old *fan-pu*. Since Chinese communist policies did not arouse the kind of national consciousness among the southern minorities that they did among those in the north and west, the CPR has been able to assume a relatively confident stance along its southern frontier in Yunnan and Kwangsi provinces.

Thailand has been sensitive to developments in the national minority regions of Yunnan despite the fact that she does not have a common frontier with the CPR. At least half a million T'ai (Thai) live in Yunnan, and the Thai government, which has been politically conservative ever since the ousting of the Prime Minister Pridi Panomyong shortly after the second world war, has been apprehensive lest a Thai government-in-exile be set up on Chinese soil. Thai fears were especially aroused by the establishment in 1953 of an autonomous region for the T'ai in the Sipsong Panna region of southern Yunnan, where China comes within 100 miles of the Thai border. At various times the former Prime Minister, Pridi, who is thought to live in Peking, has been reported as visiting the Sipsong Panna. Thai apprehensions appear to have been exaggerated, however, as it was not generally realized in Bangkok that autonomous areas for national minorities were being set up all over China, and not solely among the T'ai peoples of southern Yunnan. While fears about the activities of Thais in exile seem to have abated, the Thai government is still worried about its northern hill tribes, such as the Lahu and Lisu, which represent southern extensions of national minority groups found in the CPR. These anxieties have not caused Sino-Thai relations to be bad. They would have been bad in any case. The very fact that there is a sizeable T'ai minority in communist China, however, has provided further insurance that relations between Peking and the right-wing government in Bangkok would remain icy. Suspicions between the two countries have been mutually reinforcing.

Nothing could more clearly indicate the opposite attitudes of the Thai and Burmese governments towards Peking than the visit of the Prime Minister, U Nu, in April 1961 to the same T'ai autonomous region in southern Yunnan which had caused so much concern in Bangkok. U Nu and his family, who were on holiday in Yunnan, were accompanied by the Chinese Prime Minister Chou En-lai on their trip to the Sipsong Panna T'ai autonomous region. Their visit occurred at the time of the Thai new year, and U Nu and his party joined in the festivities.

Two substantive agreements were reached in discussions which took place at this time between U Nu and Chou En-lai. Economic co-operation between Yunnan province and Burma was to be strengthened: agricultural specialists from Burma were to study farm machinery and production in Yunnan, while Yunnanese specialists were to visit Burma to study the growing of tropical crops. At the same time it was agreed that the CPR and Burma should co-ordinate their efforts to eliminate KMT bands in Burma, which the two statesmen described as a threat to both countries.

Several of Burma's northern peoples are closely related to minority groups in Yunnan. This is especially true of the Shan (T'ai), who are practically indistinguishable from the T'ai peoples across the frontier. Minority questions are of great importance in the Union of Burma; there has been almost continuous fighting between central government forces and partisans of one or another of these non-Burman peoples, yet Rangoon has taken an interest in, rather than become alarmed by, the national minority policy of the CPR. (It must be said that this statement applies more to U Nu than to Ne Win.) During a visit to China in 1956, U Nu went to the Nationalities Institute in Peking, and in 1957 he had talks with the Vice-Chairman of the Nationality Affairs Commission of Yunnan. And he has visited several of Yunnan's autonomous areas in addition to the Sipsong Panna. On the Chinese side,

Peking did not allow itself to be deterred by the tense situation among north Burma's national groups from concluding a border agreement with Rangoon.

The influence of the frontier zone on Sino-Laotian politics has been mixed: when the government in Vientiane has been neutralist or left wing, the frontier peoples have acted as a bridge between the two countries; when the Vientiane government has been under right-wing control, the frontier peoples have been an irritant in Sino-Laotian relations. For many years Laotian politics have been dominated by the question of the Pathet Lao, a movement composed largely of non-Lao peoples on the Chinese and North Vietnamese frontiers. It has been continuously supported by Hanoi, while Peking's support seems to have been intermittent. The CPR attitude appears to be that the Pathet Lao may be useful as a way of making Chinese pressure felt in Laotian politics, but that it would dissociate itself from the Pathet Lao if a friendly government remained in office in Vientiane. When the Prime Minister, Souvanna Phouma, and Prince Souphanouvong, the Pathet Lao leader, visited China together in 1961, the two governments agreed on the establishment of diplomatic relations and the construction of a road from southern Yunnan to the northern Laotian province of Phong Saly. Souvanna Phouma was as enthusiastic about the new road as were his Chinese hosts. In the spring of the following year, however, the Chinese gave active support to a Pathet Lao offensive against Muong Sing and Nam Tha, border districts which had once been part of China.

North Vietnam is the only country on China's frontier which has adopted a national minority programme based on the CPR model. Both of North Vietnam's two autonomous regions have common borders with China: one of them, the Viet Bac Autonomous Region, extends along most of the frontier between North Vietnam and the Kwangsi Chuang Autonomous Region; the other, the T'ai Bac Autonomous Region, abuts on Yunnan province. The T'ai and Miao peoples who predominate in these autonomous regions are closely related to national minorities of south China. Trans-frontier relations between the autonomous regions of the CPR and North Vietnam have been marked throughout by expressions of comradeship and goodwill. For instance, in 1958 a delegation from the Viet Bac Autonomous Region went to Nanning to participate in the establishment of the

Kwangsi Chuang Autonomous Region; in 1959 a Yunnan provincial delegation visited the T'ai Bac Autonomous Region to celebrate the fifth anniversary of its founding.

Much more important than national-minority relations between the two countries, however, has been the direct support which the CPR has given North Vietnam, particularly in her long war with the French and, now, in her struggle with the Saigon–Washington combination. The bases for this support are mainly in Kwangsi and Yunnan, both of which are linked with North Vietnam by rail. Thus these frontier provinces have been more directly involved than have other parts of China in the CPR's relations with North Vietnam. Peking has frequently charged that United States aircraft have intruded into the region, as well as over the island of Hainan.

The involvement of Manchuria in China's relations with North Korea has been of the same nature, namely as a base for CPR support for Pyongyang. The significance of this relationship has declined steadily since the end of the Korean war and the 1958 agreement on the withdrawal of all Chinese troops from North Korea. Although Manchuria's Kirin province has a Korean population of over half a million, this minority group has not had any discernible influence on the CPR's relations with North Korea. Indeed, these Manchurian Koreans are almost never mentioned. There have been some recent indications (spring 1967) that Peking has sought to involve the North Korean regime in a renewed effort to 'liberate' the south by force, and that for his refusal to co-operate in this venture the Prime Minister, Kim Il Sung, has been attacked by the CPR as a 'revisionist'. Renewed hostilities in Korea would give the Chinese communists an opportunity to reassert themselves in North Korea.

TRANS-FRONTIER COMMUNICATIONS

The states contiguous to China have become closer neighbours as the result of the development of China's communications system. China's trans-frontier communications before 1949, such as the Japanese and Russian railways into Manchuria and the French railway into Yunnan, had been constructed almost entirely by foreign powers. An exception was the Burma road, built by the Chinese at the beginning of the Pacific War. As Owen Lattimore has pointed out, construction of the Burma road marked the first time in modern Chinese history that an important communications link had been built *outward* from China, reversing the process of imperialist penetration of China.[21] Many more such links have been forged since 1949, while the Burma road has been hard-surfaced. The new Chinese roads to Nepal and Laos have already been mentioned, as has the trans-Mongolia railway. Agreement on the construction of a new road from Sinkiang to Gilgit, in the Pakistan-administered portion of Kashmir, followed the settlement of the Kashmiri border question between the two countries. After the second world war the Hanoi–Kunming railway had to be rebuilt, and a new railway linking Hanoi with the Chinese rail system by way of Kwangsi was opened in 1954. The development of China's external communications links has been more than matched by the expansion of her internal system, in particular by new railways in western China, Tibet, and Sinkiang.

Especially important in terms of passenger travel has been the CPR's improvement of air service. The first contingent of the PLA which entered Sinkiang in late 1949 had to be flown in by Soviet aircraft, as the Chinese communists had none of their own. The national airline of the CPR now links all major cities of the country, and the domestic service is supplemented and extended at several points by international connexions. North Korea, North Vietnam, Burma, and Pakistan, in addition to the Soviet Union, are among the countries which have regular air services with the CPR. Kunming is especially important in this network, as the twice-weekly flights between Rangoon and the Yunnanese capital provide China with her most important access route to the non-communist world; there are also regular flights from Kunming to Dacca, East Pakistan.

China's neighbours can now communicate with one another, as well as with China, by means of the CPR's rail and air system. For instance, in 1961 the king and queen of Nepal visited the Mongolian People's Republic by way of Peking. In the same year the Laotian Prime Minister travelled to Hanoi via Kunming. Kunming was also a transit point for Ho Chi Minh when he went to Indonesia in 1959; later in the same year he stayed in Urumchi, the capital of Sinkiang, on his way home from a visit to the Soviet

---

[21] Owen Lattimore, 'Yunnan, Pivot of Southeast Asia', *Foreign Affairs*, Apr 1943, pp. 476–93.

x

Union. In 1957 a Burmese parliamentary delegation went on to North Vietnam after visiting China; also in 1957, a group of MPR visitors travelled through Peking *en route* to Hanoi. In 1958 the North Korean Prime Minister took the train via Antung to Peking and then flew to North Vietnam.

The impression of a regional pattern suggested by the itineraries of travellers to and through China is reinforced by the location in China's frontier regions of consulates of several governments among the states contiguous to China. The MPR consulate in Inner Mongolia and the former Soviet consulates in Sinkiang have already been mentioned. Under a 1956 agreement, Nepal was to maintain a consulate in Lhasa. The CPR has a consulate in the Burma border town of Lashio, while the Burmese maintain a consulate-general in Kunming, where there is also a Laotian consulate-general. North Vietnam has a consulate in Nanning as well as in Kunming.[22] Sometimes a neighbouring country's ambassador in Peking acts also as that country's ambassador to other neighbouring states, an example of which is the Nepalese ambassador in Peking who is also accredited to Ulan Bator and Rangoon.

In the early 1960s the CPR put her relations with her neighbours on a firmer basis by negotiating boundary treaties with the MPR and all the non-communist states contiguous to China except India (including Bhutan and Sikkim) and Laos. The settling of these boundary issues proceeded as follows:

	Agreement in principle	*Boundary treaty*	*Boundary protocol*
Burma		1960	1960
Nepal	1960	1961	1963
Mongolia		1962	1964
Pakistan	1962	1963	1965
Afghanistan		1963	1965

China has not signed boundary agreements with her other neighbours—the Soviet Union, North Korea, North Vietnam, Laos, and India. No serious frontier questions appear to have arisen with North Korea and North Vietnam, where traditional boundaries are accepted on both sides. There have, however, been altercations between Peking and Pyongyang with regard to the

[22] This listing is not exhaustive.

location of the boundary in the Changpai Shan range on the Sino-Korean frontier. Since the Vientiane government's administrative control falls far short of the China frontier, any questions relating to the Sino-Laotian border would seem to be, for the time being at least, academic. In 1963 China intimated that she did not accept the existing frontier with the Soviet Union, which had been imposed by unequal treaties; according to Soviet calculations, half a million square miles of Siberia and Soviet Central Asia were involved in the Chinese claims.[23]

The CPR described the boundary problems she had inherited as 'questions left over from history'. In settling them, Peking did not attempt to introduce claims to 'lost territories'; she kept to a minimum the number of questions which had to be resolved. In negotiating the demarcation of her boundaries, moreover, Peking's attitude was one of compromise and even generosity. Of the areas in dispute, she gave more than she received. The signing of the border treaty with the MPR was hailed in Peking as proof that all problems between communist countries could be solved 'in accordance with the principles of Marxism-Leninism and the principles guiding relations between fraternal countries laid down in the 1957 Moscow Declaration and the 1960 Moscow Statement'.[24] This was a veiled criticism of the Soviet Union, which, according to Peking, had trampled on these principles in her relations with the CPR. Similarly, New Delhi was indirectly criticized in the oratory which accompanied the demarcation of China's borders with Burma, Nepal, Pakistan, and Afghanistan. Peking hailed these settlements as victories for the 'five principles of peaceful coexistence' which India, according to the Chinese, had persistently violated.

It is not at all evident, however, that in concluding these frontier agreements with her neighbours the CPR was primarily motivated, as has sometimes been asserted, by a desire to embarrass or bring pressure upon New Delhi and Moscow for having opposed Chinese ambitions.[25] If these agreements coincided with

[23] For a discussion of this dispute, see Dennis J. Doolin, *Territorial Claims in the Sino-Soviet Conflict: Documents and Analysis* (Stanford, Calif., 1965).

[24] *Peking Review*, 28 Dec 1962.

[25] This odd (as it seems to me) interpretation is advanced by Guy Searls, 'Communist China's Border Policy: Instrument for a New Empire', *United Asia*, July 1963, pp. 469–82, and also appears to be favoured by Francis Watson, *The Frontiers of China* (London, 1966).

China's embroilment with India and the Soviet Union, they also came at a time when the CPR was shifting gears in her overall policies. The early 1960s was a time of readjustment in China's domestic programme, following the 'Great Leap Forward' and the attempt to build people's communes. Peking's control in her frontier zone had by this time been consolidated, and the national minorities were now called upon to go ahead with their socialist revolutions: this was the essence of the pertinent decisions of the tenth Plenum of the CCP central committee, held in 1962.[26] Tibet, although still trailing behind the other non-Han areas, was moving forward in the context of Chinese communist development, as was indicated by the long-delayed establishment of the Tibet Autonomous Region in September 1965, just six months after the Foreign Minister, Ch'en Yi, had journeyed to Kabul and Rawalpindi to sign the last in the series of border protocols. In the foreign policy of the CPR, the year 1960 marked a watershed as Peking moved vigorously to assert herself in the Afro-Asian world. Peking's visitors during the year included Sekou Touré of Guinea, with whom the CPR signed her first technical assistance agreement with an African country, and Che Guevara of Cuba, who won a US$60 million grant from China, the largest she had ever extended to a country outside the established communist bloc.

China's formal delimitation of her outstanding border questions can best be understood in the context of these broad political developments rather than in relation to any single objective which the CPR was pursuing at the time. The concurrent founding of the Tibet Autonomous Region is relevant to this interpretation. Tibet was the last area of the CPR to be given final administrative status. Thus within the space of a few months both the CPR's international frontiers (exclusive of those with her communist neighbours and with Laos) and internal political organization were definitively established. China thus had a trans-frontier base from which to reach farther afield.

It appears that Peking, confident of the revolution's success within her frontiers and optimistic about the prospects for welding the adjacent states of Asia (other than the Soviet Union) into a new 'Chinese family of nations', was now hopeful of becoming ascendant throughout the Afro-Asian world, which, as

[26] See the editorial on this subject in *Min-tsu t'uan-chieh* (Nationalities' unity), Nov 1962.

Chou En-lai put it, had become 'the storm centres of world revolution'.[27] The Chinese revolution, advancing from the Han Chinese core area and encompassing by stages the frontier zone and adjacent states, was being projected into the underdeveloped and non-white 'third world'. It has since become apparent that in this venture the Chinese communists overreached themselves. Following a series of severe setbacks in the foreign field, prominent among which was the thrashing taken by the Indonesian Communist Party, the Chinese communists have taken up a defensive position in their immediate frontier regions.

[27] NCNA, 30 Dec 1964.

10

Conclusions

JACK GRAY

THE contributions to this symposium span the adult life of the senior leaders of China on both sides of the Taiwan Straits. They deal with problems and events which represent the political experience of the rulers of modern China, the experience which has provided the predispositions and prejudices, the common assumptions, and the habitual reactions, of Mao Tse-tung and his fellow rulers of China. Much of this experience was concerned with problems faced by all Chinese radicals including both Nationalists and communists, and analysis of it helps to reveal what the basic *data* of politics in China have been since the first revolution of 1911.

The problems did not all reveal themselves at once, but were successively laid bare as the process of attempted revolution went on. One can express the course of Chinese political development since then as a succession of key experiences, each adding new depth to politics.

In the world of 1911, when all the great powers were constitutionally governed except Russia, which had been defeated in 1905 by Asian but constitutional Japan, there was little doubt in the minds of Chinese reformers and revolutionaries that China would become a constitutional power. The Manchus themselves had conceded this in theory, but their actual constitutional arrangements had signed the death warrant of their own power, partly because they sought to use the new constitution to strengthen themselves against their Chinese subjects in the guise of conceding a share of power to them. When the Manchus were overthrown, a parliamentary Republic was created. Within two years, however, it had manifestly failed. The inexperience of the parliamentarians played a part in this failure; every opportunity to check the ambitious President was missed, and the attempt of the KMT politician Sung Chiao-jen to turn Sun Yat-sen's alliance of secret societies, revolutionary students, and emigrant Chinese into a political party which would seek a majority from the electorate and impose a cabinet responsible to it on the President, failed—less because of the assassination of Sung himself than because of the lack of interest of his fellow leaders in the attempt. The reasons for the failure of the parliamentary experiment, however, were more profound. Like many other Asian peoples experimenting with parliamentary government, the parliamentarians were inhibited by a traditional distaste for certain things fundamental to government by these means. First, they had a distaste for parties as such—the Chinese word for a party meant a clique, a group of persons (in the bureaucracy) who used their personal connexions to disrupt the normal processes of counsel and decision-making in their own interests. Related to this was the even stronger distaste for an open struggle for power; many refused to seek power even in order to promote the policies in which they believed. This attitude was shown in Sun's failure to support Sung Chiao-jen, in the attitude of Chiang K'ang-hu and his Socialist Party,[1] in the withdrawal of the liberal wing from politics after the May Fourth Movement, and in the general weakness and ineffectiveness of the social-democratic centre of Chinese politics throughout the Nationalist period. Even the idea of the majority vote, a convention which we accept as the cornerstone of democracy, seems to people whose experience of government by discussion came from village affairs and clan councils, which tended to aim at a consensus, a very undesirable and arbitrary way of disposing of opposition. The real although paradoxical connexion between this traditional attitude and totalitarian democracy of the present Chinese type, in which the most intractable opponents have to be rejected from the body politic and the rest pressurized into an appearance of unanimity, has never really been analysed; it may well be the root of some of the many contradictions concerning democracy which appear in the thinking of Mao.

More important than these considerations, however, is the fact that by the time of the revolution of 1911 political authority had already passed to an increasing extent to the provinces of China. The defection of the provincial assemblies from the Manchus had been the decisive factor in their abdication, and the provinces were the real inheritors of power. In such a situation parliamentary

[1] See above, p. 72.

methods were as irrelevant as any others exercised in Peking, while in the provinces the complete domination of the new assemblies by a gentry electorate then almost uniformly opposed to changes of any significant sort prevented the development even at this level of any real political life. With the death of Yüan Shih-k'ai, the Peking government lost the last vestiges of authority, and the whole political problem changed. The assumption that a change of regime at the capital was the decisive step in the revolution had to be relinquished; the problem which dominated all others was the reunification of China, and the re-creation (or perhaps more properly the creation) of a centralized government. In this respect, the federalist movement[2] was revealing. It pointed up the vitality of the forces which in Chinese history had always made for provincial autonomy, the fact that national unity had traditionally depended less on a centralized state than on loyalty to the emperor as a symbol of a common ideology, and also that federal ideas (like states' rights) were much more liable to express conservatism than radicalism. The experience of the federalist movement, with which the radicals at first toyed for tactical reasons, eventually forced them sharply back to insistence—more natural for all radicals—on 'the Republic one and indivisible'. If the provinces still had to be captured for the revolution one by one, it would not be through a free association created by federalism, but by conquest; and to this the Nationalist Party turned.

Up to this point, in general all the radicals thought in terms of a political revolution imposed from above. Sun's élitist theory and the juristic preoccupations of the federalist intellectuals testify to this. By about 1920, however, this was beginning to change, less this time because a new problem was revealed than because new opportunities seemed to be emerging. The political public in China widened, and seemed to be capable of further large extension; this was the main factor. But first of all, it is worth recording (although it anticipates what will be said about the May Fourth Movement) the reaction of the Peking academic and future founder of the Chinese Communist Party, Ch'en Tu-hsiu, to China's political experience so far. In 1920, during the ferment of ideas to which the May Fourth Movement led, Bertrand Russell and John Dewey lectured in China, just when the basic intellectual controversy of modern China—pragmatism versus

---

[2] See above, ch. 4.

Marxism—had begun. As Benjamin Schwartz has pointed out,[3] according to Ch'en himself he was made a Marxist by one phrase of John Dewey—'facts have the power to make laws; laws have not the power to make facts'. Ch'en Tu-hsiu's immediate appreciation of how applicable this was to China's situation was the beginning of a new view of the revolution, implying a transformation of the whole scope of political activity. The Comintern midwives of the birth of the CCP spelled out in detail what the new scope of politics should be.

The great solvent of the limits of politics, however, and the great catalyst of change, was the May Fourth Movement, alluded to frequently in this book but never actually described. In May 1919 a student demonstration in Peking against the acceptance at Versailles of the reversion of German rights in Shantung to the Japanese, touched off a nation-wide movement of protest. Intellectuals, merchants, and urban workers made common cause in defence of China's integrity. It was the first convincing demonstration at once of the existence of widespread nationalist feeling and of something in China which could be called 'public opinion'; and it was apparently a demonstration that the masses of China, symbolized by the workers of the treaty ports who participated in the movement, were a potential force for nationalist ends, and were not by definition outside politics, traditionally the business of the élite. It was a first whiff of democratic nationalism. The movement swept on to destroy many of the restraints which had kept the pace of change slow hitherto. Confucianism was now explicitly repudiated by the young: the classical written language, difficult to read even for most literate people, was replaced for the radicals as the language of polite literature by the colloquial *pai-hua*, the spoken language written down, which was already the medium of the popular literature of drama and fiction despised by the orthodox scholar; this gave a vastly wider audience for the writings of the reformers and revolutionaries. Out of the nation-wide student unions (which were the first modern political organizations in China) grew a new level of political organization transcending the provincial, scholarly, and secret-society cliques which were the basis of existing groups. Among the new parties was the CCP, founded by men who were less concerned with socialism than with the possible use, in the political situation which May Fourth had revealed, of the political

[3] *Chinese Communism and the Rise of Mao* (Camb., Mass., 1952), p. 19.

techniques which the Bolsheviks had used with such dramatic success in Russia.

Many of the political leaders of present-day China were involved in the May Fourth Movement, including Mao Tse-tung himself. The Nationalist Party however, partly by the accident of circumstances which kept most of its leaders in the far south, was much less involved than any other political group, and was perhaps even then beginning to harden into a pattern of political thinking to which it was eventually to revert. The importance of the May Fourth Movement in Mao Tse-tung's political theory can hardly be exaggerated; it reinforced ideas of social harmony as opposed to class conflict, ideas more natural in Chinese political tradition and more attractive in view of the common subjection of all classes to foreign oppression, and determined that Mao's ideas would thereafter be conditioned by expectations about the nationalist, as much as by the class, reactions of his fellow Chinese. It was on the anniversary of May Fourth that he made the speech which first outlined the New Democracy.

At the same time as a new public for politics was discovered, a new issue with which to rouse that public was also supplied. The first study of Marx and Lenin in the wake of the movement provided, to explain China's humiliating relations with the powers, the theory of economic imperialism. Belief in the theory of economic imperialism became the shibboleth of Chinese patriotism, and was shared equally by left and right. It accounts for the paradox that in China, where there was as yet little consciousness of class conflict, the vaguely socialist (or anti-capitalist) aspirations of Chiang K'ang-hu and his Socialist Party—and for that matter of Sun Yat-sen himself—should be transformed so rapidly into a commitment to a Leninist view of China's position which was remarkably widespread and dominant by 1925, when the Communist Party itself was still insignificant in numbers and in intellectual influence.

The next major political experience was the result of these events and developments. From 1923 the Nationalist Party, strongly influenced by Marxist ideas which were by no means confined to the vigorous but limited communist group within it, and reorganized on Leninist lines with Comintern advice, gradually came to accept the idea of a revolution based largely upon the political organization of each and every pro-revolutionary class in China, including the peasants and workers. As Patrick Cavendish's chapter shows, it was at this time that the centre of gravity of party membership shifted from the emigrant groups outside China to the population of China itself, that student organizations became the most active part of the membership in the warlord areas, and that peasants and workers came to dominate the membership of those areas under the direct influence of the Nationalist Party. A new technique of revolution was developed, in which trained agitators prepared the ground in the warlord areas for the coming of the revolutionary armies, which then held the ring for a popular revolution—a technique which perhaps originated in the tolerance, by the radical warlord and secret-society leader of eastern Kwangtung, Ch'en Ch'iung-ming, of the peasant movement which was organized there largely by the vigour and initiative of the left-wing son of a local landlord, P'eng P'ai. Out of P'eng P'ai's successful movement in the area grew up in Canton the School of the Peasant Revolution (where Mao and several other since important communists taught) whose graduates went all over China to work underground in preparation for the Northern Expedition.

The most dramatic expression of this revolutionary process was seen in Hunan in 1927, in the peasant movement so graphically described by Mao Tse-tung in the famous report on conditions in Hunan which he made for the left-wing Wuhan government. Under the protection of the nationalist units which had cleared the Hsiang River valley in Hunan of warlords, the Peasant Associations took over the local government of the province, backed by 10 million peasants. Had this movement in Hunan been supported and similar movements encouraged elsewhere, an effective social revolution might have occurred within a year or two; but it was already too late. The Wuhan government was under the shadow of the dominance of the right wing of the party under Chiang Kai-shek, and although its own armies were more radical than those farther down the Yangtze, they were not so radical as to tolerate a peasant movement which might, in communist hands, end in their own expropriation. Mao's plea for support for the peasants was rejected not only by the left-wing Nationalists but by the Comintern. With the crushing of the communists in Chiang Kai-shek's Shanghai coup of April 1927, the Nationalist revolution took a different road.

The deliberate destruction by the Nationalists of their own mass organizations, including their own party organizations, described by Patrick Cavendish, was a turning-point in the history of the Nationalist movement. It was perhaps a major cause of their final failure. In a country where political and social authority was diffused among half a million villages, no amount of intelligent initiative, scholarly investigation of conditions, and well-drafted legislation was likely to change anything, unless the revolutionary government was prepared to train and to protect local democratic organizations. The very revenues necessary for reform, or even for further war to complete the unification of the country, depended upon the ability of the KMT to reform the abuses of the land-tax—the most serious problem of all; but without effective democratic control at the village level, the central government had no means whatever of penetrating the thousand-year-old jungle of local bargains, compromises, evasions, and misappropriations which made up the land-tax system. In the same way, even the moderate legislation designed to secure a reduction of rents by 25 per cent was a dead letter because the little finger of the local landlord was thicker than the loins of the national government in Nanking. The new democratic local government which here and there was attempted on Nationalist initiative, unsupported by any effort to mobilize those whose interests were most affected, was wholly distorted; the entire apparatus fell into the hands of the old ruling groups of the gentry, often through the use of the votes of their clan dependants or the votes of terrorized tenants. Where peasant associations were re-created, government—traditional or reformed—gave way to force as the threatened landlords reacted to destroy them. Eventually, in order to eliminate communist influence in the countryside, Nanking reimposed on the village the hated *pao-chia* system[4] of mutual surveillance, and this, in the hands of the local gentry, made any sort of democratic growth, however moderate, virtually impossible. The Nationalist Party, having cut off its own roots, stultified into a new-old Chinese bureaucracy, attempting to rule the villages by fiat from the cities, concerned only to maintain order and collect such taxes as they could, and ensure their own survival by compromising with the locally powerful. When Mao Tse-tung now attempts in dramatic ways to put the bureau-

[4] See above, p. 164 n. 39.

cracy which he himself has built up since 1949 under the control of new mass organizations such as the communes or the Red Guards, he is not dreaming of a future collectivist Utopia but is reacting to his experience of the decay of the KMT, of which he was once a member; when he casts post-Stalinist Russia in the KMT role, this is perhaps less rational but still understandable.

While the Nationalists were embarking on the étatist path, the communists, driven into the hills, were forced by circumstances to depend upon the organization of mass support. They began an apprenticeship in the government of the Chinese village which was to last for twenty years before they came to national power. Perhaps the first thing that should be remembered about the CCP is that the group of very young intellectuals who founded it had only six years of irresponsibility before they became the rulers of a state—a small state at first, a mountain top, but one which grew in these twenty years until it embraced a quarter of the population of China on the eve of the final civil war against the Nationalists. The survival of their state was the decisive consideration in all their policies. Three months of rule in the Chingkang mountains was enough to dispose of the most extreme of their dogmas; from then on we can watch the evolution of policies designed primarily to maintain for them the support of a majority in the villages, support upon which their continued guerrilla resistance to the Nationalists and later to the Japanese depended. In his first report from Chingkangshan in 1928, Mao Tse-tung had already repudiated the policy of the central committee in Shanghai, brought the reign of terror which they had ordered to an end, modified the redistribution of the land from rigid egalitarianism to a limited exercise from which the 'middle peasants' (the smaller independent proprietors who neither exploited nor were themselves exploited) were excluded; encouraged trade and used the Red Army to protect the local fairs; and even hinted that for economic reasons the Chinese rich peasants should, far from being wholly expropriated, be given in the land reform a share of land proportionate to their greater capital. He argued strenuously against the notion that the Red Army should be used to spread revolution over a wider area than they could consolidate, recognizing that there would be little support for any sort of revolution which would immediately be threatened by white terror when the Red Army moved on; and he sought to establish a territorial base which would provide normal revenues in place of the plunder on which the Red Army then existed. He explicitly stated that the key to the survival of the Soviet was the allegiance or at least the neutrality of the 'intermediate class'—the rich peasants, small landlords, and small traders. By 1933, when the southern Soviet was finally destroyed, communist agrarian policies had taken a form which could be used with little change in 1949 as the basis of land reform in the whole of China.

The first essay in Mao's *Selected Works* is a simple analysis, written in 1926, of the economic interests of various classes and of their consequent attitudes to politics. First he names the classes whom he regards as enemies of the revolution; these are, first, the 'compradors', those Chinese businessmen dependent for their fortunes upon participation in foreign trade dominated by foreign privileged firms, the section of Chinese society whose interests were in fact tied up with the preservation of foreign privilege. Second, the landlords, whose position Mao believed was dependent upon their co-operation with the warlords and with their age-old power to bargain with corrupt local administrations; and he believed (as almost all Chinese rightly or wrongly believed) that the major warlords were dependent upon foreign support. Therefore compradors and landlords were allies of imperialism as well as anti-revolutionary in terms of internal issues.

The second class he deals with are the 'middle bourgeoisie', whom he identifies with the 'national bourgeoisie', who were anti-imperialist because they suffered from competition with privileged foreign enterprises and who, as victims of disorder and rapacious arbitrary taxation, also opposed the warlords; but their fear of social revolution at home, irreconcilable in Mao's view with their anti-imperialism, paralysed them politically.

Then he turns to the petty bourgeoisie, among which he includes the owner-operator farmers, as well as master craftsmen, small traders, clerks, school-teachers, and students. He divides this class schematically into three—those with a surplus (and in any analysis of Chinese society the low average absolute standard of life must never be forgotten), those who in existing economic circumstances found their aspirations to improvement beyond subsistence frustrated; and those whose incomes as a result of economic decline were steadily becoming inadequate. Their political allegiance varies with their circumstances, and is unstable; most of them will usually join the winning side, only those whose incomes are in decline are consistently pro-revolutionary and they are an important revolutionary force (Mao is thinking especially of the poorer owner-operators who throughout the century were losing ground, as the steadily increasing proportion of tenant farmers and the increase of indebtedness shows).

His next category is the 'semi-proletariat', tenants and part-tenants, shop assistants and pedlars, and the smaller handicraftsmen. Again he divides this class up, and finds that their political attitudes are closely correlated with their incomes.

Finally, the proletariat, who in his view numbered 2 million, who owned no property, and suffered directly from the exploitation of employers, Chinese and foreign. It goes without saying that they are the most revolutionary class, and especially effective because of their concentration; but the *lumpenproletariat* wing, organized in their secret societies, are a problem because they are apt to be destructive and opportunist.

Except for the strong implication that a large proportion of the peasants represented a revolutionary force—by including them in the category of a semi-proletariat instead of in the orthodox way among the petty bourgeoisie—this is all orthodox and could have been written from *a priori* ideas. What gives it rather more weight and authority is Mao's experience as a Nationalist agitator engaged in United Front work and in agitation among the peasants, and more important the whole history of the revolution which Mao directed thereafter. If the victory of the communists had been, as it was superficially, a military victory, Mao's analysis of the classes of China could be written off as a series of prophecies fulfilled by main force; but the victory was a political one, the fruit of twenty years of patient handling of Chinese rural society, and crowned by the allegiance in 1949 of the majority of citizens.

This first crude analysis was only the beginning. It was to undergo a long process of refinement. One element remained throughout however, and that was the conviction that with proper political handling the vast majority of Chinese could be brought into a common united front, and that most classes of Chinese society had much to gain from the revolution; a conviction based like so much else in Chinese radical pre-conceptions, upon the May Fourth movement, the history of similar protests thereafter, and the success of the anti-Japanese boycotts.[5] It expresses also, in the division between 'comprador' and 'national' bourgeoisie—a distinction which would be difficult to sustain—the deep-rooted distrust of the new treaty-port cities which was a fundamental factor in Chinese social attitudes.

Mao's experience in Hunan at the beginning of the following year confirmed his belief that a substantial proportion of the peasants would, in hopeful circumstances, support revolutionary changes; and that they were capable to a remarkable (though still limited) extent of organizing this revolution for themselves. In 1928, however, he faced a less hopeful situation in the embattled Chingkangshan Soviet, and found there that without a victorious army to hold the ring for them, all but the poorest peasants were inclined to be quiescent or hostile. It was here also that for the first time the Communist Party attempted the redistribution of land which was the main plank in their rural programme, and ran immediately into difficulties. The middle peasants (whom Mao had included among the poorer of the petty bourgeoisie, as a potential force for revolution) were hostile to the land reform, for the very good reason that as a group they usually held land greater than the village average landholding, and egalitarian land reform would be to their disadvantage. They had to be excluded from the whole process. Successive land laws issued between 1928 and 1933 gradually modified the whole programme, and by the end it is probable that the reform usually took the simple form of the abolition of rent on existing holdings, with some adjustments of the greatest anomalies which might thus result. In the Chinese rural situation, in which the marketed surplus of agriculture seems to have come not, as in Russia, predominantly from the top 10 per cent of farmers, but equally from each class, it was necessary for the economic survival of the Chinese Soviets for the middle peasants to be induced to accept the system. It was possible to get their co-operation, given enough flexibility and moderation in policy, because they were not in fact as they were in theory a group united by common economic interests: on such questions as debt or tenancy, their interests were divided, and it was always possible to win the support of some of them and so (in most villages) to gain a majority of support in the village consisting

---

[5] Boycotts of Japanese goods as a protest against Japanese encroachments.

primarily of the poor peasants and of a varying section of the middle peasants.

The report from Chingkangshan also showed clearly that considerations of class were complicated in this area by other social factors. These, although perhaps specially severe in this remote and mountainous part of south China, were in varying degrees general throughout China. The first was the clan; the second was the racial or immigrant minority. At its most extreme (but this was by no means uncommon), the difficulty of the clan was that it was almost impossible to set up a political organization, communist or nationalist, which whatever it was called did not represent simply the clan as before. In the one-clan village, there was nothing that could be done, unless there happened to be a clan organization which had deteriorated to the point where the antagonism of poor members to a dominant clan oligarchy was a sufficient basis for a class-oriented political organization. Elsewhere, the problem was often that one or two families were numerous enough (even although still a minority) to force their will and their electees upon the whole village.

The other problem, that of the minority, was that it was difficult to create an essentially divisive political organization which did not very quickly come to be assimilated to the dominant racial division, in this case between the lowland south Chinese, and the hill-farming Hakka 'incomers'. As the latter were in general poorer as well as tougher, the Communist Party tended to become (as the T'aip'ings had done in a similar area seventy years before) a party of Hakka.

It is possible that 'incomers', groups of immigrant labourers or tenants, squatters on reclaimed land, and even seasonally migrant farm hands, may have played a very significant part in the development of the Chinese communist system. The ubiquity of such groups in Chinese society and the close traditional relationship between rebellion and comparable alienated elements, would make this a natural hypothesis; but no research has been done on this possibility as yet. It would be possible to map the occurrence of these groups with some confidence for, for example, the area of the Yangtze estuary, and then to examine the history of the revolution in the area to see if there was any correlation between the existence of incomer groups and revolt in the 1920s and 1930s, or between such groups and extremes in the implementation of policy since 1950.

Y

There was another problem of a similar kind which was even more basic in Chinese politics, and of which as yet we know little: this was the influence of the secret society. Mao mentions the secret societies as an illustration of the difficulty of dealing with the *lumpenproletariat*, which he identifies with the secret society tradition; but even now, the latest attempt to explore the relations with the Communist Party and the secret societies is not very helpful, as Mao refers to the problem only three times in his writings—perhaps for the same sort of reason as he never again refers to the *lumpenproletariat*, that is that he had decided that on the whole they were useful to the revolution although widely suspected by the population, and therefore best not talked about.

At every stage of Chinese development in the twentieth century as well as before modern times, the secret society is the basic unit of lower-class and radical protest. The White Lotus (1796), the T'aip'ings (1850), the Heaven and Earth Society (1853), the Nien in the north (1853), the Boxers (1899) were the nineteenth-century successors of earlier similar organizations of varying degrees and types of political consciousness. Fundamentally they were local friendly societies, or occupational guilds of the very poor classes, the latter type usually concerned with occupations which involved mobility and therefore divorce from settled family life and its security. In medieval Europe the most famous such organization was that of the itinerant stonemasons. In China the most conspicuous class organized in this way were the sailors, trackers, and dockers associated with transport by water; but mountain miners were also an important element. These two groups were the most politically inflammable of the secret society membership, but the habit of association in organizations (which, because they were heretical or potentially subversive were usually declared illegal) was universal in town and country alike. In the case of the Heaven and Earth Society (the Triads) the explicit aim was political—resistance to the Manchus—and it was the secret societies who provided much of the rank and file of the revolutionary forces of the 1911 revolution, which drove the Manchus out. It is probable that secret society affiliations were an important source of the strength of the warlords; for example Ch'en Ch'iung-ming in Kwangtung was a Triad leader. It was widely believed in China that Chiang Kai-shek owed his rise to prominence (and in particular the prompt acceptance of his Nanking regime by the Shanghai business community) to his membership of the Green Gang society; there is no evidence for or against this, but the T'ung-meng Hui (Revolutionary League), the predecessor of the KMT itself, was very much a secret society formed out of other such societies. And as late as 1951, resistance to the communists in Szechwan was still apparently directed by the Elder Brother Society.[6]

Many of the secret societies had an egalitarian bias—the secret brotherhood of equals offered an attractive and romantic escape from the rigid hierarchy of traditional Chinese society, while the extreme lower-class membership of many of the societies also tended to give them such a view. To this extent they should have been open to communist influence.

On the other hand, they frequently deteriorated into protection rackets of various sorts; very often they were at least involved in more or less corrupt and underhand dealings with those against whom they were supposed to protect their members, and where this was so their strong-arm capabilities might well be used by anti-communists, as they appear to have been in the most dramatic blood-letting of all, the attack on the left-wing pickets in Shanghai in 1927 in the course of Chiang Kai-shek's coup.

The Chinese communists have been almost as sparing in their references to the secret societies as Mao Tse-tung himself. Virtually nothing is known about their relations, and in the nature of secret society activity documentation is always scarce; and yet the rapid rise of the Communist Party to national leadership in north China during the anti-Japanese war, partly through the organization of local militia forces, would be most easily explained by the successful assimilation of some of the northern societies, many of which had their own armed forces and some groups of which had actually been formed for local defence against banditry.

As Patrick Cavendish notes, one of the characteristic features of mass-organization politics in China was the tendency of political groups to assume wide powers, including judicial powers. The first peasant associations in east Kwangtung, for example, dealt with a wide range of disputes among members, even dealing with matrimonial questions. This was partly the result of the anti-legalistic

[6] See Stuart Schram, 'Mao Tse-tung and Secret Societies', *CQ*, July–Sept 1966.

tradition of China: the Chinese had no inhibitions about carrying informal arbitration to the point of legal judgment; and the arbitrariness of justice in twentieth-century Chinese conditions —exemplified in the summary execution of bandits and the drumhead justice of the 'bad gentry', and more theoretically in the insistence of the Nationalists as well as the communists that they were above the law—did not encourage legalistic attitudes on the part of revolutionary bodies. It is the result also of the traditional basis of lower-class and local political and social organization in China, in which secret societies, guilds, and clans enjoyed quasi-judicial powers, which in the case of the guilds and clans were sanctioned in practice by the government, guilds and clans being accepted as mutual surety groups. One might say that, in this respect, China had a built-in tendency towards political institutions of which the classical types in Europe are the Paris Commune and the 1917 Russian soviets.

The organization of the secret societies was extremely decentralized and local. The unit was the local lodge, and there is no evidence that such higher levels of organization as existed could exert any pressures upon the lodges. If they co-operated over a wide area, as in the Triad rebellion of 1853, this was spontaneous, haphazard, and short-lived. Thus the whole tradition of political organization among the Chinese lower classes was one of small face-to-face groups which would unite in a common endeavour only when moved by widespread common interests and emotions.

This background and the anti-legalist attitudes partly derived from it help to explain the strong anarchist streak in Chinese politics. As Martin Bernal shows, anarchism was a more persistent force in Chinese politics than the extent and duration of European anarchist influence alone would lead one to expect, while in more recent times the commune system contains very obvious anarchist elements. Indeed, while it has been stressed that the Chinese communists have ruled a territorial state since an early date in their history as a party, it should equally be stressed that until 1949 the state as a form of government played a very small part in their means of political control. Their attempts to set up a state apparatus in the Kiangsi Soviet were not very successful and perhaps this was because they attached no great importance to them. The Border Regions were theroretically a part of the Nationalist state, and there was therefore a fairly strong motive for the communists in playing down the role of the state; and state power was then almost inoperative.

There is a sense in which the oldest issue in Chinese political thought, that between the Legalists and the Taoists, is still the greatest issue. If this is so, it is probably only to a secondary extent, if at all, the result of intellectual conservatism; it is primarily because certain basic facts of Chinese life have not yet decisively changed. The immense size and variety of the country prevented and still to a significant extent prevents centralized government. China is still a federation of an enormous number of relatively self-sufficient communities bound together primarily by a common ideology rather than by uniform administration. The *hsien* cadre, like the district magistrate, is still something of an intruder in a local society which would prefer to look after itself. The central government can still only get this whole mass moving by an effort of ideological exhortation, a propaganda barrage, which seems extravagant to the outside world. The local community is content most of the time to remain in a state of Taoist anarchism; the central government is driven into Legalist excesses of standardization and uniformity, and of coercion, to enforce any attempt at national policy and planning.

We are far from having the means of providing at present a rounded study of the political sociology of modern China, but some of the ideas developed out of the research which this volume represents may, in conjunction with other recent work, provide some pointers for further study.

We are constrained to accept as a working hypothesis that fundamentally, in twentieth-century conditions, and *given the actual political choices presented to them* (a most important qualification), the political attitudes of most Chinese were strongly influenced, as Mao postulated, by their economic circumstances. At the extremes of the range of economic condition, the validity of the idea will scarcely be doubted: the compradors and the landlords stood to lose by almost any change, and so did those whose fortunes came from urban rents in the treaty ports, the heavy taxation of which was prominent in all political programmes in twentieth-century China. At the other end of the scale, the vast class of farm labourers and tenants and their uprooted under-employed representatives who had flooded the cities had in the fullest sense nothing to lose but their chains. For the rest, their grievances were also essentially economic—heavy, regressive, and arbitrary taxation, expended on endless civil war and on the maintenance of a functionless bureaucracy; economic insecurity, and in many cases declining standards. The prevalence of these conditions, which operated at almost every level of income, resulted in something like a consensus on the aims of political activity; national unification, strong government, fair taxes, democratic local government, the redistribution of land, the encouragement of co-operative agriculture, state initiative in industrial development, protection from foreign economic competition.

There were at the same time obstacles to political and social change other than the existence and strength of the minority which stood to lose. Class interests were crossed by the solidarity of clans, minorities, secret societies and other voluntary groups, and by the endless proliferation in China of cliques with a local or personal basis or of patron-client relationships at all levels of society. The purely cash nexus, and the completely economic man, were still relatively scarce in China. Moreover, the prevalence of nationalist emotions itself worked against class-consciousness, as did the solidarity of the basic units of society, the village itself and the 'market area' of half-a-dozen villages which formed the natural local community in China.

Beyond these generalizations we cannot at present proceed very far. We have one excellent study of the sociology of localism;[7] we need studies of the sociology of Chinese nationalism; of the sociology of bureaucracy in China; of the social basis and relationships of the various political parties; and a study of the declining classes of Chinese society as a factor in politics. Yet the influence of all of them, still operating in Chinese society today, can be documented to a varying extent.

There is one particular feature of modern Chinese society, however, which has played such a part in modern Chinese politics until the present that the evidence of it meets us at every turn and in every Chinese newspaper; and that is the gulf between town and country. It is involved with every major Chinese problem: the relations between industry and agriculture, the place of intellectuals, the effectiveness of leadership, and the nature of educa-

[7] G. W. Skinner, 'Marketing and Social Structure in Rural China', *J. Asian Studies*, Nov 1964, Feb & May 1965.

tion. To a remarkable extent, the acid test of political reliability in China today is the answer to the question: will you serve in the countryside? Yet this question of the relations between town and country is one which has not so far been explored.

By the conclusion of the second world war, the CCP had arrived at a successful state of *rapport* with the main elements of Chinese society as described here, partly through their own skill and experience, partly by the favour of their enemies: the Japanese helped them to recruit a peasant army and make themselves the leaders of Chinese nationalism, while the KMT in the last stages of incompetence and corruption left the Chinese communists as China's sole hope of successful social change.

The communists had arrived at a successful formula for revolution in China. This was not fully proved in the Border Regions, where they did not, until the civil war began to spread in 1946, attempt to implement land reform; nor can one assume that because they had won the loyalty of the farmers of the north, their coming was therefore eagerly awaited by the peasants of the south; on the contrary, their own statements are frank in admitting that many peasants awaited their arrival with apprehension and uncertainty, feelings justified if not by the policies which the party promised at any rate fully justified by evidence in Honan and elsewhere of their failure to exercise full control over the more Utopian aspirations of their village cadres. At the same time, policies worked out in northern conditions were not applicable without change farther south, and the southern progress of the consolidation of the communist hold was accompanied by uncertainties and important modifications in policy.

With all qualifications made, however, the Chinese communist accommodation to the political facts of China was highly successful in these years, and was so profoundly different in practice from Soviet communism in relation to China's peasant majority that it can hardly be considered to be the same thing, however derivative its ideological expression appeared to be. It was the Korean war which discredited the Western observers who had long emphasized this, rather than any change in the facts; their discredit was completed when China adopted Soviet methods in the period of the first five-year plan; but events since 1958 have shown the fundamental divergence of the two systems and the capacity of the Chinese party for originality.

The Maoist formula for revolution had originated before Mao came to prominence, in the practice of the Northern Expedition, already briefly referred to.[8] In this formula, an indoctrinated army moving from county to county held the ring for a local grass-roots revolution based on the development of mass organizations. In the 1920s this had only been adumbrated, although in a most dramatic way, in Hunan in 1927. By 1949 the process was worked out in full detail.

The essential first task after the take-over—indistinguishable locally from the take-over itself—was the redistribution of the land. A routine of preparation was applied, culminating in the redistribution of the land but providing at the same time for political recruitment, political education, and the establishment of elected but party-controlled local government. This process, although based upon earlier experience, without which it could hardly have been produced, was nevertheless new, and was worked out amid profound differences and disagreements within the party during the civil war after 1946, differences based on the autonomy of the various Border Regions and civil-war fronts and on the conditions in each. The first problem was to determine the scope and nature of the redistribution of land. A vague formula produced in May 1946 led to wide divergences, varying from the reduction (with compensation) of the largest estates, to ruthlessly egalitarian apportionment of all land, apparently in some parts of Manchuria and in Shantung. In reaction to the egalitarian extreme, the reform was halted, and the Border Region policy of rent reduction revived and made the key step towards land redistribution in a new routine.

This was further elaborated in one important respect related to the changed military situation. The unexpectedly rapid collapse of the KMT forced the PLA to change its tactics from the old method of systematically consolidating and extending its rural bases, to tactics suitable for a war of movement in which they rapidly seized centres of communication, while the remnants of the KMT forces, cut off, rallied in the hills to fight on as guerrillas—a reversal of the former situation. The co-operation of the village populations was necessary in order to deal with this widespread menace to the communist rear; and this necessity was turned into a virtue by preceding political development in the

[8] e.g. above, p. 144.

village by a phase in which the poorer peasants were armed to assist in the defeat of the KMT guerrillas, and their righteous (and armed) indignation then turned on those landlords who in a natural attempt at a last-ditch defence of their position offered help and succour to the guerrillas.

The routine which emerged was expressed as a series of stages— bandit-suppression (the destruction of the Nationalist remnants); anti-despot campaign (turning the wrath of the villagers against the supporters of the guerrillas among the landlords); rent reduction (proof of the power of the poor when organized by the party); the determination of class status; the redistribution of land. This was accompanied, broadly, by stages in the institutional development of the village. The formation of militia; the establish- ment on initiative from above of preparatory committees for the formation of peasant associations; general recruitment to the Peasant Associations after the anti-despot and rent-reduction campaigns had given the peasants confidence; the establishment of elected or representative village governments to conduct land reform.

It was emphasized throughout that these were not stages and tasks which could be mechanically divided from each other, but different aspects of an organic process of political mobilization. Land reform was a form of political education; but without this political education, successful land reform was impossible. What emerged in the end was not only a land reform which had the sanction of the vast majority of the village, which was based upon local knowledge of ownership, and which therefore minimized evasions which could have prejudiced the effectiveness of the reform, but an elected village government broadly representative of all sections except the small minority under attack, and with a backbone of the natural radical village leaders whom these successive campaigns had discovered and from whom future party members were drawn to lead the village. Perhaps most important and most novel of all, a communist rural leadership of men born in the village itself was produced, as an examination of the sur- names of village cadres shows beyond doubt.

The reality was not as smooth as the theory; implementation was plagued by the tendencies of the poor to go to excesses of the traditional type (egalitarian redistribution of land, the seizure, and division of all stocks of grain and so forth), by the increasing scarcity of trained cadres as consolidation moved south, and by inadequate adaptation to different local circumstances, especially obvious in the far south where in the face of the difficulties offered by Cantonese society the land reform was in the end probably thrust through by the army in the face of widespread hostility. The Korean war and the revival of gentry hopes that 'Chiang would be back to eat his moon-cakes this year' put a new bitterness and haste into the process through the near-hysteria of the Campaign against Counter-revolutionaries of 1951. But in general the method worked. It was well related to the Chinese political realities we have discussed, and was probably as justly and moderately carried out as any such radical change in Chinese society could ever have been.

The land reform set a pattern of political methods which, as far as rural society was concerned, looked back to Border Region precedents and was continued in the campaigns for the collectivization of agriculture. In forms of organization less connected with the countryside, similar tendencies were obvious. The state apparatus was not formally created until 1953 and 1954. Law remained very much undeveloped as a means of social change and social control. There was a compromise on the issue of centralization, in which six regional authorities were created largely on the basis of the pattern of military conquest.

In 1953, when the first five-year plan was launched and a general line for the transition to socialism announced, there began a period of centralized planning and, closely related to this, a period of Soviet ascendancy in matters of organization. It was brief, and lasted at most from the beginning of the plan to the Hungarian rising of 1956; and it never dominated rural policy.

Although collectivization conformed to the postwar East European pattern of gradual socialization through mutual-aid teams and semi-socialist co-operatives to the full collectives, there were profound differences in the manner in which development was handled, differences which account for the exceptional success of the Chinese in developing and (with all allowances made) in operating collective agriculture. These sprang from the fact that the Chinese party was peasant-based and had come to power on a programme of which the best elaborated parts concerned social justice on the land; from their cautious and pragmatic view of rural change based upon twenty years of rural state-building and handling of peasant communities in this context; from the legacy of the May Fourth ideals of democratic nationalism; and finally from the particular opportunities which the Chinese rural economy provided.

About two-thirds of the party membership was and is peasant. The local leadership is, as we have seen, based upon the rule of the villages by actual villagers converted to communism, men who are as sensitive to the interests of their fellow villagers as they are to their own interests as party members. Their rural policies are based upon the two poles of just taxation and increased productivity, in contrast to the extractive, exploitative policy pursued by Stalin; it is not entirely insignificant that Mao's aim—to keep agricultural taxation at not more than 10 per cent of gross agricultural product—goes back to Mencius, and their procurement policies have been moderate[9] except perhaps in emergencies such as that of 1959–61, in which a policy of virtual requisitioning could be plausibly justified. The essence of the modifications successively made in the land reform, and of collectivization policy, was to prevent the disruption of production in the course of these changes. As far as possible, land reform took the form of the abolition of rent on existing farms so that the units of production remained the same, and collectivization took the form of local experiments whose results were then applied gradually limited throughout the surrounding area.

The collectivization movement was not based simply on the hope of extracting a greater surplus out of existing production, but on the hope of increasing production. There were three uses for the increased product: the improvement of peasants' standards of life, reinvestment within the collective itself, and eventually the achievement of a larger marketed surplus; as far as the last is concerned, the absolute amount of total procurement remained the same throughout the first five-year plan. The main pressure on the peasants was not to increase procurement norms, but to increase reinvestment; but even then, there is little doubt that at least up to 1958 the standard of living rose over the years.

The successful socialization of agriculture was based upon demonstration that collective agriculture could and did increase incomes. The demonstration took place mainly on experimental collectives, and general application of the methods demonstrated

[9] See Audrey Donnithorne, *China's Economic System* (London, 1967), p. 363.

was much less successful, although it has gradually paid off since. The key to Chinese agricultural development is the construction scheme which depends upon the use of labour underemployed in the off-season of agriculture in work requiring little capital investment, and which pays off in increased incomes in the following harvest. This would seem to be very appropriate to Chinese economic and natural conditions, and its systematic use represents China's biggest contribution to the solution of the problems of economic underdevelopment; the faults of application in China are probably more a matter of lack of trained personnel than of poor organization of the schemes themselves. The best of them, however (and at this early stage the average is not as interesting as the best), have obviously been very successful indeed. They were descended from the resettlement and reclamation schemes of the Border Regions.

Closely tied in with them was the encouragement of co-operative handicraft enterprise. In particular, handicrafts (in which expansion could be much faster in the early stages than in agriculture itself) were used to accumulate capital for investment in the construction schemes. Every means was sought to exploit local resources in this respect, in order to provide the capital for agricultural construction, which was typically of the short-gestation type described.

Thus already from 1951 onwards (and with a continuous line of precedents back to about 1943), the methods of the Great Leap Forward were being developed. The policies of 1958 were novel only in degree and intensity. In many important senses, they represent a swing back to China's own experience of economic development, as opposed to that of the Soviet Union.

The events of 1958, however, did not simply concern economic matters, even although fear of the employment problems revealed by the 1953 population census, and worry over the problem of the relatively slow pace of agricultural growth in comparison with the dramatic development of industry, were very important factors in the situation.

The condemnation of Stalin at the Soviet 20th Congress and the malaise which overtook the communist world in consequence had profound effects in China as well as in Europe. The dramatic crisis of this new development, the Hungarian rising, was echoed on a very much smaller scale in China, in strikes, withdrawals from the collectives, student riots, and other signs of discontent. Mao Tse-tung was at first sympathetic to the Hungarian rebels, until he realized that they might contract out of the military commitments of the communist bloc; but it is clear that he continued to think that there could be no smoke, either in Hungary or China, without fire, and that the causes of discontent must be dealt with. This was the background of the rectification campaign of 1957–8 and of Mao's pamphlet *On the Correct Handling of Contradictions Among the People*,[10] which admitted the conflicts of interest which must exist, although attributing them to inadequate popular appreciation of the essential identity of the interests of the individual and of society, and to the imperfect ideological education of the bureaucrats.

The result of the invitation to free criticism during the Hundred Flowers movement preceding the rectification campaign of 1957–8 is well known. The criticisms were not confined to particular individuals or to particular policies, but in some cases (notably among the frustrated leaders of the social democratic parties which were still nominally a part of the coalition) took the form of a demand for an end to the political monopoly enjoyed by the Communist Party. After a period of confusion, the party turned on the critics, whether at the personal instigation of Mao or as a result of the reaction among the bruised members of the party *apparat*, is not certain. There was a purge, widespread but mild; punishment usually took the form of a year or two years in the countryside.

The purge, however, was no answer. Mao was clearly convinced (as he had always been ready to be convinced) that the main cause of discontent was the vast state bureaucratic apparatus which had been built up since the communists took power. He now sought to short-circuit this apparatus and to provide a social system (the communes) which would reveal for all to see the fundamental harmony of social interests with long-term individual interests. In his attempts to cure China's ills, political and economic, he swung back to the precedents of the Border Regions.

There was one further complication. It already seemed possible that the Soviet Union under Khrushchev would seek a rapprochement with the United States and leave China with less support; it must already have been a question whether China could afford

[10] Peking, FLP, 1957.

to base her future—and in particular the fate of the second plan—upon hopes of a continuing high degree of co-operation from Russia. In the economic field, it was becoming obvious that the centrally-planned, capital-intensive, urban-based Soviet economic model was not wholly appropriate to China. There had already been signs that the Soviet pattern of industrial management was not uncritically accepted in China. Finally, it is possible that Mao was influenced by the fact that one of the most violent, persistent, and intense criticisms which had been made during the rectification of 1957–8 had been of Chinese dependence upon the Soviet Union, which during the second world war had been a party to treaties to China's disadvantage and which after the war had stripped Japanese industrial installations in Manchuria before the Chinese could take them over.

The history of earlier relations between the Comintern and the CCP does not suggest that there was much love lost between the Soviet and Chinese regimes; and the fact that China had been, for obvious reasons of national interest, the most strenuous supporter of the solidarity of the bloc and of Russian leadership does not necessarily mean that the CCP forgot the need for contingency planning. Of all the communist countries, China was the only one which, in the experience of the wartime Border Regions, with their decentralized and labour-intensive methods of economic development) possessed a clear and elaborated alternative to the Soviet model; one which gave hopes of self-reliance and which had continued to be practised and developed at village level if not above. It must also be remembered that, as far as politics and political leadership are concerned, Mao's basic writings on this subject were in origin polemics against a Soviet-trained and Soviet-sponsored 'bureaucratic' group within his own party. The stage was in fact already set for policy disagreements within China which would be embittered by their involvement at every point with the question of Sino-Soviet relations.

It is not certain whether Mao's panacea for China's ills, the communes as the framework of the Great Leap Forward, existed in his mind as a blueprint which he then applied in successive stages, or whether the idea grew up gradually out of events. The steps, however, are chronologically clear enough. The first was taken as a preparation for the second plan. The Chinese leaders had before them evidence that the product of the rural sector of the Chinese economy had increased by 24 per cent during the first plan, and *per capita* peasant incomes by 13 per cent. The orthodox reaction would have been to mop up as much as possible of this surplus by increased taxation of agriculture, by increased procurement, or by the manipulation of prices, and to invest this in the further development of centralized state enterprise. Mao Tse-tung argued for a different policy: to leave the absolute amount of produce taken in taxation and procurement at the same level,[11] to leave the surplus built up in the first plan, and any further increases of production during the second plan, at the disposal of the collectives, and to launch a campaign to induce the collectives to invest a large part of it in the development of local resources. His argument was that the peasants would see more point in economic development if they conducted it for themselves as far as possible.

The campaign for the development of local resources took the form of the Great Leap Forward. But involved with the many economic and political arguments for decentralized, small-scale, non-urban labour-intensive development, there was clearly another, military, argument based on the hypothesis that the Russian deterrent might not be used to protect China and that Russian equipment might not be forthcoming to modernize the Chinese armed forces further. The alternative was to assume the destruction of China's cities and centres of urban industry, to assume an army relatively simply equipped and lacking air power and mobility, and to fall back on the familiar guerrilla defence. This required a decentralized economy, a widespread ability in particular to manufacture metals, and the creation of a massive popular militia; the most striking features of the Great Leap Forward. Seen in detail and against this background, it is inapt to attempt to explain the Chinese Leap as just another example of communist euphoria which exactly paralleled that in Soviet Russia in 1928–9.

As far as economic arguments are concerned, it is worth observing that during the same years preceding 1958 economists elsewhere in the world, particularly those associated with the study of India, had been arriving at conclusions not dissimilar to those which inspired the Chinese experiments of 1958. Hirschman's

[11] Li Ch'eng-jui, *Draft History of the Agricultural Taxes of the Chinese People's Republic* (in Chinese) (Peking, 1959).

arguments[12] on the waste involved in urbanization, the discussion in India of the problem of underemployed rural labour, and the discussion of the best scale for community development, were all paralleled in China. So were the current arguments over balanced growth.

The communes came later. Perhaps the best current explanation of their origins is that Mao saw, in an *ad hoc* federation of adjoining collectives in Honan, brought together to fight the floods which threatened the harvest there in autumn 1957, a possible institutional basis for the developing Leap; but there was certainly little sign of spontaneity in the three-months' campaign which resulted in the communization of the whole of China in early 1958.

The commune system failed in its first form, whether because it was inherently unsuitable, or because it was complicated by unnecessary elements of egalitarianism, or simply by the accidental occurrence of three successive years of natural disasters, is still unknown. But its failure, the consequent demoralization, and the economic and political relaxation which followed the debacle eventually brought up once again the basic problems of Chinese politics, to be fought out in the Great Proletarian Cultural Revolution of 1966–7.

We are now in a position to ask whether recent studies, of which the contributions to this volume are examples, provide a framework of analysis of Chinese politics which is properly based upon empirical study of Chinese conditions and experience, and upon the way in which this has conditioned the expectations and assumptions of the Chinese and their leaders.

We might ask of Mao Tse-tung: What does he assume? What does he fear? What does he expect, and of what does he entertain only low expectations? We will find that his attitudes are explicable in terms of Chinese tradition, conditions, recent history, and practical political experience; and we will find that the perplexities and contradictions in that experience are woven into the tissue of Mao's thinking, and of the system which he has created.

We might begin with considering what he does not expect. First, he has no high hopes of the possibility of effective centralization: innumerable examples could be given, but it is enough to point to the very general, ideological, often essentially moral, nature of central directives and the constant insistence in such directives

[12] A. O. Hirschman, *The Strategy of Economic Development* (New Haven, Conn., 1959).

and the accompanying exegesis upon the necessity of adaptation to local conditions. The position of the army (with regional armies still settled on what they conquered in the late 1940s and still with an extraordinary degree of continuity of command since the civil war) is a further illustration. The problem of the proper proportions between central direction and local initiative has not of course been solved, and probably never will be in China, but in general there is a wide degree of decentralization. The system thus draws upon both traditional and twentieth-century (guerrilla) experience, and Mao's latest demands imply, because of their basis in the idea of a guerrilla defence, even greater decentralization than at present.

Second, Mao does not have high expectations about the possibilities of coercion. The conduct of the collectivization campaigns is a good illustration of this, in the concern to persuade, to demonstrate, to communicate, to take account of conflicting interests, and to compromise in order to gain the widest possible support. The procurement system provides further illustration; the level of compulsory purchases has been on the whole low and stable, and sales to the state beyond this norm are secured by ideological argument and pressure and by indirect means such as the discouragement of local free markets. It hardly needs to be added that while the recalcitrant minority which shows signs of active disaffection has been on occasion ruthlessly dealt with, in this respect the Chinese system is probably exceptional among communist systems for the leniency with which most political dissidents have been treated.

The third characteristic, which is as traditional in its origins as the other two, is a low expectation about the effectiveness of law. After seventeen years, there has still been no serious or sustained attempt to codify Chinese law. It may be added (what we often forget) that willingness to obey novel laws is still a rather scarce characteristic in human societies, as well as one which is absolutely basic to the operation of a free society, representing the fundamental discipline which is the condition of freedom; and the whole experience of China's attempts to reform and modernize society had already shown that new laws unsupported by new social and moral awareness or new power relations in society were futile, being merely ignored or resisted.

The obverse of Mao's low expectations of the effectiveness of

z

centralization, coercion, and law, is his high expectations concerning the possibilities of education, of personal moral reform, and of the human will acting upon conscious acceptance of the individual's place in the pattern of progress.

There is a sense in which the whole apparatus of the Chinese system is an apparatus of education. The central committee directive or the State Council decree is always merely the beginning of a long process by which at every level of society and administration the new order or the new idea is thrashed out in endless discussions, which have two related objects: to secure the conscious and voluntary acceptance of the new measure by a majority of each group or local community concerned, and to increase the general level of political consciousness at the same time. We have seen how land reform was based upon political education and issued in political education; and every other campaign since has held up this educational purpose, as well as the immediate purpose of the particular campaign. Even the failures of the Great Leap Forward were discounted because the experiments in backyard blast furnaces and similar things had, it was said, an educational value in making the peasants conscious of the simpler forms of modern technology.

The ultimate object of education directed by the party is, as James Macdonald's chapter shows, twofold—the creation of a new élite derived from the classes which have benefited from the revolution, and beyond this the creation of a politically-conscious nation capable of mass participation in politics, administration, and technical advance. This has latterly issued in and merged with a systematic attempt to destroy the barriers between those engaged in mental as opposed to physical labour, between town and country, and between industry and agriculture. These are orthodox Marxist aims, but they have not been seriously aimed at in other communist countries, and the explanation of why it should be China and China alone which has taken up this neglected part of the canon lies in Chinese conditions and Chinese tradition. That there was a gulf between the intellectual and the manual worker in China of an unusually deep kind is well known; it was expressed by Confucius himself (although Confucius did not mean what he was taken to mean: when he said the superior man does not need to be able to tell the difference between the five cereals, it is very probable that he was merely restating, epigrammatically, one of his most familiar axioms—that administration is the management of men not of things), and dramatized in the long gowns and the uncut nails of the literati. As in medieval Europe, however, this idea did not stop at a contempt for horny-handed sweating peasants; it was extended to include any sort of empirical investigation of facts. There has always been a close historical connexion between contempt for manual labour and scholasticism, and Chinese tradition is the classical case, although it is too often forgotten that there was a continuous and vigorous tradition of opposition. The division between town and country we have mentioned as perhaps the profoundest gulf in Chinese society. To traditional hostility towards the town as the citadels of the rapacious tax collector, parasitic on the land, was added in the twentieth century the jealousy felt by the war-torn hinterland for the treaty ports, peaceful and thriving under foreign protection, sucking away the life of the countryside to spend it in imports of Western luxuries consumed mostly within sight of the sea, and identified with alienated Westernized intellectuals and sycophantic compradors—a jaundiced picture, but a vivid and credible one. The Communist Party is the party of the interior, and the Nationalists the party of the coast; this, as North[13] showed, is the only measurable distinction between the two groups. Even now the towns are still the centres of privilege, where highly-paid skilled workers and superior cadres enjoy a standard of living very much greater than that of the rural population; this jealousy displayed itself very obviously in the earlier and more obviously spontaneous activities of the Red Guards.

The idea of the gulf between industry and agriculture is also one with a peculiar relevance in China. It overlaps with the gulf between town and country in so far as industry with its privileged participants and its first claim on the peasant's surplus is usually urban. The worker-peasant alliance, even in China where the procurement system is not at all obviously biased against the farmers, is an uneasy one. Urban industry stands for the sacrifices made for long-term gains which remain vague and obscure to the peasants. Mao's decision in 1957 to leave the increased incomes of the peasants in their own (collective) hands and to induce them to invest it in the development of local industry was explicitly aimed at two things: to let the peasants participate in

[13] Robert C. North, *Kuomintang and Chinese Communist Élites* (Stanford, Calif., 1952).

the development of industry themselves so that the relationship between their individual interests and their long-term interests as citizens of an industrialized state would be brought home to them; so that in fact the identity of self-love and social would be demonstrated on their own doorsteps; and to provide the peasants with the beginnings of an introduction to modern technology which alone could relieve them of that fatalism in the face of nature which China's climatic conditions have made second nature to her inhabitants, and the destruction of which is in the final analysis the first and the last lesson in Chinese communist education.

There were also good economic arguments for the attempt to develop industry in the villages: to put the underemployed to work *on the spot* where their labour will still be available to agriculture at sowing and harvest when it is needed, and to save the wastes involved in urban industrialization for building construction, the provision of urban amenities, and the transport and processing (in still primitive and enormously wasteful conditions) of the food for growing city populations. The communes and the Great Leap Forward were the first attempt to reduce the gulf between industry and agriculture. They also involved the more orthodox aspect of the idea, that is that farming should be subjected to a labour discipline and a scale of management analogous to those of the factory.

The latest attempt to demonstrate the possibilities of industrialization without urbanization is one very much involved in the Maoist campaigns since 1962 which have culminated in the Cultural Revolution. This is the Ta Ch'ing oilfield. It exemplifies the destruction of all three barriers. It is built not as a city but as a series of villages. Each village has its own farm worked by the dependants of the oil workers. Decisions (including, it is said, those involved in the creation of the oil industry from scratch after the Russian technicians were withdrawn) are taken by committees of the management, the party, and the workers, and every member of the factory takes part in productive work. Education is in the form of part-work part-study. The Ta Ch'ing system deserves more serious study than it has been given, as a complete, functioning, and apparently highly successful example of practical Maoism; but in general throughout China, the destruction of these three distinctions can be taken as the basic content of all education. The consequences of this, if it were successful, would be the destruction not only of the present middle-class élite but of all élites.

It is a point of pride with the Chinese party that China's capitalists have on the whole been turned into good proletarians by political education, and many Western observers have pointed out that this represents a somewhat heretical attitude from a Marxist point of view. It implies that there is a level of general moral consciousness in human beings which is deeper than class consciousness, upon which it is possible to operate by moral education; 'brain-washing' implies that we all, proletarian or bourgeois, had a clean brain to start with and that its cleanliness can be recovered.

In this, as in so many of the other characteristics of the system, we have again a belief which is based upon the happy coincidence of tradition and of modern experience. The central axiom of the Confucian school, which represented a compromise between the Taoist belief in the innate goodness of the natural man, and the Legalist belief in his depravity, was that while man has positive moral capacities, they can be developed only by education and the inculcation of good habits; and Confucian practice probably represented the most conscious and systematic attempt in history at the education of the sentiments. In twentieth-century China the ability of nationalist feelings to override class interests and attitudes, and the very real feelings of class guilt from which Chinese capitalists suffered, in an environment which was traditionally hostile to everything upon which capitalism is based, and in conditions in which capitalism was known only at its most predatory and vicious, provided a basis for the possible re-education—almost, one might say, for the religious conversion—of the Chinese middle classes. Indeed, it cannot be too much emphasized that Chinese communism represents for China a moral revival and in many respects a moral advance. This is one of the advantages of their situation of which the Chinese communist leaders are most conscious; both conviction and expediency combine to override Marxist orthodoxy, both upbringing and practical experience dictate that they will act as if their class enemies have souls to be saved even if salvation may take the form of the labour camp.

Even more strikingly traditional are the introspective practices by which the new morality of 'proletarian consciousness' is maintained. The good communist ends his day with a soul-searching review of what he has done and thought, and measures himself afresh against the standards which Mao Tse-tung has appointed; and it is not enough that he has done right—he must have done right for the right reasons, otherwise he may do wrong to-morrow. This ritual introspection does not go back merely to 1949, or the rectification movement of 1940–2,[14] or even to the foundations of the Communist Party in 1921: it goes back to the neo-Confucianism of the Sung dynasty, and has in fact Buddhist origins.

Related to the stress upon education and personal moral reform is the equal stress upon the potentialities of the human will. This has culminated in the recent Proletarian Cultural Revolution. Again, this has a traditional and even religious background, and again it is a tradition which chimes with twentieth-century experience of the embattled Communist Party fighting against enemies more numerous and far better equipped, maintaining their wartime economy in the Border Regions by miracles of improvisation and near-miracles of mobilization of labour; the Sino-Soviet split has given new point to the value of self-reliance, and an incentive to affirm the possibility of reaching communism without first achieving the industrial basis of abundance.

Citizens of the modern West resist the idea of a state which bases its authority less on law or on stable administrative traditions than upon an ideologically rationalized morality, preached with unremitting intensity, penetrating the private lives of citizens, and apparently often at odds with pragmatic common sense and normal routine. Many interpreters of the Chinese scene prefer to pretend that these aspects of China do not exist, or to assume that they represent the views of one man, and to confine their analysis to what they feel better able to understand, even if it is largely irrelevant. Others write the system off as being too irrational to be subject to rational analysis, and are content to catalogue instances of the apparently lunatic lengths to which ideology drives some of the exegesists of the thought of Mao Tse-tung—an amusing exercise but not very profitable.

---

[14] The rectification (*cheng-feng*) movement of 1940–2 was an attempt at party reorganization to overcome a bureaucratic tendency which was inappropriate to guerrilla conditions, and at the same time to set conditions for the successful absorption of intellectuals into the Communist Party. It served also as a means of increasing Mao's own authority over the party apparatus. It thus forms an important precedent (and one familiar to all party members) for much of the Cultural Revolution.

The resulting system is inevitably full of tensions and contradictions, of which (like so much else in the system) Mao's own thought provides the fullest expression.

The most obvious contradiction involved is that between centralization and local initiative. It has been suggested that administrative centralization in a country as large and varied as China is impossible without an intolerable degree of bureaucratization and without crippling inefficiencies; that national unity has always been fundamentally an ideological unity (another way of putting the usual judgement that Chinese nationalism in pre-modern times was 'cultural' and not racial or nation-state); and that the great issues of Chinese politics in the past were fundamentally concerned with the insoluble problem of the relationship between central government and autonomous local communities, a sort of *yang-yin* relationship. It has further been suggested that this tension inevitably increases in modern conditions when the central government seeks to produce drastic changes and can only produce them through the political manipulation of diffuse and highly localized social and political groups resistant to hierarchical organization but powerful enough to smother innovation. The work of Skinner on the traditional marketing areas of China[15] has provided a factual basis for the study of this problem, showing how economically (as markets), socially (as communities of families known to each other through market contacts, as the area within which marriage alliances generally took place, and as the effective area of clan activities), and politically (as the area of the secret-society lodge and of local gentry discussion and arbitration), this market area was basic; and Chinese communist attempts to evade it or subsume it, like the continual efforts of traditional governments before them, have not been successful. There are other contradictions with which Skinner does not deal, between centre and province, centre and district, and centre and village, which raise similar issues concerning centralization. Ideology has again become, as it always was in imperial times, the cement of China, increasingly so since the rejection in 1958 of the centralized and bureaucratic Soviet model. The aims are the maximization of communication, and the maximization of local initiative, within a consensus provided by the fundamental ideology and the enormous complex of practical

[15] n. 6 above.

recipes for political and economic action which flow from it; and as in imperial times, national policies are very often the result of local initiative.

From this essential contradiction the other, related, contradictions flow; the importance of ideology tends to limit the empiricism and pragmatism which are so obviously a part both of Mao's own thought and of Chinese attitudes, and what it does not limit it tends to conceal because only by regional and local studies on the ground, on a scale not yet attempted, can we hope to reconcile the contradiction between the ideological bent of central pronouncements and the very cautious and pragmatic policies which China has usually pursued, together with the very great variety of local arrangements which the ideology freely permits. In the same way, the contradiction between the imposition of an ideological discipline, and the inducement of conscious and voluntary acceptance of ideology and policy, is ever present; the tensions in this respect are most obvious where they are concerned with the non-communist and bourgeois intellectuals who although constituting, at the widest definition, only 2 per cent of the population, occupy a strategic position in a country where there is still massive illiteracy and where even many local communist cadres are only semi-literate.

The Great Proletarian Revolution brought all these basic issues to the forefront once more. The final objectives of the Chinese revolution—the wealth and power of the nation—were still only partially achieved. National security was still threatened; China, only nominally a nuclear power, faced the United States, the greatest nuclear and industrial nation in the world, across a ring of American bases from Korea to Vietnam, a situation militarily little different from that represented by the foreign concessions in the treaty ports and the naval stations of the powers on Chinese soil in the earlier part of the century. To this since 1957 was added the growing hostility of Soviet Russia. The Bandung unity of a large part of the uncommitted world under something like the moral leadership of China had broken up, largely it must be admitted because of the ineptitude of Chinese diplomacy; and the subsequent attempts to create new allies by the encouragement of national-liberation movements had failed. The escalation of war in Vietnam, which China sees as the consequence of a breach of the only major international agreement to which she has been a party since 1949, has provoked fears of a capitalist war of intervention extended to China herself. Russian military and technical assistance have meanwhile been withdrawn, making it virtually impossible for China to depend upon the Russian deterrent or to match American equipment.

In the economic field agriculture still lags behind industry: and 1959–61 showed dramatically that China's new defences against the vagaries of her monsoon climate are still inadequate; agricultural productivity has not only not risen to the extent hoped, but remains precarious. The vast reservoir of underemployed labour in the countryside has still not been fully put to work. The essential industries are still mainly concentrated as easy targets in eastern China. The check to technological development given by the withdrawal of Soviet technicians has still not been wholly overcome.

Throughout the twentieth century, Chinese political and social thinkers have always been impressed by the idea that China was caught in a vicious circle in which the solution of one problem depended upon the prior solution of others. National safety depended upon economic growth; economic growth very largely upon social reform; social reform upon political strength; political strength upon revenue; and revenue upon economic growth. It was partly from this well-founded idea that the holistic and totalitarian bias of Chinese politics sprang. In 1966 and 1967 it is still possible and even reasonable to take, *mutatis mutandis*, a similar view of Chinese society, on the basis of one single assumption which Mao Tse-tung makes: the assumption that in the absence of Soviet support, China must prepare to defend herself, for lack of an adequate atomic deterrent and of modern equipment, by the guerrilla methods of the anti-Japanese war.

Successful guerrilla defence depends first and foremost upon an indoctrinated army—'men who know what they fight for and love what they know'—and one capable of leading a struggle which involves the whole local civilian population. It depends also upon a vast degree of economic decentralization, which means, in Chinese terms, upon successful local economic development based upon local resources, local underemployed rural labour, and local savings—with the inevitable collectivist and egalitarian implications which at China's low levels of rural capital accumulation such a policy inevitably implies. To such a development one major obstacle is the urban-based, urban-biased intelligentsia and the cost-conscious experts, rapidly growing into an élite in which sections of the party are involved.

The gap between Mao's Yenan views and those of his opponents have widened over the years. There are now in fact three roads and not two. There is what might be called the traditional Soviet norm upon which so much of China's economic and political organization has been based since the first five-year plan. There is the Maoist road. And there is now also the liberalizing road, which has opened out of observation of changes in Soviet Russia and in Eastern Europe since the condemnation of Stalin, and in particular out of awareness of the part played by liberal imaginative writers in this process of thaw. The liberals captured a part of the party's apparatus and enjoyed until the 1966 crisis the patronage of some of the party leaders, notably of P'eng Chen. At the same time the original leadership of the party, based upon young intellectuals who had made a conscious choice of communism from known (even if ill-understood) alternatives has been replaced, at all but the top levels, by an age-group recruited into the party during the wartime guerrilla days. The simultaneous rise in strength of both liberals and hard-line Yenan men has probably sharpened the whole conflict. The fact that the alternatives to Maoism would involve the renewal of good relations with a degree of dependence upon Soviet Russia, and that there are close personal links between many of the party intelligentsia and the parties of Russia and Eastern Europe, further exacerbates the struggle.

The ideological nature of the arguments used in the Cultural Revolution should not obscure the amply documented fact that this crisis is concerned with real policy choices of a fundamental kind. Nor should the general moral tone of the Maoist pronouncements, the universality of the arguments, obscure the fact that Mao is dealing with specific Chinese problems of the kind which the contributions to this volume have raised. These can be briefly recapitulated in this context by stating, with confidence and on the basis of ample documentary evidence, that there has been growing up in China a new-old class of bureaucrats inheriting some of the worst features of China's élitist tradition, averse to practical and empirical investigation and bookish to a degree difficult for citizens of any advanced industrial country to appreciate, based in the towns and hugging the towns to such an extent that it may well be that further advance in agriculture and in rural amenities is now held up less by lack of economic resources than by lack of educated persons prepared to live in the villages, an élite content to take its place in a centralized bureaucratic hierarchy whose activities all China's modern experience suggests cannot provide an adequate substitute for well-directed local initiative. Present problems, and most fundamentally the problem of defence, make these issues urgent; but there is no doubt that Mao attacks this élite with a lusty enjoyment which derives from a life-long hatred and contempt of all they stand for, sentiments which form the most consistent part of his political writings. He expects them to look after their own interests and to line their own pockets, to regard the ordinary citizen with contempt and impatience, and to form self-protecting cliques. He expects them to have at their service many of China's writers, who are as steeped in the tradition as the bureaucrats themselves. He expects them to stay in the county seat and cut themselves off from rural realities, to think of taxation and procurement first and increased production second, to be content with routine, to play for safety, to conform outwardly but carry out policy perfunctorily, to turn the necessity of adapting policies to local conditions into an excuse for not implementing policy at all. He has the best of social and historical reasons for his expectations.

There is, however, another level of thought involved. Beneath the disputes over present urgent problems and beneath the struggle with ancient Chinese proclivities, Mao is concerned with political universals. He recognizes that China's local problems of political organization are no different in principle from the perennial basic problems of government, and in particular the problem of the aftermath of revolution when the radical leaders become a new establishment and revert to the habits of those they replaced. Mao's achievements in preventing this in China are not insignificant. In Soviet Russia, the first complaints about privilege among party leaders began to be heard before the October revolution was a year old and the party-bureaucratic die was cast within five years at most. The Chinese situation is still fluid after seventeen years. This measure of success is the result of Mao's repeatedly revived insistence on the mass line as the basis of an attempt to create a sort of crude but practical form of participating democracy, which has resulted in the creation of a population whose articulateness in politics is a byword, whose mass participation in local decisions concerning their own future has been from time to time astonishing in scale and scope, and which still throws up new revolutionary recruits, to prevent the complete crystallization of the establishment.

His means are Chinese means. They have been re-applied in the Great Proletarian Cultural Revolution, when once more an indoctrinated army (though now not without profound anxieties and divisions) has held the ring for a 'popular' revolution—this time against the party hierarchy itself; and when once more the educated youth of China, consciously and dramatically re-living the experience of their grandfathers in the May Fourth Movement, were to act as the catalyst of new and profound social changes.

Perhaps it is impossible that any revolution, in China or anywhere else, can succeed in avoiding the creation of a new élite. It may also be that the extravagant personal adulation of Mao Tse-tung, which he has so uncharacteristically encouraged since 1960 in order to offset his loss of influence with the party leadership, will in itself undermine the development of the very qualities which Mao seeks (within his Marxist framework) to inculcate—the capacity for active, critical citizenship, and the acceptance of normal modern standards of public morality, respect for facts, determination and perseverance, and personal initiative. It must be remembered, however, that history gives many examples of 'doublethink' in which uncritical devotion has motivated highly pragmatic action; this might indeed be said to have been history's most explosive mixture; and no one can visit China without being aware that the same paradox operates there.

It may be also that Mao's political aims conflict with economic rationality, not only in the sense that the Cultural Revolution has in the short term been economically costly, but that the policies it represents are finally incompatible with the rational pursuit of China's defined economic aims. Mao's defence is quite explicit. It is that 'a great spiritual force will become a great material force'; less epigramatically, that the first essential for an economic revolution in China is the dissemination throughout the population of an awareness of the unlimited economic possibilities of human inventiveness and of modern social organization. If in the short term, cost-consciousness inhibits the dissemination of this awareness, then cost-consciousness must yield. Mao may be wrong in this; but it would be a cold-hearted economist who could withhold entirely all sympathy for the idea, at a time when we have become steadily more conscious that the economic problems of underdeveloped countries are as much social and psychological as economic. On this assumption, Mao puts forward a political system whose primary aim is the mutual education of leaders and led; economic as well as political judgements of China which do not recognize this will be either trivial or irrelevant.

It is not, however, the purpose of this symposium either to predict the future development of China, or to 'apportion praise and blame', in the manner of Confucian historians themselves, to the leaders of twentieth-century China. Its aim is the more limited one of exploring some of the factors which have shaped present-day Chinese political sentiments and behaviour. Its concern is essentially with Chinese political psychology. If value judgements appear in its pages, they are those of the Chinese people, or of sections of them; if its conclusions can guide prediction, it will only be in so far as they reveal certain abiding preoccupations and presuppositions which may continue to influence the political choices which the Chinese make.

Contributors to this volume

Martin Bernal is Fellow and Assistant Tutor of King's College, Cambridge, and is writing a book on Chinese socialism and anarchism before 1914. He has contributed to various journals, including *Modern Asian Studies*, the *Journal of the Royal Asiatic Society*, *La Deuxième Internationale et l'Orient*, and the *Cambridge Review*.

Patrick Cavendish has recently been appointed Assistant Professor of History at the University of California, Santa Cruz. His Ph.D. thesis on 'The Rise of the Chinese Nationalist Party and the Foundation of the Nanking Regime, 1924–9', was accepted at Cambridge in 1968, and he is co-author with Jack Gray of *Chinese Communism in Crisis* (1968).

Dr Jerome Ch'ên is Senior Lecturer in Modern East Asian History at the University of Leeds. He is the author of *Mao and the Chinese Revolution* (1965) and is at present writing another book on Mao Tse-tung.

Jean Chesneaux is Director of Studies at the École Pratique des Hautes Études, 6me section. Among other works he has published *Le mouvement ouvrier chinois de 1919 à 1927* (1962) and, with John Lust, *Introduction aux études d'histoire contemporaine de Chine, 1898–1949* (1964).

Mark Elvin is Lecturer in the Department of Economic History, University of Glasgow. He has contributed to the Harvard *Papers on China* and is at present working on the late pre-modern Chinese economy.

John Gittings has been a Research Specialist at Chatham House and Research Fellow in Asian Affairs at the Institute of International Studies, University of Chile. He is at present an Assistant Editor of the *Far Eastern Economic Review*, Hong Kong. He is the author of *The Role of the Chinese Army* (1967) and *Survey of the Sino-Soviet Dispute: A Commentary and Extracts from the Recent Polemics, 1963–7* (1968).

Jack Gray is Senior Lecturer in Far Eastern History at the University of Glasgow and is co-author with Patrick Cavendish of *Chinese Communism in Crisis* (1968).

James Macdonald is Lecturer in Politics at the University of Leeds and his major research is on the Communist Party of China.

George Moseley has been studying at St Antony's College, Oxford, for a

D.Phil. thesis on minority questions in Yunnan and Kwangsi provinces. He is the author of *A Sino-Soviet Cultural Frontier: the Ili-Kazakh Autonomous Chou* (1966) and *The Party and the National Question* (1966), and has contributed to the *China Quarterly* and the *Far Eastern Economic Review*.

Sybille van der Sprenkel was in China from February 1948 to November 1949 (teaching for two semesters at the National Nankai University, the rest at the British Council Centre, Peking). After researching in London and Canberra (ANU) and teaching for two years in Tokyo, she revisited China in 1964, before taking up her present post as Lecturer in Sociology and Chinese Institutions at the University of Leeds. She is the author of *Legal Institutions in Manchu China*, first published in 1962, 2nd impression 1966.

Index

Note: In order to link the contributions to this book, this index stresses subjects rather than names.

DA